I0126453

Masoud Kazemzadeh
Mass Protests in Iran

De Gruyter Contemporary Social Sciences

—

Volume 38

Masoud Kazemzadeh

Mass Protests in Iran

From Resistance to Overthrow

DE GRUYTER

ISBN 978-3-11-163098-4
e-ISBN (PDF) 978-3-11-128028-8
e-ISBN (EPUB) 978-3-11-128038-7
ISSN 2747-5689
e-ISSN 2747-5697

Library of Congress Control Number: 2023938200

Bibliographic information published by the Deutsche Nationalbibliothek
The Deutsche Nationalbibliothek lists this publication in the Deutsche Nationalbibliografie;
detailed bibliographic data are available on the internet at http://dnb.dnb.de.

© 2024 Walter de Gruyter GmbH, Berlin/Boston
This volume is text- and page-identical with the hardback published in 2023.
Cover image: fotosuper / iStock / Getty Images Plus

www.degruyter.com

I dedicate this book to all those who have struggled to establish freedom, democracy, human rights, and social justice in Iran

About the Author

Masoud Kazemzadeh is Associate Professor in the Department of Political Science at Sam Houston State University. He received his B.A. in International Relations from the University of Minnesota and M.A. and Ph.D. in Political Science from the University of Southern California. He was a post-doctoral fellow at the Center for Middle Eastern Studies at Harvard University. He is the author of four books: *The Iran National Front and the Struggle for Democracy: 1949–Present* (Berlin: De Gruyter, 2022); *Iran's Foreign Policy: Elite Factionalism, Ideology, the Nuclear Weapons Program, and the United States* (London and New York: Routledge, 2020); *Islamic Fundamentalism, Feminism, and Gender Inequality in Iran Under Khomeini* (Lanham, MD: University Press of America, 2002); and *Marxism, Leninism, and Social Democracy: Ideological Premises of Dictatorship and Democracy* (Los Angeles, CA: Arta Books, 2001).

https://doi.org/10.1515/9783111280288-001

Preface and Acknowledgments

During the fall of 2022 hundreds of thousands of Iranians engaged in mass protests against the ruling dictatorship in Iran. In solidarity, tens of thousands of Iranians in diaspora participated in mass protests around the globe using the same slogans and making the same demand for the overthrow of the fundamentalist regime.

Astute observers of Iran were aware that the ruling regime in Iran was tyrannical, extremist, brutal, and terrorist. They were also aware that some Iranians did not like the fundamentalist regime. What came as surprises were that so many people bravely participated, that so many young women participated and led the protests, that the protests were so widespread, and that the protests lasted for so long. To observe tens of thousands of brave women and men stand up to one of the most reactionary, repressive, and misogynist regimes in the world, call for its overthrow, and demand the establishment of democracy, freedom, dignity, and equality was awe inspiring.

In this book, I want to answer the question why these protests are occurring. I will describe the resistance to the fundamentalist regime and the mass protests that have occurred since 1979. I will also provide analysis of the causes of these protests.

Observers, including scholars, appear surprised when a regime falls. Their surprises are recurring phenomena. They were surprised when the Shah's dictatorship fell, when Pinochet's dictatorship fell, when communist regimes in Eastern Europe fell, when the Soviet Union collapsed, when the apartheid regime in South Africa fell. There appears to be a pro-status quo bias among scholars, government officials, and political observers that clouds their judgments on the stability of dictatorial regimes.

Such a bias is understandable. A dictatorship has come to power by force or has remained in power by force. Therefore, by definition, a ruling dictatorship has been able to defeat its opponents. In democracies, when the people do not like a particular party in power, they could easily vote it out in the next elections. But because dictatorships, usually, do not allow free elections or free speech, those outside are unaware of the true popularity, strength, or weaknesses of the ruling dictatorship.

To counter the pro-status quo bias of any regime, scholars have to present objective analyses of the strengths and weaknesses of a ruling dictatorship as well as objective analyses of the strengths and weaknesses of the opposition groups and the people who oppose the dictatorship.

Revolutions and regime transitions are complex phenomena. To understand them we have to look at long-term antecedents, medium-term antecedents, and

https://doi.org/10.1515/9783111280288-002

short-term antecedents. We have to look at structural factors as well as actual human beings who make a decision to participate in one or another manner. In other words, we have to look at how individuals in what contexts make what decisions. Individuals have free will and agency, but they are able to act within certain social conditions. And these individual decisions become significant and history making when a large number of other individuals joins them in demanding change.

In Chapter 1, I will describe and analyze the long-term antecedents of the mass protests. I will discuss the totalitarian nature of the fundamentalist regime as well as its weaknesses. In Chapters 2 and 3, I will describe and analyze in great detail two major mass protests. In Chapter 2, I will discuss the 2009 fundamentalist-only elections. In that election Khamenei wanted to impose Ahmadinejad as President rather than another powerful member of the fundamentalist oligarchy. In Chapter 3, I will discuss the mass protests of December 2017–January 2018. Before those protests, the dominant discourse was "reforming the fundamentalist regime." Those who advocated democracy or advocated overthrowing the regime were in a minority. The turning point was the mass protests of December 2017. Those who advocated regime overthrow became the leaders of the opposition, and their discourse of "*sarnegooni*" [overthrow] became the dominant discourse.

In Chapter 4, I will discuss and analyze the medium-term and structural factors of the current mass protests. I will discuss and analyze the crisis of legitimacy, the crisis of succession to Supreme Leader Khamenei, and the economic crisis. In Chapter 5, I will describe and analyze the short-term antecedents of the current mass protests. I will discuss the many individuals who played major roles in the protests and how their decisions and actions have influenced and affected the protests.

In Chapter 6, I will bring the analyses in the previous chapters together. I will also discuss policy ramifications for actors outside Iran. I finished this book in late March 2023 when the outcome of the mass protests was not certain. The discussion on policy ramifications, thus, analyzes how various policies by various actors would cause the prolongation of the ruling dictatorship and what policies would increase the likelihood of overthrow of the fundamentalist regime.

About 35 pages of my earlier book, *The Iran National Front and the Struggle for Democracy: 1949–Present* (Berlin: De Gruyter, 2022) are re-published here. My analysis in that book anticipated the current mass protests; therefore, I have included those segments in my current book. I thank my editors at De Gruyter for their kind permission to re-publish those materials here. Chapter 4 was published in *Small Wars Journal* on January 3, 2018. The title of the article was "Protests in Iran: Characteristics, Causes, and Policy Ramifications."

I thank Faye Leerink, Michaela Göbels, Gerhard Boomgaarden, and Di Wardle, my fantastic editors at De Gruyter, for their efficient work. It was a pleasure working with them on this book project. I thank Penny L. Watson for her comments and suggestions on earlier versions of this book.

Contents

Chapter 1
Introduction

1.1 A Brief History of Protests Since the 1979 Revolution

The 1977–1979 protests were a broad-based popular revolution against the Shah's dictatorship. The objectives of the revolution were to establish independence, freedom, and social justice. The opposition to the Shah included secular liberal democrats and social democrats of the Iran National Front (INF), liberal Islamists (e. g., Liberation Movement of Iran), various Marxist groups, and conservative Islamists (Khomeini). As fundamentalists gained more support among the population, they changed the slogan from "Independence, Freedom, Social Justice" to "Independence, Freedom, Islamic Republic."

The Shah was widely considered to be a puppet of the British and Americans whose primary objective was to serve their colonial interests. For example, after the 1953 coup, which was organized by the CIA and MI6, the Shah returned Iran's oil that had been nationalized by Mossadegh to a consortium of major oil companies. The Shah's agreements with the oil companies were canceled by the provisional government in 1979 and Iran's oil was in the hands of Iranians again.[1] There were no freedoms of expression, of the press, or of political parties. The Shah's secret police, SAVAK, engaged in horrendous torture of dissidents including high school children and university students who had committed no crime other than reading books that the regime did not approve of. There were no free elections and the Shah had violently imposed his one-man tyranny.[2] The Shah, his family, and their cronies were engaged in outright theft, financial corruption, and graft that made them grotesquely rich while millions of the people lived in abject poverty. The Pahlavis and their *nouveaux riches* close associates lacked the *Noblesse oblige* of the upper classes or the social consciousness of the modern middle classes. Their extravagant, opulent, and pretentious lifestyles as well as their arrogance and condescending attitude toward the rest of the population alienated the overwhelming majority of the people. The demand for social justice came to mean that national wealth (state income from oil, natural gas, and the like) should be distributed fairly and legally among the population rather than siphoned off to a handful of corrupt monarchists.

---

[1] Masoud Kazemzadeh, *The Iran National Front and the Struggle for Democracy* (Berlin, Germany: De Gruyter, 2022), pp. 20–21.
[2] Ibid.

https://doi.org/10.1515/9783111280288-003

1.2 Resistance to Khomeini's Dictatorship, 1979–1981

The fall of the Shah did not usher in what many had struggled for. The so-called "*Bahar Azadi*" [Spring of Freedom] after the overthrow of the Shah's dictatorship did not last long. During the brief interlude between the monarchist and fundamentalist dictatorships, the people expressed their desire for democracy and freedom. The initial euphoria soon gave way to resistance against Khomeini and his fundamentalist supporters who envisioned a utopia different from theirs. The dystopic polity that Khomeini and his supporters were creating could not be build but upon the mass repression and oppression of millions of Iranians who were not fundamentalist. Thus, struggle ensued right after the overthrow of the hated monarchy as Khomeini and his supporters began to institute their vision of a holy polity.

As time went on, Khomeini and the fundamentalists were becoming stronger. They created the Islamic Republican Party (IRP) as their vehicle for organizing supporters of Khomeini, concentrating all power in their own hands, eliminating the non-fundamentalists, and creating a totalitarian right-wing clerical theocratic regime. They organized and armed their supporters in the Islamic Revolutionary Guard Corps (IRGC). They also created the *Basij* and plain-clothes club-wielding violent extremists called *Hezbollahis*. One of the main slogans of the fundamentalists between February 1979 and the late 1980s was: "*Hezb Faghat Hezbollah, Rahbar Faghat Ruhollah*" [Sole Party Is Party of God, Sole Leader Is Ruhollah].[3]

As the fundamentalists became stronger, Khomeini began eliminating non-fundamentalists one by one. First, they went after the feminists and female judges. Then, the free press. Then, the religious and ethnic minorities. Then, the secular, liberal, and leftist university professors and students. The IRGC, *Basij*, and Hezbollahis attacked the non-fundamentalists with knives, clubs, and guns in order to beat up, injure, or murder them. The fundamentalists routinely took non-fundamentalist political activists hostage and tortured them. By June 1981, the fundamentalists had murdered many non-fundamentalists.

Soon after the triumph of the revolution, Khomeini went after the moderate liberal Islamists such as the Prime Minister of the provisional government Mehdi Bazargan and the first elected President Dr. Abolhassan Bani Sadr.[4] After the elimination of the moderates in June 1981, the fundamentalist regime engaged

---

3 During this period, the supporters of the fundamentalist regime were called "*Hezbollahis*" and Falangists.

4 For an excellent and highly sympathetic book on Bani Sadr, see Ali Gharib, *Istad-e Bar Arman* [Standing on Principles] (2006), https://www.enghelabe-eslami.com/pdf/Gharib-Istade-bar-Arman.pdf?fbclid=IwAR2UjiHF0eHH03iyfTbTH6G81gZ8xdnfy6GcJnAHNXEm10wUZ-Iv2knFhAU.

in wholesale massacres of opponents and political prisoners, many of whom were supporters of Bani Sadr, the Islamist leftist People's Mojahedin Organization of Iran (PMOI), and Marxists.

During the First Reign of Terror between June 1981 and December 1982 somewhere between 12,000 and 20,000 political prisoners were executed. *The Economist* (October 23, 1982) provided the figure of 12,000 while the higher number was given by opposition groups.[5] Thousands more were killed in armed clashes between the regime and opposition groups.

During the Second Reign of Terror in August and September 1988, about 5,000 political prisoners were executed.[6] About 4,000 were members and supporters of the PMOI, many teenage boys and girls, who had already gone through unfair trials and been given prison sentences. About 1,000 were members of various Marxist groups (who had been born into Muslim families). PMOI prisoners were asked whether they were still supportive of their positions, whether they would be willing to execute members of the PMOI, or would be willing to walk over mines in minefields. Those PMOI political prisoners who refused to answer or gave the "wrong" answer were executed within hours or days. Members of Marxist groups were asked: if they believed in God; if they were Muslim; and if they believed that the Koran was the word of God. Those who refused to answer or said "no" were considered apostates and were executed within hours or days.[7]

The corpses were buried in unmarked mass graves throughout Iran. These gravesites became known as *"Khavaran."* The regime has refused to provide details to families about the whereabouts of the corpses of their loved ones. On several occasions when mass graves were discovered many years later, the regime destroyed the remains. Grieving mothers of the victims have been asking for information about their children. They became known as *"Madaran-e Khavaran"* [Mothers of Khavaran]. Among officials directly responsible are: Ayatollah Ruhollah Khomeini (Supreme Leader), Ahmad Khomeini (Chief of Staff for Supreme Leader), Ayatollah Abdol-Karim Moussavi Ardabili (Chief of the Judicial Branch), Ebrahim

---

5 Ramy Nima, *The Wrath of Allah: Islamic Revolution and Reaction in Iran* (London: Pluto Press, 1983), pp. 115, 158.
6 Paul Lewis, "U.N. Inquiry Says Iran Still Abuses Human Rights," *The New York Times* (November 19, 1989); and *Iran Times* (December 7, 1990), p. 1.
7 Geoffrey Robertson, *The Massacre of Political Prisoners in Iran, 1988, Report of An Inquiry*, Abdorrahman Boroumand Foundation (April 18, 2011), https://www.iranrights.org/library/document/1380/the-massacre-of-political-prisoners-in-iran-1988-report-of-an-inquiry; Amnesty International, *Blood-Soaked Secrets: Why Iran's 1988 Prison Massacres Are Ongoing Crimes Against Humanity* (London: 2017), https://www.amnesty.org/download/Documents/MDE1394212018ENGLISH.PDF, p. 10.

Raisi (a member of the "Death Board" and later Chief of the Judicial Branch, and President), and Mostafa Pour-Mohammadi (Rouhani's Minister of Justice).[8]

Amnesty International considers the 1988 massacres of political prisoners to constitute "crimes against humanity."[9] Moreover, according to Amnesty International, the regime officials have lied about the massacres or tried to justify them, refused to give the corpses of those executed to their families or tell them where the graves are, and threatened the families with violence. In September 2020, a U.N. human rights group stated that the 1988 massacre of political prisoners may constitute "crimes against humanity."[10]

1.3 Resistance and Mass Protests, 1982–2023

By mid-1982, the fundamentalist regime had succeeded in crushing the opposition groups. From then, Iran has witnessed several major mass protests.

1.3.1 May 1992, Mashhad

The first mass protests after 1982 occurred in May 1992 in the poor shantytown of Koy Toulab on the outskirts of Mashhad, Iran's second largest city. When city municipality officials ignored the pleas of the poor shanty town dwellers who had built their shacks illegally, mass riots occurred there. The people burned police cars and municipality buildings after the police killed a 12-year-old boy. Several people and members of the coercive apparatuses died in the ensuing violence. The regime executed four of the protesters. Building of illegal housing on the outskirts of large cities has been common since the early 1970s with the large-scale migration of poor rural people to major cities.

---

8 Iran Human Rights Documentation Center, *Deadly Fatwa: Iran's 1988 Prison Massacre* (February 5, 2011), https://iranhrdc.org/deadly-fatwa-irans-1988-prison-massacre/.
9 Amnesty International, *Blood-Soaked Secrets: Why Iran's 1988 Prison Massacres Are Ongoing Crimes Against Humanity* (London: 2017), https://www.amnesty.org/download/Documents/MDE1394212018ENGLISH.PDF.
10 U.N. Letter to the Iranian Government (Geneva, Switzerland: September 3, 2020), https://spcommreports.ohchr.org/TMResultsBase/DownLoadPublicCommunicationFile?gId=25503.

Most observers blame the economic policies of then-President Rafsanjani for these protests by the urban poor.[11] Ayatollah Ali Akbar Hashemi Rafsanjani was one of the main pillars of the fundamentalist regime. After Khomeini died in June 1989, Rafsanjani was able to convince the Assembly of Experts to appoint the then-President Ali Khamenei to the position of Supreme Leader. Rafsanjani then became President (1989 – 1997). By most accounts, Rafsanjani was the most powerful figure in Iran during his first term as President (1989 – 1993) and the second most powerful figure for many years after Khamenei was able to gradually increase his powers.

1.3.2 April 1995, Islamshahr

Islamshahr is a poor neighborhood on the outskirts of Tehran, where many recent rural migrants live. They commute with buses to Tehran for work on a daily basis. Rafsanjani had begun a process of economic change, such as reducing state subsidies. One of the major subsidies in Iran (before and after the revolution) has been for fuel for buses, autos, and trucks. In April 1995, the government announced reduction of subsidized fuel for buses and an increase in bus fares of 30 %. The government's announcement caused major riots by the poor in Islamshahr. The riots lasted for many days and only after massive violence was the regime able to suppress the protests. One source says that 50,000 people participated in the riots and the regime killed at least 50 people.[12]

1.3.3 November 1998, Mass Protests at Funeral of Dariush and Parvaneh Forouhar

The top two leaders of the Iran Nation Party, Dariush Forouhar and his wife Parvaneh Eskandari-Forouhar, were murdered by Ministry of Intelligence agents on November 21, 1998 in their home in Tehran. In the largest protest since June 1981, large crowds participated in their public funeral. The estimate of the number of protesters is somewhere between 50,000 and 100,000. In response to the outrage, the regime arrested Deputy Minister of Intelligence, Saeed Imami (aka Saeed Is-

---

11 Nozhan Etezadosaltaneh, "Rafsanjani's Legacy: The Father of Neoliberalism in Iran," *International Policy Digest* (January 12, 2017), https://intpolicydigest.org/rafsanjani-s-legacy-father-neo liberalism-iran/.

12 Ali Alfoneh, "More Bloodshed, Harsher Repression in Iran's Protests," *The Arab Weekly* (August 12, 2019), https://thearabweekly.com/more-bloodshed-harsher-repression-irans-protests.

lami) for organizing the murders. It is believed that the murders were ordered by the Supreme Leader Khamenei and authorized by the Minister of Intelligence Dorri Najafabadi. The regime claims that Imami committed suicide in prison. It is believed that he was murdered in order to silence him because he had begun talking and revealing a large number of assassinations and explosions carried out by the Ministry of Intelligence. This mass protest was the first pro-democracy mass protest since 1981. The protesters shouted "*Mossadegh Rahat Edameh Darad*" [Mossadegh Your Path Will Continue], and "*Forouhar Rahat Edameh Darad*" [Forouhar Your Path Will Continue].

During this mass protest, the regime did not send its coercive apparatuses to gun down the people. This was a first since July 1981. The reasons may include the following facts: (1) somewhere between 50,000 and 100,000 people were on the streets; (2) Dariush Forouhar and Parvaneh Forouhar were well-known pro-democracy non-violent activists and close associates of Mossadegh with great legitimacy; (3) Khatami had been elected President in May 1997 and was attempting to present a less violent face of the regime to both domestic and international audiences; (4) the regime was caught off-guard by the massive response of the population and did not know how to act; and (5) the protest was a one-day event. This mass protest gave rise to a template that many other mass protests emulated to protest in such a manner that the regime would not be able to use massive violence against the people.

1.3.4 July 1999, Pro-democracy Student Protests

On July 7, 1999, the judiciary announced its decision to ban the daily *Salaam*, a reformist newspaper, because it had published an article linking Saeed Imami (Deputy Minister of Intelligence) to a bill in Majles on censorship of newspapers. Reformist students at Tehran University held peaceful demonstrations condemning the ban. On the night of July 8, the police, *Basij*, and plain-clothes coercive apparatuses attacked student dormitories at Tehran University and killed one person, injuring about 200, and arresting many. In response, there were widespread protests in many universities in several major cities such as Tabriz and Esfehan. President Khatami was silent for about five days. Under threat from the IRGC, Khatami issued a public statement condemning the students. The reformist students accepted Khatami's wish and ceased their protests. But pro-democracy students continued their protests, and their slogans went beyond merely the return of the *Salaam* daily and condemned Supreme Leader Khamenei. Six days of protests were finally crushed by the IRGC with mass violence. The total number of killed, disappeared, injured, and arrested is not known.[13]

Among the leaders of the pro-democracy protesters were Roozbeh Farahanipour, Reza Mohajerinejad, Ahmad Batebi, Manouchehr Mohammadi, and Akbar Mohammadi, all of whom were for the replacement of the fundamentalist regime with a secular democratic republic.

1.3.5 June 2003, Pro-democracy Student Protests

The regime announced plans to privatize universities in early June 2003. Pro-democracy students held peaceful demonstrations condemning the plan. Their slogans, however, were for democracy, free speech, and free university tuition, and an end to police brutality. According to the regime itself, the regime arrested about 4,000 students and kept them in jail until late July to prevent commemorations of the 1999 mass protests.[14]

1.3.6 2009 – 2010, The Green Movement

The mass protests during this period were very different from those that preceded them and those that followed them. Chapter 2 will discuss and analyze the Green Movement in great detail. Suffice it to say here that the movement was under the leadership of the reformist faction of the fundamentalist regime but many outside the regime, such as those in the democratic opposition, supported the mass protests.

1.3.7 December 2017–January 2018, Mass Protest

In Chapter 3, I will discuss and analyze this mass protest in detail. This protest was a turning point. For the first time, there were slogans against the reformist faction of the oligarchy. The main slogan of the protesters was: *"Osolgara, Eslahtalab, Digeh Tamom Majera"* [Hardliners, Reformists, You Are Both Done]. Unlike the 2009 – 2010 protests (which included middle classes in large cities), large numbers

---

13 BBC News, "Six Days that Shook Iran" (July 11, 2000), http://news.bbc.co.uk/2/hi/middle_east/828696.stm.
14 Associated Press, "4000 arrests in Iran reform protests" (June 12, 2003), https://www.cbsnews.com/news/4000-arrests-in-iran-reform-protests/.

of poor people in large and medium-sized cities also participated in the mass protests. Although most slogans were in support of democracy (and a republican form of government), for the first time slogans in support of monarchy and the Pahlavi kings were shouted by many.[15]

1.3.8 November 2019, Mass Protests Against Gasoline Prices

In November 2019, the regime suddenly announced a three-fold increase in the price of gasoline. This outraged the population. The regime had made a strategic decision to reduce its subsidies for the Iranian people (e.g., fuel, food, electricity, natural gas) but it has increased its massive expenditures on its violent jihad to export its revolution and ideology (e.g., Syria, Iraq, Lebanon, Yemen, and extremist Palestinian groups such as Hamas and Palestine Islamic Jihad).

The fundamentalist regime has been using increasing levels of lethal violence against unarmed protesters to suppress dissent and protests. For example, during November 2019 protests, the regime used direct shots to the heads of protesters and used machine guns to put down peaceful protests. A report from officials stated that about 23% of those who were shot were shot in the head from a short distance.[16] The regime has refused to release official numbers but officials have said that about 200 protesters died. Reuters put the number killed at 1,500 and the U.S. government said more than 1,000.[17] A recent scholarly study conducted by three epidemiologists investigating the number of deaths due to Covid-19 looked at the number of registered deaths in each province before and after the Covid-19 epidemic emerged in Iran. Their research shows that during November 2019 the num-

---

15 Masoud Kazemzadeh, "Protests in Iran: Characteristics, Causes, and Policy Ramifications," *Small Wars Journal* (January 3, 2018), http://smallwarsjournal.com/jrnl/art/protests-iran-character istics-causes-and-policy-ramifications; and Masoud Kazemzadeh, "Five Possible Outcomes Following the Mass Protests in Iran," Radio Farda (February 6, 2018), https://en.radiofarda.com/a/iran-unrest-scenarios-war-revolution-uprising/29023446.html.

16 Iran International, *"Vakonesh Magham Dowlati Beh Koshtar Aban Mah"* [Reaction of the Government Official to the Massacre of November 2019] (April 24, 2021), https://www.youtube.com/watch?v=FiNvX16SF1M.

17 Radio Farda, *"Enteshar Amar Marg O Mir Dar Aban 98"* [Publication on the Statistics on Deaths During November 2019] (May 27, 2021), https://www.radiofarda.com/a/31276567.html; Zeitoon, *"Abaad Jadidi Az Koshtar Aban 98"* [New Dimensions of the Massacre of November 2019] (May 27, 2021), https://www.zeitoons.com/87839; and Reuters, "Special Report: Iran's Leader Ordered Crackdown on Unrest – 'Do Whatever It Takes to End It'" (December 23, 2019), https://www.reu ters.com/article/us-iran-protests-specialreport/special-report-irans-leader-ordered-crackdown-on-unrest-do-whatever-it-takes-to-end-it-idUSKBN1YR0QR.

ber of registered deaths spiked greatly. There were 4,201 more deaths in November 2019 than in October 2019. There were 4,902 more deaths in November 2019 than in December 2019. There were 6,302 more deaths in November 2019 than in November 2018. All these deaths occurred before the emergence of the epidemic of Covid-19 in Iran in early 2020.[18] An exhaustive scholarly study indicates that no known factor explains the spike in deaths in November 2019.[19] The sole factor during November 2019 was deaths due to the protests against the fundamentalist regime. These numbers suggest that the number killed during the November 2019 protests might be somewhere between 4,000 and 6,000.

In these protests, there were more slogans in support of the monarchy, which caused concerns and worries among many pro-democracy and progressive forces.

1.3.9 January 2020 Civil Society Protests

Mass protests have become more frequent and more widespread in recent years.[20] With the exception of the mass protests during 2009 – 2010 that were under the leadership of the reformist factions of the fundamentalist oligarchy, all other protests were by democratic opponents, civil society activists, or people who spontaneously joined the protests in anger against the regime for a specific policy or event. This indicates that, despite mass executions and mass repression, vast numbers of the people continue to resist the regime.

1.3.10 September 2022 – 2023, Mass Protests to Overthrow

In Chapter 4, I will discuss, in great detail, the medium-term antecedents (1–5 years) of the 2022 – 2023 mass protests. In Chapter 5, I will discuss the short-term antecedents (1–2 years) of the 2022 – 2023 protests and present a detailed analysis

---

18 Mahan Ghafari, Alireza Kadivar, and Aris Katzourakis, "Excess Deaths Associated with the Iranian COVID-19 Epidemic: A Province-Level Analysis," *International Journal of Infectious Diseases*, Vol. 107 (June 2021), pp. 101–115, https://www.sciencedirect.com/science/article/pii/S1201971221003266X.

19 Mahan Ghafari, *"Marg O Mir Aban 98: Moamae Chand Hezar Nafari Keh Ezafeand?"* [Deaths of November 2019: The Puzzle of Several Thousand Additional Deaths?], Radio Farda (May 28, 2021), https://www.radiofarda.com/a/commentary-on-death-toll-report-of-november-2019/31276714.html. Also see Ghafari, Kadivar, and Katzourakis, "Excess Deaths," op. cit.

20 Radio Farda, "Fresh Wave of Protests Starting From Universities Spread to Several Cities in Iran" (January 12, 2020), https://en.radiofarda.com/a/fresh-wave-of-protests-starting-from-universities-spread-to-several-cities-in-iran/30373141.html.

of these protests. I argue that the overthrow of the fundamentalist regime has become a likely outcome of the mass protests for the first time since 1979.

1.4 On the Nature of the Fundamentalist Regime

The fundamentalist regime has not been a one-man dictatorship. Rather, it has been an oligarchy of fundamentalist clerics and lay. The fundamentalist regime that was established after the revolution by Khomeini and his followers is a theocratic oligarchy. It is theocratic because its top rulers have to be Shia clerics. Increasingly, lay fundamentalists—members of the IRGC, who dominate the military, intelligence, and security apparatuses—have become extremely powerful. With the exception of Khomeini, who was very old and terribly ill and thus unable to rule personally, delegating the day-to-day running of the regime to his lieutenants, no one person has been able to have total power in the sense that Reza Shah Pahlavi, Mohammad Reza Shah Pahlavi had in his rule (or Saddam Hussein in Iraq or Hafiz al-Assad in Syria, or Mao in China, or Hitler in Germany). The regime has thus been an oligarchy.

Khomeini and the fundamentalists themselves used the term *"Velayat Faqih"* [Rule of a High-Ranking Shia Cleric] between 1979 and 1989 to refer to their regime. After 1989, they used the term *"Velayat Motlagh Faqih"* [Absolute Rule of a High-Ranking Shia Cleric] for their regime. Since 1997, the fundamentalists have tended to also use the terms *"democracy dini"* [religious democracy] and *"democracy Islami"* [Islamic democracy] to refer to their regime. These terms are Orwellian double-speak for a regime that has little relationship to democracy.

In this book, I use the term "fundamentalist regime" for *"Nizam Velayat Faqih."* The literal translation would be the "system of rule by a high-ranking Shia cleric." This system was established by Ayatollah Ruhollah Khomeini in Iran after the 1979 revolution.

I use the term "fundamentalists" for the supporters of Khomeini and his regime. This includes the officials and supporters of the IRP. Between February 1979 and June 1981, many non-fundamentalists were part of the post-revolution governing structure. For example, the Liberation Movement of Iran, under the leadership of Mehdi Bazargan, who served as the Prime Minister in the provisional government, was a main element within the governing structure. Also, the first elected President was Dr. Abol-Hassan Bani Sadr, a progressive liberal Islamist. The non-fundamentalists also included the secular liberal democrats and secular social democrats of the INF under the leadership of Dr. Karim Sanjabi. All the non-fundamentalists were purged from positions of power by June 1981. The fundamentalists then eliminated many non-fundamentalist groups and individuals

(e. g., Marxists, left-wing Islamists, and ethnic minority parties) through violence and mass executions.

I use the term "fundamentalist oligarchy" to refer to those who supported Khomeini's interpretation of Islam and were officials in the post-June 1981 regime. The IRP soon split into three main factions: left, center, and right. Around 1997, the left faction of the fundamentalist oligarchy (e. g., Mohammad Khatami, Mir Hussein Moussavi, and Mehdi Karrubi) chose the name "reformist," while the right faction (e. g., Ali Khamenei) became known as "hardliners" or "principles-ists." The center faction (e. g., Ali Akbar Rafsanjani and Hassan Rouhani) became known as "moderates," or "pragmatic conservatives," or "expedients."

The fundamentalist regime's ideology is a far-right totalitarian ideology. In the words of Supreme Leader Khamenei:

> One cannot assume that Islam to demand a form of social system, but does not specify the issues of governance, as well as the rule of religion and the world. When religion becomes regime, a regime that is related to the individual and the society, it becomes a constellation which has views on all individual and social issues, has an opinion, and demands; therefore, it is necessary to specify who will be on the top of this society, what should be done, and choose the Imam [Religious-Political Leader].[21]

Khamenei goes on to say that Islam is all-inclusive and has rules for both the individual and the society, including for politics, economy, domestic security, national security, and foreign policy.[22] Khamenei adds that anyone who disagrees with him is anti-Islamic. According to Khamenei: "What I want to say is that first, this [non-political Islamic] movement is in reality anti-Islamic, and primarily from the Great Powers in the world."[23]

Islamic fundamentalism is ideologically opposed to Enlightenment thought, secularism, liberalism, Marxism, feminism, and universal human rights. Islamic fundamentalism opposes the Enlightenment on the grounds that knowledge comes from revelation and not materialistic, scientific, and rational bases of knowledge. Islamic fundamentalism opposes secularism, arguing that God has re-

---

21 Imam Ali Khamenei, *"Bayanat Dar Didar Mehmanan Konferance Vahdat Islami Va Jamee Az Masoulan Nezam"* [Speech at the Islamic Unity Conference and a Group of Regime Officials] (October 24, 2021), https://farsi.khamenei.ir/speech-content?id=48891. My translation. Brief excerpts of Khamenei's speech in English is available at his site https://english.khamenei.ir/news/8739/Muslims-unity-necessary-for-realization-of-new-Islamic-Civilization. The English translation does not include some of the most significant segments. From mid-2021, the regime and Khamenei's own site refer to him with the title of "Imam."
22 Ibid.
23 Ibid.

vealed the Truth and God's Truth is superior to any human knowledge. Islamic fundamentalists want to impose (their version of) Sharia as the primary law of the land. Islamic fundamentalists oppose liberalism because (modern) liberalism respects: individual rights; civil liberties; *de jure* equality of all citizens; freedoms of expression, the press, and political parties; pluralism; religious pluralism; democracy; and secular forms of government. Islamic fundamentalists argue that, according to Sharia, there should be different laws for Muslims and non-Muslims as well as for men and women. Islamic fundamentalism opposes Marxism because of Marxism's egalitarianism. Islamic fundamentalists oppose feminists because feminists advocate equality between men and women. Islamic fundamentalists oppose universal human rights because such universal declarations are not based on Sharia but rather on secular and Western values.[24]

There are similarities between Islamic fundamentalism and European fascisms of the 1920s–1945.[25] Many Western and Iranian scholars consider the fundamentalist regime to have similarities with fascism.[26] One of the most prominent Western scholars who very early came to consider Islamic fundamentalists to be similar to fascists was the preeminent French Marxist scholar Maxime Rodinson.[27] In a major review of Rodinson's works, Professor Jean Batou analyzed Rodinson's views.[28] Batou wrote:

---

24 Ayatollah Ali Khamenei, "Speech" (January 17, 2020), http://english.khamenei.ir/news/7318/Our-Islamic-power-will-overcome-the-superficial-grandeur-of-material.
25 On characteristics of European fascisms see Roger Griffin, editor, *Fascism* (Oxford: Oxford University Press, 1995), pp. 1–12. For the classic structuralist work on the social class basis of fascism in Germany and Italy see Barrington Moore, Jr., *Social Origins of Dictatorship and Democracy: Lord and Peasant in the Making of the Modern World* (Boston: Beacon Press, 1966). For the classic psychoanalytic analysis of fascism see Erich Fromm, *Escape from Freedom* (New York: Farrar & Rinehart, 1941), ch. 6. Also see Benito Mussolini, "The Doctrine of Fascism" (1932), https://sjsu.edu/faculty/wooda/2B-HUM/Readings/The-Doctrine-of-Fascism.pdf.
26 Masoud Kazemzadeh, "Teaching the Politics of Islamic Fundamentalism," *PS: Political Science and Politics*, Vol. 31, No. 1 (1998), pp. 52–59. Some of the most sophisticated scholarly works considering the fundamentalist regime as similar to European fascism are: Said Amir Arjomand, *The Turban for the Crown: The Islamic Revolution in Iran* (Oxford and New York: Oxford University Press, 1988); and Sharif Arani, "Iran: From the Shah's Dictatorship to Khomeini's Demagogic Theocracy," *Dissent*, No. 27 (Winter 1980), pp. 9–26.
27 Jean Batou, "Maxime Rodinson Was a Revolutionary Historian of the Muslim World," Jacobin (January 31, 2021), https://www.jacobinmag.com/2021/01/maxime-rodinson-islam-middle-east. Professor Rodinson was one of the greatest scholars of Islam and the Middle East. Both of his parents (of Russian-Polish Jewish descent) died at the Auschwitz concentration camp. Professor Rodinson passed away in 2004.
28 Ibid.

In three articles published in December 1978 for *Le Monde*, he [Rodinson] described Islamic fundamentalism as a kind of "archaizing fascism" based on "the will to establish an authoritarian and totalitarian state whose political police would ferociously maintain the moral and social order," while also imposing "conformity to the norms of religious tradition as interpreted in the most conservative sense."[29]

Another great Western scholar of Iran, who very early came to recognize the fascistic nature of Islamic fundamentalism was Fred Halliday.[30] Paraphrasing Karl Kautsky's description of Nazism as the socialism of fools, Halliday describes Islamic fundamentalism as "the anti-imperialism of fools."[31] According to Walter Posch (historian and Iran expert at the National Defense Academy of the Austrian Army in Vienna), the IRGC has many similarities with the Nazi Party's Waffen-SS.[32] The role of the *Basij* for the fundamentalist regime is similar to the role of the SA Brown Shirts for the Nazi regime. Members of the *Basij* have been mobilized to beat up and suppress dissidents and opponents of the regime such as liberal democrats, Marxists, feminists, labor activists, pro-democracy university students, dissident Shia clerics, and secular women.

Increasingly, observers and scholars from diverse perspectives have also described the fundamentalist regime as similar to European fascism.[33] Many university professors inside Iran (on condition of anonymity) as well as the public use the term "banality of evil" coined by Hannah Arendt in her work *Eichmann in Jerusalem*, to describe the fundamentalist regime. Many consider President Ebrahim

---

29 Ibid.
30 Of Irish descent, Halliday became a Professor of Political Science and International Relations at the School of Oriental and African Studies, University of London. Halliday passed away in 2010.
31 Fred Halliday, "The Iranian Revolution and Its Implications," *New Left Review*, No. 166 (November/December 1987), p. 37.
32 Walter Posch, "Ideology and Strategy in the Middle East: The Case of Iran," *Survival*, Vol. 59, No. 5 (October–November 2017), p. 96, endnote 50.
33 For a recent left-liberal observer see Bijan Ghoghnoos, *"Aya 'Jomhuri Velayat Faqih' Regimi Fashisti Ast?"* [Is the "Rule of Shia Cleric Republic" a Fascist Regime?], Iran Emrooz (January 31, 2021), http://www.iran-emrooz.net/index.php/politic/more/87667/. Utilizing Hannah Arendt's definition of totalitarianism, Ghoghnoos argues that the fundamentalist regime is a form of right-wing totalitarianism similar to European fascism. In a scholarly article in a journal published by an Israeli university, Eliot Assoudeh argues that the fundamentalist regime is similar to Eastern European fascism of the 1930s–1940s. Eliot Assoudeh, "Shia Phoenix: Is Iran's Islamic Republic a Variety of Political Religion?" *The Journal for Interdisciplinary Middle Eastern Studies*, Vol. 4 (2019), pp. 57–95, https://www.ariel.ac.il/wp/jimes/shia-phoenix-is-irans-islamic-republic-a-variety-of-political-religion/.

Raisi to be very similar to Adolf Eichmann.[34] Persian translation of Arendt's *Eichmann in Jerusalem* has been a top seller in Iran.[35]

Even some European officials have recently compared fundamentalist officials to Nazi officials. In December 2020, in his speech at the European Parliament, Radoslaw Sikorski, Poland's representative to the European Parliament and former Polish Foreign Minister (2007–2014), described Iran's Foreign Minister Mohammad Javad Zarif as similar to the Nazi regime's Foreign Minister von Ribbentrop.[36] This is perhaps the most apt description of Zarif. As Nazi Germany's ambassador to the U.K., Ribbentrop had successfully kept the British out of the war against Germany when Nazis invaded Czechoslovakia and then as Nazi Germany's Foreign Minister, he signed the Nazi–Soviet non-aggression pact with Molotov, which was used to invade Poland. Zarif, similarly, was highly successful in manipulating and fooling Western policymakers and the public.[37]

The analysis that Islamic fundamentalism has similarities with European fascism should not come as a surprise. Both Khomeini and Khamenei were greatly influenced by the Muslim Brotherhood's Hassan al-Banna and Seyed Qotb.[38] Al-Banna was strongly influenced by Benito Mussolini and his fascist movement.[39]

---

34 Ghazal Golshiri, "L'incroyable succès d'Hannah Arendt en Iran," *Le Monde* (August 6, 2021), https://www.lemonde.fr/series-d-ete/article/2021/08/06/l-incroyable-succes-d-hannah-arendt-en-iran_6090745_3451060.html; and Nasser Etemadi, *"Chera Mardom Iran Ebrahim Raisi Va Ozaeh Keshvareshan Ra Shabih Eichmann Va Alman Nazi Midanand?"* [Why the Iranian People Consider Ebrahim Raisi and the Condition of Their Country to Be Similar to Eichmann and Nazi Germany], Radio France International (August 6, 2021), https://www.rfi.fr/fa/%D8%A7%DB%8C%D8%B1%D8%A7%D9%86/20210806-%DA%86%D8%B1%D8%A7-%D9%85%D8%B1%D8%AF%D9%85-%D8%A7%DB%8C%D8%B1%D8%A7%D9%86-%D8%A7%D8%A8%D8%B1%D8%A7%D9%87%DB%8C%D9%85-%D8%B1%D8%A6%DB%8C%D8%B3%DB%8C-%D9%88-%D8%A7%D9%88%D8%B6%D8%A7%D8%B9-%DA%A9%D8%B4%D9%88%D8%B1%D8%B4%D8%A7%D9%86-%D8%B1%D8%A7-%D8%B4%D8%A8%DB%8C%D9%87-%D8%A2%DB%8C%D8%B4%D9%85%D9%86-%D9%88-%D8%A2%D9%84%D9%85%D8%A7%D9%86-%D9%86%D8%A7%D8%B2%DB%8C-%D9%85%DB%8C-%D8%AF%D8%A7%D9%86%D9%86%D8%AF.

35 Ibid., Golshiri; Etemadi.

36 Radio Farda, *"Namayandeh Lahestan Dar Parleman Eropa, Zarif Ra Beh Vazir Omor Kharejeh Alman Nazi Tashbih Kard"* [The Representative to the European Parliament from Poland, Considered Zarif to be Similar to the Foreign Minister of Nazi Germany] (December 18, 2020), https://www.radiofarda.com/a/31008036.html; Radoslaw Sikorski, "Speech" (December 18, 2020), posted on You Tube https://www.youtube.com/watch?v=YjrnThhS7ZY (December 21, 2020).

37 Masoud Kazemzadeh, *The Grand Strategy of the Islamic Republic of Iran* (forthcoming).

38 Masoud Kazemzadeh, *Iran's Foreign Policy: Elite Factionalism, Ideology, the Nuclear Weapons Program, and the United States* (London: Routledge, 2020), chapters 1, 2, and 5.

Like fascism, Islamic fundamentalism is a reaction to modernity. They attract individuals and strata that feel that the processes of modernization has caused decline in their economic well-being, power, social status, and security. These individuals and strata become attracted to the use of violence and mass movement to go back to a romanticized and mythologized golden past when things were superior to the current situation. They call their advocacy and use of mass violence for rapid change a "revolution."

Like fascists, Islamic fundamentalists organize the disaffected into para-military organizations. Members in these para-military organizations get economic and psychological benefits from such memberships. They absolutely obey the Leader and they get to have power over segments of the population that are considered enemies.

Like fascists, Islamic fundamentalists are against legal equality of all citizens and peoples. Fascists and Islamic fundamentalists argue that a particular group is superior and that they want a system whereby that particular group holds positions of power and privilege. Italian fascists considered the Italian people to be such a group, German Nazis considered the Aryan race to be such a group, and the Shia fundamentalists consider the Shia fundamentalists to be such a group. As mentioned earlier, the fundamentalists use the term *"khodi"* [of one's own] to refer to Shia fundamentalists. They use the term *"ghereh khodi"* [not of one's own, the others] to refer to those who are not Shia fundamentalists. The fundamentalist constitution and laws make distinctions between Shia Muslims and others. The positions of power are designated in the fundamentalist constitution solely for the Shia. For example, the positions of Supreme Leader, Head of the Judicial Branch, and Minister of Intelligence are solely for Shia clerics. The position of President is only for male Shia. Positions of power are only for *khodi* individuals. Through *de jure* and *de facto* discriminations, *ghereh khodi* Iranians are oppressed and privilege is provided to *khodi* individuals.

The fundamentalist regime has instituted a pervasive and multi-layered system of *de jure* and *de facto* discriminations against religious minorities.[40] The first group consists of Zoroastrians, Jews, and certain Christians (Armenian and Assyrian), that are protected second-class citizens. Following the precedent of the 1906 constitution, the fundamentalist constitution allocates five seats in the Majles

---

39 Ana Belen Soage, "Hasan al-Banna or the Politicisation of Islam," *Totalitarian Movements and Political Religions*, Vol. 9, No. 1 (March 2008), pp. 21–42, https://www.researchgate.net/publication/233003241_Hasan_al-Banna_or_the_Politicisation_of_Islam.
40 Fred Petrossian, "Religious Minorities in Iran: Violence, Resistance, and Hope," Religion and IR, International Studies Association (November 29, 2021), https://religion-ir.org/blog/religious-minorities-in-iran-violence-resistance-and-hope-by-fred-petrossian.

to these religious minorities. Members of these religious minority communities throughout the country, regardless of their geographical residence, vote for a member of their community to represent them in the Majles. This representative is required to publicly support the fundamentalist constitution and policies, and publicly condemn the U.S., Israel, and global Zionism on various occasions on the floor of the Majles. Many members of this group of minorities have left Iran. For example, in 1978 there were about 85,000 Jews in Iran. In 2021, there were about 5,000 Jews left in Iran and their number is dwindling. In 1978, Iran's population was about 34 million, in 2021 it rose to about 84 million. Most Jewish Iranians have left for the U.S. and Israel, where they feel safe. Jews have been living in Iran for at least 2,700 years.

A second group consists of Sunnis and Shia Dervishes. Sunni citizens are in a legal and political limbo. The Sunnis in Iran constitute about 10 to 15% of the population and tend to be coterminous with ethnic minorities such as Kurds, Balochis, Arabs, and Turkmans. Although the Sunnis are allowed representatives in the Majles, they are victims of severe and violent repression. Virtually all the powerful positions in the state—such as provincial governors, city governors, IRGC officials, and police chiefs—are given to Shia fundamentalists. These Shia fundamentalist officials are imposed on Sunni regions and population by the regime. There has not been a single Sunni cabinet minister since 1979. The fundamentalist regime does not allow Sunnis to build new mosques and has destroyed many that were built before 1979. The Sunni Iranians complain that there are over 1 million Sunnis in Tehran, but they are not allowed to have any mosques. The Sunni places of worship in Tehran are a handful of non-mosques that were in existence before 1979. There are a large number of Sunnis in Mashhad, the second largest city in Iran. The Sunni Iranians complain that their three major Sunni mosques in Mashhad have been demolished by the fundamentalist regime, leaving the city without a major Sunni mosque. Although many fundamentalist officials, including Supreme Leader Khamenei, publicly talk about unity between Shia and Sunni Muslims, in actual fact they have pursued a policy of harsh repression of Iranian Sunnis. The fundamentalist regime has secretly assassinated critical Sunni *ulama*. It has also provided funds to those Sunni *ulama* who support the fundamentalist regime. The fundamentalist regime has followed a similar policy toward the Shia Dervishes (who tend to be mostly Persian and Azerbaijanis), who have also been victims of harsh, violent repression.

The third group consists of Bahais, Christian converts, followers of Yarsan, and Mandaeans. The fundamentalist regime considers members of the third group to be "politically problematic individuals."[41] By law, the fundamentalist regime has attempted to violently suppress and eradicate these religious minorities. After the revolution, the fundamentalists arrested and executed about 200 leaders of the Bahai community.[42] Bahais are banned from university admission and government jobs. Christian converts have been jailed for many years. The Ministry of Intelligence has also assassinated many Christian converts (e.g., Mehdi Dibaj). According to one expert on religious minorities in Iran:

> Based on the ideological perspective of theocracy in Iran, these citizens are considered "politically problematic individuals", just like Nazi Germany that, based on its ideology of racism, considered the Jews to be a political problem not because of their activities and beliefs, but because of their very existence.
>
> The Islamic Republic has condemned the religious beliefs and identities of citizens belonging to religious minorities, even denying their right to exist.[43]

I include agnostics and atheists in the third group. Although the fundamentalist regime is uncomfortable about agnostics and atheists in general, it is particularly hostile to those who were born into Shia families. According to most Shia *ulama*, the punishment for Shia Muslims who become agnostic or atheist is execution. The fundamentalist regime has used that Shia Sharia law to persecute such Iranians.

Although fascism and Islamic fundamentalism contain atavistic and obscurantist elements, they are not total rejections of all things modern. Both fascists and Islamic fundamentalists strongly admire and embrace the most advanced military technologies (e.g., missiles, jetfighters, nuclear weapons, and tanks). Fascism and Islamic fundamentalism are reactionary adaptations to the modern world. Fascists and Islamic fundamentalists feel threatened by certain aspects of modernity and globalization, and they are mass violent movements to forcefully change the situation to their benefit.

Like fascism, Islamic fundamentalist ideology is explicitly corporatist and organic (i.e., society is conceived of an organic body where all parts have to cooperate in order to ensure the healthy functioning of the system). Such a political system regards its leader as the brain of the polity that has the right to order others and others have to obey. This form of corporatist ideology explicitly denies civil liberties and the right of dissent. Thus, individuals are crushed for the sake of the Islamic state. Like fascism, Islamic fundamentalism attempts to create a cult of personality of its leader. Like fascism, Islamic fundamentalism denies the saliency of

---

41 Ibid.
42 Ibid.
43 Ibid.

class struggle and class consciousness and utilizes class-derived rhetoric to mobilize certain classes against certain groups and scapegoats.

Islamic fundamentalists excel in manipulating prejudices (usually against religious and ethnic minorities) and xenophobic fears of the masses. Islamic fundamentalists have succeeded in mobilizing the masses not through appealing to their best and most noble desires (e.g., tolerance, coexistence, amity, compassion, mercy), but rather to their basest (e.g., hate, prejudice, revenge, envy).

The fundamentalist regime, under the auspices of the Ministry of Foreign Affairs, has organized seminars on the Holocaust inviting Europeans who deny the Holocaust to attend. For example, the regime held an official conference on the Holocaust on December 11–12, 2006.[44] It is significant to add that the conference was organized by Mohammad Ali Ramin, who was a top advisor to then-President Mahmoud Ahmadinejad and was the Secretary of *"Rayeheh Khosh Khedmat,"* the electoral list of supporters of Ahmadinejad for the 2006 elections.[45] In a lecture at the University of Gilan on May 30, 2006, Mr. Ramin said:

> Among the Jews there have always been harmful and wicked elements who killed God's prophets and stood against justice and rights, and this ethnic group has done the most damage to the human society throughout history, and another group among them has engaged in conspiracies, inflicting harm and cruelties on other nations and ethnic groups. … There are many accusations against the Jews throughout history, among them that they are the cause of spreading of diseases such as plague and typhus, because the Jews are very dirty persons.[46]

Ayatollah Ruhollah Khomeini blamed the Jews and foreigners for what he considered evil policies in Iran. Before October 1964, Khomeini explicitly used the terms *"Yahud"* [Jew, Judaism] and *"ajaneb"* [foreigners, aliens] in his official proclamations. However, after October 1964, he used the terms "Zionists," "imperialists," and "colonialists" instead. For example, he issued an official call in March 1963 condemning voting rights for women. Khomeini repeatedly attacked *ajaneb* [foreigners] for the Shah's policies.[47] Khomeini proclaimed:

> The ruling regime in Iran has attacked the holy laws of Islam and has the intention of attacking the certain laws of the Qoran, and the honors of Muslims are about to be violated and the

---

44 See www.adelaideinstitute.org/2006December/contents_program1.htm.

45 For some of Mr. Ramin's views see www.memri.org/bin/opener_latest.cgi?ID=SD140807.

46 BBC Persian, *"Taasis Bonyad Jahani Holocast Dar Tehran"* [Establishment of the Global Foundation of the Holocaust in Tehran] (December 14, 2006), www.bbc.co.uk/persian/iran/story/2006/12/061214_mf_holocaust.shtml. My translation.

47 Ayatollah Ruhollah Khomeini, *"Elamieh Imam Khomeini Beh Monasebat Tahrim Nourooz 1342"* [Statement of Imam Khomeini for the Boycott of 1963 Iranian Persian New Year] (March 1963), https://psri.ir/?id=7fjcxlg1.

tyrannical regime with policies that are against Sharia and the constitution wants to dishonor the chaste women and humiliate the Iranian nation. The tyrannical regime wants to pass and carry out [laws] on equality between women and men. This means undermining the necessary laws of Islam and the Holy Qoran. ...

The target of the *ajaneb* are the Qoran and clerics. The dirty hands of the *ajaneb* have the objective of using the hands of the government to remove the Qoran and to attack the clerics. We have to be attacked for the benefit of *Yahud* [Jew, Judaism], America, and Palestine [presumably referring to Israel], go to prison, be eliminated, be sacrificed for the evil wishes of the *ajaneb*.

Oh God, save the Holy Qoran and the honor of the Muslims from the evils of *ajaneb*.[48]

It is true that the Kennedy administration had put pressure on the Shah to make certain reforms such as the female franchise. Khomeini's attacks on Jews were not based on anything Jews had done. It appears that Khomeini simply blamed Jews for what he perceived to be evil such as the female franchise. What is even more interesting is that, in October 1963, Khomeini sent a secret letter to President Kennedy asking that the U.S. should support him [Khomeini] rather than the regime of the Shah.[49] Khomeini's secret letter to President Kennedy was delivered by a cleric, Ayatollah Hajj Mirza Khalil Kamarei, who took Khomeini's letter to the U.S. Embassy in Tehran. According to research conducted by BBC investigative journalist, Kambiz Fattahi, Khomeini's letter arrived in Washington on November 6, 1963. President Kennedy was assassinated on November 22, 1963. There does not exist any public information on whether President Kennedy read the letter or the U.S. government ever responded to this letter. A CIA analysis refers to the letter that Ayatollah Khomeini sent President Kennedy.[50]

After October 1964, Khomeini attacks the U.S. directly and uses terms like "imperialist" and "colonialist." It is not clear who told Khomeini in 1964 to use terms like "Zionist" rather than "Jew" or "Jewish," and "imperialist" and "colonialist" rather than "foreigner."

Like many right-wing Shia clerics in Iran, Khomeini was extremely and viciously anti-Bahai. In his public sermons and written proclamations, Khomeini blamed Jews for assisting Bahais. In 1963, in a public sermon, Khomeini directly attacked the Shah for having provided funds to some Bahais to attend a conference

---

48 Ibid.
49 Kambiz Fattahi, *"Payam Mahramaneh Ayatollah Khomeini Beh Dowlat Kennedy"* [The Secret Message from Ayatollah Khomeini to the Kennedy Administration], BBC Persian (June 1, 2016), https://www.bbc.com/persian/iran/2016/06/160601_kf_khomeini_carter_kennedy.
50 U.S. Government, CIA, "Islam in Iran" (August 31, 1979), http://news.files.bbci.co.uk/ws/documents/persian/bbc_persian_islam_in_iran.pdf, p. 67.

in London. The following is Khomeini's sermon (translation is by the fundamentalist regime's website of Khomeini's speeches and writings):

> But who are the advisers now? Israel! Our counselors are Jews! In the Dunya newspaper they themselves acknowledged the donation of five hundred dollars to each of two thousand Baha'is (the wretch hadn't better deny this since it was actually in the press); that's five hundred dollars from the wealth of this Muslim nation- in addition to offering a one-thousand-and-twe [sic] tumans discount on each of their air fares. And what was this for? It was for their journey to London to participate in an anti-Islamic meeting. They were thus afforded the highest respect. On the contrary, our pilgrims have to bear the most severe hardships and sometimes even have to offer bribes just to obtain permission for their journey; and even then only a few are actually successful. What intimidation they are subjected to on the outward journey and how many difficulties they have to face during their return journey! Moreover, whilst there at Minah and Mecca, they have to tolerate the objections and protests of a contemptible official who demands the apprehension of someone for truthfully stating that Islam is threatened by the Jews. My God man, are you indeed a Jew? And our country, is that Jewish too?[51]

Khomeini attacks the Shah as "a Jew" and his regime as "Jewish." To use "Jew" and "Jewish" as insults (for allegedly the regime had provided funds to Bahais to attend a conference in London) may be described as anti-Jewish racism.[52] After October 1964, Khomeini tends to use terms like "Zionist" rather than "Jew" for his attacks on opponents. After October 1964, he tends to distinguish two groups of Jews. One group of Jews who support the creation of the State of Israel. Khomeini calls them Zionists and they are considered the enemy. Khomeini has said that these Jews might be descendants of those Jews who have resisted Islamic rule and have conspired against Islam for the past 1,400 years.[53] A second group of Jews have accepted living as second-class citizens within *"balad Islam"* [the Islamic realm]. Khomeini has echoed the traditional Islamic view that Moses was one of the main

51 Ayatollah Ruhollah Khomeini, *"Sokhanrani Dar Jame Rouhanioun Qom"* [Speech to the Clerics at Qom] (May 2, 1963), https://emam.com/posts/view/134/%D8%B3%D8%AE%D9%86%D8%B1%D8%A7%D9%86%DB%8C-%D8%AF%D8%B1-%D8%AC%D9%85%D8%B9-%D8%B1%D9%88%D8%AD%D8%A7%D9%86%DB%8C%D9%88%D9%86-%D9%82%D9%85-%28%D8%A7%D8%B1%D8%B2%DB%8C%D8%A8%DB%8C-%D9%82%DB%8C%D8%A7%D9%85-%D9%85%D9%84%D8%AA%29.
52 In Europe and the U.S., the term "anti-Semitism" is used for what I call "anti-Jewish racism." The reason I avoid the term "anti-Semitism" is that Arabs are also considered to be Semitic. Clearly, Khomeini is not anti-Arab, for the Prophet Mohammad and the Shia Imam were Arabs. Although the Jewish people (or the Arab people or the Polish people) are not a race, virulent attacks against a particular group are usually described as "racist."
53 Grand Ayatollah Ruhollah Khomeini, "Speech" (1984), the video of the speech available on You Tube (May 18, 2014), https://www.youtube.com/watch?v=0EmAxl1Ksv0&list=RD0EmAxl1Ksv0&start_radio=1&rv=0EmAxl1Ksv0&t=399; and Grand Ayatollah Ruhollah Khomeini, "Speech" (no date), posted on You Tube (August 31, 2014), https://www.youtube.com/watch?v=C8nX-IZiWFY.

prophets of Allah, and that Jews are people of the book and should be protected in Islamic lands, so long as they accept their role as second-class citizens.

Like fascism, Islamic fundamentalism views political violence not as a necessary evil, but as a desirable tool to subjugate and intimidate domestic and foreign opponents. Religious rituals and liturgy have been manipulated to create a cult of violence that glamorizes violence. Like fascists, Islamic fundamentalists violently attack ethnic and religious minorities, feminists, liberals, leftists, labor unions, professional associations, and homosexuals.

In several speeches Khomeini criticized *"democratha va melliun"* [democrats and nationalists] for being under the influence of the West by criticizing violence against dissidents as violations of human rights. Khomeini said that these people were wrong and did not understand Islam. Khomeini said: "Islam includes teachings and punishments. ... For example, the Prophet Mohammad told Imam Ali to behead 700 Jews of Banu Qarayza."[54]

Like European fascists in Germany and Italy, Islamic fundamentalists pursue extremely bellicose, militarist, and expansionist foreign policies. Khomeini and Khamenei have been attempting to export their fundamentalist revolution and political system to other countries using violence and terrorist proxies. The Shia fundamentalists want to dominate the region and bring their governments under their control.[55] Khomeini famously said that Islam says *"Jang Jang Ta Raf'ah Fitna"* [War, War Until the Elimination of Rebellion].[56] Khomeini justified the continuance of war against Saddam Hussein with the slogans *"Jang Jang Ta Raf'ah In*

---

54 Grand Ayatollah Ruhollah Khomeini, "Speech" (1984), the video of the speech available on You Tube (May 18, 2014), https://www.youtube.com/watch?v=0EmAxl1Ksv0&list=RD0EmAxl1Ksv0&start_radio=1&rv=0EmAxl1Ksv0&t=399; and Grand Ayatollah Ruhollah Khomeini, "Speech" (no date), posted on You Tube (August 31, 2014), https://www.youtube.com/watch?v=C8nX-IZiWFY. Banu Qurayza or Bani Quraizah was a Jewish tribe in Medina. The tribe was defeated in a war against the Prophet Mohammad's forces. The Shia believe that Imam Ali personally cut off the heads of 700 male members of the group. It is not clear how true or exaggerated the story is. What is analytically significant here is that Khomeini used this story several times to argue that those who say that Islam is a religion of peace are wrong. Khomeini argues that Islam includes the use of great violence.
55 IRGC Gen. Qassem Soleymani, "Speech," Fars News Agency (March 29, 2014). The speech was delivered on February 16, 2014, http://www.farsnews.com/newstext.php?nn=13930108000154. *Kayhan*, *"Ma'muriyat-e niru-ye qods towse'eh-ye enghelab-e eslami dar jahan ast"* [The Quds Force's Mission is to Expand the Islamic Revolution Throughout the World] (October 2, 2014), http://kayhan.ir/fa/news/24370. For translations of excerpts of the above see Masoud Kazemzadeh, *The Grand Strategy of the Islamic Republic of Iran* (forthcoming).
56 In this context, *"fitna"* or *"fitnah"* refers to opposition to Islam, or discord, or rebellion.

Fitna" [War, War Until the Elimination of This Fitna] and "*Rah-e Qods Az Karbala Migozarad*" [The Road to Jerusalem Goes Through Karbala].[57]

Islam enjoys a rich tradition that includes both mercifulness and peace as well as violence and aggressive war. Moderate and liberal Muslims regard the merciful and peaceful aspects of Islam to constitute Islam's primary message and soul, while violence is interpreted as exceptional and historical. Islamic fundamentalists, on the contrary, regard jihad and violence to be primary aspects of Islam, while peace and mercifulness are interpreted as minor aspects practiced only after infidels have been vanquished and dominated.

It is necessary to emphasize that the highest-ranking clerics in Shia Islam have opposed the fundamentalists. For example, the highest-ranking Shia cleric in Iran during the revolutionary period was Grand Ayatollah Kazem Shariatmadari, who strongly opposed Khomeini, the fundamentalist regime, and the fundamentalist constitution. The two highest-ranking Shia clerics in the Shia world since 1979 have been Grand Ayatollah Abol-Qassem Khoi and Grand Ayatollah Ali Sistani. Both of Iranian origin, Khoi and Sistani have strongly opposed Khomeini and the fundamentalist regime, lived in Najaf, Iraq, and refused to move to Iran.

There are some major differences between European fascism and Islamic fundamentalism. European fascists are extreme nationalists. Ideologically, Islamic fundamentalists are pre-modern, pre-Westphalian, anti-Westphalian, and pan-Islamists. Ideologically, Islamic fundamentalists do not recognize the legitimacy of the nation-state and nationalism, although they have made pragmatic adjustments. Ideologically, the fundamentalists regard the only legitimate entity to be the *Ummah* (the Islamic community). For the Shia fundamentalists, the theocratic leader is called *Vali Faqih* or Imam. In the West, the term "Supreme Leader" is used to refer to the *Vali Faqih*, or *Rahbar Moazam Enghelab*.[58] For the Sunni fundamentalists, the theocratic leader is called *Khalifah* or Caliph. For example, the Shia fundamentalists regard the Supreme Leader Ali Khamenei (and before him, Ruhollah Khomeini) to be the leader of all Muslims. When Shia fundamentalists talk about Islamic unity, they mean that all Muslims (Sunni and Shia alike) should follow the leadership of the Supreme Leader. The fundamentalist constitution emphasizes this notion.[59] The fundamentalists emphasize that the Islamic Revolution-

---

57 Grand Ayatollah Ruhollah Khomeini, "Speech" (1985), You Tube (May 27, 2015), https://www.youtube.com/watch?v=8uhI1FUeVxA.

58 The term "*Vali*" means "leader." The term "*Faqih*" refers to a high-ranking Shia cleric who has specialized in Islamic law. The term "*Rahbar*" means "leader." The term "*Moazam*" means "Supreme" or "Great." The term "*Enghelab*" means "Revolution."

59 See the fundamentalist constitution at https://www.constituteproject.org/constitution/Iran_1989.pdf?lang=en.

ary Guard Corps purposefully does not contain the word "Iran" in its title.[60] In fact, the membership of the IRGC includes Shia from many nationalities such as Lebanese, Iraqi, Pakistani, and Afghans.[61] Khomeini's "Last Will and Testament" goes even further and argues that Sunni Islam is theologically false, that the only true Islam is the Shia denomination, and thus all Muslims should embrace Shia Islam.[62] There are *de jure* and *de facto* discriminations against Sunni Muslims by the Shia fundamentalist regime in Iran. Sunni fundamentalists (e.g., ISIS, Taliban) discriminate against Shia Muslims under their control.

Although the fundamentalist regime has many similarities with European fascist regimes, it has not been successful in imposing a stable system. One reason is the oligarchic nature of the regime. The fundamentalist regime tried to create a fascistic party (the Islamic Republican Party), but due to intense factional differences as well as Ayatollah Ruhollah Khomeini's old age and illness, the regime had to dismantle the party in 1987. A second reason is the lack of reputation by Ali Khamenei to create a successful cult of personality and impose his personal rule. A third reason is the regime's failures in economy, culture, and governance. A fourth reason is technological changes such as the internet, satellite television, and cell phones, which have enabled and empowered the people to undermine the regime's ability to impose its monopoly of news and analysis. A fifth reason is the resistance by the people to the regime's ideology (e.g., female hijab [Islamic headcover for women]). And sixth, the resistance by the various opposition groups and parties

---

60 Fadavi, IRGC Gen. Ali, "*Sardar Fadavi: 'Sepah Pasdaran Enghelab Islami' Hich Kalamee Dar Edameh Khod Nadarad Hatta Iran*" [Gen. Fadavi: "The Islamic Revolutionary Guards Corps" Does Not Have Any Words After Its Title, Even Iran], Bahar News (April 22, 2018), https://www.baharnews.ir/news/148310/%D8%B3%D8%B1%D8%AF%D8%B1-%D9%81%D8%AF%D9%88%DB%8C-%D8%B3%D9%BE%D8%A7%D9%BE-%D8%A7%D8%B3%D8%A7%D8%B1%D8%A7%D9%86-%D8%A7%D9%86%D9%82%D9%84%D8%A8-%D8%A7%D8%B3%D9%84%D8%A7%D9%85%DB%8C-%D9%87%DB%8C%DA%86-%DA%A9%D9%84%D9%85%D9%87-%D8%A7%DB%8C-%D8%A7%D8%AF%D8%A7%D9%85%D9%87-%D8%AE%D9%88%D8%AF-%D9%86%D8%AF%D8%A7%D8%B1%D8%AF-%D8%AD%D8%AA%DB%8C-%D8%A7%DB%8C%D8%B1%D8%A7%D9%86.

61 IRGC, "*Razmandegan Bedon-e Marz Ra Behtar Beshnasid: Niroyeh Qods Sepah Chegoneh Shekl Gereft?*" [Get to Know Better the Fighters Without Borders: How Was the Qods Force Formed?], Fars News (January 25, 2020), https://www.farsnews.ir/news/13981105000470/; and IRGC, "'*Razmandegan Bedon-e Marz' Dar Meydan Razm: Niroyeh Qods Dar Kodam Jang-ha Hozoor Yaft?*" ["Fighters Without Borders" on the Battlefield: Qods Force Was Present in Which Wars?], Fars News (January 26, 2020), https://www.farsnews.ir/news/13981106000522/. Also see Ayatollah Ali Khamenei, "Speech" (January 17, 2020), http://english.khamenei.ir/news/7318/Our-Islamic-power-will-overcome-the-superficial-grandeur-of-material.

62 Ayatollah Ruhollah Khomeini, "Last Will and Testament" (February 15, 1983), released after his death in June 1989, https://www.al-islam.org/imam-khomeini-s-last-will-and-testament.

(e. g., the INF) to the regime and their providing hope for the people for an alternative and better future.

1.5 Intra-elite Factionalism

Intra-elite factionalism is fueled by class differences, policy preferences, and personal ambitions for power. There are three main factions among the fundamentalists: right (hardline), center (moderate), and left (reformist).[63]

The right faction is better known in the West as hardliners. Their leader is the Supreme Leader Ali Khamenei. The center faction of the fundamentalist oligarchy has also been called *"Kargozaran Sazandegi"* [Executives of Construction]. This faction is also referred to as "moderates." The leaders of this faction include Ali Akbar Hashemi Rafsanjani and Hassan Rouhani.

The left faction of the fundamentalist oligarchy was called *"Peyrove Khate Imam"* [Supporters of Imam Khomeini's Line]. Since 1997, the left faction of the fundamentalist oligarchy has been called reformist. The left faction was the most anti-democratic, violent, anti-American, and repressive faction between 1979 and the early 1990s. The leaders of this faction have included: Ahmad Khomeini (responsible for the massacre of political prisoners in 1988); Ayatollah Sadegh Khalkhali (the head of the revolutionary courts, known in the West as the "hanging judge," the leader of Fadaian Islam, one of Khomeini's closest confidants before and after the revolution);[64] Ayatollah Hadi Ghaffari; Ayatollah Abdol-Karim Moussavi Ardabili; Ayatollah Mohammad Moussavi Khoeiniha (the leaders of fundamentalist students who took over the American Embassy and their liaison with Ayatollah Khomeini); Hojatolislam Mohammad Khatami (President 1997–2005); Mir-Hussein Moussavi (Prime Minister 1981–1989); Hojatolislam Mehdi Karrubi (Speaker of Majles); and Ayatollah Ali Akbar Mohtashami-pour (ambassador to Syria, one of the main founders of the Lebanese Hezbollah, Interior Minister for Mir-Hussein Moussavi's government, member of Majles, top official for Mir-Hussein Moussavi's presidential campaign in 2009).

Mohammad Khatami, Mir-Hussein Moussavi, and Hassan Rouhani were among the top fundamentalist officials between 1979 and 1989, who promoted extreme reactionary policies and violence against dissidents and opponents. As Prime Minister, Moussavi issued a policy for female government employees,

---

63 Kazemzadeh, *Iran's Foreign Policy*, op. cit., pp. 1–45.
64 Ayatollah Sadegh Khalkhali, "All the People Who Are Opposed to Our Revolution Must Die," Interview, *MERIP Reports*, No. 104 (March–April 1982), pp. 30–31.

which ordered mandatory hijab to be chador (and not the less restrictive scarf and manteau). Moussavi's order even mandated the color of chador for women. His wife, Zahra Rahnavard, was appointed editor-in-chief of the largest women's magazine and under her leadership the weekly promoted the most reactionary, fundamentalist, misogynist views, including on hijab. Khatami was appointed the editor-in-chief of the *Kayhan*, Iran's largest daily. Khatami wrote a number of vicious attacks on the moderate Mehdi Bazargan and his government. Khatami was also a member of the Majles. At the podium of the Majles, Khatami advocated creating a wall on the streets segregating women from men. Rouhani was a member of the Majles. In the Majles he advocated public executions on the streets in order to teach a lesson to dissidents.[65]

Most of the fundamentalist students who attacked the U.S. Embassy on November 4, 1979 and took its diplomats hostage for 444 days were members of the reformist faction.[66] The top three fundamentalist student leaders who planned, organized, and carried out the take-over of the American Embassy were Habibollah Bitaraf, Mohsen Mirdamadi, and Ebrahim Asgharzadeh. The number one leader of the fundamentalist students, Bitaraf, became governor of the province of Yazd and Minister of Energy under President Khatami (1997–2005). The number two, Mirdamadi, became governor of Khuzestan province, member of Majles, and the Secretary-General of the largest reformist fundamentalist party, the Islamic Iran Participation Front (IIPF). The number three, Asgharzadeh, became member of Majles and top official at *"Vezarat Ershad Va Tablighat Islami"* [the Ministry of Islamic Guidance and Propaganda]. Asgharzadeh is one of the few fundamentalists who has apologized to Abbas Amir-Entezam for the false allegations of spying for the CIA. Saeed Hajjarian became one of the founders of the Ministry of Intelligence, Deputy Minister of Intelligence, and the theoretician of the reformist faction in 1997. Mohsen Aminzadeh became Deputy Foreign Minister (1997–2005) during President Khatami's rule and the most influential foreign policy official during that period. Reza Khatami, the younger brother of President Khatami, became the Secretary-General of the IIPF. Masoumeh Ebtekar, the spokeswoman of the hostage takers, became Deputy to the President on environmental affairs under Khatami and Rouhani. She continues to strongly support the hostage taking.[67] Mohammad Hashemi Isfehani (Ebtekar's husband) became the Foreign

---

65 For documents, videos, and photos of the articles see the video documentary at https://www.facebook.com/hassan.behgar.5/videos/4875496775803694.
66 Iranian Students' News Agency (ISNA), *"Sarnevesht Daneshjooyan Eshghalkonandeh Sefarat America"* [What Became of the Students Occupying the American Embassy] (November 3, 2016), https://www.isna.ir/news/95081309267.
67 Ibid.

Operations Head of the Ministry of Intelligence. He was personally tasked with leading a group of assassins to assassinate Hadi Khorsandi (Iran's leading satirist and a supporter of Dr. Bakhtiar), who was living in exile in Britain. The British security forces foiled the operations.[68] Abbas Abdi, one of the more outspoken fundamentalist students, has been a top advisor to Karrubi. Abdi remains a strong supporter of the hostage taking and continues to make false allegations against Amir-Entezam. Abdi is one of the most reactionary and dictatorial leaders of the reformist fundamentalist faction. Abdi was among the top reformist leaders during 2018 and 2019 that publicly condemned the protesters and publicly called for the violent suppression of the protests.

Other reformist members of the fundamentalist oligarchy have also played very violent and dictatorial roles when the left faction of the fundamentalist oligarchy had the upper hand. Mostafa Tajzadeh was a top prosecutor in revolutionary courts in the 1980s, during the worst violations of human rights in the fundamentalist regime. Sadegh Zibakalam was a top fundamentalist official in the Cultural Revolution when the fundamentalists violently attacked the universities and purged secular, liberal, and leftist professors, students, and staff.

Between 1981 and 1989, Supreme Leader Ruhollah Khomeini was ill and was able only occasionally to intervene in detail of policy. Five top members of the oligarchy ruled the country: Ahmad Khomeini, Rafsanjani, Khamenei, Mir-Hussein Moussavi, and Moussavi Ardabili. Until Khomeini's death in 1989, the left (or reformist) faction had the upper hand in the regime. Between 1989 and the mid-1990s Rafsanjani and his expedient faction had the upper hand. In the years between 1981 and 1989, the left fundamentalists had the upper hand. These years were by far the most repressive years of the regime.[69] Between 1989 and 1995, expedients (Rafsanjani) had the upper hand. This period was the second worst period in terms of repression and dictatorship. Since 1995, Khamenei and the hardline faction have gained the upper hand. This period has been the least repressive period under the fundamentalists. Khamenei has been far more tolerant of criticism than either Khomeini (1979–1989) or Rafsanjani (when he was the most powerful fig-

68 Shappi Khorsandi, "My Family Values," *The Guardian* (October 23, 2015), interview, https://www.theguardian.com/lifeandstyle/2015/oct/23/shappi-khorsandi-my-family-values. The would-be assassin, Abol-Qassem Mesbahi, defected and gave the information to Bani Sadr, the former President in exile in France. The court testimony of Mr. Mesbahi was crucial in convicting top officials of the fundamentalist regime in the Mykonos restaurant trial in Berlin for assassination of dissidents in Europe.

69 Masoud Kazemzadeh, "Ayatollah Rafsanjani's Death and Trump Policy on Iran," *Small Wars Journal* (January 18, 2017), https://smallwarsjournal.com/jrnl/art/ayatollah-rafsanjani%E2%80%99s-death-and-trump-policy-on-iran.

ure, 1989–1995). Mass executions and assassination of dissidents were far more prevalent in the Khomeini and Rafsanjani periods than in Khamenei's period.

Each faction believes that its policies will better serve the interests of the fundamentalist regime. The reformist faction proposes to reduce political repression, reduce cultural repression, and make less adventurist and violent foreign policies. The reformists want to make (minor) reforms in order to preserve the fundamentalist regime and the fundamentalist constitution. The reformists oppose replacing the ruling fundamentalist dictatorship with democracy. They continue to support the fundamentalist regime, the extremely anti-democratic fundamentalist constitution (which grants a Shia cleric enormous powers as *Vali Faqih*), and strongly support Khomeini (under whom they had the upper hand in most state institutions). Mohammad Khatami has explicitly said that he opposes democracy, that the Iranian people are not capable of democracy, and that he strongly supports the fundamentalist constitution.[70] Mehdi Karrubi, too, has repeatedly supported the fundamentalist constitution, fundamentalist rule, and Khomeini's rule. On October 5, 2021, in a gathering at Gholam-Hussein Karbaschi's home, Karrubi said: "I ask the Holy and Supreme God, to provide victory to all the supporters of Islam, to put this great movement that the Imam [Khomeini] created, on a path that Inshallah will continue. To preserve the basic principle of the regime and Inshallah get rid of its shortcomings."[71] Mir-Hussein Moussavi infamously referred to Khomeini's period as *"Dowran Talaee Imam"* [The Golden Period of the Imam]. Moussavi was Prime Minister for about eight years under Khomeini when the regime's worst atrocities were occurring, including mass executions of teenagers. According to Amnesty International, Moussavi played a role in distorting the truth about the

---

70 Mohammad Khatami, "Speech," You Tube (2014), https://www.youtube.com/watch?v=KiygQj96DrQ.
71 Mehdi Karrubi, "Speech," *"Avalin Sokhanrani Karrubi Pas Az 11 Sal"* [The First Speech by Karrubi After 11 Years], Ensaf News (October 5, 2021), http://www.ensafnews.com/312263/%D8%A7%D9%88%D9%84%DB%8C%D9%86-%D8%B3%D8%AE%D9%86%D8%B1%D8%A7%D9%86%DB%8C-%DA%A9%D8%B1%D9%88%D8%A8%DB%8C-%D9%BE%D8%B3-%D8%A7%D8%B2-%DB%B1%DB%B1-%D8%B3%D8%A7%D9%84-%D8%B9%DB%8C%D9%88%D8%A8-%D9%86/. Karbaschi is the Secretary-General of the Executives of Construction Party, the party created by Rafsanjani. Karbaschi has been a top supporter of Karrubi since 2008. The words chosen by Karrubi are: *"Asl nezam mahfooz bemanad."* Karrubi's words unambiguously and strongly mean that one should work to preserve the basics and principles of the regime such as its constitution and the fundamentalist clerical supreme power.

massacre of political prisoners in August–September 1988, during the Second Reign of Terror.[72]

The expedient faction proposes what is called the Chinese model: increase political repression, reduce cultural repression, make IMF-style economic policies, and reduce confrontation with the United States. The hardline faction proposes to increase political repression, increase cultural repression, increase confrontation with the U.S. and E.U., as well as expand the Islamic Republic of Iran's (IRI) influence in the Middle East region through violent proxies. The hardline faction believes that reduction of repression would result in collapse of the regime in Iran as it occurred in the former Soviet Union. The crises engulfing the regime have further inflamed intra-elite struggles.

The hardliners orchestrated the election on June 18, 2021 to make certain that Ebrahim Raisi would become President. Raisi is one of the more extreme members of the hardline faction. He was born on December 14, 1960.[73] His father was a mid-ranking cleric. He attended only six years of primary school. Then he began attending seminaries. When the revolution occurred in 1979, he was 18 years old. He began working with the fundamentalists after the revolution. Raisi held a series of positions in the judiciary from revolutionary prosecutor to judge. He was responsible for the execution of thousands. He was a member of the so-called "Death Board" in Tehran and Karaj during the Second Reign of Terror in August–September 1988 when about 5,000 political prisoners were summarily mass executed. The "Death Board" consisted of three individuals who would ask several questions and then decide whether the political prisoners would live or be executed. On Saturday June 19, 2021, when the regime announced that Raisi had won the election, Amnesty International and Human Rights Watch called for probes for crimes against humanity committed by Raisi.[74]

By August 2021, the hardline faction controlled all levers of power in Iran: Supreme Leader, President, Majles, Council of Guardians, Assembly of Experts, Council for Expediency of the System, and IRGC. This not only cements hardline control of the regime in the short term but, in the long term, also eliminates the likelihood of a non-hardline candidate becoming the next Supreme Leader after Khamenei dies.

---

72 Amnesty International, "Iran: Top Government Officials Distorted the Truth about 1988 Prison Massacres" (December 12, 2018), https://www.amnesty.org/en/latest/press-release/2018/12/iran-top-government-officials-distorted-the-truth-about-1988-prison-massacres/.

73 Raisi's biography at his website https://raisi.ir/page/biography.

74 Reuters, "Rights Groups Call for Probe into Iran's Raisi for Crimes Against Humanity" (June 19, 2021), https://www.reuters.com/world/middle-east/amnesty-calls-investigation-into-irans-raisi-crimes-against-humanity-2021-06-19/.

The expulsion of reformist and expedient factions from the top positions of power and the monopolization of power in the hands of hardliners has advantages and disadvantages for the fundamentalist regime both domestically and internationally. The marginalization of reformists and expedients eliminates the hope of many inside Iran that gradual and small changes are possible. This would benefit the opposition (e.g., democratic opposition) that wants to replace the ruling fundamentalist regime with another form of political system (e.g., democracy). When another uprising occurs such as those that occurred in 2017 and 2019, the likelihood of more people going to the streets and joining the uprising increases. Ebrahim Raisi's presidency indicates that Khamenei and hardliners have reached the conclusion that they fear mass uprisings and believe the best way to keep power is through brute force.

Raisi's presidency also makes it harder for the U.S. and Europeans to make concessions to the fundamentalist regime. One of the main arguments for the appeasement of the fundamentalist regime has been that, by doing so, the U.S. and E.U. would increase the power of the reformists and moderates (expedients) within the fundamentalist regime. The presidencies of Khatami and Rouhani had made those arguments plausible for many. Raisi's presidency would undermine the plausibility of such arguments.

The INF had called for boycott of this election, as it had all the elections since 1980, with only two exceptions. The INF had called the people to vote for Mohammad Khatami for reelection to the presidency in 2001 and for reformists for Majles elections in 1998. The INF argued that the people had moved on from choosing between "bad" (i.e., reformists, expedients, or less extremist hardliners) and "worse" (i.e., hardliners or more extreme hardliners). The INF believes that the Iranian people deserve freedom, democracy, and human rights. The INF advocates replacing the current dictatorship with a democracy. By participating and voting, one would be proviing legitimacy to the fundamentalist regime. Therefore, the INF called for boycott of the elections.[75]

75 Jebhe Melli Iran, *Mellat Iran Az Entekhab Bein Bad Va Badtar Oboor Kardeh Ast* [The Iranian Nation Has Moved On From Choosing Between Bad and Worse] (April 7, 2021), https://melliun.org/iran/257087. Also see Hussein Moussavian, "Interview," Iran National Front-Organizations Abroad TV, Channel One (June 20, 2021), https://www.youtube.com/watch?v=XflRlCIejVk.

Chapter 2
The Green Movement, 2009–2010

The June 12, 2009 presidential election in Iran was a turning point in Iranian politics. It greatly increased the internal divisions among the ruling elites and propelled various factions and individuals to more pronounced and violent confrontations for power. In this chapter, I analyze the nature of the protests between June 2009 and June 2010. Two major events in July 2009 were significant because they indicated that the hardliners did not succeed in intimidating their opponents into submission. The first event was the protests on July 9, 2009, the 10th anniversary of the student uprising in 1999. The second event was the Friday sermon on July 17, 2009 by Ayatollah Ali Akbar Hashemi Rafsanjani. Repression succeeded in controlling the situation. However, the opposition continued to bring significant numbers of protesters to the streets on major historical anniversaries. Despite violence and threats of violence, the opponents repeatedly defied the hardline faction and participated in massive protests on September 18, 2009, November 4, 2009, throughout December 2009, and, to a lesser extent, on February 11, 2010, May 2, 2010, and May 3, 2010.

This chapter describes and analyzes the demands and roles of the main individuals, groups, and strata in this conflict. This chapter concludes that after a year of struggle, none of the main groups was able to achieve its primary objective, thus leading to stalemate and paralysis.

The crisis which began in June 2009 is unprecedented in the history of intra-elite power struggles among the fundamentalists. One primary issue dividing the oligarchy during the 2009–2010 mass protests was the distribution of power and the proper role of the Supreme Leader.

2.1 What was the Fight About? Distribution of Power and the Proper Role of the Supreme Leader

The constitution grants huge amounts of power to the Supreme Leader. But it also grants executive power to the President. Until June 2009, intra-elite competitions were conducted behind the scenes, to reveal themselves when the Council of Guardians would disqualify members of rival factions from running for a particular position such as the presidency, Majles, or the Assembly of Experts. In the previous 30 years, many such disqualifications had been the norm. Less clear has been the veracity of the announced results. For example, Ayatollah Rafsanjani's website published a report which revealed that in the Majles elections in 1999,

https://doi.org/10.1515/9783111280288-004

the initial result stated that he came in 30th in Tehran, but after a recount of only 20% of the ballots by the Council of Guardians, he came in 19th. The top 30 vote getters would win seats in the Majles. The report concluded by stating: "Don't you know that when this embarrassing episode occurred which would undermine the basis of the elections, the esteemed Supreme Leader ordered the stopping of the recount?"[1]

It was widely expected that the Supreme Leader would follow the norm and the letter of the constitution. The putative electoral fraud in June 2009 and the mass arrests of reformist elements of the oligarchy are regarded by many as a coup d'état unprecedented in the history of intra-elite conduct since the revolution. According to a high-level hardline official in the intelligence and security establishment, on June 9, 2009 (19 Khordad 1388 in the Iranian calendar), the security institutions were given a "general arrest warrant" to arrest anyone whom they suspected of being involved in a forthcoming "soft coup" after the election.[2] This general arrest warrant was issued three days before the election. The general warrant was the basis for the mass arrest of the leaders of the reformist faction of the oligarchy that were supporting Moussavi or Karrubi and refused to accept Ahmadinejad's reelection.[3] This arrest warrant raises the question of why the hardliners were planning for a crackdown before any protests occurred.

Dr. Alireza Beheshti is a senior advisor to Moussavi and one of his top officials at his election headquarters. Beheshti described what occurred on the day of the election to two reporters of *Eatemaad* newspaper:

> We had close to 40,000 volunteers to monitor the election and we asked for observation identity cards for them, but of these only about 25,000 were able to be present at the ballot boxes.

1 BBC Persian, *"Entesharat Nokat Tazeh Dar Mored Ayatollah Khamenei"* [The Publication of New Things About Ayatollah Khamenei] (June 11, 2010), http://www.bbc.co.uk/persian/iran/2010/06/100611_l10_rafsanjani_mohajerani_khamenei_disclosure.shtml.
2 Aftab News, *"Goft O Goo Ba Maqam Bolandpayeh Amniyati, Shakhsi Bedon Naam Va Aks"* [Discussions with a High-Level Security Official, A Person with No Name and Photo] (April 20, 2010), http://aftabnews.ir/vdcjvheh.uqeaxzsffu.html. Aftab News is one of the main fundamentalist establishment sources of news. The person being interviewed is a hardliner and a top official in the intelligence and security establishment who was closely involved in the interrogations of the top reformists after the June 12, 2009 crackdown. Keyvan Mehregan, *"Goftogoo Ba Mohammad Reza Khatami: Maa Jomhuri Islami Khah Hastim"* [Interview with Mohammad Reza Khatami: We Are Islamic Republicans], *Eatemaad* newspaper, reposted at Green Wave Blog, (August 7, 2009), http://greenwavearchive.blogspot.com/2009/08/blog-post_9237.html. Mohammad Reza Khatami is the younger brother of the former President Mohammad Khatami. He is married to a granddaughter of Ayatollah Khomeini. He was also the Secretary-General of the largest reformist fundamentalist party, the Islamic Participation Front of Iran.
3 Ibid., Aftab News.

The rest were not given observation identity cards or were not allowed to be present. Even of these (25,000), many were expelled when the counting of the ballots began. They made many obstacles to prevent monitoring. ... On the night of the election [June 12], they turned off cell phone text messaging, and they turned off our more than 300 regular telephone landlines of the headquarters for the monitoring of the votes. ... Around 2:00 p.m., we felt that something different [from normal] was occurring. ... One of the suspicious actions was the invasion of Moussavi's headquarters on the day of the election [June 12] and their closing. For example, the Central Headquarters of the Moussavi campaign in Mirhadi as well as the election headquarters in Qeytariyeh were closed without any clear reason. Officials have not given us any explanations. ... Many of our people in connection with the votes were arrested on the day of the election [June 12], and within two days after the election, all the members of the Moussavi election headquarters were in prison.[4]

This study shows that what occurred between June 12, 2009 and June 2010 was not a coup of one man. Rather, it was a "coup" by several powerful but unpopular hardline factions against other factions within the ruling fundamentalist oligarchy.[5] With this "coup," the hardliners broke all norms in order to sideline the reformist faction (led by former President Khatami, Moussavi, and Karrubi) and the expedient faction (led by the powerful Hashemi Rafsanjani).

Those who opposed increasing the powers of the Supreme Leader included Rafsanjani, Khatami, Moussavi, and Karrubi. Those who wanted to increase the powers of the Supreme Leader included Khamenei, Ahmadinejad, Ayatollah Mesbah Yazdi, Ayatollah Ahmad Jennati, and Ayatollah Mohammad Yazdi. Ahmadinejad changed his position later and became critical of Khamenei. In much of 2009–2010, Ayatollah Mohammad Yazdi took the lead in countering Rafsanjani and supporting Khamenei and Ahmadinejad inside the Assembly of Experts and the press. Ayatollah Mohammad Yazdi had been one of the most powerful members of the oligarchy. He was appointed Chairman of Judicial Branch by Khamenei. He served in that position for 10 years. He had been a powerful member of the Assembly of Experts. During 2009–2010, he served as the Secretary of the Assembly of Experts, the second most powerful position in that body. He had also been one of the six clerical members of the Council of Guardians. On April 22, 2010, Ayatollah Mohammad Yazdi stated:

4 Keyvan Mehregan and Amin Alam-alhody, "'Pas Az Entekhabat' Dar Goftogoo Ba Alireza Beheshti" ["After the Election" Interview with Alireza Beheshti], *Eatemaad* newspaper, republished at Iran Emrooz (August 22, 2009), http://www.iran-emrooz.net/index.php?/news2/print/19156.
5 After the revolution, all the factions within the fundamentalist oligarchy called themselves "*maktabi*" [doctrinaire]. Today, those referred to as hardliners prefer to use the term "*osol-gara*" [advocates of principles] or "*mohafezehkar*" [conservative]. Today, those referred to as "reformists" call themselves "*eslah-talab*."

Some with the intention of weakening the position of the Supreme Leader have the objective of limiting his prerogatives. ... Their goals are to be able to determine the powers [*taeen taklif*] and constantly say the Leader has to do this action and not do that action. ... Terms such as fatwa by council or ijtihad by council, the right to rule, international organizations, and human rights are among the words used based on which some want to limit the powers of the Supreme Leader. They say that for the work of the Supreme Leader we should have a term-limit or the Assembly of Experts should determine the years of each Leader. ... Unfortunately, some of the top statesmen of the country pay attention to these arguments. ... Everybody should be aware that the sole view that is determining is that of the Supreme Leader and one has to look up to it and not fall for the deceptions of other individuals.[6]

Ayatollah Ahmad Jennati provided the same rationale. Jennati is one of the four or five most powerful figures in Iran. In addition to being the Head of the Council of Guardians, Jennati is a senior member of the Assembly of Experts, and one of five Friday prayer speakers in Tehran. Jennati stated:

In case they won [the election], they sought to weaken the position of the Supreme Leader [*Velayat Faqih*], and in case they lost [the election] to create a ruckus and claim fraud and change the atmosphere and undermine the elections. ... The conditions of the election last year were different and before 1388 [Iranian calendar year March 20, 2009 to March 20, 2010], the enemies inside and outside the country had planned to take advantage of the elections and question the basic principles of the system, the Rule of the Cleric, and the Islamic governance. ... The enemies sought to gain their objectives in this election that had evaded them during the imposed war [Iran–Iraq war of 1980–1988]. ... The plan of the enemies was clear to the Supreme Leader, and he knew that the enemies are attempting a soft overthrow.[7]

Jennati artfully, and erroneously, mixed up the reformist demand for circumscribing the powers of the Supreme Leader (making it constitutional) with abolishing it. Jennati is fully aware that Rafsanjani, Khatami, Moussavi, and Karrubi strongly and unequivocally support the institution of *Velayat Faqih* [the Rule of the Cleric] as well as the Islamic Republic, a system which they themselves helped create. Rafsanjani was the Chairman of the Assembly of Experts and Chair of the Council for

---

6 Raja News, "*Enteqadat Sarih Ayatollah Yazdi: Mikhahand Baray Rahbari Taain Taklif Konand*" [Explicit Criticisms of Ayatollah Yazdi: They Want {The Power} to Tell The Supreme Leader What To Do] (April 23, 2010), http://www.rajanews.com/Detail.asp?id=48204. Raja News is an extremist hardline news agency close to former President Ahmadinejad.

7 Islamic Republic of Iran, Ministry of Interior, Bushehr province, "*Ayatollah Jennati: Saran-e Fetneh Dar Sadad Tazief Rahbari Va Velayat Faqih Boodand*" [Ayatollah Jennati: The Leaders of the Sedition Sought to Undermine the Supreme Leader and the Rule of the Cleric] (April 15, 2010), http://www.ost-boushehr.ir/fa/pages/?cid=1183. This is published on the official site of the Ministry of Interior in Bushehr province.

the Expediency of the System. Rafsanjani was also a former speaker of the Majles (early 1980s to 1989) and a two-term President (1989 – 1997). Khatami was a close confidant of Ayatollah Khomeini. Khatami drafted many of Khomeini's statements during the revolution. He also served two terms as President (1997–2005). Moussavi was one of the top leaders of the Islamic Republican Party, which helped eliminate rivals to Khomeini and helped consolidate Khomeini's power. Moussavi served as the editor-in-chief of *Jumhuri Islami*, the daily which served as the official voice of the IRP. Moussavi served as Prime Minister during the crucial years between 1981 and 1989. In 2009, Moussavi was a member of the Council for the Expediency of the System, whose members are appointed by the Supreme Leader. Karrubi was a very close and trusted confidant of Khomeini before and after the revolution. Khomeini appointed Karrubi to head the powerful *Bonyad Shahid* [Martyrs Foundation] and the annual Haj pilgrimage to Mecca. Karrubi also served twice as speaker of the Majles.

Moreover, family members of some of the founders and icons of the regime have publicly opposed Ahmadinejad and supported reformists. Hojatolislam Hassan Khomeini is a grandson of Ayatollah Ruhollah Khomeini, the founder of the Islamic Republic. Hassan Khomeini is the spokesman of the Khomeini family, Director of Khomeini's Mausoleum (used in some official ceremonies), Head of the Khomeini Jamaran Office and Housing Complex, and Director of *"Moasesseh Tanzim Va Nashr Asar Imam"* [Foundation for the Compilation and Publication of Khomeini's Perspectives]. Hassan Khomeini has publicly snubbed Ahmadinejad, refused to participate in his 2009 inauguration, criticized hardline policies, and on numerous occasions sided with various reformists (including both Moussavi and Karrubi). Zahra Eshraqi (Ayatollah Khomeini's granddaughter) and her husband Reza Khatami (former President Khatami's younger brother) were briefly imprisoned for the support of reformists.[8] Mohammad Taheri, who is married to Naimeh Eshraqi (another granddaughter of Ayatollah Khomeini) was also briefly imprisoned.[9] Yasser Khomeini, another grandson of the founder of the regime, publicly expressed his support for the reformists in 2011.

Ayatollah Mohammad Beheshti was one of the main founders of the Islamic Republic. Beheshti founded and headed the Islamic Republican Party. Beheshti

---

8 JARAS, *"22 Bahman Zabz- Reza Khatami Va Zahra Eshraqi Azad Shodand"* [Green February 11: Reza Khatami and Zahra Eshraqi Were Released] (February 11, 2010), http://www.rahesabz.net/ story/10023/. The two were briefly imprisoned in order to prevent them from joining the protest march on February 11. Reza Khatami was also arrested immediately after the June 12 election.
9 Nasrin Alavi, "This Magic Green Bracelet: Ayatollah Khomeini's Grandsons Supporting the Reformers?" *New Internationalist*, January 2010, http://www.newint.org/features/web-exclusive/2010/ 01/20/magic-green-bracelet/.

also served as the first Head of the Judicial Branch. His son, Alireza Beheshti, is a senior advisor to Moussavi. He was imprisoned in the aftermath of the protests and suffered a heart attack while in custody. The hardliners banned Ayatollah Beheshti's publications in the Book Faire in May 2010.[10]

The regime has created icons of several *Basij* members who fought in the war with Iraq and were martyred. Two of the most famous are Bakeri and Ebrahim Hemmat. Their photos are plastered on roads, and many schools and roads are named after them. The family members of these celebrated martyrs publicly supported the reformists as well as strongly condemning the repression of the protesters and the harsh treatment of them by the regime.[11]

Hassan Yunessi, the son of the former Minister of Intelligence, Hojatolislam Ali Yunessi, was arrested during the February 20, 2011 demonstrations and held for months.[12] Hassan Yunessi is a lawyer who defended many of the protesters. He has been subjected to severe interrogations. The child of IRGC Gen. Ali Fazli has also been arrested and put in prison during protests. Gen. Fazli was at the time the Commander of the Seyyed ol-Shohada IRGC base in Tehran, which was the primary IRGC anti-riot coercive apparatus responsible for putting down the protests in Tehran. Pro-Ahmadinejad websites revealed that the son of Ali Larijani (the powerful Speaker of Majles) had been arrested on December 28, 2009 and during the September 2009 protests. Mohsen Ruholamini, the son of Abdol-Hussein Ruholamini, a prominent hardliner close to former IRGC Commander-in-Chief Mohsen Rezaee, was tortured to death in June 2009. Mohsen Ruholamini was among the protesters during June 2009. Two sons of the prominent high-ranking reformist cleric, Ayatollah Bayat Zanjani, were arrested during the February 14, 2011 protests. Narges Kolhar, the daughter of Mehdi Kolhar, publicly condemned Ahmadinejad, supported the Green Movement, left Iran, and defected to Germany. Mehdi Kolhar was at the time the media advisor and close associate of Ahmadinejad.[13] The above are the children of the most powerful men in the Islamic Republic.

---

10 BBC Persian, *"Jologiri Az Barpaee Ghorfeh Asar Ayatollah Beheshti Dar Namayeshgah Ketab Tehran"* [Preventing the Publisher of the Publication of Ayatollah Beheshti Holding Its Booth At the Tehran Book Faire] (May 5, 2010), http://www.bbc.co.uk/persian/lg/iran/2010/05/100505_l07_ iran89_politics_bookfair89_beheshti.shtml.

11 Bakeri, *"Pedar Jaan Jayat Inja Aslan Khali Nist"* [Dear Father Your Place Is Not Here], Kaleme (May 18, 2010), http://www.kaleme.com/1389/02/28/klm-19784; Khabar Online, *"Hamsar Shahid Hemmat"* [The Wife of Martyred Hemmat] (May 23, 2010), http://www.khabaronline.ir/news-63698.aspx.

12 Hussein Kermani, *"Zohor Aghazadeh-hay Nogara Va Motarez Beh Pedar Khandeh Nezam"* [The Appearance of the Modernist Children of the Ruling Elite and Their Protests Against the Godfather of the System], Deutsche Welle (April 10, 2011), http://www.dw-world.de/dw/article/0,,6499727,00. html?maca=per-rss-per-all-1491-rdf.

13 Ibid.

They are familiar with the behind-the-scenes secrets of the regime. They are among the most privileged beneficiaries.

For the first time in the history of intra-elite struggles, Ahmadinejad and other powerful hardliners used a language which portended a bloody purge of Rafsanjani and his pragmatic conservatives as well as the reformist elements of the oligarchy. During the last days of the campaign and the live televised debates, Ahmadinejad repeatedly targeted Rafsanjani and his family members, along with other corrupt officials within the oligarchy. These threats escalated immediately after the election.[14] Rafsanjani did not quietly accept defeat and did not resign from all the positions of power. Instead, he decided to put up a fight. Rafsanjani's wife and daughter publicly asked for mass protests.

Moussavi, Karrubi, and Khatami, too, repeatedly appealed to the people to protest on the streets. Moussavi and Karrubi made official requests for a permit to hold rallies on June 15. The authorities denied the requests. Because Moussavi and Karrubi were denied the ability to have access to mass media, the people were not aware of the decision. The reformists were surprised by the massive numbers. Therefore, they simply joined the demonstration.[15] Moussavi, Karrubi, and Khatami were present at the demonstration. On June 15, 2009, the largest demonstration since the revolution occurred in Tehran. The estimates range between 2 million and 3 million people.[16]

---

14 IRNA, *"Jashn Piroozi Mellat: 'Ahmadi Bot Shekan', Bot-e Bozorg Ro Beshkan"* [The Great Celebration of the Nation: 'Ahmadinejad the Idol Smasher', Smash the Big Idol], (June 14, 2009), http://www.irna.ir/View/FullStory/?NewsId=546770; IRNA, *"Sokhanan Rais Jumhur Dar Meidan Vali Asr Tehran"* [The Speech of the President in Vali Asr Square Tehran] (June 14, 2009), http://www.irna.ir/View/FullStory/?NewsId=546894; IRNA, *"Nokhostin Sokhanan Pas Az Piroozi Dar Entekhabat Riyasat Jumhuri; Ahmadinejad: Dorani Jadid Dar Tarikh Mellat Iran Aghaz Shod"* [The First Speech After the Victory in the Presidential Elections; Ahmadinejad: A New Era Has Begun in the History of the Iranian Nation] (June 14, 2009), http://www.irna.ir/View/FullStory/?NewsId=545489. IRNA is the official news agency. It is controlled by the hardliners appointed by the Supreme Leader.

15 Keyvan Mehregan and Amin Alam-alhody, *"'Pas Az Entekhabat' Dar Goftogoo Ba Alireza Beheshti"* ['After the Election' Interview with Alireza Beheshti], *Eatemaad* newspaper, republished at Iran Emrooz (August 22, 2009), http://www.iran-emrooz.net/index.php?/news2/print/19156.

16 The estimate of 2 million to 3 million was made by the *Time* magazine reporter on the ground in Tehran. Nahid Siamdoust, "Tehran's Rallying Cry: 'We Are the People of Iran,'" *Time* magazine (June 15, 2009), http://www.time.com/time/world/article/0,8599,1904764,00.html?xid=rss-topstories. Most other observers gave the same range. Tehran's mayor, Mohammad Baqer Qalibaf has provided the estimate of 3 million. Qalibaf is a hardliner who does not support Ahmadinejad. Reformist Mohammad Reza Khatami has given an estimate of "more than 3 million." Keyvan Mehregan, *"Goftogoo Ba Mohammad Reza Khatami: Maa Jomhuri Islami Khah Hastim"* [Interview with Mohammad Reza Khatami: We Are Islamic Republicans], *Eatemaad* newspaper, reposted at Green Wave Blog (August 7, 2009), http://greenwavearchive.blogspot.com/2009/08/blog-post_9237.html.

Some reformist leaders believe that the massive protests saved them from a mass bloody purge. In the words of Mostafa Tajzadeh:

> My friends, myself, and numerous election activists, who are alive thanks to God's mercy, are in great debt to those history making protests on June 15, which not only exposed the electoral coup de'etat, but also revealed the iron fist beneath the velvet glove, and not only saved me and those like me, but also saved Iran and Islam and ... that which might have occurred if the protests of millions did not occur. ... On that day, the people not only saved our lives, but also all the freedom-seeking and justice-seeking efforts and struggles of the past century and opened the path for tomorrow.[17]

2.2 Supporters of Ahmadinejad's Reelection

The following individuals and groups supported Mahmoud Ahmadinejad's reelection: (1) the Supreme Leader, Ali Khamenei; (2) the IRGC and *Basij*; (3) Ayatollah Mesbah Yazdi and his supporters; (4) Mojtaba Khamenei, the Supreme Leader's son; (5) hardline fundamentalists who oppose détente with the United States; and (6) Ahmadinejad's inner circle.

2.2.1 The Supreme Leader, Ali Khamenei

For the June 2009 presidential election, the Council of Guardians allowed only three trusted members of the oligarchy to compete against Ahmadinejad.[18] One candidate was Mir Hussein Moussavi, whose loyalty to the system was unquestioned.[19] Another was Mehdi Karrubi, a fundamentalist cleric regarded as one of the most conservative members of the reformist camp. It was assumed that neither would be able to galvanize a population that had shown great apathy in the previous few years.

Intense hatred for Ahmadinejad's foreign policy which unnecessarily antagonized others, and his denial of the Holocaust which has brought great shame for Iranians, together with a deteriorating economy, increased political repression, and increased social restrictions, galvanized the middle classes in order to get Ah-

---

17 Mostafa Tajzadeh, *"Pedar, Madar, Ma Baz Ham Motahamim!"* [Father, Mother, We Are Accused, Again!], Iran Emrooz (June 15, 2010), http://www.iran-emrooz.net/image1/Tajzadeh20106.pdf.
18 Walter Posch, *Prospects for Iran's 2009 Presidential Elections* (Washington, D.C.: The Middle East Institute Policy Brief 24, June 2009).
19 Mehrzad Boroujerdi, "Iran's Potato Revolution," *Foreign Policy* web exclusive (May 2009), available at: http://www.foreignpolicy.com/story/cms.php?story_id=4921.

madinejad out. Ahmadinejad's performance in sensational television debates, where he clearly defeated his two reformist rivals, did not, however, reduce enthusiasm and support for the reformists.[20]

Ahmadinejad's performance injected his supporters with enthusiasm and increased his support among some. However, his rude and extremely aggressive attacks on Moussavi, his wife, and Karrubi enraged many in the population and probably convinced them to participate in the election and vote for Moussavi or Karrubi. Apparently, Ahmadinejad's great advantages in controlling state machinery did not succeed in winning him the majority of the votes needed to legitimately win the election. There is little doubt that massive fraud occurred.[21] Even the hardline-controlled Council of Guardians conceded that in 50 cities, the votes cast were over 100% of eligible voters. The Council of Guardians' spokesman said that the irregularity was "over 3 million." But he added that: "it has yet to be determined whether the amount is decisive in the election result."[22] This explanation was intended to show that although fraud had occurred, it was too small to change the result.

It was widely expected that the Supreme Leader would follow the norm and the letter of the constitution. The disputed election is regarded by many as a coup d'état unprecedented in the history of intra-elite conduct in Iran. After the election, Khamenei publicly and fully supported Ahmadinejad and strongly confronted Moussavi, Karrubi, and Khatami. A Moussavi or Karrubi presidency would have decreased the power of Khamenei.

2.2.2 IRGC and *Basij*

The IRGC is not merely a military organization.[23] In the words of Gen. Mohammad Ali Aziz Jaafari, the Commander-in-Chief of the IRGC: "the IRGC, before being a

---

20 The complete collection of the videos of the debates is available at http://www.mardomak.org/election88/debate.
21 The Moussavi campaign released a comprehensive and detailed report on the alleged fraud. Moussavi Campaign, *Gozaresh Tafzili Komiteh Sianat Az Araye Mir Hussein Moussavi* [Detailed Report of the Committee for the Defense of the Votes of Mir Hussein Moussavi] (July 4, 2009), http://news.iran-emrooz.net/index.php?/news1/18633/.
22 Press TV, "Guardian Council: Over 100% voted in 50 cities" (June 21, 2009), http://www.presstv.ir/detail.aspx?id=98711&sectionid=351020101. Press TV is the official state English-language satellite program.
23 The constitution of the IRGC is available at http://www.tooba-ir.org/_Book/BookFehrest.asp?BookID=225&ParentID=61149. An extensive compilation of laws, rules, and bylaws of the IRGC and *Basij* is available at http://www.tooba-ir.org/_Book/bookfehrest.asp?Bookid=225.

military organization is a security-political organization, whose existential philosophy is the defense of the revolution and its achievements."[24] It was clear that the IRGC leadership and *Basij* forces supported Ahmadinejad in the crisis.[25] It is also significant to add that, during the first term of his presidency, when Ahmadinejad was criticized by some hardline elements for his domestic and foreign policies, the top IRGC officials publicly defended him. For example, Gen. Hassan Firoozabadi, the Chairman of the Joint Chiefs of Staff (the highest military officer commanding IRGC, *Basij*, regular armed forces, and the police), consistently and publicly defended Ahmadinejad.[26] Gen. Firoozabadi has been a reliable ally of Khamenei since the latter was President. Khamenei has appointed Firoozabadi to all his major offices, including the highest military office in Iran.

The Fars News, a semi-official news agency funded by the IRGC, strongly promotes extremist conservative hardline positions, closely associated with IRGC top leadership. Fars News strongly supported Ahmadinejad in the post-election crisis.

Someanalysts have argued that the prime mover of the putative fraud has been the IRGC with Ahmadinejad as its main representative, and that the Supreme Leader has been following the lead and pressure of the IRGC. Although the available evidence does show that the IRGC and *Basij* strongly oppose the reformists and support Khamenei and Ahmadinejad, so far convincing evidence that the June crisis was a coup by the IRGC has not been uncovered. The assertion that the June 2009 election was a coup by the IRGC against the clerical system has great analytical, political, and policy ramifications. If the analysis in this chapter is correct, the IRGC did not make a coup against the clerics in June 2009. Rather, the IRGC was simply one among several groups that under the leadership of the hardline clerics made a coup against other segments of the ruling oligarchy. If the argument that the IRGC leadership made the coup is correct, then its leaders should be the ones calling the shots. However, if the IRGC was not the primary mover, then one should be able to show that other actors more powerful than the IRGC could have the final word on some issues of prime significance.

---

24 Fars News, "*Sarlashkar Jaafari: Farmandehan Sepah Baray Ayandeh Enqelab Khod Ra Amadeh Konand*" [Gen. Jaafari: Commanders of the IRGC Should Prepare for the Future of the Revolution] (May 26, 2010), http://www.farsnews.com/newstext.php?nn=8903051665.
25 The official views of the IRGC leadership are available in their weekly theoretical publication *Sobhe Sadegh*. This is published by the headquarters of the Supreme Leader's Representative in the IRGC. The publication is available online at: http://www.sobhesadegh.ir/Sadegh.htm.
26 Deutsche Welle, "*Defaa Rais Setad Kole Nirohay Mosalah Az Ahmadinejad*" [The Chairman of the Joint Chiefs of Staff Defends Ahmadinejad] (August 19, 2007), www.dw-world.de/popups/popup_printcontent/0,,2744095,00.html.

It is highly significant to note that for twelve months after the June 2009 election, Khamenei did not consent to the arrest of reformist leaders despite repeated public calls by IRGC-related hardliners. This clearly indicates that the leaders of the IRGC did not have the final say in such sensitive matters. Conversely, this clearly shows that it was the Supreme Leader who was determining the most sensitive issue. The Supreme National Security Council met immediately after the election to decide how to control the situation. It is reported that Ahmadinejad argued for the arrests of Moussavi and Karrubi, but the majority of the council decided against it for fear of a popular reaction that the regime might not be able to control.[27] On July 4, 2009, Hussein Shariatmadari, editor-in-chief of the hardline daily, *Kayhan*, and an extremist hardliner demanded in his editorial that Moussavi and Khatami be tried for "horrible crimes and treason."[28] Shariatmadari wrote: "His [Moussavi's] aim is to escape from definite punishment for the murder of innocent individuals, inciting riots and rebellions, hiring some thugs and ruffians to attack the lives, property and honor of the people, clear collaboration with foreigners, performing the role of the fifth column inside the country, and scores of other undeniable crimes."[29] Earlier, Fatemeh Rajabi, the outspoken wife of Gholam Hussein Elham, the then-spokesman of Ahmadinejad's government, had publicly demanded the prosecution of Rafsanjani, Khatami, Moussavi, Karrubi, and Karbaschi as leaders of a coup against the regime.[30] Mrs. Rajabi published a note publicly advocating the *"eadam enqelabi"* [revolutionary execution] of Mohammad Khatami.[31]

---

27 *Norooz, "Bar-rasi Tarh Bazdasht Mir Hussein Moussavi Dar Setad kou De Taa"* [Considering Arresting Mir Hussein Moussavi By the Headquarters of the Coup de Etat], republished at Iran Emrooz (August, 14, 2009), http://www.iran-emrooz.net/index.php?news1/print/19096. This report was initially published by *Norooz*, which is a reliable publication inside Iran. The report indicates that Ahmadinejad wanted to have Moussavi and 10 other individuals arrested, including Ali Akbar Mohtashamipour, Mehdi Karrubi, Mohsen Alviri, Reza Khatami, and one of Rafsanjani's sons. Also see Mitra Shojaee, *"16 Azar Va Ehtemal Dastgiri Moussavi va Karrubi"* [December 7 and the Possibility of the Arrests of Moussavi and Karrubi], Deutsche Welle (November 25, 2009), http://www.dw-world.de/dw/article/0,,4929214,00.html?maca=per-rss-per-all-1491-rdf.

28 Hussein Shariatmadari, *"Hezb Ya Sotune Panjum?! (Yaddasht Rooz)"* [Party or Fifth Column?! (Comment of the Day)], *Kayhan* (July 4, 2009), http://www.kayhannews.ir/880413/2.htm#other200. For an English translation see Ali Akbar Dareini, "Iranian Hardliner Calls Opposition Leader US Agent," Associated Press, (July 4, 2009), http://news.yahoo.com/s/ap/20090704/ap_on_re_mi_ea/ml_iran_election.

29 Ibid., Shariatmadari. For an English translation see Thomas Erdbrink, "Iranian Details Alleged Fraud: Mousavi Is Also Accused of Treason," *The Washington Post* (July 5, 2009), http://www.washingtonpost.com/wp-dyn/content/article/2009/07/04/AR2009070402685.html?hpid=topnews.

30 Parsine News Site, *"Fatemeh Rajabi Khastar Bazdasht 'Hasemi, Khatami, Karrubi Va Moussavi' Shod"* [Fatemeh Rajabi Demanded Arrests of 'Hashemi, Khatami, Karrubi, and Moussavi'] (June 14,

Threats of arresting the reformist leaders continued. Mehdi Taeb, the brother of Hojatolislam Hussein Taeb (the IRGC's Intelligence Chief), in a speech to the *Basij* conference in Golestan province said that the arrests of Rafsanjani, Khatami, Moussavi, and Karrubi would not cause any problems for the regime. Mehdi Taeb also said that about 14 years earlier, they had arrested Rafsanjani's son, Mehdi Hashemi, for organizing a prostitution ring which was training prostitutes to trap regime officials. Mehdi Taeb added that Rafsanjani used his influence to release his son and transfer the Ministry of Intelligence personnel, and that the prostitutes of the said ring were working in Moussavi's campaign.[32] Mehdi Rafsanjani left Iran in summer 2009. Iran's chief prosecutor has publicly asked Mehdi Rafsanjani to return to Iran to answer the accusations.[33] The hardliners continued their harsh attacks on Rafsanjani and his family members in 2010.[34]

As the crisis continued, many hardline elements publicly called for the arrest of reformist leaders. The mass popular protests continued at Qods Day demonstrations in late September 2009 and during the demonstrations at the anniversary of the take-over of the American Embassy on November 4, 2009. In late November, threats of arresting reformist leaders increased, especially as the regime feared the arrival of December 7, 2009, the anniversary of the killing of university students in 1953, which is commemorated as University Student Day.[35] Large numbers of university students were arrested in November 2009 in order to intimidate students and undermine the organization of the protests on December 7, but Moussavi, Karrubi, Khatami, and Rafsanjani were not arrested despite repeated calls by the extreme members of the hardline camp.[36]

2009), http://www.parsine.com/pages/?cid=8335. Mrs. Rajabi is the author of Ahmadinejad's biography entitled *Ahmadinejad: The Miracle of the Third Millennium.*

31 Yalda Arasteh, *"Hoshdar Sepah Dar Astaneh Khordad: Cheh Kasi Saran Eslahat Ra Terror Mikonad?"* [The Warning of the IRGC Approaching Anniversary of June: Who Assassinates the Reformist Leaders?], JARAS (May 10, 2010), http://www.rahesabz.net/story/15184/.

32 Al-Arabiya, *"Taeb Baradar Moaven Sepah Az Bi-Khatari Dastgiri Rafsanjani Sokhan Goft; Baradar Movaen Sepah Pesar Hashemi Ra Beh Rah Andazi Khaneh Fesad Moteham Kard"* [Taeb the Brother of the IRGC Deputy Remarked on the Lack of Danger in Arresting Hashemi; Brother of IRGC Deputy Accused Hashemi's Son of Organizing A House of Prostitution] (November 25, 2009), http://www.alarabiya.net/articles/2009/11/25/92341.html#.

33 Brian Murphy, "Iran Seeks to Quiet Critic Inside Ruling System," Associated Press (November 25, 2009).

34 For a comprehensive attack see: RAHVA, *"Hameh Farzandan Khanevadeh Hashemi"* [All the Children of the Hashemi Family] (June 15, 2010), http://rahva.ir/104/10267-89.html. RAHVA is an extremist hardline website. It regularly makes harsh attacks on Rafsanjani and the reformists.

35 Ibid.

36 International Campaign for Human Rights in Iran, "Crackdown on Students Ahead of National Student Day" (November 24, 2009), http://www.iranhumanrights.org/2009/11/crackdownstudentday/;

In numerous incidents, hardliners engaged in intimidations and violence against Karrubi, Moussavi, and his wife Dr. Zahra Rahnavard. In January hardline elements fired gun shots at Karrubi's vehicle and on March 14, 2010, they vandalized his home in Tehran.[37] In May 2010, the state-appointed chief of Moussavi's security was arrested and imprisoned. Haj Ahmad Yazdanfar, a high-ranking IRGC officer, had been the Chief of Security for Moussavi since 1981, when Moussavi was Prime Minister. The regime denied that Yazdanfar had been arrested and instead claimed that his duties as Chief Security Officer had ended. In an interview published on May 23, 2010, Moussavi said:

> If someone's assignment has ended, this would be officially communicated to him, not that when he is going to do his *namaz* [prayer] be arrested in the middle of the street and taken to military headquarters. Mr. Yazdanfar had been a member of the security team since 1360 [1981]. He had been one of the old and very good brothers in the IRGC and had been performing his duties. He is also the brother of two martyred, and is very devout, and committed and self-sacrificing in this performing his responsibilities. In the past thirty years, he could have accepted high positions and well-paying jobs, but did not accept those,

---

Hussein Mohammadi, *"Barkhord Ba Jonbesh Daneshjooe Dar Mosahebeh Ba Bahareh Hedayat"* [Confronting the Student Movement in an Interview with Bahareh Hedayat], Rooz Online (November 25, 2009), http://www.roozonline.com/persian/news/newsitem/article////107/-0742b448ce.html; Reuters, "Iran Detains Scores Of Students, Rights Group Says" (November 25, 2009), http://www.reuters.com/article/topNews/idUSTRE5AO1ZH20091125; Amir Kabir University Students News, *"Gozaresh Bazdasht Daneshjooyan Tey Aban Mah; Bazdasht 60 Daneshjoo Dar Yek Mah"* [Report on the Arrests of Students During the Month of Aban: Arrests of 60 Students in One Month] (November 4, 2009), http://www.autnews.es/node/4364; Amir Kabir University Students News, *"Ehzar-e Nazdik Beh 100 Daneshjoy Daneshgah Azad Ahwaz"* [Arraignments of Close to 100 Students of the Free University of Ahwaz] (November 4, 2009), http://www.autnews.es/node/4375.

37 AFP, "'Thugs' Vandalized Apartment of Iran's Karroubi" (March 15, 2010), http://www.google.com/hostednews/afp/article/ALeqM5inF2uzaSRQ8lXw6r7p_uLL45hW3 A; Payvand, "Photos: Assailants Attack Iranian Opposition Leader's Home" (March 15, 2010), http://www.payvand.com/news/10/mar/1147.html. A group calling itself *"Setad Mardomi Peygiri Mojazat Saran Fetneh"* [People's Headquarters for the Demand for Punishment of the Leaders of the Sedition] held protests in front of the home of Karrubi, vandalized his home, and smashed its windows. The group spray painted the house with the slogans "Death to Karrubi," "Death to Moussavi," "Death to Khatami," and held signs with the remarks "Illiterate Karrubi is puppet of Mossad" [Israel's intelligence agency]. The security camera at Karrubi's home appears to show coordination between the police and the attackers. The attack occurred on Sunday March 14 and the videos of the attack had been placed on YouTube by March 15. This video is from the security camera http://www.youtube.com/watch?v=w2CHkdgykag; and this video was shot the following day http://www.youtube.com/watch?v=1otHmKEZg5A.

and did not leave. He stood for what he believed. By arresting Mr. Yazdanfar, they [the regime] have placed themselves in a major harm and I do not know where this project will end.[38]

Many hardline IRGC officials had been publicly speculating that terrorists might assassinate reformist leaders in order to blame the regime.[39] Moussavi is pointing out that by arresting the trusted chief of his security, if he (Moussavi) were assassinated, then many would blame the regime. The numerous warnings of assassinations were understood as threats of assassination in order to intimidate reformist leaders.

As will be shown later, some hardliners known as *osolgarayan efrati* (extremist fundamentalist, or extremist hardliners) publicly and repeatedly demanded arrests of *"saran fitneh"* [leaders of the sedition], referring to Moussavi, Karrubi, Khatami, and Rafsanjani. Despite these repeated calls, Khamenei did not consent to the arrests of these leaders. Khamenei's refusal created great unease and confusion among the extreme hardliners, among whom absolute obedience to the Supreme Leader is the cardinal belief.[40] Finally Moussavi and Karrubi were arrested and placed under house arrest on February 14, 2011.

Also of significance is that in the 12 months following the election, there were some high-ranking IRGC officers who had not publicly condemned the actions of opponents of the Ahmadinejad reelection as *"fitneh"* [sedition]. In great frustration, Gen. Yahya Safavi, the former Commander-in-Chief of the IRGC, a hardliner and a senior advisor to the Supreme Leader, criticized such IRGC high-ranking officers (who refused to condemn Moussavi and Karrubi) in late May 2010.[41] Moreover, there are credible reports of high-ranking officers (e. g., generals and colo-

---

38 Moussavi, *"Beh Mardom Bazgardid Angah Sobh Omid Fara Khahad Resid"* [Return To The People Then The Morning of Hope Will Arrive], Kaleme (May 23, 2010), http://www.kaleme.com/1389/03/02/klm-20224.

39 Rahe Sabz, *"Hoshdar Sepah Dar Astaneh Khordad; Cheh Kasi Saran Eslahat Ra Terror Mikonad?"* [Warning of the IRGC As June Approaches; Who Will Assassinate the Reformist Leaders?] (May 10, 2010), http://www.rahesabz.net/story/15184.

40 Ayatollah Mesbah Yazdi's official website, *"Porsesh Va Pasokh Jam'i Az Daneshjooyan Basiji Ba Alameh Mesbah Yazdi"* [Question and Answer between a Group of *Basij* Students with Alameh Mesbah Yazdi] (December 31, 2009), http://mesbahyazdi.org/farsi/?../farsi/speeches/ques-dAns/q-a4.htm.

41 Fars News Agency, *"Chera Barkhi Sardaran Dar Barabar Fetneh-hay Akhir Mozea Roshani Nemigirand?"* [Why Some High-Ranking Officers Do Not Take Clear Position on the Recent Sedition] (May 31, 2010), http://www.farsnews.com/newstext.php?nn=8903070179.

nels) in the IRGC who escaped Iran because of their strong opposition to the top leadership.[42]

In a seminar for the security officials on July 24, 2010, Gen. Mohammad Ali Jaafari (the Commander-in-Chief of the IRGC) publicly acknowledged that many IRGC members had supported "leaders of the sedition."[43] Gen. Jaafari was asked why the IRGC officials who supported the leaders of sedition were not confronted. Jaafari responded: "many of their confusions have been solved and they have become convinced that their actions were wrong, and this is better than physical confrontation and their elimination."[44]

During the presidential campaign in mid-2009, several former top IRGC commanders had publicly supported Moussavi. These included Mohsen Rashid, the former Chairman of the IRGC's Center for the Study of War, and Mohammad Ezlati-Moghadam, the Chairman of *Komiteh Easargaran* [Self-Sacrificers Committee]. Both Rashid and Ezlati-Moghadam were commanders of the IRGC during the war with Iraq in the 1980s. Ezlati-Moghadam was imprisoned after the June 2009 election.[45]

According to the highly credible news site JARAS (based outside Iran and closely connected to the reformists inside), the Supreme Leader Ayatollah Khamenei formed a committee to decide what to do with the IRGC high-ranking officials who supported Moussavi during the campaign or did not support the harsh crackdown in the post-election period. The committee was composed of Hojatolislam Mojtaba Khamenei (the Supreme Leader's son), Gen. Hassan Firoozabadi (Chairman of all the armed forces), Gen. Mohammad Reza Naqdi (Commander of *Basij*), and Hojatolislam Hussein Taeb (the Head of the Intelligence Organization of the IRGC). This committee decided to retire about 250 IRGC officers, which in-

---

42 Angus Stickler and Maggie O'Kane, "Former Elite Officers Reveal Tensions In Iran Regime," *The Guardian* (June 11, 2010), http://www.guardian.co.uk/world/2010/jun/11/iran-revolutionary-guards-regime.

43 Fars News Agency, *"Sarlashkar Jafaari Dar Hamayesh Morabiyan Amadegi Defaii"* [Gen. Jafaar in the Seminar for Coaches of Defense Readiness] (July 24, 2010), http://www.farsnews.com/news text.php?nn=8905020568; Deutsche Welle, *"Azan Farmandeh Kol Sepah Beh Vojod 'Pasdaran Hami Fetneh'"* [Admission of the Commander-in-Chief of the IRGC About the Existence of 'IRGC Officials Who Support the Sedition'] (July 25, 2010), http://www.dw-world.de/dw/article/0,,5835486,00.html? maca=per-rss-per_politik-4076-xml-mrss.

44 Ibid., Fars News Agency. My translation. The word *"hazf"* [elimination] in Persian, as in English, could mean either dismissing them from their job at the IRGC or physical elimination.

45 Radio Farda, *"Jaafari: Eqna Pasdaran Hami Fetneh Behtar Az Hazf Anhaast"* [Jaafari: Convincing the IRGC Members Who Support the Sedition Is Better Than Eliminating Them] (July 25, 2010), http://www.radiofarda.com/content/F8_SEPAH_JAFARI_MEMBERS_SUPPORTING_OPPOSITION/ 2108863.html.

cluded high-ranking commanders who had participated in the war with Iraq. The purged officers included Gen. Hussein Alawi, Gen. Hussein Dehqan, Gen. Mostafa Ajarloo, and Gen. Morteza Qorbani. These high-ranking IRGC officers did not support the harsh crackdowns despite repeated attempts to persuade them. They were fired directly by the Supreme Leader.[46]

This analysis shows that the June 2009 election was not a coup by the IRGC. A coup by the IRGC, however, is a possibility in the future. It is significant to add that the political and economic power of the IRGC has increased dramatically in recent years and that the IRGC fears a reformist government may threaten its powers and privileges. The economic activities of the IRGC began after the war with Iraq ended.[47] Then-President Rafsanjani encouraged this move into economic activity. In addition to above-ground economic activities, "the IRGC is also widely rumoured to control a near monopoly over the smuggling of alcohol, cigarettes and satellite dishes, among other things in great demand."[48] In the same article, *The Economist* quotes a member of the parliament as estimating "these black-market deals net it $12 billion a year."[49] The economic activities of the IRGC grew greatly under President Ahmadinejad (2005 onward). These activities grew even more in 2009 – 2010.[50] For example, in one acquisition, the IRGC's related companies purchased 51% of shares of the communications industry for $8 billion. In the 1980s, the state and the *bonyads* [foundations] controlled the Iranian economy. The bonyads are economic foundations created after the revolution and are under the control of the clergy. They are answerable solely to the Supreme Leader, who appoints their Heads. They do not pay taxes but receive funds from the state. The 1990s witnessed the rise of fantastically rich families composed of high-ranking clerics who were at

---

46 JARAS, *"Bazneshastegi 250 Sardar Pasdar Hami Mir Hussein Moussavi"* [The Retiring of 250 IRGC Commanders Who Supported Mir Hussein Moussavi] (July 26, 2010), http://www.rahesabz.net/story/20243/.

47 On the rise of IRGC's economic activities see Ali Alfoneh, "How Intertwined Are the Revolutionary Guards in Iran's Economy?," American Enterprise Institute, Outlook Series, No. 3, (October 2007), http://www.aei.org/outlook/26991.

48 *The Economist*, "Showing Who's the Boss: Iran's Hard Men Purge Opponents and Line Their Pockets" (August 27, 2009), http://www.economist.com/world/middle-east/displaystory.cfm?story_id=14327633&source=login_payBarrier.

49 Ibid.

50 Deutsche Welle, *"Defaa Rais Majles Az Faaliyathay Eqtesadi Sepah"* [The Speaker of the Majles Defends the Economic Activities of the IRGC] (May 13, 2010), http://www.dw-world.de/popups/popup_printcontent/0,,5568997,00.html; Ardalan Siami, *"Sal 88 Sal Sepahi Shodan Eqtesad"* [The Year 2009 – 2010 The Year IRGC Dominated the Economy], Rooz Online (March 19, 2010), http://www.roozonline.com/persian/news/newsitem/article/2010/march/19//88-12.html.

the helm of various state institutions, and their children.[51] In the aftermath of American sanctions on Iran, Dubai emerged as one of Iran's main trading partners. There are about 9,000 registered Iranian businesses and about 400,000 Iranian nationals live there. Some believe that the IRGC controls much of Iran's business interests in Dubai.[52] Since 2005, it has been the IRGC that has emerged as the most powerful economic actor in the Iranian economy, along with the state itself.

During 2005–2007, the *Basij* was integrated into the IRGC. In 2006, Gen. Jaafari was appointed the Commander-in-Chief of the IRGC. For the first time, the Commander-in-Chief of the IRGC was also the Head of the *Basij*. In the past few years, the Commanders of the *Basij* and IRGC have claimed that their budgets have increased greatly. The official weekly publication of the IRGC, *Sobh Sadeq*, claimed that for the year 1387 (March 21, 2007–March 21, 2008), the year before the 2009 election, the budget for the *Basij* increased by 200 %.[53] Another official publication, *Barnameh*, the publication of the Planning and Strategic Monitoring department, which functions under the Office of the President, stated that in the year 1388 (March 21, 2008 to March 21, 2009), the budget for the *Basij* was increased by 45,238,000,000 touman (about $45 million) again.[54] In July 2010, the Commander of *Basij*, Gen. Mohammad Reza Naqdi, stated that in that year 7,000 new *Basij* bases would be created and the budget for *Basij* bases would increase between two and seven times their current budget.[55] The question that remains is that, if the hugely increased economic powers of the IRGC were threatened, would the IRGC simply accept them or would they stage a coup against the system. That situation may or may not arise.

It is significant to note that between late 2010 and April 2011, senior leaders in the IRGC and *Basij*, as well as the powerful hardline *Kayhan* paper moved away from Ahmadinejad when Ahmadinejad began having conflicts with Khamenei.

---

51 Paul Klebnikov, "Millionaire Mullahs," *Forbes* (July 21, 2003), http://www.forbes.com/global/2003/0721/024.html.

52 Morris M. Mottale, "The Birth of a New Class," Al Jazeera (April 22, 2010), http://english.aljazeera.net/focus/2010/04/2010421104845169224.html. I thank Karmen C. King for referring this article to me.

53 Javad Talei, "*Na-aramihay Iran Va Afzaesh Entezarat Mali Police Va Basij*" [Disorders in Iran and the Increased Financial Expectations of the Police and *Basij*], Deutsche Welle (January 15, 2010), http://www.dw-world.de/dw/article/0,,5128185,00.html.

54 Ibid.

55 Fars News Agency, "*Rais Sazeman Basij Mostazafin Khabar Dad: Ehdas 7,000 Paygah Moqavemat Basij Dar Sal Jari*" [The Commander of the *Basij* Presented the News: 7,000 *Basij* Resistance Bases Will Be Constructed This Year] (July 29, 2010), http://www.farsnews.net/newstext.php?nn=8905061538.

All the above clearly indicate that the June 2009 event was not a coup by the IRGC. At all times, the IRGC remained fully subservient to the Supreme Leader. Subsequent events show that the IRGC, *Basij*, and *Kayhan* have acted as powerful extremist hardline entities, which lobbied the Supreme Leader for violent action against the reformists. And when splits developed between Ahmadinejad and the Supreme Leader, these powerful extremist hardline entities followed the dictates of the Supreme Leader. They were not happy at many of the decisions of the Supreme Leader, but at no time did they disobey his orders.

2.2.3 Ayatollah Mesbah Yazdi and His Supporters

There have been powerful members of the oligarchy who have been working to transform the Islamic "Republic" into an Islamic "government," arguing that republican features of the constitution are Western constructs alien to the pure Islamic form of government created by the Prophet Mohammad. This group wants to make the powers of the Supreme Leader absolute. Ayatollah Mohammad Taqi Mesbah Yazdi was the most sophisticated theoretician of this group before his death.[56] Mesbah was the most erudite of all clerics in the extreme hardline camp. In addition, he possessed great administrative and organizational skills.[57]

Mesbah's book—entitled *Hokumat Islami Va Velayat Faqih* [Islamic Government and the Rule of the Cleric] and published by *Sazeman Tablighat Islami* [Organization of Islamic Guidance], one of the government's main publishing houses —is the most sophisticated and forceful presentation of the idea of Islamic government.[58] In a major public display of mutual admiration and support, Khamenei personally paid a visit to Mesbah at his home. Mesbah bowed to kiss Khamenei's foot but was only allowed by Khamenei to kiss his hand. Sitting next to Mesbah, Khamenei strongly praised his writings and ideas.[59] Mesbah taught at the Haqqani seminary school. Its alums include Minister of Intelligence Hojatolislam Gholam-Hussein Mohseni Ezhei and Inspector-General Hojatolislam Mustafa Pour-Moham-

---

56 Ayatollah Mesbah Yazdi's website is http://www.mesbahyazdi.org/.
57 See Zammaneh radio's Mohammad Tajdolati interview with Hassan Yousef Eshkevari, Part I (April 28, 2010), http://zamaaneh.com/analysis/2010/04/post_1457.html. Eshkevari is one of the most prominent clerics in Iran associated with liberal and reformist circles. He was defrocked by the Special Clerical Court due to his critical views. He now classifies himself as *"roshanfekr dini"* [religious intellectual].
58 Ostaad Mohammad Taqi Mesbah Yazdi, *Hokumat Islami Va Velayat Faqih* (Tehran: Markaz Chap Va Nashr Sazeman Tablighat Islami, 1369 [1991]).
59 See http://www.youtube.com/watch?v=Qv5FK7zid7U.

madi.[60] Ahmadinejad was extremely close to Mesbah. Mesbah was an influential member of the Assembly of Experts. Many in the hardline faction want to see Mesbah become Supreme Leader after Khamenei passes away.

According to Mohammad Hashemi, the attacks on Ayatollah Rafsanjani are orchestrated by those forces who want to replace the Islamic Republic with Mesbah's version of an Islamic government. Mohammad Hashemi is a high-level insider. He is the younger brother of Rafsanjani. He was appointed the Head of the state television and radio monopoly by Ayatollah Khomeini. He has been a member of the Expediency Council. In Hashemi's words: "Some do not want this [Islamic Republic], and for this reason they have to get rid of Mr. Hashemi [Rafsanjani] to get to the Islamic government [*hokumat Islami*], and for this they make false accusations and slander [against Rafsanjani] to get what they want. These people do not recognize any rights for the people in the governing structure."[61]

2.2.4 Mojtaba Khamenei and Succession

Many consider a prime, but covert, driver of the June 2009 events to have been Mojtaba Khamenei, the son of the Supreme Leader. Mojtaba is a cleric, extremely conservative, and highly political.[62] He is the second son of the Supreme Leader.[63]

---

60 Pour-Mohammadi was a deputy to the Minister of Intelligence in 1988 and responsible for the massacre of political prisoners. He also served as Minister of the Interior in Ahmadinejad's cabinet but was forced out due to differences with him. Human Rights Watch, "Ministers of Murder: Iran's New Security Cabinet" (December 2005), http://hrw.org/backgrounder/mena/iran1205/. BBC Persian, "*Ayatollah Montazeri Naghshe Pour-Mohammadi Dar Edamhay Sal 67 Ra Taeed Kard*" [Ayatollah Montazeri Confirmed the Role of Pour-Mohammadi in the Executions of the Year 1998] (December 16, 2005), http://www.bbc.co.uk/persian/iran/story/2005/12/051216_mf_si_hrw.shtml.
61 Tabnak, "*Mohammad Hashemi: Roozhay Sakhti Bar Ayatollah Migozarad*" [Mohammad Hashemi: Harsh Days for the Ayatollah] (August 14, 2009), http://www.tabnak.ir/fa/pages/?cid=59551.
62 Hussein Kermani, "*Zohor Aghazadeh-hay Nogara Va Motarez Beh Pedar Khandeh Nezam*" [The Appearance of the Modernist Children of the Ruling Elite and Their Protests Against the Godfather of the System], Deutsche Welle (April 10, 2011), http://www.dw-world.de/dw/article/0,,6499727,00.html?maca=per-rss-per-all-1491-rdf. The above report interviews Mehdi Mahdavi Azad, who during 2009 was the managing editor of one of the news agencies in Iran, and reports the reports he received from that period. In an interview with Hamid Reza Forozanfar, a grandson of the sister of Khamenei, who had spent time with his cousin Mojtaba Khamenei, Mr. Forozanfar confirms that Mojtaba is now playing a prominent role and that he regards himself as of such a high status that he does not pray behind Ayatollah Jennati. To pray behind a person is public acceptance of that person's superior religious authority. If Mr. Forozanfar's report about his cousin is true, this means that Mojtaba does have ambition to become the next Supreme Leader. See the interview with Khodnevis (April 8, 2011), http://www.khodnevis.org/persian/%D8%B1%D8%B3%D8%A7%

He was a student of Ayatollah Mesbah. It is reported that his degree of *"ijtehad"* [the right to issue fatwa] has been granted by Mesbah.[64] In 2005, Mehdi Karrubi published a public letter and blamed Mojtaba Khamenei for fraud in that election which lowered his votes and increased those of Ahmadinejad in the first round. Karrubi then resigned his position as advisor to the Supreme Leader as well as his position in the Council for the Expediency of the System.[65] Both Karrubi and Rafsanjani were candidates in the 2005 presidential elections, and both claimed that Ahmadinejad's declared victory was due to cheating.[66]

Many reports, relying upon those who used to work in the Office of the Supreme Leader and those who used to work for the Ministry of Intelligence, state that Mojtaba issues orders which others in the Office of the Supreme Leader convey to the relevant officials to be carried out.[67]

Many believe that Mojtaba wants to be the next Supreme Leader, and his father quietly supports his ambition. However, Mojtaba was simply too young and his clerical credentials too low to assume such a position in 2009.[68] When Ayatollah

---

D9%86%D9%87%E2%80%8C%D9%87%D8%A7%DB%8C-%D8%AE%D9%88%D8%AF%D9%85%D8%A7%D9%86%DB%8C/%D8%B3%DB%8C%D8%A7%D8%B3%D8%AA/12119--عوض-خامنهای-مجتبی-"انفر روز فر.
html."است-پاکار-خامنهای-هادی-،شده".

63 Iran Emrooz, *"Seyyed Mojtaba Khamenei Kist?"* [Who is Seyyed Mojtaba Khamenei?] (July 4, 2010), http://www.iran-emrooz.net/index.php?/politic2/print/18644.

64 Ibid.

65 Maryam Manzouri, *"Mehdi Karrubi Farzand Rahbar Jomuri Islamic Ra Beh Eamal Nofoz Dar Entekhabat Moteham Kard Ayatollah Ali Khamenei Goft Ejazeh Nemidahad Afradi Dar Keshvar Bohran Eajad Konand"* [Mehdi Karrubi Accused the Son of the Supreme Leader of the Islamic Republic of Influencing the Elections, Ayatollah Ali Khamenei Said that He Will Not Allow Individuals to Create Crisis in the Country], Radio Farda (June 20, 2005), http://www.radiofarda.com/content/article/303458.html.

66 Iran Emrooz, *"Mohammad Atrianfar: Hamchenan Moataghedam Keh Mahmoud Ahmadinejad Baramadeh Az Aray Omumi Mardom Naboodeh Va Az Nazar Orfi Rais Jomhur Boodan Oo Mahal Tardid Ast"* [Atrianfar: I Still Believe that Mahmoud Ahmadinejad Did Not Get the Vote of the People and From the Perspective of the Common Law There Is Doubt that He Can Be Regarded the President] (June 23, 2006), www.iran-emrooz.net/index.php?/news2/print/9000/.

67 Deutsche Welle, *"Peyda Va Penhan Daftar Ayatollah Khamenei"* [Hidden and Open Aspects of the Office of Ayatollah Khamenei] (July 23, 2010), http://www.dw-world.de/dw/article/0,,5832999,00.html?maca=per-rss-per_politik-4076-xml-mrss.

68 Maziar Radmanesh, *"Seyyed Mojtaba Khamenei Kist?"* [Who is Seyyed Mojtaba Khamenei?], Rooz online (July 4, 2009), http://www.roozonline.com/persian/sotun/sotun-item/article/2009/july/04//-74f76da028.html; Julian Borger, "Mojtaba Khamenei: Gatekeeper to Iran's Supreme Leader," *The Guardian* (June 22, 2009), http://www.guardian.co.uk/world/2009/jun/22/mojtaba-khamenei-iran-protest; and Julian Borger, "Khamenei's Son Takes Control of Iran's Anti-protest Militia," *The Guardian* (July 8, 2009), http://www.guardian.co.uk/world/2009/jul/08/khamenei-son-controls-iran-militia.

Ruhollah Khomeini was the Supreme Leader, his powerful son, Ahmad Khomeini, served as his Chief of Staff, and commanded great power. Ahmad Khomeini's bid to become Supreme Leader was thwarted by the Assembly of Experts, which chose Ali Khamenei instead. Ahmad Khomeini's power waned until he died unexpectedly at the age of 50.[69] His death was declared a heart attack.

It is speculated that Mojtaba fears the ascendancy of expedient and reformist clerics because such a scenario would increase the likelihood of such a cleric becoming the next Supreme Leader, and Mojtaba would be permanently marginalized. The significance of bloodline in succession of Imams in Shia Islam, as well as the Persian tradition of sons becoming the next king, may allow Mojtaba to maneuver himself into the position of Supreme Leader. And if that was not possible immediately, and Mesbah became the next Supreme Leader, that would pave the way for Mojtaba to become President or some other powerful position. Mojtaba would then be a main contender for the position of Supreme Leader after Mesbah passes away.

Much of Mojtaba Khamenei's activities are shrouded in secrecy. In mid-June 2009, the British government announced that, due to U.N. Security Council and E.U. sanctions on the Iranian government, the British government had frozen $1.6 billion in Iranian government assets.[70] The British government did not disclose the exact nature of the assets. Highly regarded British journalists, however, published reports based on "unsourced reports" that the assets were funds which belonged to Mojtaba Khamenei and that the British banks had frozen those funds.[71] Further reports either substantiating or debunking these reports have not surfaced at the time of writing this book.

Events since 2009 have substantiated the view that Mojtaba wants to be the next Supreme Leader and wields great power behind the scenes.

---

69 Eric Pace, "Ahmed Khomeini Is Dead; Son of Ayatollah Khomeini," *The New York Times* (March 18, 1995); Baquer Moin, "Obituary: Ahmad Khomeini," *The Independent* (March 18, 1995), http://www.independent.co.uk/news/people/obituaryahmad-khomeini-1611695.html.
70 Adrian Croft, "Britain Has Frozen $1.6 Billion in Iranian Assets," Reuters (June 18, 2009), http://www.reuters.com/article/idUSTRE55H5Z620090618.
71 Simon Tisdall, "Allegations from Tehran Straining Already Rocky Relations with the West," *The Irish Times* (June 23, 2009), http://www.irishtimes.com/newspaper/world/2009/0623/1224249338747.html.

2.2.5 Hardline Fundamentalists Who Oppose Détente with the United States

Every Friday, the Iranian regime holds a mass prayer at the campus of the University of Tehran, where one of the highest officials delivers either the consensus position of the ruling oligarchy or the position of one of its main factions. On January 16, 2009, the Friday prayer was conducted by the powerful Ayatollah Jennati.[72] In his speech on January 16, Jennati, referring to then Israeli Foreign Minister Tzipi Livni, said: "When I see her face, I wish someone would waste a bullet on her."[73] Jennati added: "The world is on a slope of collapse. One is shocked when a president (Obama) sits, smiles, and says 'my concern is to find a dog for my daughter.' Really shame on you and on those who voted for you."[74]

Jennati also attacked the governments of Egypt and Saudi Arabia. He said:

> Disgrace be upon Islamic countries that neither possess faith, nor courage, nor manliness, nor popular support, the worst of which are Saudi Arabia and Egypt, one of them is a puppet of the United States and the other one is an ally of Israel. ... The leaders of these countries have to be afraid of popular uprisings and God's anger gripping them. ... We are hopeful that the day will come that in the words of the esteemed Supreme Leader, we will celebrate Hamas's victory in Jerusalem.[75]

During the official rally after the January 16, 2009 mass prayer, the slogan "*Marg bar Obama*" [Death to Obama] was added to the usual slogan of "*Marg bar Amrika*" [Death to America]. The video of the event was available on YouTube.[76] A target sign was painted on photographs of Obama and Livni with the words "*monafeghan*

---

72 Fars News Agency, "*Rahpemai Zede Zeihonisti Pas az Marasem Namza Jomeh Tehran*" [Anti-Zionist Rally After the Friday Prayer Ceremonies] (January 16, 2009), http://www1.farsnews.com/imgrep.php?nn=8710270933.

73 The quoted segment is my translation from the video of Ayatollah Jannati originally broadcast on Channel 1, Iranian TV, and placed on the MEMRI site: http://www.memritv.org/clip/en/1986.htm?auth=ea4d243656d2616d0cd5788ad984764f (accessed January 31, 2009). For slightly different translations see: Associated Press, "Iranian Cleric Calls for Shooting Israeli FM," republished in *The International Herald Tribune* (January 17, 2009), http://www.iht.com/articles/ap/2009/01/17/news/ML-Iran-Israel.php.

74 Ibid.

75 *Rooznameh Iran*, "*Taghdir Khatib Jomeh Tehran Az Talash-hay Diplomatic Dowlat Baray Nejat Ghazeh*" [Friday Prayer Speaker Applauding the Government for Its Diplomatic Efforts to Rescue Gaza] (January 17, 2009), http://www.iran-newspaper.com/1387/871028/html/internal.htm#s944718. *Rooznameh Iran* is the official paper of record of the Iranian government.

76 http://www.youtube.com/watch?v=1HnTsiB6zIc&eurl (accessed January 19, 2009). The video has since been removed.

omat" [the hypocrites of the Islamic people] as a reference to Obama.[77] Then Obama's photos were burned, dragged in the street, and some had shoes thrown at them.[78]

In addition to Obama and Livni, photos of King Abdallah of Saudi Arabia, President Hosni Mubarak of Egypt, and King Abdallah of Jordan were included with the phrase "wanted dead or alive" in both Persian and English. Nooses were placed around effigies of the Arab leaders and the effigies were then hanged.[79]

The event indicates that this faction under Jennati's leadership was extremely hostile to Obama and strongly opposed any negotiations with the United States. On January 29, Jennati strongly condemned those who supported rapprochement with the U.S. as "troublemakers" who belonged to "hated groups."[80] Jennati added: "I am warning some of society's most abandoned and hated groups who are intending to establish relations with the U.S., want to meet with Obama and give the U.S. president a green light: do not go in this direction. You are just troublemakers. Do not damage yourselves more. Do not rely on America and do not hurt people."[81]

These very hostile remarks came in January 2009, during the Israeli military strikes on Hamas and other Palestinian militants in Gaza. Then-President Elect Obama had expressed his support for Israel. Similar hostile sentiments were again on display on April 9, 2009. On this day, hardline students held a rally in front of the former U.S. Embassy in Tehran on the occasion of the "30th anniversary of breaking diplomatic relations between Iran and the U.S."[82] This occurred at a time when President Obama had already made several public and private remarks indicating that he recognized the Islamic Republic political system and would like to engage in negotiations and agreements based on mutual interests and mutual respect.

During the protests on April 9, 2009, hardline students burned photos of President Obama with former Presidents Jimmy Carter, George Bush, Bill Clinton, and

---

77 The term *"monafeghan"* [hypocrites] is one of the most despised terms used by the regime, usually reserved for those who pretend to be Muslim but are the enemy of real Muslims.
78 The following are photos of the event: http://www1.farsnews.com/plarg.php?nn=M417844.jpg; http://www1.farsnews.com/plarg.php?nn=M417836.jpg; http://www1.farsnews.com/plarg.php?nn=M417845.jpg (all accessed February 2, 2009).
79 The following are photos: http://www1.farsnews.com/plarg.php?nn=M417854.jpg; http://www1.farsnews.com/plarg.php?nn=M417837.jpg; http://www1.farsnews.com/plarg.php?nn=M417846.jpg; http://www1.farsnews.com/plarg.php?nn=M417852.jpg (all accessed February 2, 2009).
80 Robert Tait, "Iran Should Keep Its Distance from US, Says Senior Cleric," *The Guardian* (January 29, 2009), http://www.guardian.co.uk/world/2009/jan/29/iran-us-obama.
81 Ibid.
82 Golnaz Esfandiari, "'Death to Obama' Chants In Iran," Radio Free Europe/Radio Liberty (April 9, 2009), http://www.rferl.org/content/Death_To_Obama_Chants_In_Iran/1605628.html.

George W. Bush, as well as photos of Obama and former Israeli Prime Minister Ol-mert.[83] The slogans shouted by the students included: *"Marg bar Obama"* [Death to Obama], *"Marg bar Tagheeir Amricai"* [Death to American Version of Change], *"Da-neshjoo Bidar Ast, Az Obama Bizar Ast"* [Students are Aware, They Hate Obama], *"Tagheer Amricai, Farib-e Amricai"* [American Change is American Deception], *"Marg bar Sazeshkar"* [Death to Compromiser], *"Islam Pirooz Ast, Sharq va Gharb Nabood Ast"* [Islam is Victorious, the West and the East is Obliterated], and *"Marg bar Ghalam-bedast Mozdor"* [Death to Puppet Writers].[84]

2.2.6 Ahmadinejad's Inner Circle

Ahmadinejad and his inner circle should be understood as a group among the fun-damentalist oligarchy. Ahmadinejad has gathered a number of highly loyal advi-sors and friends. Between 2005 and 2009, Khamenei was quietly but fully suppor-tive of Ahmadinejad. In all likelihood, the reason was that he wanted to undermine the reformists and reduce the power of Rafsanjani. Khamenei continued to public-ly strongly support Ahmadinejad until early 2011. Tensions arose in mid-2010 to early 2011 between Khamenei and Ahmadinejad.

Ahmadinejad is very different from many in the hardline camp. On economic issues, for example, Ahmadinejad's policies between 2005 and early 2010 were strongly to support the poor. The statist economic policies benefiting the poor via subsidies and spending were promoted by the so-called Left Fundamentalists between 1979 and the early 1990s. In the early 1990s, Rafsanjani allied with the Right Fundamentalists (in the Council of Guardians) to peacefully purge the Left Fundamentalists from positions of power. Rafsanjani pursued policies to reduce subsidies for the poor and IMF-style economic reforms (which benefited the so-called fundamentalist *nouveaux riches*). The Left Fundamentalists transformed themselves into reformists between 1992 and 1997. They abandoned their statist

---

83 Fars News Agency, *"Tajamo Daneshjoyan dar Salrooz Ghate Rabeteh Iran va Amrica"* [Gathering of Students on the Anniversary of the Breaking of Relations between Iran and America] (April 9, 2009), http://www.farsnews.net/imgrep.php?nn=8801200623. Also see: http://www.farsnews.net/plarg.php?nn=M517526.jpg; http://www.farsnews.net/plarg.php?nn=M517528.jpg; and ttp://www.far-snews.net/plarg.php?nn=M517534.jpg.
84 Iran Press News, *"Shoar-e 'Marg bar Obama' dar Tazahorat Tehran"* [The Slogan of "Death to Obama" at Demonstrations in Tehran] (April 9, 2009), http://www.iranpressnews.com/source/057215.htm. Also see: Fars News Agency, *"Tajamo Daneshjooyan Tehrani Moghabel Laneh Jasoosi Sabeq Amrica Aghaz Shod"* [Gathering of Students from Tehran began in Front of the Former Den of Spies of America] (April 9, 2009), http://www.farsnews.com/newstext.php?nn=8801200232.

economic policies and instead emphasized political liberalization and reduction of social restrictions.

The Right Fundamentalists, or what became known as conservatives, or hard-liners, were more supportive of policies to help the bazaaris (small shopkeepers), and emphasized traditional conservative social issues such as stricter enforcement of hijab, but restrictions on Western music, and hairstyles, films, and the like. The reformist fundamentalists won all the elections for the presidency, Majles, and local offices after 1997. Ahmadinejad reversed the electoral fortunes of the reformists by appealing to the poor, who had been abandoned since around 1992 by all the factions. Khamenei and other conservative hardline elements supported Ahmadinejad in order to keep the Left Reformists out of the presidency. The huge increase in the price of oil allowed Ahmadinejad to spend huge amount in handouts to the rural and urban poor between 2005 and 2008. Ahmadinejad enjoyed real support among vast sectors of the poor in urban and rural areas in 2005. It appears that he lost some support due to the deteriorating economic situation later on.

On a few other minor issues, there were differences between Ahmadinejad and the hardliners. But these issues did not cause much conflict until early 2011. During the 2005 election campaign Ahmadinejad stated that it is not the business of the government how the people dress or which hairstyles they choose, issues which the conservatives are obsessed about and regard as symbols of Western decadence. In 2007, Ahmadinejad drew the ire of the conservative clerics when he said that women should be allowed to attend games at soccer stadiums. He was forced to withdraw his position after a backlash from the conservatives.

2.3 Opponents of Ahmadinejad

There are several major groups that oppose Ahmadinejad and the so-called June 2009 coup. Each has its own concerns and demands. Their confluence caused the June 2009 crisis. These groups include: (1) Rafsanjani; (2) reformist elements of the ruling oligarchy such as Khatami and Karrubi; (3) elements of the establishment such as Moussavi; (4) many young men and women who appear genuinely to believe in Moussavi bringing freedom; (5) secular modern middle classes; and (6) the "solid opposition."

2.3.1 Ayatollah Ali Akbar Hashemi Rafsanjani

Rafsanjani was one of the main pillars of the Islamic Republic. He was the Chairman of the Assembly of Experts as well as the Chairman of the Council for the Expediency of the System. A wily and elastic politician, Rafsanjani has been described as extremist (1979–1989), moderate (1989–1997), pragmatic (circa 1997–2000), and pragmatic conservative (circa 2000–2009). From 2005, he strongly opposed Ahmadinejad.

Until 2009, Rafsanjani had promoted what may be called the Chinese model as the solution to the crisis in the Islamic Republic. Rafsanjani had been identified with increasing repression of opponents of the regime, especially with assassinating them inside and outside Iran, as well as Tiananmen Square-style massacres to intimidate the population into submission. Rafsanjani and Ali Fallahian (his Minister of Intelligence) are believed to have masterminded the assassinations of non-violent, pro-democracy activists and writers both inside and outside Iran. Rafsanjani had advocated increasing repression of the more radical members of the reformist faction. He advocated improving political and economic relations with the E.U., Japan, and Canada, and reducing tensions with the United States. He advocated reducing subsidies to the poor and making "rational" economic policies (creating one exchange rate instead of several) and IMF-style economic reforms.

Rafsanjani's support base included many clerics within the establishment, many technocrats, and the *nouveaux riches*.[85] They regard Ahmadinejad's domestic policies to have both harmed their interests and the economy. Moreover, they fear that Ahmadinejad's foreign policies might provoke a war with the U.S. or Israel, or more severe economic sanctions.[86]

In a truly remarkable comment during the Persian month of Azar (October–November 2009), Rafsanjani said: "The Iranian people are believers and Muslims, if they want us, we will govern them, and if they do not want us, we should leave [power]."[87] In March 2010, Rafsanjani stated: "In the present era, with the growth and spread of media, any governing system which lacks a popular base could not last."[88] In late February 2010, Rafsanjani's influential daughter, Faezeh Hashemi

---

85 The official websites of Rafsanjani are: http://www.hashemirafsanjani.ir/?lang=1 and http://www. rafsanjani.ir/ (both accessed last on February 11, 2010). BBC Persian, *"Jame'eh Rouhaniyat Mobarez Az Rafsanjani Hemayat Mikonad"* [The Society of Combatant Clergy Supports Rafsanjani] (March 7, 2010), http://www.bbc.co.uk/persian/lg/iran/2010/03/100307_l39_rafsanjani_salek.shtml.

86 Kasra Naji, *Ahmadinejad: The Secret History of Iran's Radical Leader* (Berkeley: University of California Press, 2008), pp. 60–89.

87 Radio Farda, *"Rafsanjani: Hokomat Keh Payeh Mardomi Nadashteh Bashad Paydar Nemimanad"* [Rafsanjani: A Governing System Which Lacks Popular Base Will Not Last] (March 11, 2010), http://www.radiofarda.com/content/F8_RASANJANI_DEMOCRACY/1980196.html.

88 Ibid. The word used by Rafsanjani is *"hokomat,"* which means "governing system." In Iran, this term is different from *"dowlat,"* which means "government" or "administration." The term *"hokomat"* refers to the entire system of the Islamic Republic and not to the administration of Ahmadinejad.

Rafsanjani, stated in an interview with Rooz Online (which was one of the most credible news outlets established outside Iran by many democrats and reformists who had fled Iran in recent months and years): "You could also consider him [Ayatollah Rafsanjani] as one of the Greens."[89] She went on to add that her father had been standing by people's rights in his own way because he had "foresight and knows what is expedient for the current situation of the society ... in the current situation any compromise without consideration of the people's rights and damages they have suffered is questionable."[90] It should be emphasized that Rafsanjani's comments should not be interpreted as opposition to the system. As one of the most powerful members of the system, he was strongly committed to the Islamic Republic.[91]

2.3.2 Reformists Elements of the Oligarchy

In 1992 the conservative faction in the Council of Guardians and then-President Rafsanjani used their control of the Council of Guardians to purge the left-wing fundamentalists. For example, 40 left-wing fundamentalist members of the 3rd Majles (1988–1992) were forbidden to run for the 4th Majles (1992–1996) election. Between 1992 and 1997, former left-wing fundamentalists metamorphosed into the so-called reformist fundamentalists.

Khatami's coalition in 1997 was composed of almost two dozen sub-factions. The main groups were: *"Rouhaniun Mobarez"* (Combatant Clerics),[92] *"Sazeman Mojahedin Enghelab Islami"* (Organization of the Mojahedin of the Islamic Revolution, or OMIR), and the Islamic Iran Participation Front. The Combatant Clerics is the most traditional and least reformist, and the IIPF is the least traditional and the most reformist within the main groups in the reformist camp. Before 1997, the Combatant Clerics and OMIR advocated statist economic policies; violent, virulent

---

89 Payvand Iran News, "Ayatollah Rafsanjani Said to Stand Firm on Upholding People's Rights" (March 1, 2010), http://www.payvand.com/news/10/mar/1002.html.
90 Ibid.
91 For example, see Rafsanjani's strong support for the system and the Supreme Leader: Iranian Labour News Agency (ILNA), *"Rahbari Mikhahad Sahneh Kheili Dagh Nashavad Va Kasi Asib Nabinad"* [The Supreme Leader Does Not Want to See the Situation Heated Up, and Anyone Harmed] (February 23, 2010), http://www.ilna.ir/newsText.aspx?ID=109649.
92 The former left faction and now reformist group *"Rouhanioun Mobarez"* (Combatant **Clerics**) should not be confused with right faction, now hardline group *"Rouhaniyat Mobarez"* (Combatant **Clergy**). The former (**Clerics**) split from the latter (**Clergy**) in the early 1980s and made a small change in the name.

anti-Americanism; and repression of dissidents at home.[93] In 1991, both Combatant Clerics and OMIR called for Iran to abandon neutrality and side with Saddam Hussein in the U.S. war against Saddam, and then in August 1991 they called for the recognition of the coup against Gorbachev.[94] The IIPF has advocated improving relations with the United States. Interestingly, many of the leaders of the IIPF, such as Reza Khatami, Abbas Abdi, and Mohsen Mirdamadi, were the top leaders of the fundamentalist students who took American diplomats hostage in 1979–1981.[95] The Secretary-General of the IIPF until 2006, Dr. Mohammad Reza Khatami, is the younger brother of President Khatami and is married to Ayatollah Khomeini's granddaughter. Mirdamadi, another top leader of hostage takers, became the Secretary-General of the IIPF in 2006.

Former President Khatami is a cleric with the rank of Hojatolislam and is a top leader of the Combatant Clerics. The Secretary-General of Combatant Clerics was Hojatolislam Mehdi Karrubi who was Speaker of the 6th Majles, and head of *Bonyad Mostazafin* [The Foundation of the Deprived], among many other top positions. Karrubi ran for the presidency in 2005. Hojatolislam Mohtashami-Pour is another leader of the Combatant Clerics, and the former ambassador to Syria who helped create the Lebanese Hezbollah. Another top leader of Combatant Clerics is Hojatolislam Moussavi Khoeiniha, who organized and led the taking of American diplomats hostage in 1979.

Although there had been a real reduction of repression under his presidency, Khatami cannot be classified as a democrat. Khatami has explicitly opposed the replacement of clerical rule with democracy. Khatami only calls for *"Mardomsalai*

---

93 Abbas Kakavandi, a hardline fundamentalist writing in the conservative daily *Resalat*, threatened to reveal the names of reformist fundamentalists who in the 1979–1991 period engaged in "violent and fascistic behaviors such as using metal files to rub lipstick off the lips of women, throwing acid on the faces of women not fully observing the hijab, assaulting the dissidents especially in universities, the sort of things they did in their positions as interrogators and prosecutors, creating shock troops." Abbas Kakavandi, *Resalat* (15 Mordad 1381 in Iranian calendar, August 6, 2002), excerpts in Farsi available at http://www.iran-emrooz.de/yaddasht/bagerz810516.html, my translation.

94 Mohsen Milani, "Iran's Active Neutrality During the Kuwaiti Crisis: Reasons and Ramifications," *New Political Science*, Vols. 21–22 (1992), pp. 41–60; and Scott Macleod and Azadeh Moaveni, "Confronting the Dark Past," *Time Magazine* Europe (July 10, 2000), http://www.time.com/time/eu rope/webonly/mideast/...khoeiniha_intvu.htm. Also among the reformists was Ayatollah Sadeq Khalkhali, the so-called hanging judge, who issued the execution orders of hundreds in summary executions after the ascendancy of fundamentalists to power.

95 Abdi and Ebtekar continue to support their actions in taking American diplomats hostage. That action undermined the moderates in the provisional government and helped consolidate the rule of fundamentalists under Khomeini and his fundamentalist supporters in the Islamic Republican Party (later dissolved).

Dini" (Religious Democracy), by which he advocates only those who are fundamentalist (supporting Khomeini's *Velayat Faqih*) being able to hold office. Basically, Khatami wants the hardliners to allow full participation by all fundamentalist factions and wants to reform the fundamentalist regime to prolong the rule of fundamentalists. From1997, under the leadership of Khatami, the reformists have advocated reduction of repression and freedom for all fundamentalist factions to participate in positions of power. Khatami's position between June 2009 and June 2010 remained the same. He continually emphasized support for the fundamentalist constitution and rights only for supporters of the *"nezam"* [system].

The hardline faction believes that it can preserve and prolong fundamentalist rule with an increase in repression: if they have to use large-scale massacres to intimidate the people into submission, they should do so. The hardliners fear that a reduction of repression would cascade out of control, as occurred in the USSR and Eastern European communist regimes. Khatami's nickname, "Ayatollah Gorbachev," had made the hardliners even more nervous and tenacious in their resistance to a reduction of repression. The hardliners constantly threaten the people with increasing violence and repression if the people continue criticizing the ruling regime.

On economic policy, major conflicts exist among the sub-factions that constitute the reformist camp, with some sub-factions promoting liberalization while others promote statist policies. The braver individuals in this camp have expressed the desirability of compelling *bonyads* [economic foundations under the control of the clerics appointed by the Supreme Leader] to show transparency, including being monitored by the government and paying taxes. Hardliners strongly oppose any changes in the bonyads, which serve as a huge source of wealth for the hardline clerics as well as employment and benefits for their social base.

On foreign policy the picture was clearer. Khatami, with substantial support from the reformist camp, had successfully pursued a policy of détente with Arab governments such as those in Saudi Arabia, Jordan, Morocco, and Egypt.[96]

---

96 Late 2004 witnessed a reversal of earlier détente with Arab governments largely due to the rise of hardliners to power in Iran and their interference in the internal affairs of Iraq. Egypt froze relations again after its officials accused Iranian officials of assisting Egyptian fundamentalists in planning to assassinate Egyptian officials. King Abdullah II of Jordan also publicly pointed the finger at the Iranian regime for interference in the internal affairs of Iraq. The revelations of the clandestine nuclear program of the Iranian regime also rattled many Arab governments who feared a nuclear regime in Iran would be a serious threat to their stability and existence. See the excellent analysis by Ahmad Zeid-Abadi, *"Iran va Arab: Doore Tazei az Bi-eatemadi"* [Iran and Arab: A New Round of None-trust], BBC Persian (December 26, 2004). This article is no longer available on the BBC site. Dr. Zeid-Abadi is highly articulate and is associated with the Nationalist-Religious Alliance (see below). Zeid-Abadi was imprisoned after the elections. Despite

Some of these policies were criticized by the more extremist elements in the hard-line camp. For example, when Khatami's government tried to change the name of one of the main streets in Tehran, which was named after the assassin of President Sadat, the more extremist elements of the hardline camp objected.[97]

Khatami, with support from other factions (Rafsanjani and many hardliners), also pursued improved relations with European powers, especially Germany, France, and Britain, some of which had been frayed in the wake of convictions of leaders of the regime in state-sponsored assassinations of Iranian opposition leaders in Germany, France, Austria, and Italy before Khatami took office. Although Khatami wanted to improve relations with the United States, the Supreme Leader vetoed that policy.[98]

From early 1997 to the present, the reformist mantra has been that if the hardliners allowed them to run for the presidency and Majles, this would undermine the foreign threats to the entire regime. The words of Mohsen Mirdamadi are typical of the reformist leitmotif:

> If presidential elections are going to be like the 7th Majles elections, the Americans will regard the regime as not supported by the people and vulnerable to foreign pressures. Therefore, it looks like the new threatening words by the United States against Iran, are a start of new analysis of Iran's environment for the upcoming election and may begin a very serious confrontation if the elections are weak. On this basis, it is possible for the United States to increase its hostility and to even enter the implementation phase (of overthrowing), which cannot be predicted now. ... The nature of the 1997 elections postponed foreign threats for a prolonged time. ... This forthcoming election can determine the nature of American relations with Iran. ... They [the Americans] will have to determine whether their confrontation with Iran is a confrontation with the people or merely with the regime. If it is with the people, it will have a long-term negative impact for the United States.[99]

To everyone's surprise, during the 1997 presidential campaign Khatami adopted the language of the pro-democracy opposition and talked about democracy, freedom, civil society, and the rule of law. During the election for the presidency in

---

great pressure put on him in prison, he continued his resistance in prison. The Facebook page of his supporters is http://www.facebook.com/#!/FreeAhmadZeidabadi?ref=ts.

97 Sadat's assassin, named Khaled Islamboli, is regarded as a martyred hero by hardliners. The Egyptian government requested a change in the name of the street as a precondition for normalization of relations.

98 Naji, *Ahmadinejad*, op. cit., p. 189.

99 Iranian Students' News Agency (ISNA) interview with Mohsen Mirdamadi, February 19, 2005, my translation. Mirdamadi was also the Chairman of the Foreign Relations Committee in the 6th Majles. The report is no longer available online. Mirdamadi's Facebook page is http://www.facebook.com/drmirdamadi.

1997, the Majles elections in 2000, and the election for the presidency in 2001 reformists talked about such demands. By echoing these non-fundamentalist slogans and demands, the reformist members of the fundamentalist oligarchy garnered huge numbers of votes and edged out their hardline rivals. The hardliners strongly resented the reformists for making such promises. The hardliners believed that such promises jeopardized the survival of the regime.

Those who echoed the demands for freedom and democracy gained about 70 % of the votes in these elections. In the presidential elections of 1997, nearly 88 % of eligible voters participated, and of these, about 70 % voted for Khatami. Again in 2001, about 71 % of those who voted, voted for Khatami.

In 2009, the reformist elements of the fundamentalist oligarchy believed that the regime could be better if it reduced repression and allowed more space for cultural expression. They pursue détente with the United States and the West. Former President Khatami best represents this group.[100]

On February 8, 2009, Khatami officially announced his candidacy for the June 12, 2009 election.[101] After Moussavi announced his candidacy for the presidency in 2009, Khatami withdrew from the race and personally supported Moussavi and encouraged his supporters to support Moussavi. In the aftermath of the disputed election, several websites published the views and policies of the reformists.[102]

2.3.3 Hojatolislam Mehdi Karrubi

Karrubi was regarded as one of the most conservative leaders in the reformist faction. From 2006, however, Karrubi became increasingly "liberal."[103] After June 2009, Karrubi exhibited great courage in his resistance to the hardliners despite real danger to his life. Many clerics within the establishment support this group. The middle classes and lower middle classes in urban areas support this group.

---

100 The official website of Khatami is http://www.khatami.ir/. Khatami heads his think-tank, the Baran Foundation. The website of his think-tank is: http://baran.org.ir.

101 IRNA, "*Khatami Namzadi Khod Ra Rasman Ealam Kard*" [Khatami Officially Announced His Candidacy] (February 8, 2009), http://www5.irna.ir/View/FullStory/?NewsId=346045.

102 These websites included: Jonbesh Rahe Sabz (JARAS) http://www.rahesabz.net/; Emrooz [Today] http://www.emruznews.com/; Tahavole Sabz [Green Evolution] http://www.tahavolesabz.net/; and Neday-e Sabz-e Azadi [The Green Voice of Freedom] http://www.irangreenvoice.com/.

103 Karrubi established his own newspaper (*Eatemaad Melli*) and party (Hezb Eatemaad Melli Iran). His party's official news site, called Saham News, is http://sahamnews.org/. The paper's website is http://www.etemadmelli.org/. The party's official paper is *Eatemaad Melli*. Karrubi's official personal website is http://www.karroubi.ir/.

Some reformists, under the leadership of Khatami, supported Moussavi in the 2009 election, while others supported Karrubi.

2.3.4 Mir-Hussein Moussavi

Moussavi is one of the main founders of the Islamic Republic.[104] Before the revolution, he was involved in Islamist groups which were not fundamentalist. But during the revolutionary process, he joined the fundamentalist supporters of Ayatollah Khomeini. Moussavi was among the original founders of the IRP. He served as the Political Secretary of the IRP and the editor-in-chief of its paper, *Rooznameh Jomhuri Islami*. The IRP played crucial roles in the undermining of the moderates in the provisional government of Mehdi Bazargan and the government of President Bani Sadr, and in consolidating Khomeini's dictatorship. Moussavi served as Foreign Minister in the first fundamentalist cabinet under Prime Minister Mohammad Ali Rajaii with President Bahonar. When Bahonar and Rajaii were killed in 1981, Khamenei was made President and Moussavi was made Prime Minister. After Khomeini died in 1989, Khamenei became the Supreme Leader. The position of Prime Minister was abolished in 1989. Supreme Leader Khamenei appointed Moussavi to the Council for the Expediency of the System in 1989. In July 2010, Moussavi was a member of the Council for the Expediency but was dismissed afterwards. Moussavi also served as advisor to Presidents Rafsanjani (1989–1997) and Khatami (1997–2005). He was also a member of the Supreme Council of the Cultural Revolution until Ahmadinejad dismissed him after the disputed election.

Until late April 2009, Moussavi was calling himself *osolgaray eslahtalab* [reformist hardliner].[105] Prominent elements of the establishment such as Moussavi, who was not identified with either Rafsanjani or the reformists, became very worried about the way Ahmadinejad was conducting domestic and foreign affairs. Many in the lower middle classes, lower classes, and some hardliners have been close to this group.

It is believed that many in the Ministry of Intelligence and state bureaucracy believed that a Moussavi presidency would have been beneficial to the Islamic Re-

---

104 A brief, but excellent, biography is available at: BBC Persian, *"Zendeginameh Namzadha: Mir-Hussein Moussavi"* [Biography of the Candidates: Mir-Hussein Moussavi] (May 21, 2009), http://www.bbc.co.uk/persian/iran/2009/05/090521_og_ir88_mosavi.shtml.

105 Moussavi's website is Kaleme [Word] http://www.kaleme.org/; Moussavi's Facebook page is http://www.facebook.com/mousavi. The Facebook page contains some of Moussavi's statements and interviews in English. Kaleme belongs to Moussavi. The Moussavi Facebook page is managed by his supporters.

public. The most prominent official of the Ministry of Intelligence who was a top official in Moussavi's campaign headquarters was Akbar Khosh-koosh.[106] According to Jahan News, an extremist hardline site, Khosh-koosh played a pivotal role in the post-election events. Akbar Ganji had published reports naming Khosh-koosh as one of the main officials responsible for the assassinations of dissidents outside Iran.[107] Shortly after the election, Ahmadinejad fired more than 20 high-ranking officials of the Ministry of Intelligence. Those fired included Haj Habibollah (Deputy to the Minister of Intelligence for Special Affairs) and Khazaee (Deputy to the Minister of Intelligence for Counterespionage). Each of these two high-ranking officials had served in the Ministry for more than 20 years.[108] It is widely believed that these officials were supporters of Moussavi's reelection.

Another high-ranking official of the Ministry of Intelligence who is a supporter of Moussavi is Hojatolislam Mohammad Reza Nour-Allahyan. A cleric, Nour-Allahyan was a Deputy to the Minister of Intelligence, an official in the Office of the Supreme Leader (until the June 2009 election), and the person responsible for the Shia seminaries outside Iran. He participated in the war against Iraq, and two of his brothers were killed in that war. During the funeral of Moussavi's father, on March 31, 2011, Nour-Allahyan was severely beaten up by the security forces, arrested, and taken to the Evin prison.[109]

The internal problems in the Ministry of Intelligence continued well after the June 2009 crisis. Ahmadinejad fired Gholam-Hussein Mohseni Ejei (a hardliner close to the Supreme Leader) in 2009, apparently because he was not fully supportive of Ahmadinejad. Later on, Ahmadinejad said that "if the Minister of Intelli-

---

106 Jahan News, "*Ranzgoshaee Az Yek Tasliyat*" [Decoding the Secret of Expressing Condolences] (May 13, 2010), http://www.jahannews.com/vdcfcmdyxw6dyta.igiw.html.

107 Ganji is a former fundamentalist official who broke with the regime. He was an investigative journalist who exposed the officials behind assassinations of dissidents inside and outside Iran.

108 Bahram Rafiee, "*Tagheer Gostardeh Masoolin Amniyati Va Nezami Keshvar*" [Massive Changes the Security and Military Officials], Rooz Online (August 4, 2009), http://www.roozonline.com/per sian/news/newsitem/article/2009/august/04//-ad05e8de0f.html. The Head of the police in the country was Esmail Ahmadi Moqadam, who is a brother-in-law of Ahmadinejad. Moqadam purged Heads of police in four provinces in the aftermath of the protests. The reasons for the dismissals were not clear.

109 Kaleme, "*Eateraf Zolnour Beh natavani jaryan Eqtedar-Gara Az Sazemandehi Janiyat*" [Admission of Zolnour to Not Being Able to Gather Popular Support by the Hardliners] (April 18, 2011), http://www.kaleme.com/1390/01/29/klm-55429/; and Deutsche Welle, "*Negarani Do Rouhani Nezami Az Mahar Jonbesh Eaterazi*" [Worries of Two Clerics in the Armed Forces About Containing the Protest Movement] (April 19, 2011), http://www.dw-world.de/dw/article/0,,6507336,00.html?maca= per-rss-per-all-1491-rdf.

gence had done his mission correctly, we would not have these harmful events on the streets."[110] The Supreme Leader quickly appointed Ejei to become the Chief Prosecutor of the Country as well as the Spokesman of the Judicial Branch. In Shahrivar 1388 (circa September 2009), Hojatolislam Heydar Moslehi was appointed to the Ministry of Intelligence. At the same time, the Intelligence [*Edareh*] Office of the IRGC was elevated to the Intelligence [*Sazeman*] Organization of the IRGC. An extremist hardliner, Hojatolislam Hussein Taeb, was appointed the Chief of this more powerful department. Taeb had been the Commander of *Basij*. He was dismissed during the presidency of Rafsanjani because he was too extremist and too violent. Many have accused Taeb of personally raping young female political prisoners such as Ms. Taraneh Moussavi. The Intelligence Organization of the IRGC, under full control of extreme hardline elements, played a leading role after the June 2009 crisis in arresting and torturing protesters. The Ministry of Intelligence, however, was staffed with professional, experienced intelligence officers and reportedly many who were not supportive of the extremist hardline faction. Apparently, many of the personnel of the Ministry of Intelligence were supportive of other factions (e.g., hardliners not supportive of Ahmadinejad, pragmatic conservatives, and reformists). The Supreme Leader made a publicized six-hour visit to the Ministry of Intelligence in mid-Esfand 1389 (circa early March 2011). The Supreme Leader emphasized that the Ministry of Intelligence should not have tendencies supportive of any of the factions. Khamenei said that it is "necessary" for the Ministry of Intelligence to have "a perspective which is above factions and above groups, and be unified."[111] Six weeks later, on April 17, 2011, the Minister of Intelligence, Moslehi offered his resignation. The resignation was accepted by Ahmadinejad, but the Supreme Leader immediately refused the resignation and asked Moslehi to remain the Minister of Intelligence.[112] It is believed that the resignation–reinstatement had to do with high-level personnel in the Ministry and their factional alliance. Different powerful hardline factions presented their critique of the episode.[113]

---

110 Deutsche Welle, "*Barkenari Va Ebqa Dobareh Vazir Etelaat Iran dar Yek Rooz*" [Dismissal and Reinstatement of the Minister of Intelligence of Iran in One Day] (April 17, 2011), http://www.dw-world.de/dw/article/0,,6505906,00.html?maca=per-rss-per-all-1491-rdf.

111 Radio Farda, "*Mokhalefat Rahbar Jomhuri Islami Ba Kenaregiri Heydar Moslehi Az Vezarat Etellaat*" [Opposition of the Supreme Leader of the Islamic Republic with the Resignation of Heydar Moslehi from the Ministry of Intelligence] (April 17, 2011), http://www.radiofarda.com/content/f7_iran_supreme_leader_acts_against_moslehi_resign/4747130.html.

112 Ibid.

113 Deutsche Welle, "'*Fetneh Nofozihay Dowlati*' *Dar Azl Moslehi*" ['Sedition of Those Who Have Infiltrated the Government' in the Dismissal of Moslehi] (April 19, 2011), http://www.dw-world.de/dw/article/0,,15001857,00.html?maca=per-rss-per-all-1491-rdf.

During the presidential campaign in mid-2009, several former top IRGC commanders had publicly supported Moussavi. They included Mohsen Rashid (the former Chairman of the IRGC's Center for the Study of War) and Mohammad Ezlati-Moghadam (Chairman of *Komiteh Easargaran* [Self-Sacrificers Committee]). Both Rashid and Ezlati-Moghadam were commanders of the IRGC during the war with Iraq in the 1980s. Ezlati-Moghadam was imprisoned after the June 2009 election.[114] As mentioned earlier, many family members of commanders of the IRGC and *Basij* during the war with Iraq publicly supported Moussavi. They included the families of Hemmat, Bakeri, and Zeinoldin. Moreover, according to published reports in highly reliable sources, about 250 IRGC commanders were fired by Khamenei for their support for Moussavi or their opposition to harsh crackdowns after the election.

Many have pointed to Moussavi's actions when he was Prime Minister as evidence that there is little difference between Moussavi and hardliners. For example, one expert has argued that Moussavi was responsible for the attacks on Americans in Lebanon which caused more than 200 deaths.[115] One of Moussavi's closest lieutenants is Hojatolislam Ali Akbar Mohtashami-Pour, the former ambassador to Syria who helped create Lebanese Hezbollah in 1982.

Many have argued that when Moussavi was Prime Minister, the regime engaged in its most brutal and repressive actions. Moussavi was Prime Minister during the First Reign of Terror (1981 – 1983), when somewhere between 10,000 and 20,000 political prisoners were executed, and the Second Reign of Terror (August–October 1988) when about 5,000 political prisoners who had already been given prison sentences were executed.[116] For the mass executions of political prisoners in 1988, a commission was formed which included the Minister of Intelligence, who served under Moussavi in his cabinet.

In May 2009 a university student asked Moussavi whether he would support reforming those aspects of the constitution that are dictatorial. Moussavi replied: "I am explicitly against reforming the Constitution. I saw who signed that Consti-

---

114 Radio Farda, *"Jafaari: Eqna Pasdaran Hami Fetneh Behtar Az Hazf Anhaast"* [Jafaari: Convincing the IRGC Members Who Support the Sedition Is Better Than Eliminating Them] (July 25, 2010), http://www.radiofarda.com/content/F8_SEPAH_JAFARI_MEMBERS_SUPPORTING_OPPOSITION/2108863.html.

115 Jeff Stein, "Mousavi, Celebrated in Iranian Protests, Was the Butcher of Beirut," *CQ Politics blog* (June 22, 2009), available at: http://blogs.cqpolitics.com/spytalk/2009/06/mousavi-celebrated-in-iranian.html.

116 For an excellent analysis of human rights violations in this period see Reza Afshari, *Human Rights in Iran: The Abuse of Cultural Relativism* (Philadelphia: University of Pennsylvania Press, 2001).

tution. I am not saying you are an infidel [*kafar*], but these positions will not take us to a good place. ... I totally believe in this Constitution and will be devoted to it."[117]

Throughout the campaign and the post-election protests, Moussavi and his supporters have repeatedly and explicitly stated that they want to reform the system (the Islamic Republic with its principle of *Velayat Faqih*, the rule of a Shia cleric as the Supreme Leader) in order to preserve it. Moussavi's official website, which reflects his views, stated: "the central [leadership] cell and the huge body of the Green Movement has always emphasized its reformist and principled positions on the path of the return to the principles and values of the 1979 revolution and creating conditions for the realization of the Constitution of the Islamic Republic."[118] Moussavi gradually changed his position and accepted the notion of revising some aspects of the constitution. In 2023, Moussavi issued a statement supporting abolishing the fundamentalist constitution and the fundamentalist regime (see Chapter 5).

2.3.5 The Youth Social Base Who Voted for Moussavi

Many young men and women in their teens and early 20s appear genuinely to believe in Moussavi bringing social freedoms such as stopping the moral patrols harassing the youth for their clothing, listening to music, and the like. They come from various social classes and with varied degrees of religiosity. It appears that Moussavi's wife, Dr. Zahra Rahnavard, was one of the main factors that galvanized support for her husband among the youth. Rahnavard has a Ph.D. in political science. She served as President of the all-female al-Zahra University until 2005, when Ahmadinejad became President.[119] Not only did she campaign publicly for her hus-

---

117 Akhbar Rooz, "*Porsesh Daneshjuyan Az Kandiaday Jebhe Mosherekat: Koshtar Sal-e 67, Mir Hussein Javab Bedeh!*" [Students' Questions of the Candidate of the Participation Front: The Massacre of the Year 1988, Mir Hussein Provide an Answer!] (May 5, 2009), http://akhbar-rooz.com/news.jsp?essayId=20689.

118 Kaleme Political Group, "*Tavafoq Na-Neveshteh Oposisioun Zede Enqelab Va Halqeh Mahfeli Qatl-hay Zanjirei*" [The Unwritten Agreement between the Counter-Revolutionary Opposition and the Private Circle of Chain Murders], Kaleme (March 15, 2010), http://www.kaleme.com/1388/12/24/klm-14326. This article contained two parts. One part was a harsh attack on monarchists. The other was a harsh counterattack on the extremist hardliners in the *Kayhan* paper who were accusing Moussavi of being in league with those who want to overthrow the Islamic system. In both parts, the article situates Moussavi's segment of the Green Movement as the real defender of the Islamic Republic and its constitution.

119 Rahnavard's Facebook page is http://www.facebook.com/zrahnavard.

band, but she held her husband's hand in public, unprecedented acts among officials in Iran.[120] These symbolic gestures presented Moussavi as a modern and moderate person. These characteristics resonated extremely well among the young who crave modernity. Ironically, Rahnavard was closely associated with Khomeini's traditionalist policies restricting women's rights.

After the revolution Ayatollah Khomeini pursued patriarchal policies such as the violent imposition of the compulsory hijab, dismissal of all female judges, and restrictions on women's entrance to universities.[121] For example, before the revolution, women were excluded from only two majors in higher education: mining and religious studies. After Khomeini's "Islamization" of the universities, women were prohibited from studying in 91 of the 169 majors offered in Iranian universities and other institutions of higher education. In other words, women were forbidden to take classes in 54% of the majors offered in higher education. In addition, ceiling percentages were established on the maximum number of women who could be admitted to other fields. These ceilings ranged from 10 to 50%; in other words, males were guaranteed at least 50 to 90% of the seats in majors which did not exclude women.[122]

For many young women (and men), unaware of Rahnavard's role during the establishment of Khomeini's patriarchal policies, Rahnavard appeared as modern and progressive. It needs to be emphasized that although Rahnavard's views have been traditional and patriarchal, they have been far less patriarchal than the ultra-patriarchal policies of Ahmadinejad's administration. Some believe that Rahnavard has genuinely evolved toward a more modern position on women's issues in recent years.

For the occasion of International Women's Day, Rahnavard made remarks that were somewhat progressive although they were very carefully couched in Islamic terms and made references to women's sacrifices for the Islamic revolution and the regime during the war with Iraq.[123] In addition to praising female relatives

120 See some of the photos at http://www.ghalamnews.ir/images/2009/5/2009_5_30_18_46_44.jpg; http://www.payvand.com/news/09/jun/1076.html; and http://www.ghalamnews.ir/images/2009/5/img_7549.jpg.
121 Masoud Kazemzadeh, *Islamic Fundamentalism, Feminism, and Gender Inequality in Iran Under Khomeini* (Lanham, MD: University Press of America, 2002), pp. 9–10, 17–30. Most restrictions on female entrance to universities were abolished in the late 1980s. By the late 1990s, women constituted a majority of university students.
122 Ibid., pp. 27–28.
123 Zahra Rahnavard, *"Kojayeh Tarikh Sarzamin Maa Bedoon Zan Irani Dar Ooj Ast?"* [Where in the History of Our Land Have There Been Great Heights Without Iranian Women?], Kaleme (March 6, 2010), http://www.kaleme.com/1388/12/15/klm-13282. For brief excerpts in English see: Radio Za-

of the Prophet Mohammad, Rahnavard also praised female heroines of pre-Islamic Iran. She also criticized a new bill on polygamy as well as discriminatory laws on custody of children. More significant than Rahnavard's statement for International Women's Day was that she attended a meeting with some of Iran's foremost women's rights and feminist activists on March 8, 2010.[124]

2.3.6 Secular Modern Middle Classes

The secular modern middle classes of all ages, but especially youth and women, oppose the fundamentalist regime. They tend to be liberal, feminist, and progressive. They tend to boycott the elections. They viewed the opposition as too divided and weak to present a real alternative to the regime. This segment had assumed that incremental reforms are possible in the system. This segment hoped for reduced social restrictions, improved economic situation, and better relations with the United States. This segment of the population was willing to participate in the election to choose "bad" (Moussavi or Karrubi) over "worse" (Ahmadinejad). They believed that life would be meaningfully better under the reformist members of the oligarchy compared with life under Ahmadinejad and the hardliners. They enthusiastically participated in the election of Khatami in 1997 and 2001. They did not participate in the local elections in 2003 or presidential election in 2005, which allowed hardliners in 2003 and Ahmadinejad in 2005 easy wins.

For example, in the 1999 local elections around the country 34 million people voted. In the 2003 local elections around the country only 16 million voted. In the 1999 local election for the city of Tehran 1.4 million voted. The top 15 vote getters would be elected to the Tehran city council, with the following six as reserve members (who would assume membership if any of the top 15 resigned or left the seat). Ahmadinejad, who was a candidate for the Tehran city council, came in 23rd. In the 2003 local election for Tehran only about 560,000 voted. The turnout in Tehran was

---

maaneh, "Zahra Rahnavard Condemns Discriminatory Laws Against Women" (March 6, 2010), http://www.zamaaneh.com/enzam/2010/03/zahra-rahnavard-issued-a.html.

124 Feminist School, *"Qate'nameh Payani Jam'i Az Faalan Jonbesh Zanan Dar Gerdhamai Sabz Beh Monasebat 8 Mars' Va Gozaresh Tasviri Az Marasem In Rooz"* [The Declaration of 'A Group of Women's Movement Activists for the Green Meeting For March 8' and a Photo Report of the Ceremonies of This Day] (March 8, 2010), http://iranfemschool.net/spip.php?article4425; Payvand Iran News, "Iranian Women Activists Call for End to Discrimination" (March 9, 2010), http://www.payvand.com/news/10/mar/1082.html; Payvand Iran News, "Statement by Iranian Women for International Women's Day" (March 15, 2010), http://www.payvand.com/news/10/mar/1128.html.

12 % of eligible voters. Because most people boycotted the election, the hardliners (whose base obviously votes regularly) won the overwhelming majority of seats.[125]

In the presidential election in 2005 in Tehran, about 45 % of eligible voters did not participate in the run-off election. About 30 % of the eligible voters in the country did not participate in the same 2005 run-off election.[126] In the June 2009 election, Moussavi and Karrubi and their campaigns successfully appealed for support from this segment of the population.[127] In the 2009 election, this segment played major roles in the campaigns of Moussavi and Karrubi. The government claimed that 85 % of eligible voters participated in the 2009 election. The data released by the Ministry of the Interior and the Council of Guardians in 2009 simply cannot be regarded as reliable. Nevertheless, it is clear that the campaign of Moussavi and Karrubi succeeded in convincing large numbers to vote.

2.3.7 The Solid Opposition

I use the term "solid opposition" in contradistinction to the term "reformist opposition." By "solid opposition," I refer to those who unequivocally oppose the system of *Velayat Faqih* and demand a different form of government. The solid opposition includes liberal democrats and social democrats of the INF, monarchists, the PMOI, various Marxist organizations, and various ethnic parties.[128]

The secular democratic forces wish to replace the Islamic Republic with a democratic system, with a separation of religion and state, and elections for all the major positions of power. Many Western observers confuse the terms "reformist" and "democrat." The two groups are very different in Iran. The term "reformist" refers to those within the fundamentalist oligarchy who want to reform the system in order to preserve and prolong the system of clerical rule. The most prominent leader is Khatami.

125 All the data in this paragraph are from Naji, *Ahmadinejad*, op. cit., pp. 42 – 28.
126 Golnaz Esfandiari, "Reformers Hope Iran's 'Silent Voters' Will Be Heard in June," Radio Free Europe/Radio Liberty (May 28, 2009), http://www.rferl.org/content/Reformers_Hope_Irans_Silent_Voters_Will_Be_Heard_In_June/1741914.html.
127 Ibid.
128 Masoud Kazemzadeh, "Opposition Groups," in Mehran Kamrava and Manochehr Dorraj, editors., *Iran Today: An Encyclopedia of Life in the Islamic Republic.* Vol. II (Westport, CT: Greenwood Press, 2008), pp. 363 – 367; Masoud Kazemzadeh, "The Perils and Costs of a Grand Bargain with the Islamic Republic of Iran," *American Foreign Policy Interests*, Vol. 29, No. 5 (September–October 2007), pp. 301 – 327; and Kazemzadeh, *The Iran National Front*, op. cit.

The term "democrat" refers to those who want to replace the rule of clerics with a democracy, where the Iranian people can vote for whomever they want. The most prominent among these inside Iran is the INF.[129] The INF was established by Mossadegh in 1949. It is the oldest and largest pro-democracy organization in Iran. The INF struggles to establish a secular democratic republic and comprises secular liberal democrats and social democrats.

Iranian democrats demand free elections for all Iranians. But the reformists only want "free elections" for the supporters of the fundamentalist constitution. In Khatami's words:

> By free elections, our intention is not to refute monitoring, but that this monitoring ought to be such which is consistent with the spirit of the [fundamentalist] Constitution. ... The condition for free elections is for activities of groups and parties to be free within the framework of the [fundamentalist] Constitution. ... If individuals who are committed to the [fundamentalist] Constitution, which is the basis of the order, not only are they free to be active, but the society and the governing system is duty-bound to defend their rights and encourage them.[130]

There are also other forces that strongly and unequivocally oppose the Islamic Republic. The monarchists want to replace the Islamic Republic with a monarchical system with Reza Pahlavi, the son of the last Pahlavi monarch, as king.[131] The PMOI is by far the best organized and most disciplined group in Iran. It is capable of carrying out military operations inside Iran and of mobilizing many thousands of its supporters abroad. Because of its ideology, history, and leadership, the vast majority of Iranians resent and fear it. It is clear that the PMOI could neither win any major elections, nor could overthrow the regime; it is also clear, however, that it has enough muscle, organization, and committed members to be a spoiler in Iranian politics.[132]

Some groups in the solid opposition, such as various ethnic parties among Kurds and Baluchis, were relatively silent during this period in 2009 and 2010. The same was true among the far-left communist groups.

Most organizations in the solid opposition called on the people to boycott the June 2009 election. They argued that voting for one of the candidates approved by the Council of Guardians and the Supreme Leader would be interpreted as granting legitimacy to the regime. However, from the very night of June 12, when they

---

129 Ibid., Kazemzadeh, *The Iran National Front.*

130 Seyyed Mohammad Khatami, *"Hazf Jaryanat Beh Maani An Ast Keh Dar Keshvar Moshgel Vojod Darad"* [The Elimination of Groups Means That There Are Problems in the Country], Baran Foundation Website (May 4, 2010), http://baran.org.ir/?sn=news&pt=full&id=2754.

131 Reza Pahlavi's website is http://www.rezapahlavi.org/.

132 The organization's website is http://www.mojahedin.org/pagesen/index.aspx.

considered the counting of votes as fraudulent, the solid opposition strongly participated in the struggle to counter what soon became termed a "coup." The solid opposition unequivocally opposed Ahmadinejad, and after the election most in the solid opposition gave provisional support to the reformists who were resisting Ahmadinejad's government.

There are some groups that vacillate between the democratic opposition and the reformist faction of the oligarchy. The most prominent and largest are the National-Religious Alliance and the Iran Freedom Movement. The National-Religious Alliance is a collection of liberal-minded activists who attempt to combine Islam and democracy as their political ideology.[133] The Iran Freedom Movement began as a split from the INF in 1961.[134]

2.4 From Difference to Conflict

The differences over personal ambitions for power, constitutional form, and distribution of power, as well as domestic and foreign policies, have created great chasms among various factions within the ruling oligarchy. The serious and irreversible consequences of each side's victory created unprecedented tension between the two sides. The disputed 2009 election brought the differences into open and unprecedented conflict.

The hardliners used great violence against non-violent protesters in the immediate aftermath of the election. The regime stated that 20 persons, including eight *Basij* members, were killed between June 12 and July 9, 2009. Many believe the actual numbers to be higher.[135] The regime could not name a single member of the *Basij* that died in the process. The regime also arrested somewhere between 1,000 and 2,000 activists during this period.

In addition, the regime arrested large numbers of reformist leaders. Among those arrested were Hojatolislam Mohammad Ali Abtahi,[136] Mostafa Tajzadeh,[137]

---

133 The website of the Nationalist-Religious Alliance is http://www.mellimazhabi.org/.

134 The Facebook page of the group's supporters is http://www.facebook.com/group.php?gid=121085368980.

135 Farnaz Fassihi, "Inside the Iranian Crackdown," *The Wall Street Journal* (July 13, 2009).

136 Abtahi's Facebook page is available at http://www.facebook.com/mohammad.ali.abtahi. His blog is available at http://www.webneveshteha.com/.

137 Tajzadeh's Facebook page is available at http://www.facebook.com/Mostafa.Tajzadeh. He was arrested immediately after the election and was imprisoned for more than 280 days. One of the first things he did after being furloughed was to open a page inviting the readers of his Facebook page to ask him questions about the election, and the post-election events. See http://www.facebook.com/note.php?note_id=113606981991063.

Mohsen Aminzadeh, Saeed Hajjarian, Dr. Abdollah Ramezanzadeh, and Alireza Beheshti. During Khatami's presidency, Abtahi was First Vice-President, Tajzadeh was Deputy Minister of the Interior (the second highest official in the Ministry), Aminzadeh was Deputy Minister of Foreign Affairs (the second highest official in the Ministry), and Ramezanzadeh was spokesman for the administration. Hajjarian had served as a senior advisor to Khatami; earlier he had served as Deputy Minister of Intelligence. Alireza Beheshti is the son of Ayatollah Beheshti, one of the founders of the Islamic Republic, who was the Secretary General of the IRP and Head of the Judicial Branch. Alireza Beheshti was kept in prison for a long time, where he suffered a non-fatal heart attack in late January 2010. Many others were also briefly detained, such as Mohammad Reza Khatami (younger brother of President Khatami) and Faezeh Rafsanjani (Rafsanjani's daughter).

Many had assumed that due to great disparity in resources, the hardliners could easily crush opposition to Ahmadinejad's reelection. However, two events in July served as turning points: July 9 protests and Rafsanjani's speech on July 17. Subsequent events show that no side has been able to achieve its main goals, thus leading to a stalemate and paralysis.

2.4.1 July 9 Protests

The regime was fearful that the 10th anniversary of the July 9, 1999 uprising might become a turning point in the current struggle. So, it issued unusually dire threats to anyone who would protest on this day. The regime brought its full force to the streets to make sure that there would be absolutely no protests. However, on July 9, 2009, thousands of men and women defied the regime and came to the streets and shouted: "Death to the dictator."[138] The word "dictator" presumably was used to refer to Ahmadinejad. By July 2009, the ruling theocracy had lost its political legitimacy and ideological hegemony among vast sectors of the population, but not its ability to coerce the population into submission.

---

138 Thomas Erdbrink, "Protesters Clash With Police in Iran: Demonstrators Endure Batons, Tear Gas As They Try to Mark 1999 Unrest," *The Washington Post* (July 10, 2009); Michael Slackman, "Iran Protesters Take to Streets Despite Threats," *The New York Times* (July 10, 2009); and Farnaz Fassihi, "Iran Protesters Defy Clampdown," *The Wall Street Journal* (July 10, 2009).

2.4.2 Hashemi Rafsanjani's July 17 Speech

On Friday July 17, 2009, Rafsanjani gave the official Friday sermon. He had been silent since June 12. The reformists called upon the people to attend the ceremony, which is conducted at the University of Tehran. It is estimated that about 1 million people attended (they stood outside on the streets leading to the university). The people outside the enclosed place openly defied the official line repeatedly. When an official instructed the people to shout the slogan "Death to America," the people shouted: "Death to Russia." When he instructed the people to shout, "Death to Britain," or "Death to Israel," the people shouted: "Death to Russia."[139] The people were very upset that the Russian government had been providing support to the regime, especially at the U.N. Security Council, as well as being one of the main governments that immediately congratulated Ahmadinejad's election. In addition to Russia, the people also chanted "Death to China." China has also been supportive of the Iranian government.

When the official instructed the people to shout *"khooni ke dar rag-e maast, hedyeh be **Rahbar-e** maast"* [the blood that runs in our veins is our gift to **the Leader**], the people shouted *"khooni ke dar rag-e maast, hedyeh be **mellat-e** maast"* [the blood that runs in our veins is our gift to **our people**].[140] On their own, before the sermon began, the people shouted *"Hashemi, Hashemi, sokot koni, khaeni"* [Hashemi, Hashemi, if you remain silent, you are a traitor].[141]

The hardliners in the auditorium did make a few protests, but they mostly remained quiet. The presence of about a million people outside and many inside the covered auditorium created an environment for Rafsanjani to present his views. It was not known whether he would publicly support the Supreme Leader and call the election fair, or if he would use the occasion to fully support Moussavi's challenge. In a remarkable speech, he was able to couch support for Moussavi as a solution for unity.[142] He brilliantly used the example of the governments of the Prophet Mohammad and of the First Shia Imam Ali to argue that without the explicit consent and support of the people, one could not have an Islamic government.

---

139 See http://www.youtube.com/watch?v=CzO2Nd8PzLA.
140 See http://www.youtube.com/watch?v=GPIpBdwJYaE.
141 See http://www.youtube.com/watch?v=QXzMUmzZ_y8.
142 The full text in Persian is available at Rafsanjani's site: http://www.hashemirafsanjani.ir/?type=dynamic&lang=1&id=1227. The entire speech is also available on YouTube in seven parts: http://www.youtube.com/watch?v=6d0GbvQRDp8; http://www.youtube.com/watch?v=FC9KvuZx-h4; http://www.youtube.com/watch?v=54wMNO6Zf6Q; http://www.youtube.com/watch?v=pzGYkjXIXfI; http://www.youtube.com/watch?v=-ZqJmK9RQ5E; http://www.youtube.com/watch?v=8I57hKlB49k; and http://www.youtube.com/watch?v=OvFG5Cl6Irw.

After about one hour of discussing historical examples, he ended with stating that many have doubts about the veracity of the election results. Rafsanjani used the term *"bohran"* [crisis] to describe the events since June 2009. The hardliners used the term *"fitneh"* [sedition, conspiracy] and repeatedly referred to the events as foreign-sponsored "velvet revolutions" to overthrow the Islamic system. The term *"bohran"* connotes a situation engendered by decisions of the government and others, which could be resolved by wise decisions. The term *"fitneh"* is an old Islamic term, *"fitna"*, which connotes a conspiracy by enemies determined to destroy Islam, an enemy which has to be crushed. Rafsanjani proposed a solution that included freeing all those imprisoned since June 12, allowing free debate in state television, and allowing peaceful demonstrators to use their right to protest, as well as taking care of and honoring the families of those killed since the election.

Although Rafsanjani did not go as far as the democratic opposition demanded (freeing all political prisoners and holding free democratic elections), or even what the reformists within the oligarchy demanded (holding a new election between Moussavi and Ahmadinejad), Rafsanjani's remarks made the reformists happy and the hardliners very angry.[143] Khatami praised Rafsanjani's remarks and called for a referendum on the legitimacy of Ahmadinejad's election.[144]

All the commentaries in hardline venues over the following days criticized Rafsanjani. The powerful Ayatollah Mohammad Yazdi (member of the Council of Guardians as well as Secretary of the Assembly of Experts) criticized Rafsanjani.[145]

IRNA, the official state news agency, is run by the government of Ahmadinejad, although it is expected to reflect the policies of the entire system. On July 18 and 19, all the reports on the Friday prayer published by IRNA attacked Rafsanjani.[146]

Similarly, on July 18 and 19, all the commentaries published by the Fars News Agency explicitly criticized Rafsanjani.[147] The Fars News Agency reflects the views of the hardline faction and the IRGC leadership. In addition, on the left sidebar of

---

143 Borzou Daragahi and Ramin Mostaghim, "Iranian Protesters Galvanized by Sermon," *The Los Angeles Times* (July 18, 2009).

144 Robert F. Worth, "Ex-President in Iran Seeks Referendum," *The New York Times* (July 20, 2009).

145 Part 1 of the speech: http://www.irna.ir/View/FullStory/?NewsId=593503; Part 2 of the speech: http://www.irna.ir/View/FullStory/?NewsId=593795.

146 See http://www.irna.ir/View/FullStory/?NewsId=595235; http://www.irna.ir/View/FullStory/?NewsId=594029; http://www.irna.ir/View/FullStory/?NewsId=595211. For the most critical attack see http://www.irna.ir/View/FullStory/?NewsId=594348.

147 See http://www.farsnews.net/newstext.php?nn=8804280242; http://www.farsnews.net/newstext.php?nn=8804271423; http://www.farsnews.net/newstext.php?nn=8804280431.

its site, the Fars News Agency re-posted earlier stories critical of Rafsanjani or his position. One report was the June 19, 2009 Friday prayer by Khamenei.[148] Another report was a direct criticism by Ayatollah Mohammad Yazdi on Rafsanjani's letter, an open letter Rafsanjani had written to Khamenei after Ahmadinejad made serious personal attacks on him and his family members during the presidential debates.[149] Others included reports undermining Rafsanjani's position and that of Moussavi.[150]

The direct criticisms of Rafsanjani continued. On July 20, Khamenei criticized Rafsanjani without naming him directly. Khamenei said: "The elite should be watchful, since they have been faced with a big test. Failing the test will cause their collapse. ... Anybody who drives the society toward insecurity and disorder is a hated person in the view of the Iranian nation, whoever he is."[151] On July 22, the Fars News Agency published a letter signed by 306 of the clerics in Qom supporting Ayatollah Yazdi and criticizing Rafsanjani.[152]

The reaction of the hardliners was immediate and strong. They had used great violence in order to put down the uprising. They had imprisoned most of the top officials of the reformist faction of the ruling oligarchy. Despite their dire threats to intimidate the people from protesting on July 9, the people came out in large numbers. If the hardliners had intended to carry out a massive purge of their reformist rivals, the massive street protests had undermined that plan. The street demonstrations indicated that a bloodier repression could backfire and threaten the entire system with collapse. They had not arrested Rafsanjani, Moussavi, Karrubi, or Khatami. The hardliners needed Rafsanjani to submit to what Khamenei had demanded in his June 19 Friday sermon: full acceptance of the election result.[153] Anything

---

148 See http://www.farsnews.net/newstext.php?nn=8803290701.

149 See http://www.farsnews.net/newstext.php?nn=8803200002.

150 See http://www.farsnews.net/newstext.php?nn=8804120167; http://www.farsnews.net/newstext.php?nn=8804091286; http://www.farsnews.net/newstext.php?nn=8804130969; http://www.farsnews.net/newstext.php?nn=8804081380; http://www.farsnews.net/newstext.php?nn=8804060966; http://www.farsnews.net/newstext.php?nn=8803310021.

151 Ali Akbar Dareini and Lee Keath, "Iran Election Dispute Escalates to New Phase" Associated Press (July 20, 2009). Also see Robert F. Worth, "Iran's Chief Cleric Warns Political Leaders Over Election Criticism," *The New York Times* (July 21, 2009).

152 Fars News Agency, *"Dar Nameii Khatab Beh Ayatollah Yazdi Soorat Gereft; Hemayat 306 Ostaad Howzeh Az Mavazeh Ayatollah Yazdi Dar Ertebat Baa Hashemi"* [In a Letter Addressed to Ayatollah Yazdi That Occurred; Support of 306 Seminary Teachers of the Positions of Ayatollah Yazdi in Regard to Hashemi] (July 22, 2009), http://www.farsnews.net/newstext.php?nn=8804310610.

153 Fars News Agency, *"Rahbar Moazam Enqelab Islami Dar Azimtarin Namaz Jomeh Tehran"* [The Great Leader of the Islamic Revolution at the Greatest Friday Prayer in Tehran] (June 19, 2009), http://www.farsnews.net/newstext.php?nn=8803290701. For the full sermon in English translation see http://www.youtube.com/watch?v=hLiBp8qxuMA.

less would be a challenge to the Supreme Leader's authority. Rafsanjani's speech demanding the release of those arrested since June 12 would undermine the hardliners' repression. It would allow the reformists and others to continue the challenge.

Gholam-Hussein Elham concluded that:

> If he [Rafsanjani] had not stood behind the crisis, this crisis would not have had the ability to last. ... Now the warnings [of the leaders of the crisis] have ended, and they have shown in practice that they are not in the path delineated by the Supreme Leader; therefore, they are responsible for their actions and they should pay the price of these, and the people will not waste their time with these deviations and will eventually eliminate these movements from the head of the revolution.[154]

Elham was one of the most powerful individuals among the extremist hardliners close to Ahmadinejad. He has been a non-clergy member of the Council of Guardians, Minister of Justice, and spokesman of the Ahmadinejad government.

These two events in July undermined the hardliners' plans. Although initially reformist elements in the oligarchy and Rafsanjani's supporters within the state apparatus supported the protests, the actual Green Movement is a much broader grassroots movement that arose to challenge what many in Iran called "*kodetay 22 Khordad*" [June 12 coup d'état]. What emerged was a movement which encompassed many groups, parties, strata, and social classes. Moussavi, Karrubi, and Khatami remained some of the main leaders of this movement. But they could not control the slogans and demands, which various groups and large sectors of the protesting public kept publicly shouting. The government banned any protests by the opposition. Because the opposition could not get permission to hold its own rallies, they decided to call upon their supporters to hold rallies during those days on which the regime held official rallies.

The Islamic Republic claims that the overwhelming majority of the people support it and that those who oppose the Islamic Republic constitute an insignificant minority. Because there are no free and democratic elections in Iran, many in the opposition claim that they in actuality represent the majority. To show that its claim is true, the regime mobilizes the people to participate in official rallies. The stated numbers of people who participate in these official rallies are then used as evidence that the majority of the people support the Islamic Republic. Some of these days include Qods Day (the last Friday in the month of Moharram),

---

154 JARAS, "*Elham: Hashemi Rafsanjani Tabe' Rahbari Nabood*" [Elham: Hashemi Rafsanjani Was Not Submitting to the Leader] (March 24, 2010), http://www.rahesabz.net/story/12630.

November 4, Ashura, and February 11. These days are official holidays, and the regime attempts to bring as many to these rallies as possible.

2.4.3 The Social Sciences and Show Trials

On August 30, 2009, the Supreme Leader attacked the humanities and social sciences.[155] Khamenei lamented that 2million of the 3.5 million university students in Iran studied humanities and social sciences. Khamenei stated:

> This makes us worried. Many of the perspectives in the humanities and social sciences are based on philosophies whose foundations are based on materialism, on regarding human beings as animal, and on the lack of individuals' responsibility toward God almighty, as well as on not having a foundation which holds a moral perspective on the human and the world. ... These will lead to doubt and to disbelief in the divine and the Islamic foundations of our values.[156]

The Supreme Council of the Cultural Revolution, the body that monitors and oversees the universities in Iran, was then tasked to propose policies on the Supreme Leader's concerns. The Supreme Leader repeated his concerns on several occasions.[157] Other hardline conservatives echoed the Supreme Leader's demands. For example, see the comments of Ayatollah Mohammad Imami Kashani, the powerful conservative Friday Prayer leader of Tehran on the following Friday.[158] Tehran's Friday prayer leader, Kazem Seddigi, said: "There is need for another revolution in the universities, like the first one."[159] Seddigi called for a complete overhaul of the humanities and social sciences and asked "pious professors who

155 Golnaz Esfandiari, "Supreme Leader Stokes Fears of New Cultural Revolution in Iran," Radio Free Europe/Radio Liberty (September 3, 2009), www.rferl.org/content/Fears_Of_A_New_Cultural_Revolution_In_Iran/1814207.html; Michael Slackman, "Purge of Iranian Universities Is Feared," *The New York Times* (September 1, 2009).

156 Ali Khamenei, *"Bayanat Dar Didar Asatid Daneshgah"* [Remarks in the Meeting with University Professors] (August 30, 2009), http://farsi.khamenei.ir/speech-content?id=7959, my translation.

157 For example, see his remarks in late October 2009: http://www.iranian.com/main/2009/oct/khamenei-islam-humanities. The video was originally made by http://IranNegah.com.

158 BBC Persian, *"Edameyeh Enteqadha Az Tadris Olum Ensani Gharbi Dar Iran"* [The Continuation of Criticisms on Teaching the Western Humanities and Social Sciences in Iran] (September 4, 2009), http://www.bbc.co.uk/persian/iran/2009/09/090904_op_ememikashani-azghadi_humanities.shtml.

159 Radio Zamaaneh, "Iran Universities Target of Conservative Attacks" (October 23, 2009), http://www.zamaaneh.com/enzam/2009/10/iran-universities-target.html.

are knowledgeable in Islamic issues"[160] to write textbooks based on the Quran and Islamic laws.

After the June 12, 2009 election, many of the reformist members of the oligarchy were arrested and compelled to make public confessions in show trials and television appearances. They included Hajjarian, who was one of the founders of the Ministry of Intelligence and rose to serve as Deputy Minister of Intelligence. He is regarded as the main theoretician of the reform movement as well as the brain behind Khatami's electoral strategy in 1997. In the show trial and televised roundtable, Hajjarian confessed that he made an error by reading Western social science works and singled out Max Weber for causing him to err in his analysis and judgment. In the televised roundtable held at the Evin prison, and broadcast on September 22, 2009, Hajjarian stated:

> The Western thought has its connections with its own traditions although there have been some splits; however, we have forgotten our own traditions in the Islamic system and have become imprisoned in the Western world, and in the inverted trend from our need to Western technology have fallen into the trap of social sciences and Western philosophy, and this is the point of our disconnect from our own traditions. And now perhaps in Islamic societies, especially in our society, to be traditional is regarded to be equal to be [ommol][161] hick.[162]

Hajjarian went on to state:

> Many of these dear ones, who teach social sciences at Iranian universities, have gotten their higher education in the West, and there was an environment where they received the collection of their intellectual package. ... I do not want to say that they are cadres of the West, but unconsciously an Iranian professor who has been educated in the West and has not been provided an arena for critique, had received a collection of teachings that presents these teachings as though they are total [divine] revelations. ... Whether we like it or not, for all practical purposes, many of these dear individuals [professors], who have not had the occasion to criticize Western perspectives and thoughts and have brought these [Western] collections and present them, they become like an all-encompassing cadre who act on behalf of Western perspectives and represent Western thought. ... When you use such a literature that was developed in the Western thought in Iranian universities, which ought to have compatibility with religious literature, whether you want it or not, for all practical purposes you undermine and destroy your national identity and your university. ... The Western liberal thought arrives through valuable individuals like these professors who were not able to criticize their re-

---

160 Ibid.

161 This Persian word *ommol* is a demeaning term for those who are backward.

162 Saeed Hajjarian, "Television Roundtable Hajjarian, Atrianfar, and Shariati," broadcast from Evin prison on IRIB (Islamic Republic of Iran Broadcasting), Channel One (September 22, 2009), large excerpts available at: http://www.farsnews.com/newstext.php?nn=8806311665. My translation.

ceived education. These [Western liberal thoughts] sit in our brains and thoughts and funda-
mentally mess up all the beliefs, and one feels that it has become the backyard of the Western
world. ... In the end, in order for me to say what kind of society is our society, and what is the
nature of our government, I had no choice but to seek tools for producing [analysis]. Well, we
did not have such tools, so I went to the original sources that could provide an explanation on,
for example, the nature of the government in the Third World. For instance, I [came across]
the theory of Sultanism, which harmed the system, and the deviations came from here.[163]

By late August 2009, the government had not succeeded in forcing the population
and the reformist candidates to accept the announced election result. The hardliners feared that university students and faculty would mobilize resistance to the
government's efforts.[164] Closing the universities under the pretext of Islamization
of curricula would give the government more time to intimidate its opponents and
restore order. However, the closing of the universities would also signal the failure
of the regime to restore normalcy. The Supreme Leader's remarks at that sensitive
juncture indicated the extreme worry the regime had about restoring order.

Khamenei's attacks on social sciences were intended to undermine reformists
by portraying them as being influenced by Western thought. The public trials were
intended to intimidate the population, especially the modern middle classes. Khamenei's remarks and the public trials were also intended to provide a rationale for
the mobilization of the hardliners' social base.

2.4.4 September 18, 2009, Qods Day

After coming to power, Ayatollah Khomeini declared that the last Friday of the Islamic month of Ramadan should be commemorated as Qods Day [Jerusalem Day]

---

163 Saeed Hajjarian, "Television Roundtable Hajjarian, Atrianfar, and Shariati," broadcast from
Evin prison on IRIB (Islamic Republic of Iran Broadcasting), Channel One (September 22, 2009),
large excerpts available at http://www.farsnews.com/newstext.php?nn=8806311672. My translation.
164 BBC, "Tehran Students Protest on Campus" (September 28, 2009), http://news.bbc.co.uk/2/hi/
middle_east/8279193.stm; Golnaz Esfandiari, "Iran's Campuses On Edge As University Doors Open,"
Radio Free Europe/Radio Liberty (September 23, 2009), www.rferl.org/content/Irans_Campuses_On_
Edge_As_University_Doors_Open/1829627.html; Radio Zamaaneh, "Eateraz Tahkim Vahdat Beh
'Apartheid Elmi'" [The Office for Consolidation of Unity Objects to 'Scientific Apartheid'] (September 21, 2009), http://zamaaneh.com/news/2009/09/post_10568.html; Time Magazine online, "As Students Return, Iran's Regime Braces for More Protests" (September 17, 2009), http://www.time.
com/time/world/article/0,8599,1924412,00.html?xid=rss-topstories; Leyla Tayeri, "Goftogoy Rooz Ba
Dabir Daftar Tahkim Vahdat: Daneshgah Saket Nemimanad"[Discussions of Rooz with the Secretary
of the Office for Consolidation of Unity: University Will Not Be Silent], Rooz Online (September 21,
2009), www.roozonline.com/persian/news/newsitem/article////107/-62742948d2.html.

in opposition to Israel. On this day, the regime holds rallies and marches to express opposition to Israel and support to those fighting Israel. In 2009, this day coincided with September 18. In the aftermath of the June crisis, the government banned all protests by the Green Movement. The reformist groups as well as the democratic opposition groups asked people to participate in the marches, wear green as a symbol of their opposition to the election, and to shout their own slogans.

Before the rallies, one of the groups which invited the people to participate asked the people to shout: *"Naa Ghazeh, Naa Lobnan, Janam Fadayeh Iran"* [No to Gaza, No to Lebanon, My Life for Iran], which became one of the dominant slogans of the protesters. This slogan made Moussavi uncomfortable, he who stated that one could and should care both for Iran and the plight of others. These slogans and the plans for the protests were made by social networking sites such as Facebook, Twitter, and opposition websites.

2.4.5 November 4, 2009, the Anniversary of Taking Americans Hostage

On November 4, 1979, fundamentalist students took over the American Embassy in Tehran and held Americans hostage for 444 days. Every year, November 4 is celebrated by the regime. Among the official slogans have been: *"Marg Bar Amrika"* [Death to America], *"Marg Bar Engelis"* [Death to England], and *"Marg Bar Israel"* [Death to Israel]. Again, Moussavi, Karrubi, Khatami, and others in the Green Movement asked the people to participate in the rallies and shout their own slogans.[165]

Massive numbers of Iranians participated in large demonstrations in many large cities against the regime. Official slogans of the regime were: "Death to America" and "Death to Israel," which the supporters of the regime shouted. The opposition had printed its own fliers with "Death to no one." However, the protesters repeated the earlier slogan of "Death to Russia." Spontaneously, the people, however, began a new slogan: *"Obama Obama, Ya Baa Onaa, Ya Baa Maa"* [Obama Obama, Either with Them, or with Us.][166] The protesters explicitly demanded

---

165 Robert F. Worth and Nazila Fathi, "Opposition in Iran Urges Continuing Challenge," *The New York Times* (November 2, 2009); Borzou Daragahi, "Iran Students Carry on Protests," *The Los Angeles Times* (November 3, 2009), http://www.latimes.com/news/nationworld/world/la-fg-iran-protests3-2009nov03,0,1803055,print.story.
166 Golnaz Esfandiari, "Protesters, Police Clash in Tehran on Anniversary of U.S. Embassy Takeover," Radio Free Europe/Radio Liberty (November 4, 2009), http://www.rferl.org/content/Protesters_Security_Forces_Clash_In_Tehran_On_Anniversary_Of_US_Embassy_Takeover_/1869186.html?page=1#relatedInfoContainer.

that the Obama administration stop providing what they regarded as recognition to the Ahmadinejad government, and instead to explicitly express its support for the Green Movement. In reaction to the call for support by the Iranian people, White House spokesman Robert Gibbs said: "We obviously have been and are following the reports of this and hope greatly that violence will not spread."[167]

The very first time the slogan *"Esteghlal, Azadi, Jomhuri Irani"* [Independence, Freedom, **Iranian** Republic] was shouted was on July 30, 2009.[168] The main slogan of the 1979 revolution which emerged late in the revolutionary process (about October or November 1978) was *"Esteghlal, Azadi, Jumhuri Islami"* [Independence, Freedom, **Islamic** Republic]. This slogan was shouted during Qods Day as well. But it was during November that this slogan was shouted by truly vast numbers. The emergence of this slogan during November 2009 as one of the main slogans of the people indicated that the demands had moved from merely reforms within the system to the democratic demand to replace the fundamentalist regime's "Islamic Republic" with "Iranian Republic." In other words, this slogan demanded the abolition of the *Velayat Faqih*'s office and other fundamentalist institutions such as the Council of Guardians and the Assembly of Experts. This slogan was quickly supported by the democratic opposition in August.[169] From this time onward, the hardliners constantly condemned Moussavi and reformists for being part of a movement many of whose supporters demanded an "Iranian Republic," which is not the Islamic Republic. Moussavi indicated that he disagreed with this slogan.[170]

Soon, another slogan, *"Naa Sharqi, Naa Gharbi, Jumhuri Irani"* [Neither Eastern, Nor Western, **Iranian** Republic] became popular. This slogan also mirrored the regime's slogan of *"Naa Sharqi, Naa Gharbi, Jumhuri Islami"* [Neither Eastern, Nor Western, Islamic Republic]. An interesting and imaginative number of posters were created by various Green Movement constituencies.[171] By November, clearly the protesters had become very angry at the regime and their demands reflected

---

167 Lou Kesten, "White House Monitoring Crackdown in Iran," Associated Press (November 4, 2009).

168 The video of the people was immediately placed on YouTube http://www.youtube.com/watch?v=e0zquYsjE6k.

169 Personal communications with democratic republican forces inside Iran. Outside Iran, the Iran National Front-Abroad immediately placed this slogan on its website, http://www.jebhemelli.net/. In its official proclamation, Iran National Front-Abroad unequivocally embraced the demand "Iranian Republic," and expressed its cautious support for Moussavi and Karrubi as long as they continued their resistance to the Khamenei–Ahmadinejad coup. See Iran National Front-Abroad, *"Ahdaf Va Rahkarhay Jonbesh Melli Iranian"* [Goals and Plans of the Nationalist Movement of Iranians], August 18, 2009, http://www.iranazad.info/jebhehkharej/jkh09/08/27mordad.htm.

170 See http://news.gooya.com/politics/archives/2009/10/095191.php.

171 See http://payvand.com/blog/blog/2009/10/27/posters-students-day-nov-4th-2009/.

their desires. Many embraced these pro-democracy slogans, which the hardliners correctly termed "*sakhtar shekan.*" The word "*sakhtar*" means "structure" or "foundation" and refers to the foundations of the system. The word "*shekan*" means "to smash" or "to crush." Again, the reformist elements of the Green Movement expressed their opposition to these pro-democracy demands of the people on the streets, while the democratic elements of the solid opposition (e.g., the Iran National Front) warmly embraced them.

2.4.6 December, National Student Day, Death of Grand Ayatollah Montazeri, and Ashura

University students had emerged as the most vociferous opponents of the Islamic Republic. The government began arresting hundreds of student leaders in November because it was concerned about the students organizing mass protests for the annual National Student Day on December 7.[172] The government even severely restricted internet connections on December 5, two full days before the anniversary, in order to reduce the ability of the students to use it to organize protests and send the news to the outside world.[173] On many sensitive days, the government had closed down cell phone connections and slowed down internet connections for several hours, but it was the first time that two days before the event such communications had been so restricted. The National Student Day is a particularly sensitive day. This was even more the case in 2009 because if the students were able to gather in thousands in protest after more than five months since the June election,

---

172 International Campaign for Human Rights in Iran, "Crackdown on Students Ahead of National Student Day" (November 24, 2009), http://www.iranhumanrights.org/2009/11/crackdownstudentday/; Hussein Mohammadi, "*Barkhord Ba Jonbesh Daneshjooe Dar Mosahebeh Ba Bahareh Hedayat*" [Confronting the Student Movement in an Interview with Bahareh Hedayat], Rooz Online (November 25, 2009), http://www.roozonline.com/persian/news/newsitem/article////107/-0742b448ce.html; Reuters, "Iran Detains Scores of Students, Rights Group Says" (November 25, 2009), http://www.reuters.com/article/topNews/idUSTRE5AO1ZH20091125; Amir Kabir University Students News, "*Gozaresh Bazdasht Daneshjooyan Tey Aban Mah; Bazdasht 60 Daneshjoo Dar Yek Mah*" [Report on the Arrests of Students During the Month of Aban: Arrests of 60 Students in One Month] (November 4, 2009), http://www.autnews.es/node/4364; Amir Kabir University Students News, "*Ehzar-e Nazdik Beh 100 Daneshjoy Daneshgah Azad Ahwaz*" [Arraignments of Close to 100 Students of the Free University of Ahwaz] (November 4, 2009), http://www.autnews.es/node/4375; and Scheherezade Faramarzi, "Iran Cracks Down on Dissent in Universities," Associated Press (December 4, 2009), http://news.yahoo.com/s/ap/20091204/ap_on_re_mi_ea/ml_iran_university_crackdown.
173 AFP, "Internet Down in Iran Ahead of Planned Protests" (December 5, 2009), http://news.yahoo.com/s/afp/20091205/wl_mideast_afp/iranpoliticsinternet_20091205174520.

it would show that the government had not succeeded in intimidating the students into acquiescing to Ahmadinejad's election. Despite all these measures, the students succeeded in attracting many thousands to their rallies.[174] Many ordinary citizens joined the student protests. The failure of the government to stop the protests on this day despite repeated threats and massive measures, showed the weakness of the regime and the strength of the opposition. Coming after similar experiences since June, this widespread perception further emboldened the people that overthrow of the whole system, rather than merely reforming it, was possible.[175]

Late December 2009 witnessed a number of unprecedented events, including attacks on the funeral processions and commemoration of a *marja taqlid* (source of emulation, a very high ranked cleric, whose fatwas are followed by many) and killing of people on Ashura. The participation of the traditional strata of the population had been more limited until December 2009, although many leaders of these traditional sectors were among the leaders of the Green Movement. In December the more traditional religious sectors dramatically increased their participation in the protest movement. The trigger was the death of Grand Ayatollah Hussein Ali Montazeri.[176] Grand Ayatollah Montazeri died on Sunday December 20, 2009. In Shia custom, the day after death is the funeral. The mourning ceremonies are held on the third day, seventh day, and the fortieth day. The funeral was thus on December 21, the third on December 23, and the seventh on December 27. The seventh coincided with Ashura, the day Imam Hussein, the Third Shia Imam, was killed in Karbala in 680 AD. Ashura is commemorated by Shia and is the most emotional day for Shia who mourn the death of Imam Hussein by his Sunni rival

---

174 Ali Akbar Dareini, "Iran Student Protests Bring Out Tens of Thousands," Associated Press (December 7, 2009), http://news.yahoo.com/s/ap/20091207/ap_on_re_mi_ea/ml_iran/print; Robin Wright, "Latest Iran Protests Show a Resilient Opposition," *Time Magazine* online (December 7, 2009), http://www.time.com/time/world/article/0,8599,1946038,00.html?xid=rss-world&utm_source=feedburner&utm_medium=feed&utm_campaign=Feed%3A+time%2Fworld+%28TIME%3A+Top+World+Stories%29; and Robert Mackey, "Latest Updates on New Protests in Iran," *The New York Times* blog (December 7, 2009), http://thelede.blogs.nytimes.com/2009/12/07/latest-updates-on-new-protests-in-iran/?scp=3&sq=Iran&st=cse. Photos of the event are available at "Photos: Iran Students Stage Nationwide Protests," Payvand Iran News (December 7, 2009), http://www.payvand.com/news/09/dec/1070.html. Videos of the protests are available at http://www.iranian.com/main/2009/dec/16-azar-2009 and http://www.iranian.com/main/2009/dec/16-azar-reports.

175 For example, see the opinion of one of the leaders of the pro-democracy movement in Iran, who published his analysis in *The Wall Street Journal*. Heshmat Tabarzadi, "What I See on the Frontline in Iran: Regime Change is Now Our Movement's Rallying Cry," *The Wall Street Journal* (December 17, 2009). Tabarzadi was one of the leaders of the student uprising in July 1999. He was arrested in late December 2009.

176 Montazeri's official website is http://www.amontazeri.com/farsi/default.asp. Montazeri's Facebook page is http://www.facebook.com/GrandAyatollahMontazeri.

Yazid (Yazid is one of the most hated figures for the Shia).[177] Ashura is the tenth day in the month of Moharram in the Arabic-Islamic calendar. It is the apogee of the mourning for the killing of Imam Hussein. One day earlier, the ninth of Moharram, is called Tasua and other ceremonies related to Ashura are held.

Montazeri's funeral on Monday December 21 was huge despite the regime's efforts to deter mass mourning.[178] According to the former Head of Montazeri's office, the estimate was between 1 million and 1.5 million mourners.[179] The official funeral was in the shrine city of Qom, where most seminaries are located and where Montazeri lived. By this time, the slogans of the masses had become very hostile to Khamenei and openly called for his overthrow.[180] From this day forward, the anger of the protesters was targeted at Khamenei.

When the regime's loudspeaker announced the message of the Supreme Leader Khamenei, the crowd became very angry and immediately began booing and shouted: "Marg bar dictator" [Death to the Dictator] and "Khamenei Qatel-e Velayat-ash Batel-e" [Khamenei is a Murderer, His Rule is Invalid].[181] At the processions at Qom, the main slogans included: "Moharram Mah-e Khon-e, Kar-e Yazid Tamomeh" [The Month of Moharram is the Month of Blood, Yazid is Finished]; and "En Mah, Mah-e Khon-e, Seyyed Ali Sarnegoneh" [This Month is the Month of Blood, Seyyed Ali is Overthrown]. The slogan "Death to the Dictator" had been used on previous occasions, but these other slogans were new. Also, the slogan "Marg Bar Khamenei" [Death to Khamenei] was used.

At Montazeri's hometown of Najafabad, a small town outside of Isfahan, the protesters shouted: "Montazeri Mazloom, Rahat Edameh Darad; Hata Agar Dictator Bar Maa Gololeh Barad" [Innocent Montazeri, Your Path Will Be Continued; Even if the Dictator Will Rain Bullets on Us].[182]

---

177 Sunnis, too, have ceremonies on Ashura, the tenth day of Muharram. It is for an entirely different reason, which began during the time of the Prophet Mohammad. For Sunnis, Ashura is not a mourning occasion. Many Sunnis hold an optional fast.

178 Robert Tait, "Funeral of Iranian Cleric Montazeri Turns into Political Protest," The Guardian (December 21, 2009), http://www.guardian.co.uk/world/2009/dec/21/iran-funeral-ayatollah-montazeri-protest.

179 Mardomak, "Goftogo Baa Seyyed Hadi Hashemi" [Interview with Seyyed Hadi Hashemi] (December 25, 2009), http://www.mardomak.biz/news/Interview_with_Montazeri_ExOfficeman/.

180 For excellent collections of YouTube videos see: http://www.iranian.com/main/2009/dec/montazeri-funeral; and http://www.iranian.com/main/blog/shifteh-ansari/reactions-ayatollah-montazeris-death.

181 See http://www.youtube.com/watch?v=M61NhkeNqzA; and http://www.youtube.com/watch?v=_Yx-BfcM1dQ.

182 See http://www.youtube.com/watch?v=_aXTqEkDb4w.

Ayatollah Seyyed Jalaleddin Taheri announced that he would hold a ceremony for Montazeri in Isfahan on Wednesday December 23. Taheri was one of the most senior clerics in Iran. He was a member of the Assembly of Experts and was Imam Jomeh of Isfahan. In July 2002, Taheri resigned his posts as Imam Jomeh and member of the Assembly of Experts, and harshly criticized and condemned the hardliners.[183] During the December 23 ceremony, anti-regime protests continued, despite the regime's violent efforts to suppress them.[184] According to eyewitnesses, the regime deployed more than 2,000 special security forces in front of the Seyyed Mosque, the mosque chosen by Taheri for the ceremonies. The regime forbade Ayatollah Taheri from leaving his home in order to attend the ceremonies at the Seyyed Mosque. With the help of the people who came to his house, Taheri succeeded in leaving his home by car, but could not reach the mosque. The government security forces forcefully blocked the six different roads by which Taheri's car could have reached the mosque. Special security forces and plain-clothes forces beat up large numbers of people who had gathered for the ceremony and more than 50 were arrested.[185]

The slogans in Isfahan on December 23 and 24 included: *"Tajavoz, Khianat; Marge Bar In Velayat"* [Rape, Treason; Death to this Rule]. By *"In Velayat"* [This Rule], the protesters referred to the rule of the Supreme Leader. Other slogans were: *"In Mah, Mah-e Khon-e; Yazid Sarnegoneh"* [This Month is the Month of Blood; Yazid is Overthrown] and *"In Mah, Mah-e Khon-e; Regime Sarnegoneh"* [This Month is the Month of Blood; the Regime is Overthrown].

On December 24, protesters also held protests in the traditional bazaar Tehran neighborhood of Toopkhaneh.[186] One estimate put the number of protesters at around 2,000.[187] Protests were also held in Mashhad and Zanjan, despite clashes

---

183 Jim Muir, "Cleric Denounces Iran 'Chaos,'" BBC (July 10, 2002), http://news.bbc.co.uk/2/hi/2119775.stm.

184 For a collection of videos of the protests see http://www.iranian.com/main/2009/dec/protests-ban-defiance. The above collection (note 182) also includes videos of protests in Tehran.

185 Rouydad News, *"Eateraz Mardomi Dar Isfehan: Mardom Mohasereh Manzel Ayatollah Taheri Raa Shekastand"* [The Protests by the People in Isfahan: The People Broke Down the Encirclement of the Home of Ayatollah Taheri] (December 24, 2009), http://rouydadnews.com/pages/877.php. For Ayatollah Taheri's own words see http://www.youtube.com/watch?v=jqAbHrM5e6I and http://www.youtube.com/watch?v=-4wieJGqg5U.

186 See http://www.youtube.com/watch?v=2D1mwQlkilU; http://www.youtube.com/watch?v=XIX YwICrS6Y; and http://www.youtube.com/watch?v=I_Mrn8h_Qws.

187 Deutsche Welle, *"Tadarok Marasem Haftom Ayatollah Montazeri"* [Preparation for the Ceremonies for the Seventh of Ayatollah Montazeri] (December 25, 2009), http://www.dw-world.de/dw/article/0,,5056115,00.html?maca=per-rss-per_politik-4076-xml-mrss; Borzou Daragahi and Ramin

with security forces. In Zanjan, the protests were at the invitation of Ayatollah Asa-dollah Bayat Zanjani. Ayatollah Zanjani is a highly respected and highly ranked cleric critical of the regime. Many believe that he might replace Montazeri as the *marja taghlid* for his followers.

On Tasua, which coincided with December 26, 2009, Mohammad Khatami was invited by the family of Ayatollah Khomeini to deliver the sermon at Jamaran, a huge building complex which had served as Khomeini's home, office, and Hussei-niyeh lecture hall after the revolution. Khomeini's family members had been pub-licly supporting the reformist wing of the oligarchy including Khatami, Moussavi, and Karrubi. The invitation to Khatami to deliver the Tasua sermon at Khomeini's home was another public gesture of support to reformists by Khomeini's family. In an unprecedented action, plain-clothes forces (*lebas shakhsiha*) attacked the pro-ceedings at Jamaran. The videos of this attack were immediately placed on You-Tube.[188] Plain-clothes forces are under the control of hardliners and are composed of *Basij* and IRGC out of uniform. This indicates that, for the hardliners, even Kho-meini's home is not a sanctuary, safe from hardline violence. According to eyewit-nesses, outside of the Jamaran building, a large crowd had gathered to listen to Khatami. The crowd was attacked by official special police and plain-clothes forces that used tear gas and electric batons.[189] December 26 witnessed protests in work-ing-class south Tehran, wealthy north Tehran, and other middle-class neighbor-hoods in central Tehran.[190]

On Ashura, December 27, much of Tehran, including neighborhoods of various social classes, participated in the protests.[191] The protests were massive, and the violence was brutal. *Basij* and plain-clothes forces used live ammunition. Accord-

---

Mostaghim, "Tehran Protesters Clash with Iranian Security Forces," *The Los Angeles Times* (Decem-ber 25, 2009).

188 Part 1: http://www.youtube.com/watch?v=62ST2KDlCPE; and part 2: http://www.youtube.com/watch?v=PBSfqGhJ7UY.

189 Fereshteh Qazi, "*Hamleh Nirohay Dowlati Beh Manzel Ayatollah Khomeini*" [Government Forces Attack Khomeini's House], Rooz Online (December 27, 2009), http://www.roozonline.com/persian/news/newsitem/article////107/-e179c444ec.html.

190 Nazila Fathi, "Tehran Protesters Defy Ban and Clash With Police," *The New York Times* (De-cember 27, 2009); Robert Tait, "Iranians' Green Revolution Refuses to Wither and Die," *The Guard-ian* online (December 27, 2009), http://www.guardian.co.uk/world/2009/dec/27/iran-tehran-ayotollah-khamenei-protests.

191 *Norooz News*, "*Tanin Allah O Akbar Sabzha Tehran Ra Larzand*" [The Echo of God Is Great by the Greens Shook Tehran] (December 27, 2009), http://noroznews.info/news/15886.php. *Norooz News* is published by the Islamic Iran Participation Front, the largest reformist party within the fundamentalist oligarchy. It was led by President Khatami's younger brother, Dr. Mohammad Reza Khatami.

ing to opposition sources, the government forces killed about 8 protesters, injured many more, and arrested more than 300. In addition, a nephew of Moussavi, 34-year-old Ali Moussavi Habibi, was assassinated.[192] By the next day, reported arrests had reached around 1,100, including large numbers of prominent reformist activists, democratic opposition figures, and civil society activists.

During the December 27 Ashura protests, on several occasions the people overwhelmed the special riot police and *Basij* members, captured them, and beat them up.[193] Despite the extreme brutality of the riot police, when they surrendered to the people, many protesters stopped beating them and saved their lives by circling them with protesters wearing green. The riot police usually took off their helmets and put on green headgear. In one dramatic event, about 30 riot police surrendered to more than several thousand protesters.[194] At other venues, protesters succeeded in setting on fire the motorbikes of *Basij* and police cars.[195] They also attacked a police van, kicked the police driver out, and freed the arrested protesters.[196] Vast areas of Tehran were in total control of the people, and no signs of coercive apparatuses were present.[197] Government control had collapsed in vast areas of Tehran. However, neither the reformist leadership, nor the democratic opposition leadership, took the lead to guide the people.

On this day, four were killed in Tabriz and one in Shiraz. Martial law was declared in Najafabad, Montazeri's hometown. Over the following days, top associates of Moussavi and Karrubi were arrested. There were also violent attacks on offices and mosques belonging to top clerics associated with the reformists. For example, plain-clothes forces violently attacked and closed the offices and mosque belonging to Grand Ayatollah Dastgheyb in Shiraz. Security forces prevented Grand Ayatollah Dastgheyb from flying from Tehran to Shiraz to take control of

---

192 Robert F. Worth and Nazila Fathi, "Death Toll Rises to 10 as Clashes in Iran Intensify," *The New York Times* (December 28, 2009).

193 For one of the more dramatic instances see the following video: http://www.youtube.com/watch?v=DlCCSyTT7js.

194 For the battle between the protesters and the riot police see http://www.youtube.com/watch?v=HqGYnjqHdOw. A few minutes earlier one of the protesters had been killed by a massive injury to the head; this killing had further enraged the protesters.

195 For a good collection of videos of the December 27 protests see http://www.iranian.com/main/2009/dec/people-fight-back.

196 The video of the rescue was placed on YouTube: http://www.youtube.com/watch?v=-HlYKkRzdNk.

197 For an excellent video with English narration see http://www.youtube.com/watch?v=q91cK5twvQU.

the situation. Grand Ayatollah Dastgheyb is a prominent fundamentalist cleric and a member of the Assembly of Experts.[198]

The widespread use of the slogan "Iranian Republic" indicated increased support for the secular, and the solid opposition. The events of Ashura showed that vast numbers inside Iran wished to see a change of regime and not a mere change of President or even the replacement of Khamenei with another cleric in his position.

2.4.7 From Ashura to February 11: Crisis, Paralysis, and Response

In reaction to the Ashura protests, which had witnessed great violence, the regime implemented new measures. On December 30, 2009 (9 Day 1388 in the Iranian calendar), the regime mobilized as many people as it could in a state-sponsored rally in order to illustrate the number of its supporters. This was intended to show that large numbers of the people supported the regime, boost the morale of its supporters, intimidate the opposition, and illustrate to the world that it intended to fight against its domestic opponents. This tactic had been used 10 years earlier in reaction to the pro-democracy student uprising in July 1999. On July 14, 1999, the regime mobilized its supporters for a mass rally in Tehran. The December 30 rally provided the regime with the claim that the people supported it. A conflict arose between opponents and supporters of the regime on the numbers that actually attended, and those that the regime was able to mobilize.

Despite the regime's claims, the photos did indicate that the number was much smaller than the number of people the regime had been able to mobilize in earlier times.

After more than six months of massive repression, it became clear that the Green Movement had not been crushed. The regime was facing serious internal and external challenges, and it appeared that, as time went by, the position of the regime was weakening. In the aftermath of Ashura protests some hardline elements again demanded arrest and prosecution of Moussavi and Karrubi. Obviously, the imprisonment of the top reformist cadres and their show trials had not deterred the protests. A public debate among the hardliners ensued on what to do.[199] I see four main groups within the hardline camp, that propose different responses.

---

[198] For the original news in Persian see http://www.parlemannews.ir/?n=6862; for an English version see: Payvand Iran News, "Iran: Grand Ayatollah Dastgheyb Prevented from Traveling to Shiraz" (January 3, 2010), http://www.payvand.com/news/10/jan/1023.html.

[199] Some of these debates were broadcast live on national television. For an example, see http://www.irannegah.com/Video.aspx?id=1481.

The first group consists of strong supporters of Ahmadinejad and the so-called June 12 coup. This group is called *"osulgarayan efrati"* [extremist hardliners]. This group includes top leaders of the IRGC and *Basij*, Ayatollah Mesbah, Ayatollah Jennati, Mojtaba Khamenei, Hojatolislam Ruhollah Husseinian, and Hussein Shariatmadari and his newspaper *Kayhan*. Their views are expressed in the IRNA, Fars News Agency, Islamic Republic of Iran Broadcasting (IRIB, the state television and radio monopoly), and the *Kayhan* daily. This group has been the most vociferous group in the hardline camp. They have been behind the show trials. They have been advocating arrests of Moussavi, Karrubi, Khatami, some of Rafsanjani's children, and sometimes Rafsanjani himself. Their criticism has been that the regime has not used enough violence. They believe that great violence could easily put down the resistance. One member of this group, Hojatolislam Ruhollah Husseinian, resigned his seat in the Majles on January 6, 2010, because he said that the regime was not showing enough resolve to put down the reformists. In particular, he was critical of some reformists (e.g., Hojatolislam Ali Akbar Mohtashami-Pour) being given leading positions in the Majles committees.[200] Husseinian was one of the leaders of the most extremist group in the Majles. He was the judge who issued large numbers of executions. He also was the most prominent official who publicly defended Saeed Imami (Deputy Minister of Intelligence) for the assassination of dissidents in 1999. A few days after his resignation, Husseinian withdrew his public support for Imami.

A second faction may be called the moderate or pragmatic hardliners. This group includes the following: Mohsen Rezaee, former Supreme Commander of the IRGC; Ali Larijani, Speaker of the Majles; Sadeq Larijani, the Head of the Judicial Branch; Nateq Nouri; Habibollah Asgaroladi-Mosalman, leader of the Islamic Coalition Party and a powerful, wealthy bazaar merchant; and Ali Motahhari, the powerful hardline member of the Majles and son of Grand Ayatollah Motahhari, one of the main founders of the Islamic Republic. Mehr News Agency publishes the views of this group,[201] which fears that continued crisis could lead to a collapse of the regime and thus advocates reconciliation with Rafsanjani and Moussavi. Khabar Online also reflects the views of Ali Larijani, one of the most prominent members of this sub-faction.[202] Although they all strongly support Kha-

200 Hojatolislam Ali Akbar Mohtashami-Pour is a former Minister of the Interior and the former ambassador to Syria who helped create the Lebanese Hezbollah in 1982. In 1982, Mohtashami-Pour lobbied Ayatollah Khomeini to join the war against Israel but failed to convince him to do so. Mohtashami-Pour is one of the top advisors and associates of Moussavi.
201 The website is http://www.mehrnews.com/fa/. Their English-language section is http://www.mehrnews.com/en/.
202 See http://khabaronline.ir/default.aspx.

menei, they are lukewarm toward Ahmadinejad. Some supporters of Ahmadinejad have argued that a group led by Ali Larijani has been leading an anti-Ahmadinejad campaign.[203]

In December 2010, Ahmadinejad succeeded in dismissing Manuchehr Mottaki, the Foreign Minister. Although the constitution gives the power to appoint (then confirmed by majority vote of Majles) and dismiss the members of the cabinet, in practice, four members of the cabinet (Ministers of Intelligence, Foreign Affairs, Interior, and Defense) have to be appointed by the consent of the Supreme Leader (and usually report directly to the Supreme Leader instead of the President). Mottaki was a close ally of Ali Larijani, and the dismissal was a successful attempt by Ahmadinejad to undermine Larijani. Ahmadinejad's firing of Mottaki was done in a humiliating manner. Mottaki was fired when he was on an official visit to Senegal and heard of his dismissal from the President of Senegal.[204] In April 2011, another Ali Larijani ally, Minister of Intelligence Moslehi, resigned. His resignation was accepted by Ahmadinejad, but the Supreme Leader opposed the resignation, and Moslehi continued in his post.

A third group may be termed anti-Ahmadinejad hardliners. Many in the hardline camp have always been critical of Ahmadinejad and his policies. They include Tehran mayor, IRGC Gen. Mohammad Baqer Qalibaf. Members of this group have been very quiet since June 2009. One possible solution to the crisis may be the replacement of Ahmadinejad with another hardliner such as Gen. Qalibaf or Ali Larijani.

The fourth group includes Supreme Leader Khamenei. Members of this group want the reformists to submit to the Supreme Leader and accept Ahmadinejad as legitimate President. Members of this group have shown great hesitance to arrest reformist leaders and cause more massive bloodshed. Apparently, they are concerned that arrests of reformist leaders and/or massive violence could backfire and result in collapse of the regime. They seem to think that time is on their side and measured repression could control the protesters and compel the reformists to submit to the Supreme Leader. Khamenei proposes measured violence but warns that too much violence, especially those acts not authorized and directed by

---

203 BBC Persian, "*Mahkomiyat Dobareh Moaven Siasi Daftar Rais Jomhur Iran Beh Tahamol Zendan*" [Sentencing of the Political Deputy of the Office of the President of Iran to Prison, Again] (April 20, 2010), http://www.bbc.co.uk/persian/iran/2010/04/100420_l10_behdad_hosseinkhan_sentenced.shtml.
204 *The Economist*, "Iran's Foreign Minister: Thank You and Good Bye" (December 16, 2010), http://www.economist.com/node/17733215.

officials, might benefit the opponents.[205] In his speech in January 2010, Khamenei forcefully demanded that those elites in the system (referring to Moussavi, Karrubi, Khatami, and Rafsanjani) stop taking vague positions and instead explicitly make their position on the system clear.[206] In no uncertain terms, Khamenei wanted these reformists to make public their positions clearly and unambiguously. Khamenei wanted the reformists to condemn the slogans of the secular and the solid opposition. Moussavi's Communique 17 had already distanced him from those shouting the slogans demanding an "Iranian Republic." Khatami had also already criticized those slogans. Khatami again declared his support for the 1979 constitution and the system, and demanded that Khamenei be the leader of all the people instead of supporting only one faction.[207] Rafsanjani stated that the current problems could only be solved by Khamenei himself.[208]

The Green Movement was composed of many divergent groups with widely divergent hopes, demands, and policies. Some wished to see minor reforms while others wished to replace the Islamic Republic with a secular democracy. Moussavi, Karrubi, and Khatami wished to pursue reforms; they were fully committed to the preservation of the Islamic Republic and its constitution.

On January 1, 2010, about three weeks before Khamenei's demand to make their positions clear, Moussavi had already issued his famous Communique 17,

---

205 Ali Khamenei, *"Bayanat Dar Didar Mardom Qom Dar Salgard Qiyam 19 Dey"* [Remarks in the Meeting with the People of Qom on the Anniversary of January 9 Uprising], Khamenei's website (January 9, 2010), http://farsi.khamenei.ir/speech-content?id=8599. For an excellent summary in English see: Borzou Daragahi, "Iran's Supreme Leader Tells Militias Not To Meddle," *The Los Angeles Times* (January 10, 2010), http://www.latimes.com/news/nation-and-world/la-fg-iran-khamenei10-2010jan10,0,5472926.story.

206 Khamenei, *"Didar Ba Aazaye Shoray Hamahangi Tablighat Islami"* [Meeting with the Members of the Coordinating Council of Islamic Publicity], Khamenei's website (January 19, 2010), http://farsi.khamenei.ir/speech-content?id=8629. Short excerpts in English translation are available at http://www.iranreview.org/content/view/5263/1/ and http://www.zamaaneh.com/enzam/2010/01/iran-leader-urges-opposit.html.

207 BBC Persian, *"Khatami: Ma Mikhahim Rahbari, Rahbar Hameh Mardom Bashad"* [We Want the Leadership, to Be the Leader of All the People] (February 1, 2010), http://www.bbc.co.uk/persian/lg/iran/2010/02/100201_l10_ir88_khatami_khamenei.shtml; and Payvand Iran News, "Khatami: The Response to Civil Protests is Not Repression, Prison, and Execution" (February 2, 2010), http://www.payvand.com/news/10/feb/1013.html.

208 Radio Farda, *"Hashemi Rafsanjani: Massael Mojod Ba Tadbir Rahbari Qabel Hal Va Fasl Ast"* [Hashemi Rafsanjani: The Current Problems Can Be Solved by the Wisdom of the Leader] (January 23, 2010), http://www.radiofarda.com/content/o2_rafsanjani_on_iran_crisis/1937710.html.

which became known as his Five Point Plan to resolve the crisis.[209] Absent were the demands for the abolition of the presidential election result, and declaration of his (Moussavi's) victory. He also accepted Ahmadinejad's government, and merely asked that it be a responsible government. There were also numerous explicit declarations of support for the 1979 constitution. The demands were somewhat similar to those made by Rafsanjani in his July 17 speech. Moussavi asked for the promulgation of a transparent election law that would gain the trust of the people; freeing of political prisoners; freedom of the press and media; and recognizing the right of the people to hold legal assemblies and establish parties (a right that was mentioned in Article 27 of the constitution but never respected including when Moussavi was Prime Minister). Moussavi added that he did not demand that these be implemented immediately and simultaneously. Moussavi's plan was a retreat, but not a surrender. Similar statements by Rafsanjani, Khatami, and Karrubi followed in the following two weeks.[210]

Moussavi's plan, however, accentuated the internal differences among the hardliners. It pitted those who wanted to use more massive violence against those who feared that more violence would be counter-productive and could result in the collapse of the regime. Accepting Moussavi's plan could undermine the ability of Ahmadinejad to rule comfortably and would create conditions for the return to power by the reformists in the following elections. Khamenei's acceptance of Moussavi's demands would require abandoning the extremist faction and acquiescing to a return to power of reformists.

It is not clear what would be the impact of the hardliners on the freeing of political prisoners. Imprisonment and threats of imprisonment are the primary methods to control a population that intensely opposes the regime. Accepting the freedom of the press also would badly undermine the hardliners. Accepting the right of assembly would allow the massive majority to legally gather free from state violence. And if the hardliners accepted fair electoral laws, they would lose to their reformist rivals.

By accepting Moussavi's Five Point Plan, the extremist wing of hardliners would lose power; therefore, these hardline elements would oppose it. However, there are many hardline members of the fundamentalist oligarchy who place the survival of the regime above the narrow interests of the hardline elements. Moussavi's plan created public divisions among the hardliners. Mohsen Rezaee,

---

209 Mir Hussein Moussavi, *"Bayanieyh 17, Rah Halhay Panjganeh Baray Khoruj Az Bohran"* [Communique 17, Five Point Plan Solution For Getting Out of the Crisis], Iran Emrooz (January 1, 2010), http://news.iran-emrooz.net/index.php?/news1/20455/.
210 Payvand Iran News, "Iranian Opposition Leaders React to Deepening Crisis" (January 12, 2010), http://payvand.com/news/10/jan/1107.html.

who had been siding with Khamenei since June 2009, wrote Khamenei a public letter. Rezaee wrote: "The retreat of Mr. Mir Hussein Moussavi from denying the government of Mr. Ahmadinejad and his constructive suggestions in regard to the Majles and the Judicial branch to act according to their legal mandates in keeping the government responsive, although late, nevertheless could be the beginning of a new unifying move from the protesting front with others."[211] Rezaee was immediately attacked by the extreme wing of the hardline camp.[212]

Another hardliner, Ali Motahhari, supported reconciliation and advocated that both Moussavi and Ahmadinejad publicly admit their mistakes. Motahhari strongly criticized the accusations against the top reformists and criticized the use of massive violence.[213]

The daily *Rooznameh Jumhuri Islami* is regarded as the main establishment paper. In its January 9, 2010 editorial, entitled *"Raah Baaz Ast"* [The Path is Open], the paper criticized the extremists in the first group who have been closing the door to reconciliation with Moussavi.[214] This editorial received wide re-publication on other sites inside Iran and was featured prominently on Moussavi's website, Kaleme.[215] The editorial stated:

> [A]ll sides accept they have made mistakes … all regard as a principle the preservation of the system, and for the achievement of this objective, anywhere they can, they should show forgiveness. … Are we going to witness a civil war and brother killing brother … this flood that has begun, if not stopped, will take with it everything. … A faction, which possesses power in the country, the only thing that it does is beating war drums and condemns and prohibits any attempt of reconciliation. Among the innovations of this faction is putting everyone on the throats of others and all the attacks are on the system, and it has placed itself far away

---

211 Mohsen Rezaee, *"Nameh Dr. Rezaee Beh Rahbar Moazam Enqelab"* [The Letter of Dr. Rezaee to the Esteemed Leader of the Revolution], Rezee's website (January 1, 2010), http://www.rezaee.ir/fa/pages/?cid=8627.

212 An interesting video was placed on YouTube in which the hardliners attack Rezaee, Moussavi, and Rafsanjani. They make veiled references to Rezaee, Moussavi, and Rafsanjani of pressuring Khomeini to drink the poison and accept cease-fire with Iraq in 1988. In 1988, Rezaee was the Commander-in-Chief of the IRGC, Moussavi was Prime Minister, and Rafsanjani was the Speaker of the Majles. They also make a parallel with current events. The person shown making some of the accusations is Dr. Hassan Abbasi, the extreme hardline former IRGC officer, who is close to Ahmadinejad and one of the top strategists of the hardline camp. See http://www.youtube.com/watch?v=WhDJPSDea1g.

213 Iran Emrooz, *"Hamleh Beh Hashemi Az Tribune Majles"* [Attack on Hashemi from the Majles's Tribune] (January 7, 2010), http://www.iran-emrooz.net/index.php?/news2/20543/; see the video of Ali Motahhari on IRIB at http://www.youtube.com/watch?v=TnuymdsqSC4.

214 Editorial, *"Raah Baaz Ast"* [The Path is Open], *Rooznameh Jumhuri Islami* (January 9, 2010), http://www.jomhourieslami.com/1388/13881019/index.html.

215 See http://www.kaleme.org/1388/10/19/klm-7715.

from the attacks and is waiting to catch its own fish in the muddy waters. One can say that putting more fuel on this hot fire is not providing service to the system, God's religion, the prophet, or the people. The divisions have now penetrated the hardline camp and this extremist faction condemns any wise remarks on the path of unity and resolution of the problems. Even when these come from inside this hardline camp from well-known individuals, the extremists throw all sorts of accusations and destroy him in various ways. Violence and confrontation not only will not solve any of the problems but would make the issues even more complex.[216]

Moussavi's Five Point Plan has the potential to alienate secular forces in the opposition and vast segments of the population. Secular democratic forces do not want to struggle and die in order to help a reformed Islamic Republic. They want their sacrifices to be for the establishment of democracy. However, these concerns were mitigated by the weakness of the opposition on the one hand, and the great sympathies that were generated for Moussavi in the aftermath of the assassination of his nephew on December 27, and arrest of his brother-in-law (Zahra Rahnavard's brother), on the other. Moreover, Moussavi's personal courage in the face of potential arrest or assassination caused many democratic opposition groups to withhold their criticisms. Nevertheless, Moussavi's Five Point Plan alienates him from the massive number of secular and democratic Iranians, especially those on the streets. Many secular democrats are worried that what occurred in 1978–1979 could happen again. Khomeini sought and received support from secular democrats before coming to power but slaughtered them after gaining power. If Khamenei accepted Moussavi's plan and the situation stabilized, then Moussavi could lose support from large segments of the modern middle classes.

Karrubi changed his position several times. On January 11, 2010, Karrubi released his Five Point Plan.[217] Karrubi demanded: (1) those who committed crimes against the people since the election should confess and ask for forgiveness; (2) the deviations in the system should be remedied by adherence to the constitution, international conventions signed by Iran, respect for freedoms of the press and for political prisoners and reforms; (3) avoidance of violence; (4) investigation into the root causes of the crisis; and (5) readiness to debate any representative of the re-

---

216 Editorial, *"Raah Baaz Ast"* [The Path is Open], *Rooznameh Jumhuri Islami* (January 9, 2010), http://www.jomhourieslami.com/1388/13881019/index.html. My translation.

217 Mehdi Karrubi, *"Rahkarhay Mehdi Karrubi Jahat Khoroj Az Bohran"* [Mehdi Karrubi's Solution for Exiting the Crisis], Iran Emrooz (January 11, 2010), http://news.iran-emrooz.net/index.php?/news1/20604. For English translation of the five points see: Payvand Iran News, "Opposition Leader Karroubi Delivers Proposal to Resolve Iran's Crisis" (January 11, 2010), http://payvand.com/news/10/jan/1101.html.

gime. Soon Karrubi retreated slightly from his earlier position. Karrubi stated that he believed that there was cheating in the election but because the Supreme Leader had *"tanfeez"* [affirmed] Ahmadinejad as President, he would accept Ahmadinejad as President.[218] Soon afterwards, Karrubi said that he continued his work against Ahmadinejad, and that his earlier statement did not mean that he would stop his activities against Ahmadinejad.

Moussavi's Communique 17 and Karrubi's statement gave rise to hardline characterization of their positions as surrender and acceptance of Ahmadinejad as the legitimate President. It also gave rise to disappointment among some in the opposition. Rahnavard (Moussavi's wife) gave an interview with Rooz Online.[219] In the interview, Rahnavard dispels the notion that Moussavi has recognized the Ahmadinejad administration. She states:

> I believe that from the tone of this statement we can clearly see that Mr. Moussavi does not recognize a government that was established based on fraud. ... I don't see any compromise in that statement, rather it lays out the minimum desires and aspirations of the people of Iran that the current regime could easily fulfill. ... I want to emphasize the fact that we neither acknowledge the legitimacy of Ahmadinejad's government, nor are we making any behind the scenes compromises.[220]

Rahnavard emphasizes that the demands in the Communique 17/Five Point Plan were the minimum demands. She concedes that these demands could be fulfilled by the regime. Rahnavard said that there have been no behind-the-scenes compromises. This indicates that the reformist faction has not surrendered and intends to continue the struggle against the hardliners.

After what appeared to be retreats in early to mid-January, the remarks by Moussavi, Karrubi, and Khatami became stronger leading up to the 31st anniversa-

---

218 JARAS, *"Karrubi: Dar Entekhabat Taghalob Shodeh va Mohkam Bar Harf Khod Estadeam"* [Karrubi: There Has Been Cheating in the Election and I Stand Strong on My Position] (January 25, 2010), http://www.rahesabz.net/story/8684/.

219 Fereshteh Qazi, *"Zahra Rahnavard Dar Mosahebeh ba Rooz: Sazesh Nemikonim, Beh Rasmiyat Nemishenasim"* [Zahra Rahnavard in Interview with Rooz: We Will Not Compromise, We Will Recognize], Rooz Online (January 26, 2010), http://www.roozonline.com/persian/news/newsitem/article/2010/january/26//br-br.html.

220 The English translation of the interview is from Moussavi's Facebook page: http://www.facebook.com/note.php?note_id=276918527611&id=79757303129&ref=mf; also available at http://www.irannewsdigest.com/2010/01/26/rahnavard-we-don't-compromise-or-recognise-ahmadinejad's-government/. Moussavi's Facebook page is maintained by his supporters.

ry of the revolution on February 11.[221] On January 28, 2010, the regime executed 19-year-old Arash Rahmanipour and 37-year-old Mohammad Reza Ali-Zamani on charges of participating in anti-government activities. The regime also announced that more executions of those convicted in opposing the government would follow.[222] Moussavi and Karrubi immediately condemned these executions and publicly called for mass participation in the February 11 demonstrations.[223] After it was revealed that the two had been imprisoned before the June election, and therefore could not have possibly been involved in the street protests, the regime announced that they belonged to a monarchist group which had detonated a bomb the previous year which had killed several people. The executions were widely viewed as a warning to the Iranian people who opposed the regime that the regime would execute those who opposed it.

Rafsanjani's position became less clear during this period. Rafsanjani did not call for support for the reformist position, nor did he make any statement recognizing Ahmadinejad's government. Instead, Rafsanjani warned about how internal division could be used by outside enemies of the revolution and that only the Supreme Leader could resolve the crisis.[224]

As February 11 approached, Moussavi made his position more explicit. In his interview with his news website, Kaleme, Moussavi made several very significant statements. Moussavi strongly criticized the moves toward dictatorship in the Islamic Republic. He suggested that these dictatorial moves were not compatible with the constitution of the IRI. Referring to Khamenei without naming him, Moussavi suggested that all return to the constitution as the best way to resolve the crisis. Moussavi harshly and unequivocally criticized and condemned the notion of moving beyond the constitution, implicitly referring to the slogan "Iranian Republic" and demands for a secular democracy. He also harshly criticized the monar-

221 Kaleme, *"Goftogoye Kaleme Ba Mir-Hussein Moussavi Piramoon Masayel Mohem Keshvar"* [Discussion of Kaleme with Mir-Hussein Moussavi About the Significant Problems in the Country] (February 2, 2010), http://www.sabztab.blogfa.com/post-161.aspx.
222 Nazila Fathi, "Iran, With Opposition Protests Continuing, Executes More Prisoners," *The New York Times* (February 2, 2010).
223 JARAS, *"Mir-Hussein Moussavi Va Mehdi Karrubi Eadamhay Akhir Ra Mahkoom Kardand"* [Mir-Hussein Moussavi and Mehdi Karrubi Condemned the Recent Executions], JARAS (January 30, 2010), http://www.rahesabz.net/story/9089/.
224 Parcham, *"Hashemi: 22 Bahman Motealeq Beh Hameh Vafadarain Nezam Ast"* [Hashemi: February 11 Belongs to All Faithful to the System] (February 10, 2010), http://www.parcham.ir/vdcd.j052yt0kxa26y.html; Farda News, *"Hoshdar Hashemi: Mardom Va Masoulan Movazeb Bashand"* [Hashemi's Warning: The People and the Officials Should be Careful] (February 10, 2010), http://www.fardanews.com/fa/pages/?cid=103370; also see http://www.youtube.com/watch?v=2TwAXD2S51E.

chists as one of those groups who wanted a change in the constitution. Moussavi opposed the proposal of an Islamic Republic without the IRI's constitution, a proposal backed by some of his supporters such as Hojatolislam Mohsen Kadivar (who at the time was at Duke University). Moussavi said that the IRI's constitution was not a divine revelation and that some aspects of it could be changed, as was done in 1989.[225] This was a major evolution for Moussavi, who had earlier explicitly opposed any changes to the anti-democratic aspects of the constitution.

February 11, the anniversary of the revolution, was a day for each side to show its strength. The reformists had called upon the people to massively participate in the protests. The regime deployed all its resources to bring its supporters to the rally and prevent the opposition supporters from participating in the rally. On this day, the hardliners gained a victory. The regime succeeded in mobilizing massive numbers to participate in its rallies, containing the protests without resorting to mass killings, and preventing the mass violence which had occurred on Ashura. Despite its extensive efforts during the previous six weeks, however, the regime failed to prevent the opponents from defying the regime.[226] In other words, eight months after the election, despite all its efforts, the regime had failed to end the crisis, its primary and overarching objective.

The hardliners portrayed the rally as a huge success. Fars News Agency claimed that 50 million people had participated in the rally.[227] All the available videos and photos of the event clearly undermine this claim. A dispute arose on the numbers of participants. Google made available satellite photos of the event which showed that Azadi Square was sparsely populated 10 minutes before Ahmadine-

225 Kaleme, *"Goftogoye Kaleme Ba Mir-Hussein Moussavi Piramoon Masayel Mohem Keshvar"* [Discussion of Kaleme with Mir-Hussein Moussavi About the Significant Problems in the Country] (February 2, 2010), http://www.sabztab.blogfa.com/post-161.aspx.
226 Martin Fletcher, "Iran Crushes Opposition Protests with Violence," *Times* online (February 11, 2010), http://www.timesonline.co.uk/tol/news/world/middle_east/article7023684.ece; Alan Cowell and Michael Slackman, "Iran Controls Protests and Defies West on Nuclear Fuel," *The New York Times* (February 11, 2010), http://www.nytimes.com/2010/02/12/world/middleeast/12iran.html?hp; Al Jazeera English, "Iran Blocks Opposition Protests" (February 11, 2010), http://english.aljazeera.net/news/middleeast/2010/02/20102117332284608.html; and Borzou Daragahi and Ramin Mostaghim, "Pro-government Demonstrators Overshadow Opposition in Iran," *The Los Angeles Times* (February 12, 2010), http://www.latimes.com/news/nation-and-world/la-fg-iran-protests12-2010feb12,0,2941207.story. Large numbers of videos of the February 11 protests (many from the pro-democracy opposition) are available at http://www.iranian.com/main/2010/feb/protests-22-bahman. About 70 videos of the protests on February 11, 2010, are available from a reformist site, see http://www.hambastegi.com/70_video_clips_of_green_movement.htm.
227 Fars News Agency, *"Refrandom 50 Million Nafari Mardom Iran Jahan Ra Mabhoot Khod Kard"* [A Referendum of 50 Million Persons of the Iranian People Amazed the World] (February 11, 2010), http://www.farsnews.com/newstext.php?nn=8811220307.

jad's speech. However, the Google photo does show large numbers of people in the streets leading to Azadi Square. The Google photo indicates that at least a few hundred thousand were present on the streets leading to Azadi Square.[228] Moreover, Google also posted a video of the image which clearly showed large numbers of buses parked close to the Square, indicating that those present were bused into the event rather than having arrived spontaneously themselves.[229] The hardliners claimed that all those on the streets were supporters of the Supreme Leader and President Ahmadinejad. Supporters of the hardliners placed on YouTube a sophisticated montage of videos showing very large numbers of protesters in support of the regime (accompanied by rap music attacking the Green Movement).[230]

Moussavi and Karrubi said that large numbers of supporters of the Green Movement participated in the rally but due to the threats of violence by the security forces did not reveal their identities. Moussavi and Karrubi criticized the hardliners for usurping the rally as their own and the violence of the security forces.[231]

The reformists did not succeed in capturing the streets as they had accomplished on June 15, September 18, November 4, and in December. However, the reformist opposition succeeded in bringing large numbers onto the streets shouting slogans in support of Moussavi.[232] The regime's use of massive force as well as intimidation tactics succeeded in thwarting the Green Movement from capturing the streets. The regime used violence against Karrubi, arrested his son, and smashed the windows of Karrubi's auto. Mrs. Rahnavard was beaten up. The people intervened and rescued her from the regime's forces. The intervention of the regime's forces also prevented Moussavi and Khatami from joining the protesters. The regime also temporarily arrested Mrs. Zahra Eshraqi (granddaughter of Ayatollah Khomeini) and her husband Mohammad Reza Khatami (the younger brother of former President Khatami).[233] The massive presence of the coercive apparatuses

---

228 See http://google-latlong.blogspot.com/2010/02/view-into-tehran.html.
229 Gooya, *"Aaks-hay Mahvareh Google Az Jamiyat 22 Bahman + Esteqrar Otobus-hay Dowlati"* [The Photos of Google's Satellites From the Population on February 11 + Placement of Government's Buses] (February 12, 2010), http://news.gooya.com/didaniha/archives/2010/02/100390.php. Also see Kazem Alamdari, *"Neshanei Digar Az Shekast Estrategic Jumhuri Islami"* [Another Indication of the Strategic Defeat of the Islamic Republic], Iran Emrooz (February 16, 2010), http://www.iran-emrooz.net/index.php?/politic/more/21088/.
230 See http://www.youtube.com/watch?v=HbYqckFvUJI.
231 BBC Persian, *"Enteqad Moussavi Va Karrubi Az 'Mosadereh' Rahpeymaii 22 Bahman"* [Criticisms of Moussavi and Karrubi of "Usurpation" of the February 11 Rally] (February 18, 2010), http://www.bbc.co.uk/persian/iran/2010/02/100218_l10_mousavi_karubi_22bahman.shtml.
232 See http://www.youtube.com/watch?v=n8Vd-b9S1RE.
233 Iran Emrooz, *"Hamleh Beh Karrubi, Khatami, Moussavi va Rahnavard, Jahat Jologiri Az Hozoor Anha Dar Tazahorat Mardom"* [Attacks on Karrubi, Khatami, Moussavi, and Rahnavard in

succeeded in preventing the protesters from joining the rallies.[234] The evidence which appeared soon afterwards showed that, despite the regime's claims, large numbers of people joined the protests, although not as large as in earlier demonstrations.

The secular opposition also showed its strength by holding protests shouting the slogan demanding an "Iranian" republic, although compared with the Ashura protests, there were far fewer protests by the secular opposition. Supporters of the secular opposition burned a motorcycle belonging to the security forces and shouted *"Marg Bar Dictator"* [Death to the Dictator], *"Khamenei Qateleh, Velayatash Batelleh"* [Khamenei is a Murderer, His Rule is Voided], *"Esteqlal, Azadi, Jumhuri Irani"* [Independence, Freedom, Iranian Republic].[235] As in all the protests since June 12, the protesters supporting the reformist opposition and the secular opposition cooperated extremely well with each other.[236] For example, in many protests the protesters sang *"Yar-e Dabestani"* [Grade School Friends], which has become the anthem of both democratic opposition and young members of reformist groups.[237]

A pattern seems to have emerged. The regime arrests large numbers. Many are furloughed, or temporarily released on bail. As new protests are called, more activists are arrested while those in prison are again furloughed or released on bail.[238] Although many extremist hardliners make public calls for the arrest and

---

Order to Prevent Them from Participating in the People's Protests] (February 11, 2010), http://www.iran-emrooz.net/index.php?/news2/21038/.

234 Martin Fletcher, "Iranian Regime Ships in Support for Anniversary Celebrations," *Times* online (February 12, 2010), http://www.timesonline.co.uk/tol/news/world/middle_east/article7024206.ece.

235 See the video from the February 11 protests in Tehran: http://www.youtube.com/watch?v=ja0qDrfvqp0. Also see http://www.youtube.com/watch?v=i95pEWw0WL4: the people chanted *"Koshteh Nadadim Keh Sazesh Konim, Rahbar-e Qatel Ro Setayesh Konim"* [We Did Not Get Killed, So That We Would Compromise, and Praise the Murderer Supreme Leader].

236 Unlike inside Iran, outside Iran there have been serious tensions between the reformist opposition and the secular and solid opposition groups. One main reason may be that inside Iran, most of the solid opposition seems to constitute secular liberal republicans, whereas those outside Iran include monarchists, PMOI, and leftists in addition to liberal republicans. It has been easier for the liberal democrats to cooperate with reformists than for the monarchists and PMOI to do so. Indeed, many reformists such as Moussavi have explicitly condemned the PMOI. In his Communique 17, the sole group that Moussavi explicitly condemned was the PMOI.

237 See http://www.youtube.com/watch?v=2YV1kUGfO2s. One could also hear calls for a referendum (on the form of the political system), which is the slogan of the democratic opposition and the solid opposition. Also see http://www.youtube.com/watch?v=PVBwNzJTDMg.

238 Nazilah Fathi, "6 More Iranian Activists Reported Arrested," *The New York Times* (March 3, 2010).

punishment of the top leaders such as Moussavi, Karrubi, Khatami, and Rafsanja-ni, they have not been arrested. February 11, once again, showed the paralysis in Iran: none of the main players (hardline regime, reformist opposition, secular op-position) was able to accomplish all their main goals.

2.4.8 May 1, 2010, International Workers' Day, and May 2, 2010, National Teachers' Day

On May 1, 2020—International Workers' Day—and May 2, 2010—National Teach-ers' Day—despite calls by the opposition and several major labor unions and teachers' unions, only relatively minor protests occurred.[239] Certainly the regime's effective repressive tactics played a part, but by and large the workers and teach-ers did not join the protests.[240] On May 1 and 2, large numbers of university stu-dents, especially at the University of Tehran, held protests.[241] The slogans shouted by the university students included: *"Marg Bar Dictator"* [Death to the Dictator]; *"Ya Marg Ya Azadi"* [Either Death or Freedom]; *"Daneshjoo, Karegar, Etehhad Eteh-had"* [Student, Worker, Unite, Unite]; *"Azadi, Edalat, Ean Ast Shoar-e Mellat"* [Free-dom, Justice, This is the Slogan of the Nation]; *"Dictator Haya Kon, Daneshgah Raa Raha Kon"* [Dictator Have Shame, Leave the University Alone]; *"Dowlat Mozdor Nemikhaym, Police Mozdor Nemikhaym"* [We Do Not Want Mercenary Govern-ment, We Do Not Want Mercenary Police]; *"Khoni Keh Dar Rag Maast, Hediyeh Beh Mellat Mast"* [The Blood in Our Veins, is Our Gift to Our Nation]; and *"Marg bar Ean Dowlat Mardom Farib"* [Death to this Demagogic Government].[242]

---

239 Samnak Aqai, *"Gozareshi Az Bargozari Rooze Kargar Dar Keshvar: Kargaran Amandand"* [A Report on the Participation on the Workers' Day in the Country: Workers Came], Rooz Online (May 2, 2010), www.roozonline.com/persian/news/newsitem/article/2010/may/02/-0583b70fa8.html. On the major labor unions calling for marches, see their joint call available at *"Qatnameh Mosh-tarek Rooz Jahani Kargar"* [Joint Declaration on the International Workers' Day], http://www.syn dicavahed.net/index.php?option=com_content&task=view&id=241&Itemid=10; for English transla-tion see http://www.nosweat.org.uk/story/2010/04/28/iranian-may-day-statement.
240 Parsa Piltan, *"Yek Sal Sarkoob Moaleman Moatarez Dar Iran"* [One Year of Repression of the Protesting Teachers in Iran], BBC Persian (May 1, 2010), http://www.bbc.co.uk/persian/lg/iran/2010/05/100501_u02-pp-teachers-day.shtml.
241 For a video of the protests see http://www.youtube.com/watch?v=assCWrbzfVs&feature. Pho-tos, videos, and commentary are available at http://www.iran-emrooz.net/index.php?/news1/22220/.
242 Ibid. Compilations and translations are mine.

2.4.9 June 2010

June 4, 2010 was the 21st anniversary of the death of Ayatollah Khomeini. June 5 (15 Khordad in the Iranian calendar) is the anniversary of a major uprising in 1963 when Ayatollah Khomeini publicly opposed the Shah's reform proposals for land reform (taking land from the large landowners and distributing it to peasants), the female franchise, and changing the law from taking an oath to the Quran to taking an oath to a holy book (which would have allowed non-Muslims to gain high positions in the government). The fundamentalists regard the June 5, 1963 protests against these reforms to be the beginning of Khomeini's movement. Since 1989, there have been three days of commemoration on June 3, 4, and 5. Khomeini's grandson, Hojatolislam Seyyed Hassan Khomeini, who is the spokesman of the Khomeini family and the Director of the Khomeini Mausoleum, had been directing the events in the previous few years. Major conflicts had emerged between Hassan Khomeini and the hardliners since the June 2009 election. They included Hassan Khomeini refusing to be present at the inauguration ceremonies of Ahmadinejad; inviting Mohammad Khatami to speak at the official Residence of Ayatollah Khomeini at Jamaran; paying his respects to Alireza Beheshti (Moussavi's top advisor and son of one of the founders of the Islamic Republic) after he was released from prison; attending the wedding of a son of the Secretary-General of the main reformist party, Islamic Iran Participation Front, where he sat at the same table with Moussavi and Karrubi; and publicly criticizing the Head of the state television monopoly for "distorting" the words of Ayatollah Khomeini.[243] Hardliners had criticized Hassan Khomeini. The Head of the state television monopoly accused Hassan Khomeini of being in collusion with those who want to "overthrow" the regime and called his actions a "grave mistake."[244]

Instead of the usual three-day ceremonies, in 2010 only one ceremony was held at Khomeini's Mausoleum, and the IRGC was given a major role in conducting the ceremonies. At the ceremony something unprecedented occurred. Hassan Khomeini's talk was disrupted by a crowd of hardline supporters of Ahmadinejad and the Supreme Leader. Ahmadinejad was to talk first, then Hassan Khomeini, and then the Supreme Leader. Ahmadinejad arrived late and spoke much longer

---

243 Hussein Bastani, *"Aya Rahbar Iran Az Hamleh Beh Hassan Khomeini Razi Bood?"* [Did the Supreme Leader of Iran Consent to the Attack on Hassan Khomeini?], BBC Persian (June 7, 2010), http://www.bbc.co.uk/persian/iran/2010/06/100607_l39_hassankhomeini_rahbar.shtml; and Hussein Bastani, *"Eteham: Khabar Gereftan Az 'Molaqathay Khososi Imam'"* [Accusation: Getting News of 'Khomeini's Private Meetings'], BBC Persian (March 7, 2010), http://www.bbc.co.uk/persian/iran/2010/03/100307_l39_khanevadeh_khomeini_vataneemrooz.shtml.
244 Ibid., Bastani, *"Eteham."*

than his allotted time. Despite several times being reminded by Hojatolislam Mohammad Ali Ansari, the official organizer of the event, that he had gone over his limit, he ended his speech by saying to now listen to the Supreme Leader, although the following speaker was Hassan Khomeini.[245] A crowd situated in front of the speaker booed Hassan Khomeini and did not allow him to finish his speech. One of the slogans was *"Navadeh Ruhollah, Seyyed Hassan Nasrollah"* [Grandson of Ruhollah, Seyyed Hassan Nasrollah]. Ruhollah is the first name of Ayatollah Ruhollah Khomeini, and Nasrollah is the Secretary-General of the Hezbollah in Lebanon. They also shouted slogans against Moussavi and Rafsanjani, including *"Marg Bar Moussavi"* [Death to Moussavi].[246] When Hassan Khomeini stopped his speech, the disrupting crowd began their jubilation and cheered. All these shocking events occurred on the day commemorating the death of Ayatollah Khomeini, ostensibly one of the saddest days in the Islamic Republic's history to Khomeini's grandson, who is the spokesman of the family, at the mausoleum of which he is the Director. Hassan Khomeini's father, Ahmad Khomeini, is also buried in that mausoleum.

Such an insult to the spokesman of the Khomeini family in front of the Supreme Leader was unprecedented and indicated the great divide among the ruling elites. Khamenei kissed Hassan Khomeini and then began his own speech. In his speech, not only did the Supreme Leader not condemn his supporters, but he harshly attacked the reformists. In the following days, all the major reformist groups strongly condemned the insult to Hassan Khomeini. Virtually all the reformists regarded the disrupting group as being a highly organized group who had been instructed and trained to do this. They blamed Ahmadinejad as among those who pre-planned this insult to Hassan Khomeini.[247]

Ali Motahhari, the hardline member of the Majles, criticized the disruption. Ali Motahhari is the son of Ayatollah Morteza Motahhari, who was the main intellectual of the fundamentalist camp, who played a prominent role in the founding of the Islamic Republic. Ayatollah Motahhari was assassinated after the revolution. Ali Motahhari issued a statement and stated that the disruption was a "bitter

---

245 Radio Farda, *"Dabir Setad Markazi Bozorgdasht Ayatollah Khomeini, Joziyat Ekhlal Dar Sokhanrani Hassan Khomeini Ra Montashar Kard"* [The Secretary of the Central Headquarters of the Commemoration of Ayatollah Khomeini Published the Details of the Disruptions of Hassan Khomeini's Speech] (June 8, 2010), http://www.radiofarda.com/archive/news/20100608/143/143.html?id=2065482.
246 Radio Farda, *"Vakonesh Mokhalefan Va Havadaran Dowlat Beh Qateq Sokhanrani Hassan Khomeini"* [Reactions of Opponents and Supporters of the Government to the Disruption of Hassan Khomeini's Speech] (June 5, 2010), http://www.radiofarda.com/content/f6_Iran_Khomeini_Reactions/2063035.html.
247 Ibid.

event," that it was "pre-planned," and that "the President personally had the primary role in this."[248] Some hardline members of the Majles said that they wanted to expel Motahhari from the Majles and that the judiciary should investigate him. Motahhari responded that if he was expelled from the hardline faction, he would create a third faction composed of some of the members of the hardline and reformist factions.[249]

The first anniversary of the election was to be another major confrontation between the hardline regime and its opponents. It was widely expected that massive numbers would march on the first anniversary of the June 12 election to show, again, that the protest movement was strong and did not submit to the government. Moussavi and Karrubi for a long time had been talking about the anniversary. Several weeks before the anniversary, the two announced that they had officially asked for a permit to hold a "silent march" on the anniversary. All the major reformist groups also made official requests for permission from the Ministry of the Interior and the Tehran local government. On June 10, 2010, Moussavi and Karrubi made the surprise announcement that because the authorities refused to issue a permit, they were calling off their march in order to prevent bloodshed. To everyone's surprise, they did not have an alternative plan of action. Moussavi and Karrubi held an 87-minute video press conference via the internet with several reformist sites and groups.[250] Shortly thereafter, Moussavi issued his Statement Number 18.[251] In this long statement, entitled a charter for the Green Movement, Moussavi reiterated his strong support for the fundamentalist constitution and working within the parameters of the system of the Islamic Republic. Although it is well known that many of the protesters on the streets were strongly secular and demanded an "Iranian Republic," which meant a secular republic, Moussavi's charter explicitly excluded the seculars from the Green Movement and explicitly considered the Green Movement an Islamist movement. The charter contains a sec-

---

248 Parleman News, *"Ali Motahhari: Shakhs Ahmadinejad Dar Memaneaat Az Sokhanrani Seyyed Hassan Khomeini Naqsh Dasht"* [Ali Motahhari: Ahmadinejad Personally Had a Role in Preventing the Speech of Seyyed Hassan Khomeini] (June 5, 2010), http://new.parlemannews.net/index.aspx?n= 11645. Parleman News is the official website of the reformist faction in the Majles.

249 BBC Persian, *"Ali Motahhari: Agar Osolgarayan Ekhrajam Konanad, Ferakciuni Jadid Tashkil Midaham"* [Ali Motahhari: If the Hardliners Expel Me, I Will Create a New Faction] (June 8, 2010), http://www.bbc.co.uk/persian/iran/2010/06/100608_l07_iran89_motahari_parliament.shtml.

250 See the interview conducted and placed on YouTube on June 11, 2010, http://www.youtube.com/ watch?v=GQoF5Q_QZSA&feature.

251 Moussavi, *"Matn Bayaniyeh Shomareh 18 Va Manshoori Baray Jonbesh Sabz: Ba Qamati Sarafraz Garcheh Majrooh Va Habs Keshideh Eastadehim"* [Content of the Statement Number 18 and Charter for the Green Movement; Standing Tall Although Wounded and Detained], Kaleme (June 15, 2010), http://www.kaleme.com/1389/03/25/klm-22913.

tion entitled *"Hoviyat Sabz"* [Green Identity]. The charter explicitly describes its *"hoviyat"* [identity] as *"Irani-Islami"* [Islamic-Iranian]. The charter states:

> The Green Movement along with accepting plurality within the movement, is adamant about the continuation of the presence of the compassionate religion that is full of mercy, kindness, morality, ethics and honoring the human, and the path for strengthening of religious values in the society are in strengthening the ethical and compassionate aspects of the sublime religion of Islam and the System of the Islamic Republic. ...
>
> The Green Movement is an Islamic-Iranian movement [*jonbeshi Irani-Islami*] that is seeking to gain a prosperous, free, and advanced Iran. Based on this, any Iranian individual who accepts the collective *Towhidi* [Divine Unitary] wisdom as the foundation of the struggle for the establishment of a better tomorrow for one's country, is among the activists of the Green Movement.[252]

On June 20, Karrubi released his statement.[253] Karrubi restated his opposition to the hardliners (including the Supreme Leader), his support for the constitution, and his promise to stand with the people (who were opposing the hardliners) to the end.

The cancellation of the protest march on the anniversary of the election was a major retreat by Moussavi and Karrubi. The charter by Moussavi also alienated the secular opposition, which was the backbone of much of the protests. Some believe that the primary intention of Moussavi is to undermine the support base of the hardliners by showing them that the Green Movement would actually help the regime. This strategy would also deprive the hardline leadership of arresting him and Karrubi. This strategy, however, badly undermined Moussavi in the eyes of the secular forces. Moussavi has made numerous critical remarks against other opposition groups.

2.4.10 February 2011, Revival of the Green Movement and Arrests of Moussavi and Karrubi

The relative quiet between January 2010 and January 2011 made it appear that the hardliners had succeeded in smashing the Green Movement. Many had erroneously interpreted the relative quiet as the successful crushing of the Green Movement.

---

252 Ibid. My translation.
253 Karrubi, *"Bayaniyeh Mohem Mehdi Karrubi Dar Mored Ekhtiyarat Velayat Faqih"* [The Significant Statement of Mehdi Karrubi on the Powers of the Supreme Leader], Saham News (June 20, 2010), http://www.sahamnews.org/?p=4091. An English translation of parts of Karrubi's statement is available at http://www.zamaaneh.com/enzam/2010/06/opposition-leader-critici-2.html.

But the events in February showed that the resentments were smoldering during that period. The trigger came with the unexpected protests in January 2011 in Tunisia and Egypt. Moussavi and Karrubi called for protests on February 14, 2011 to show support for and solidarity with the protest movements in Tunisia and Egypt. Despite the heavy presence of coercive apparatuses, massive numbers showed up. Some estimates were in the hundreds of thousands. My estimate, based on extensive YouTube evidence, clearly shows that many tens of thousands in Tehran participated. Perhaps the number may have even reached 100,000, but the figure of hundreds of thousands seems to be an exaggeration.

In April, Hojatolislam Ali Saeedi, the Representative of the Supreme Leader to the IRGC, and Hojatolislam Mojtaba Zolnour, Deputy Representative of the Supreme Leader to the IRGC, had stated that the regime was surprised at the very large numbers of protesters. Zolnour told a private gathering of clerics in Qom:

> To tell the truth, we cannot provide a permit for any gathering or march to them because as soon as they find any opportunity, they can gather a huge population. An example of this was on February 14, 2011 during which at the beginning the police personnel were frightened by the large population, and that the forces from IRGC and *Basij* had not gotten into action on time, it is not clear what would have happened. ... Initially parts of the coercive apparatuses were afraid and frightened and there was lack of coordination, but gradually, under the leadership of the Supreme Leader and the necessary coordination, the crisis was contained.[254]

The regime itself was shocked at the unexpectedly large numbers of protesters. In response the hardliners took Moussavi, Ms. Zahra Rahnavard-Moussavi, Karrubi, and Ms. Fatemeh Karrubi from their homes. For a while it was not clear where the four had been taken. The regime claimed that they were under house arrest, and that all their communications with the outside world had been cut, including contacts with their children. Apparently, the four had been taken to "safe-houses" belonging to some coercive apparatus not far from their own homes. Later on, their children were allowed a brief visit.

Minor protests followed. During the protests, the people burned state-owned (police, Tehran municipality, *Basij*, and IRGC) automobiles. The pro-Ahmadinejad

---

254 Kaleme, *"Eateraf Zolnour Beh natavani jaryan Eqtedar-Gara Az Sazemandehi Janiyat"* [Admission of Zolnour to Not Being Able to Gather Popular Support by the Hardliners] (April 18, 2011), http://www.kaleme.com/1390/01/29/klm-55429/; and Deutsche Welle, *"Negarani Do Rouhani Nezami Az Mahar Jonbesh Eaterazi"* [Worries of Two Clerics in the Armed Forces About Containing the Protest Movement] (April 19, 2011), http://www.dw-world.de/dw/article/0,,6507336,00.html?maca= per-rss-per-all-1491-rdf.

news agency, Raja News, states that on March 15, 2011, the people burned 15 autos.[255]

When Moussavi's father passed away in March 2011, Moussavi was neither allowed to see his father for the last time nor attend the funeral. Moussavi was allowed only a visit of a few minutes to see the body of his father after he had passed away. The funeral of Moussavi's father was held on March 31, 2011. During the funeral the security forces beat up those who shouted slogans against the regime or in support of Moussavi. Rafsanjani (still the Chairman of the Council for the Expediency of the System) issued a public statement expressing his condolences to Moussavi and calling him *"khadem"* [one who had provided great service] to Islam, the Islamic Republic, and to the revolution. Although under pressure from hardliners, Rafsanjani lost the Chairmanship of the Council for the Expediency of the System, he was still willing and able to publicly support the person whom the hardliners were calling the Chief of Sedition.

Moussavi, Rahnavard, and Karrubi were placed under house arrest and remain so until the time of writing in March 2023. Khatami is free but state media do not cover his views and there are some restrictions of his movements. Moussavi and Rahnavard do not enjoy the support they once had among millions of people. However, they are respected by many in the opposition, for the fact that they did not submit to Khamenei.

2.4.11 Conflict Between Ahmadinejad and Khamenei

There had existed some very minor differences between Ahmadinejad's inner circle and those close to the Supreme Leader and some other hardliners. These differences grew dramatically in mid-2010. Sometime between March and April 2011 the conflict between the President and the Supreme Leader erupted into the open, with news sites allied to each camp publishing details of their differences with language reserved for enemies.

On April 17, 2011, the Minister of Intelligence, Hojatolislam Heydar Moslehi, offered his resignation. The resignation was accepted by Ahmadinejad, but the Supreme Leader immediately refused the resignation and asked Moslehi to remain the Minister of Intelligence.[256] Different powerful hardline factions presented

---

255 Raja News, *"Kahesh Talafat Chaharshanbeh Souri Emsal/Zedde Enqelab Az Roo Miravad?"* [Reduction of Casualties of This Year's Charharshanbeh Souri/Will Anti-Revolutionaries Have Shame?] (March 19, 2011), http://www.rajanews.com/detail.asp?id=82236.
256 Ibid.

their critique of the episode.[257] The Supreme Leader explained the differences in an article in the *Sobh Sadeq*, the theoretical weekly of the IRGC. The target audience of the *Sobh Sadeq* is mid- to high-ranking officers in the IRGC. The article was authored by the Hojatolislam Saeedi, who is the Supreme Leader's Representative (SLR) to the IRGC. The SLR is the IRI's equivalent to the USSR's Political-Ideological Commissars. His role is to monitor the allegiance of the IRGC to the Supreme Leader.[258] According to Saeedi, Ahmadinejad's inner circle convinced Ahmadinejad to force Moslehi to resign or be fired. Saeedi offered two reasons. One was that Moslehi had fired one of the Deputies to the Minister of Intelligence who was close to Ahmadinejad's inner circle. A second reason, Saeedi said, was that earlier, an analyst in the Ministry had written a report stating that a group had infiltrated the Ministry which was influenced by the beliefs of the Hojjatieh Society. Saeedi wrote that the analyst was fired by the Ahmadinejad inner circle, and from then on Ahmadinejad's inner circle turned sour on Moslehi. And if the firing of Foreign Minister Mottaki had not encountered such a negative reaction, the inner circle might have fired Moslehi at the time the analyst was fired as well. Saeedi used the term *"baand"* to refer to Ahmadinejad's inner circle. This term has a negative connotation and is best translated as "gang." Most significantly, Saeedi called this group *"jaryan enherafi."* The term *"jaryan"* means "current" or "group." And the term *"enherafi"* means "deviant." The term *"jaryan enherafi"* [deviant current] began to be used in early 2011 by hardliners close to the Supreme Leader against Ahmadinejad's inner circle.

Saeedi criticized Ahmadinejad for not consulting the Supreme Leader before firing Foreign Minister Mottaki and Intelligence Minister Moslehi. Much of the criticism targeted the inner circle. Saeedi quoted the criticism of Ayatollah Mesbah on the possibility that the inner circle included members of the Freemasons. Although it seems bizarre to Westerners, the allegation of being infiltrated by the Freemasons is one of the worst attacks by the hardline elements and is synonymous with working for the spy agencies of Israel, the U.K., and the U.S. This harsh attack by Mesbah was a most serious threat to Ahmadinejad to stop acting autonomously from the Supreme Leader and fully and unequivocally submit to him in all matters.

---

257 Deutsche Welle, *"Fetneh Nofozihay Dowlati' Dar Azl Moslehi"* ["Sedition of Those Who Have Infiltrated the Government" in the Dismissal of Moslehi] (April 19, 2011), http://www.dw-world.de/dw/article/0,,15001857,00.html?maca=per-rss-per-all-1491-rdf.

258 Mehdi Saeedi, *"Bazi Hashiyeh Sazan Bah Manafeh Melli"* [Playing with the National Interests by the Band], *Sobh Sadeq*, http://www.sobhesadegh.ir/Sadegh.htm, republished at Iran Emrooz (April 26, 2011), http://www.iran-emrooz.net/index.php?/news2/28274/.

The conflict reached an unprecedented height in late April and early May 2011. To show his displeasure, Ahmadinejad did not go to work for 11 days. He did not attend two meetings of the cabinet which Moslehi attended. During this time, unprecedented public and vulgar attacks were launched by hardline elements against Ahmadinejad and his supporters. Various hardline elements openly expressed their support for the absolute power of the Supreme Leader. On May 5, 2011, Gen. Jaafari, the Commander-in-Chief of the IRGC stated: "To remain in the path of the revolution means absolute obedience to the Supreme Leader and any person from any class or position or responsibility that he possesses must bow his head to the order of the Supreme Leader; otherwise, he has not understood the meaning of the Islamic Revolution and Velayat Faqih [the Rule of Supreme Leadership]."[259]

2.4.12 Political Paralysis

By early 2010, a stalemate had been reached. The reformists failed to overturn the announced election result but succeeded in capturing the streets on several occasions. Reformist tactics probably accentuated the internal conflicts of the hardliners. The retreats by Moussavi and Karrubi, however, alienated the secular forces from them.

The demands for an Iranian republic (i.e., a secular and democratic republican system) continued to increase, but the various democratic groups within the solid opposition failed to create a common platform or gather around one leadership. Therefore, their great potential remained unrealized. Modern middle classes and modern working classes, both with long secular attachments and history, remain to be organized by the democratic opposition. By and large, other members of the solid opposition (monarchists, PMOI, Marxists) tended to remain on the sidelines.

In the aftermath of the disputed election, students, professors, women's groups, and human rights organizations joined the struggle.[260] Glaringly absent were the workers' organizations and teachers.

---

259 Khabar Online, *"Farmandah Sepah: Mardom Enheraf Az Masir Enqelab Va Rahbari Ra Tahamol Nemikonand"* [IRGC Commander: The People Will Not Tolerate Deviation from the Path of Revolution and Leader] (May 5, 2011), http://khabaronline.ir/news-148846.aspx.

260 On the joining of the women's movement with the protest movement see the interview conducted with one of Iran's foremost feminist activists, Noushin Ahmadi Khorasani, with one of the major feminist organizations, *Madreseh Feministi* [Feminist School]. Available at http://www.iran-emrooz.net/index.php?/politic2/more/21973/.

There was little doubt in June 2009 that the economic situation was very bad and was getting worse. The price of oil was very high between 2004 and mid-2008. The government received $55 billion in export of oil and natural gas in the 2005–2006 fiscal year, in comparison to $23 billion in the 2002–2003 fiscal year.[261] The price of oil reached a peak of $147 per barrel in July 2008. It declined to about $40 in early 2009. Between late 2009 and early 2010, it mostly fluctuated between $70 and $80 per barrel. The price of oil jumped to over $100 a barrel in early 2011. During the first four years of Ahmadinejad's government, Iran received $278.79 billion in oil income. For the five years of Ahmadinejad's government, Iran received more than $340 billion in oil income alone. According to the Iranian Labour News Agency's (ILNA's) calculations, in the first four years of Ahmadinejad's government, Iran received more oil income than in the previous 16 years combined. Iran's oil income during Iranian calendar years 1360–1368 [1981–1989] was $102.72 billion; during 1368–1376 [1989–1997] was $123.6 billion; and during 1376–1384 [1997–2005] was $176 billion dollars.[262]

According to official data, in 2008 the annual inflation rate was about 30% and unemployment almost 11%.[263] Many believe the real rates to have been much higher. Out of a population of 70 million, at least 14 million live below the poverty line, defined as per capita monthly income of about $100. In the three years 2006–2009, according to one high-ranking official, the government withdrew about $46 billion from the reserve fund (established in order to provide a cushion when the price of oil drops). The fund stood at just $7 billion in mid-2009.[264]

Part of the economic problem was due to Ahmadinejad's policies which injected massive amounts of money (from the high oil prices between 2005 to late 2008) into short-term projects. It was probably intended to boost political support for the regime among the poor in large cities and medium-sized towns. Previous administrations under President Rafsanjani (1989–1997) and President Khatami (1997–2005) did try to help local industrial production and non-oil exports. Ahmadine-

261 Bill Samii, "Iran: Weak Economy Challenges Populist President," Eurasianet (July 23, 2006), www.eurasianet.org/departments/business/articles/pp072306.shtml.

262 ILNA, *"Dar 5 Sal Gozashteh 340 Millianrd Dollar Daramad Nafti Kasb Shodeh Ast"* [During the Past 5 Years Oil Income Has Been 340 Billion Dollars] (June 9, 2010), http://www.ilna.ir/newsText. aspx?ID=128346. ILNA is an official news agency devoted to labor news. ILNA has remained relatively autonomous from Ahmadinejad's faction and has produced reports not supported by Ahmadinejad's government. Ayatollah Khomeini's powerful grandson, Hojatolislam Hassan Khomeini, has publicly lent his support to ILNA, thus undermining Ahmadinejad's government from placing his own loyalists at its helm.

263 Hossein Aryan, "Falling Price of Oil Compounds Iranian President's Problems," Radio Free Europe/Radio Liberty (October 29, 2008), http://www.rferl.org/content/By_Hossein_Aryan/1336169.html.
264 The data are from Hossein Aryan, ibid.

jad's policies seemed to have been intended to quickly gain or re-energize the support of the regime among the poor, who had suffered in the previous 16 years under the presidencies of Rafsanjani and Khatami. Therefore, Ahmadinejad's policies on the one hand injected massive amounts of cash into the economy while, on the other, undermining domestic production and investments (by domestic and international investors). These policies made products more expensive and scarcer. They substantially increased the inflation rate. In order to combat inflation and satisfy demand for goods generated by his policies, Ahmadinejad's government reduced import duties on 63 goods, including agricultural goods (such as rice, tea, and sugar).[265] These policies also caused bankruptcies among domestic industries. However, the importers (usually connected to centers of power) have profited greatly.[266] According to the Customs Office, imports for the Iranian year 1387 (March 20, 2008 to March 20, 2009) were $56 billion.[267] This constituted the highest import in Iran's history. The imports for 1387 were 30% higher than those of the previous year (March 20, 2007 to March 20, 2008). According to the Central Bank of Iran (CBI), during Ahmadinejad's first four years of presidency, Iran's imports reached $220 billion.[268] The Customs Office, which works directly under the administration, has provided the figure of $185 billion for the same period. Whichever figure is true, it constitutes a record high in imports for any President since the 1979 revolution.

The policies of the Ahmadinejad government had caused chaos in many industries. For example, these policies are regarded by many experts in Iran to have caused the "astronomical rise" in the price of red meat, as well as shock and plunge in the domestic animal husbandry industry.[269] According to experts, Iranian consumers pay exorbitant prices for red meat while domestic producers are

---

265 Behzad Kashmiripour, *"Afzayesh Varedat; Rah Mahar Tavvarom?"* [Increasing Imports; The Way to Contain Inflation?], Deutsche Welle (June 14, 2008), http://www.dw-world.de/dw/article/0,,3412457,00.html.
266 Javad Talei, *"Hazf Yarabeh-ha Va Ehtemal Naa-Aramihay Gostardeh Dar Iran"* [Eliminating Subsidies and the Possibilities for Widespread Instability in Iran], Deutsche Welle (October 28, 2010), http://www.dw-world.de/dw/article/0,,4835454,00.html.
267 Behzad Kashmiripour, *"Karnameh Saderat Va Varedat Iran Dar Sal 1387"* [Imports and Exports Results of Iran in the Year 1387], Deutsche Welle (April 12, 2009), http://www.dw-world.de/dw/article/0,,4171924,00.html.
268 Javad Talei, *"Hazf Yarabeh-ha Va Ehtemal Naa-Aramihay Gostardeh Dar Iran"* [Eliminating Subsidies and the Possibilities for Widespread Instability in Iran], Deutsche Welle (October 28, 2009), http://www.dw-world.de/dw/article/0,,4835454,00.html.
269 Ali Pirvali, *"Sanat Damparvari Iran Dar Shook Va Soqoot"* [Iran's Animal Husbandry Industry in the Circuit of Shock and Plunge], ILNA (March 28, 2010), http://www.ilna.ir/newsText.aspx?ID=114469.

facing serious challenges and many are on the verge of bankruptcy.[270] However, the importers (closely connected to centers of power) have made huge profits. According to ILNA, some critics believe: "the existence of importation mafia is one of the factors which has impacted the red meat market."[271]

As long as the price of oil was high, the Iranian government was able to manage the shortage of goods through imports and abate the problem of inflation with increased subsidies. However, with the unexpected drop in the price of oil in late 2008, the government began to lack enough funds to carry out those measures.

According to the government's data, the economic situation began deteriorating in late 2008 and the decline was projected to continue for 2010.[272] The government had the goal of annual economic growth of 8% for the Iranian calendar year of 1388 (March 20, 2009 to March 20, 2010). However, the annual growth in 1387 (March 20, 2008 to March 20, 2009) was 2.3% and the preliminary data for 1388 were estimated to be between 1.5 and 2%. According to Ahmad Tavakoli, who is a powerful hardline member of the Majles: "our economic recession began in 1387 and if next year economic growth is not negative, it will be close to zero."[273] According to the Iranian government's Statistical Center of Iran, the unemployment rate rose in January 2010 to 11.3%. It was up 1.8% compared with the previous year.[274] The Iranian government claims that the inflation rate in 2010 fell to 12.2%.[275] According to the data released by the IMF in April 2011, the real GDP

---

270 Ibid.

271 Ibid.

272 Mehr News, *"Roshd Eghtesadi Parsal 2.3 Darsad Bood; Ehtemal Roshd Manfi Ya Sefr Dar Sal 89"* [Economic Growth Rate Was 2.3 Percent Last Year; The Possibility of Growth for the Year 2010–2011 Either Negative or Zero] (February 20, 2010), http://www.mehrnews.com/fa/newsdetail.aspx?pr=a&NewsID=1037312.

273 Ibid.

274 Payvand Iran News, "Iran Unemployment Rate Hits 11.3%" (January 11, 2010), http://www.payvand.com/news/10/jan/1106.html.

275 Press TV, "Iran's Inflation Rate Falls to 12.2 Percent" (February 11, 2010), http://www.presstv.ir/detail.aspx?id=118386&sectionid=351020102. Many believe the actual inflation rate might be twice the announced official rate. Jahangir Amuzegar, "The Rial Problem," *Foreign Policy* web edition (February 11, 2010), http://www.foreignpolicy.com/articles/2010/02/11/the_rial_problem. According to Amuzegar, the inflation rate reached 29.5% in September 2009. During the presidential televised debates in June, Ahmadinejad claimed that the inflation rate was 15%. Moussavi showed a document from Iran's Central Bank indicating that the inflation rate was around 25%. Nahid Siamdoust, "Ahead of Iran Election, President's Rivals Gain Hope," *Time Magazine* online (June 11, 2009), http://www.time.com/time/world/article/0,8599,1903841,00.html.

growth rate in 2010 was 1% and inflation was 12.5%.[276] The IMF report projected the real GDP growth for 2011 to be zero and the inflation rate 22.5%.

The reduction in income, due to lower crude oil prices (since late 2008 and early 2009) and the bad economy in Iran, has forced the government to reduce subsidies. The government spends about 100 billion dollars a year in subsidizing refined petroleum, heating oil, utilities (e.g., electricity, water), bus fares, and foodstuffs (bread, rice, cooking oil).[277] A dispute emerged between Ahmadinejad and the Majles (controlled by the hardliners) on how much and over what intervals to cut the subsidies.[278] Some of the concerns over the proposed massive cuts in subsidies included inflation, serious economic dislocations, and disorder among the poor.[279]

According to ILNA, Iran has suffered major reduction in attracting direct foreign investments (FDI) in recent years.[280] This dramatic reduction in FDI occurred while Iran's neighbors succeeded in dramatically increasing FDI. The ILNA report states that in 2002, FDI in Iran was $3.66 billion. In 2008, FDI declined to $1.49 billion. The Fourth Development Plan had envisaged FDI to be around $3.17 billion. ILNA cites comparable data for Saudi Arabia, Turkey, Egypt, Kazakhstan, and Pakistan. For Saudi Arabia, FDI rose from $450 million in 2002 to $38.22 billion in 2008. For Turkey, FDI rose from about $1 billion in 2002 to about $18.28 billion in 2008. For Kazakhstan, FDI rose from $2.59 billion to $14.54 billion in 2008. For Egypt, FDI rose from less than $1 billion in 2002 to $9.5 billion in 2008. For Pakistan, FDI rose from less than $1 billion in 2002 to $5.44 billion in 2008. The ILNA report concludes

276 IMF, "Islamic Republic of Iran and the IMF" (April 16, 2011), http://www.imf.org/external/country/irn/index.htm. The report entitled "World Economic Outlook" is available at http://www.imf.org/external/pubs/ft/weo/2011/01/index.htm.
277 Mehr News, "Ahmadinejad Proposes Referendum on Subsidy Reform Plan," (March 20, 2010), http://www.mehrnews.com/en/NewsDetail.aspx?NewsID=1054038.
278 BBC Persian, *"Pasokh Eqtesad-danan Majles Iran Beh Ahmadinejad"* [The Response of the Economists in Iran's Majles to Ahmadinejad] (March 20, 2010), http://www.bbc.co.uk/persian/lg/iran/2010/03/100320_l10_ahmadinejad_subsidies_tavakoli_naderan_mesbahi_reax.shtml.
279 Javad Talei, *"Hazf Yarabeh-ha Va Ehtemal Naa-Aramihay Gostardeh Dar Iran"* [Eliminating Subsidies and the Possibilities for Widespread Instability in Iran], Deutsche Welle (October 28, 2009), http://www.dw-world.de/dw/article/0,,4835454,00.html; BBC Persian, *"Pasokh Eqtesad-danan Majles Iran Beh Ahmadinejad"* [The Response of the Economists in Iran's Majles to Ahmadinejad] (March 20, 2010), http://www.bbc.co.uk/persian/lg/iran/2010/03/100320_l10_ahmadinejad_subsidies_tavakoli_naderan_mesbahi_reax.shtml.
280 ILNA, *"Sarmayehha Mizbani Irani Ra Doost Nadarand: Kahesh Shadid Sarmayeh-Gozari Khareji Iran Az Sal 2002 ta 2008"* [Investments Do Not Like Iranian Hosts: Severe Reductions in Foreign Investments in Iran Between 2002 and 2008] (June 6, 2010), http://www.ilna.ir/newsText.aspx?ID=127547.

by stating: "The trend for all these countries has been positive and only for Iran due to severe economic crises, it also witnesses decline in investment indices."[281]

Decline in oil prices, the effects of sanctions on the Iranian economy, and bad economic policies of Ahmadinejad's government have led to a very bad economic situation in 2010.

2.5 Conclusion

The 2009–2010 mass protests were a turning point in Iranian history. Initially, the demand of the protesters was simply for the votes to be counted. In other words, the demand was for Moussavi to be declared President instead of Ahmadinejad. As the hardliners used massive violence, the demands of the protesters became increasingly democratic. By December 2009, the protesters had targeted Khamenei and demanded his removal.

The post-election protest movement was composed of diverse groups and strata with diverse demands. Some wished merely to reform the system while many wished to replace the clerical regime with democracy. Many protesters explicitly demanded the overthrow of the system. Although many individuals in the reform segment of the Green Movement have been hostile to Khamenei, they do not wish for the overthrow of the system. What is significant is that, by November, demands for the replacement of the Islamic Republic with an Iranian Republic (i. e., a secular democratic system) had gained ascendancy.

On February 11, the regime showed that it could control the streets. The reformist leaders have hesitated, on several occasions, to make bold moves. For example, on June 15, 2009, they could have easily led the 3 million protesters to take over the Presidential Palace or even the Residence of the Supreme Leader. Or on Ashura, when state security collapsed in much of the capital, the reformist leaders could have led the protesters to take over major state buildings. On the anniversary of the election, they called off their call for protests instead of personally leading the protests. Some believe that the reformist leaders are simply weak. Others believe that the reformists are part of the system, and they merely wish for minor reform and oppose moves that would cause the collapse of the system. Still others think that the reformists wish to avoid bloodshed and their strategy is to convince the Supreme Leader to compromise.

The dominant feature of the post-election crisis is the unintended consequences of political leaders' decisions. Supreme Leader Khamenei had assumed that his

---

281 Ibid.

words were final, and the reformist members of the oligarchy would submit to his orders. Two reformist candidates, Moussavi and Karrubi, refused to submit—unexpectedly and bravely. It was unimaginable that the reformist members of the fundamentalist oligarchy, whose privileges depend on the maintenance of the current regime, would call upon the people to openly defy the Supreme Leader and protest on the streets until the election was nullified; but they did. It was assumed that a population intimidated into silence by a violent regime would not risk their lives, liberties, and jobs, engaging in prolonged mass protests; but they did, and did so courageously. The democratic opposition, whose ideals animate the masses, and whose slogans the people shout, has shown great lack of competence. The masses on the streets have not followed the advice of the democratic opposition although they have engaged in actions that most benefit the democratic opposition.

The events of July 9 showed that the people were willing to risk their lives defying the hardliners. Rafsanjani's speech undermined the efforts of the hardliners to crush any challenge to the Supreme Leader's order for all to respect the announced election result. Continued protests indicate the increasing loss of legitimacy of the regime and the willingness of the people to resist the regime.

Between June 2009 and June 2010, hardliners were weakened by the loss of legitimacy, loss of many members, and severe internal conflicts. They have contained the situation but failed to crush it. During this period, the reformists failed to capture power despite the massive support of the population, leading to much disappointment among their bases.

Chapter 3
Mass Protests, December 2017 – January 2018

The protests that began on Thursday December 28, 2017 were the largest such protests since 2009.[1] Within days, the protests had spread to about 40 cities. The 2017–2018 protests were very different from those in 2009.

The protests in 2009 began with the reformist members of the ruling fundamentalist oligarchy who were unhappy with the election results announced by the regime. The reformist fundamentalists believed that they had received more votes than the hardline Ahmadinejad. The reformist fundamentalists wanted to mobilize the people to put pressure on the hardline Supreme Leader Ayatollah Ali Khamenei to reverse course and allow their candidate to assume the presidency. Soon, however, the protests became more complicated. One group, under the leadership of the reformist fundamentalists, kept the same demands and its slogans were simply asking for Khamenei to allow Mir-Hussein Moussavi to become President.

Another group, without any organized leadership, promoted pro-democracy demands and used slogans such as: *"Marg bar Khamenei"* [Death to Khamenei]; *"Marg bar Dictator"* [Death to the Dictator]; *"Marg bar Asl Velayat Faqih"* [Death to the Principle of Rule by a Shia Cleric]; *"Zendanee Siasi Azad Bayad Gardad"* [Free Political Prisoners]; *"Na Ghazeh, Na Lobnan, Janam Faday Iran"* [Neither Gaza, Nor Lebanon, My Life for Iran]; and *"Esteghlal, Azadi, Jumhuri Irani"* [Independence, Freedom, Iranian Republic]. The term "Iranian Republic" was used in contradistinction to the term "Islamic Republic," indicating that their demands were beyond mere reform within the fundamentalist regime, and they wanted a democracy. Despite tensions among them, nevertheless, both sides cooperated closely against the hardline fundamentalist faction. The 2009 protesters came largely from the middle classes. The working classes were, by and large, absent from the protests.

For the presidential elections in 2013 and 2017, Khamenei allowed all three main fundamentalist factions (reformist, expedient, and hardline) to have approved candidates. The reformist fundamentalist candidates (Mohammad Reza Aref in 2013 and Eshagh Jahangiri in 2017) withdrew from the race and threw their support behind Hassan Rouhani, the main leader of the expedient faction. Reformist fundamentalists have become junior partners with the expedient faction

---

1 Radio Farda, "Latest On Continuing Unrest In Iran—*Basij* Enters the Foray to Crack Down" (December 31, 2017), https://en.radiofarda.com/a/28947733.html.

https://doi.org/10.1515/9783111280288-005

both in Rouhani's cabinet and in the Islamic Consultative Assembly (the funda-mentalist-only parliament).

The 2017–2018 protests were different in four major respects from the 2009 protests. First, the protesters were targeting not only Khamenei but also Rouhani. One of the main slogans of the current protests was *"Marg bar Rouhani"* [Death to Rouhani]. Another slogan was *"Esteghlal, Azadi, Jumhuri Irani"* [Independence, Freedom, Iranian Republic]. The protesters were attacking the whole regime, in-cluding all three factions. The reformist fundamentalists have condemned the pro-democracy and anti-regime protests.

Second, the protesters were supporters of various opposition groups such as the Iran National Front (a coalition of liberal democrats and social democrats), monarchists, the PMOI (also known as MKO, NCRI, MeK), and the Democratic Party of Iranian Kurdistan. In addition to the usual pro-democracy slogan "Inde-pendence, Freedom, and Iranian Republic," in three cities slogans in support of monarchy were also heard.

Third, and perhaps most significantly, there were large numbers of working-class participants in the protests. One of their slogans is *"Marg bar Gerani"* [Death to High Prices]. Some of the slogans include words such as *"Akhund Sar-maydar"* [Capitalist Shia Clerics] and *"Dozd"* [Thief]. What is most interesting is that economic grievances and political grievances were coalescing to make a pow-erful protest movement. The protesters blamed their economic woes on the astro-nomical theft by fundamentalist rulers who control most financial institutions and banks. Unlike the 2009 protests, these protests have targeted banks and have smashed bank windows. And, like the protests of 2009, these current protests also targeted police vehicles and *Basij* headquarters.

Fourth, during the 2009 protests slogans condemning the fundamentalist re-gime's foreign policy played only a minor role. As mentioned earlier, one of the slogans wase "Neither Gaza, Nor Lebanon, My Life for Iran." Also, when the re-gime asked the people on the anniversary of the take-over of the U.S. Embassy in Tehran to shout, "Death to America," the protesters shouted "Death to Russia." During the 2017–2018 protests, however, slogans condemning the regime's foreign policy were playing very prominent roles. One of the main slogans of the 2017–2018 protests was *"Sorieh Ra Raha Kon, Fekri Be Hale Ma Kon"* [Leave Syria Alone, Do Something For Us]. This reflects the recognition that the enormous sums the regime spends in Syria (as well as in Iraq, Lebanon, and elsewhere) are at the cost of the welfare of the Iranian people who suffer poverty, unemploy-ment, and high prices.

3.1 Causes

There are three main causes for the 2017–2018 protests. First, the fundamentalist regime is dictatorial, reactionary, extremist, and terrorist. The overwhelming majority of the Iranian people want a political system that is democratic, modern, and moderate, as well as to live in peace with the world and the people in the region. Therefore, the fundamentalist regime lacks legitimacy in the eyes of the vast majority of the population. The people, thus, look for opportunities to express their opposition to the regime.

Second, for the previous four-and-a-half years, President Rouhani had been making grandiose promises to greatly improve the economic situation, reduce repression, tackle official corruption, and avoid wars. Rouhani had hugely increased the expectation of the people that such reforms were feasible within the fundamentalist system. The huge gap between expectation and reality is fueling the current protests. The huge windfall from the nuclear deal has gone mostly to fundamentalist rulers through outright theft, budget provisions to the coercive apparatuses (IRGC, *Basij*), and spent on the regime's proxies and wars in Syria, Iraq, Lebanon, Yemen, Bahrain, Palestine, and elsewhere. The overwhelming majority of the people have seen their own finances decline while the fundamentalist elites are becoming grotesquely wealthy. Although repression has slightly abated under Rouhani in comparison with the period under Ahmadinejad, the regime continues to be terribly repressive and dictatorial. Moreover, corruption by officials has boomed. The regime also keeps spending huge amounts on its bellicose adventurism abroad. Since early November, several prominent figures have expressed regret for having voted for Rouhani, which has been followed by an avalanche of people on social media expressing their regret as well. Ali Karimi, Iran's most beloved soccer star, was one such figure.

Third, President Trump's hostile rhetoric against the fundamentalist regime seems to have emboldened the Iranian people. President Obama's policy of appeasement of Khamenei had a terribly demoralizing effect on the Iranian people who oppose the fundamentalist regime. The Iranian people believe, rightly or wrongly, that they have an ally in the White House. This perception has formed due in some measure to the policies and rhetoric of the Trump administration. Also, there has been a major change in Voice of America (VOA) Persian-language satellite television. During the Obama administration, VOA's coverage tended to give a great deal of coverage to the views of those who were close to the expedient and reformist factions of the fundamentalist regime. During the Obama years, I was one of the few who was repeatedly invited to provide analysis that was critical of Obama's appeasement policy. Soon after Trump became President, VOA greatly increased coverage of various opposition groups, particularly the monarchists and the PMOI.

3.2 Policy Ramifications

President Trump and Vice-President Mike Pence wrote excellent tweets supporting the Iranian people.[2] The State Department spokeswoman also released a well-written statement supporting the Iranian people and condemning the repression of the people by the fundamentalist regime. Several Republicans in Congress (Senators Tom Cotton, Orrin Hatch, and Ted Cruz, and Speaker Paul Ryan, Congresswoman Ileana Ros-Lehtinen, and Congressman Mike Gallagher) also wrote in support of the Iranian people in their Twitter accounts.[3]

Hillary Clinton has also supported the Iranian protesters.[4] However, conspicuous by its absence has been support (as of the third day of protests) from Democrats in Congress. This is surprising because there are Democrats who historically have strongly condemned the fundamentalist regime and supported the Iranian pro-democracy demands. For example, Senators Robert Menendez, Ben Cardin, and Chuck Schumer, as well as Congressmen Brad Sherman and Elliot Engle.

Strong bipartisan support for the pro-democracy protests in Iran would have positive ramifications. First, the people would feel that the world hears them. This means that their sacrifices would not be in vain. As more people join protests, that would increase the self-confidence of the people in their strength. Second, the fundamentalist regime would become aware of the costs of repression. As more governments around the world and more political parties and political figures express support for democracy in Iran, the costs of repression for the fundamentalist regime go up.

It is too early to know the results of the current protests. The regime may succeed in crushing the current protests as it did the protests in 1981, 1998, 2003, and 2009. Or it may not. However, after each mass protest movement, the fundamen-

---

2 VOA, *"Hemayat President Trump Az Motarezan Dar Iran"* [President Trump's Support for Protesters in Iran] (December 29, 2017), https://ir.voanews.com/a/us-iran-protest-/4185384.html; VOA, *"Vakonesh Hillary Clinton Beh Eaterazha Dar Iran"* [Hillary Clinton's Reaction on the Protests in Iran] (December 31, 2017), https://ir.voanews.com/a/us-iran-protet-pence-clinton-/4186242.html.

3 VOA, *"Vakonesh Aazaey Kongreh Beh Eterazha Dar Iran"* [Reaction of Members of Congress to Protests in Iran] (December 30, 2017), https://ir.voanews.com/a/us-iran-congress-/4185301.html.

4 VOA, *"Vakonesh Hillary Clinton Beh Eaterazha Dar Iran"* [Hillary Clinton's Reaction on the Protests in Iran] (December 31, 2017), https://ir.voanews.com/a/us-iran-protet-pence-clinton-/4186242.html.

talists become a little weaker and mass grievances grow more acute. In a totalitarian regime, where there is no freedom of expression, free press, free political parties, or free elections, the ruling regime has to base its claim of popular support on the myth of mass support. In such regimes, the government claims that it has mass support despite lack of freedom and democracy. Such regimes attribute dissent to a small proportion of the population and accuse them of treason and being agents of foreign powers. So, when masses of people brave repression and protest on the streets they are undermining the propaganda and the legitimacy of the totalitarian regime.

At certain junctures in history, large numbers of men and women decide that they would rather stand and fight for their rights than live as slaves on their knees. They may succeed or fail to defeat the forces of repression and tyranny. These brave men and women in Iran today are literally risking their lives and liberties fighting against one of the most brutal regimes in the world. At a very minimum, we owe these men and women our support.

Chapter 4
The Political Situation in 2022

The fundamentalist regime is suffering from serious crises. These include a severe crisis of legitimacy, crisis of succession to the Supreme Leader, economic crisis, intra-elite factionalism, and confrontation with powerful foreign opponents. These crises have made the regime more unstable than before.

4.1 Crisis of Legitimacy

There is no reliable way to measure the support for or opposition to the regime. There are no free and democratic elections in Iran. Only members of the fundamentalist oligarchy are allowed to run in the elections. The data the regime presents on elections are not even accepted by members of the oligarchy. For example, in the 2009 presidential election, two top members of the fundamentalist oligarchy (Mir-Hussein Moussavi and Mehdi Karrubi) refused to accept the results the regime announced. Opinion surveys using phone interviews or door-to-door interviews are not credible in a country that is highly repressive and dictatorial.[1] Therefore, we can only guess the support bases of the regime and the opposition.

According to Sadegh Zibakalam, only 10 to 20 % of the population supports the regime.[2] Zibakalam is the most famous Political Science Professor at the University of Tehran. What makes Zibakalam's estimate significant is not his faculty position, but his status as one of the top intellectuals of the reformist and expedient factions of the fundamentalist regime. Zibakalam has been close to President Hassan Rouhani and Ayatollah Akbar Rafsanjani. Rafsanjani was one of the most powerful members of the ruling oligarchy, a two-term President, the Head of the Assembly of Experts that chose Khamenei for the position of Supreme Leader, and the Head of the Expediency Council (which allowed him access to the true vote counts). Zi-

---

1 Several scholars have attempted to conduct surveys and other ways to measure the attitudes of the Iranian people using various methods such as online surveys. For the best example, see Pooyan Tamimi Arab and Ammar Maleki, "Iran's Secular Shift: New Survey Reveals Huge Change in Religious Beliefs," The Conversation (September 10, 2020), https://theconversation.com/irans-secular-shift-new-survey-reveals-huge-changes-in-religious-beliefs-145253. For other examples of various observers who have attempted to measure indications of the attitudes of the Iranian people, see Kazemzadeh, "The Perils and Costs of a Grand Bargain," op. cit.
2 Sadegh Zibakalam, "If a Referendum was Held Today, Over 70 % Would Say No to an Islamic Republic," Deutsche Welle (January 5, 2018), https://www.youtube.com/watch?v=GuXyEtMgAOI.

https://doi.org/10.1515/9783111280288-006

bakalam, himself, was one of the top fundamentalists who was responsible for the purge of universities from professors and students who were liberal, secular, or Marxist during the "Islamic Cultural Revolution" in the early 1980s. In an interview with the Persian-language program of the German state news agency Deutsche Welle, Zibakalam said: "If there was a referendum on the Islamic Republic … over 70 percent of the people would vote no to the Islamic Republic, and the officials of the regime know this as well."[3] Many observers believe that the regime's base of support is less than 20% of the population.[4]

Iranians have been voting with their feet. According to the International Monetary Fund, Iran has had the largest "brain drain" in the world since the 1990s, with about 150,000 to 180,000 leaving the country annually.[5] An article in the *Los Angeles Times* places the number of Iranians leaving annually at 180,000.[6] According to the Medical Council of Iran, about 3,000 physicians emigrated from Iran in 2020.[7] One physician tells the *Los Angeles Times* correspondent in Tehran that about 30% of his colleagues have left Iran for Western Europe and North America since 2009.[8] According to Ali-Reza Monadi, Chairman of the Education and Research Committee of the Majles, in the Iranian calendar year 1398 (March 21, 2019 to March 19, 2020), about 900 university professors emigrated from Iran.[9] According to one official at Tehran Nurses' Organization, about 500 nurses officially file papers to leave Iran each month.[10] The official added that many nurses leave without filing officially.[11]

---

3 Ibid.

4 For indications on the social base of the regime, see MasoudKazemzadeh, "The Perils and Costs of a Grand Bargain," op. cit.; and Masoud Kazemzadeh, "Five Possible Outcomes Following the Mass Protests in Iran," Radio Farda (February 6, 2018), https://en.radiofarda.com/a/iran-unrest-scenarios-war-revolution-uprising/29023446.html.

5 Golnaz Esfandiari, "Iran: Coping With the World's Highest Rate of Brain Drain," Radio Farda (March 8, 2004), https://www.rferl.org/a/1051803.html; *Financial Tribune*, "Brain Drain Continues in Iran" (November 9, 2016), https://financialtribune.com/articles/people/53254/brain-drain-continues.

6 Omid Khazani, "Just When They're Needed Most, Iran's Doctors are Leaving in Droves," *The Los Angeles Times* (May 23, 2021), https://www.latimes.com/world-nation/story/2021-05-23/iran-brain-drain-doctors-exodus-covid-pandemic.

7 Ibid.

8 Ibid.

9 Iranian Students' News Agency (ISNA), "*Monadi: 900 Ostad Dar Sal 98 Az Iran Kharej Shodand*" [Mondai: 900 Professors Left Iran in the Year 2019–2020] (March 6, 2021), https://www.isna.ir/news/99121612250.

10 Iran International, "*Nezam Parastari Tehran: Mahaneh 500 Parastar Be Dalil Hoghogh Paeen Az Iran Mohajerat Mikonand*" [Tehran Nurses' Organization: Every Month 500 Nurses Emigrate From Iran Due to Low Wages] (April 11, 2021), https://iranintl.com/%D8%AA%D8%A7%D8%B2%D9%87-%DA%86%D9%87-%D8%AE%D8%A8%D8%B1/%D9%86%D8%B8%D8%A7%D9%85-%D9%BE%D8%

Many who have left Iran cite oppressive political and social policies of the fundamentalist regime for their decision to leave.[12] More recently, many cite the economic conditions after the sanctions that were imposed by the Trump administration.[13]

4.2 Crisis of Succession to the Supreme Leader

The fundamentalist system has concentrated enormous powers in the hands of the position of Supreme Leader. Khamenei has been Supreme Leader since 1989. Khamenei was born in 1939. In 2021, at age 82, he has been the Supreme Leader for 32 years. It is not clear who will be the next Supreme Leader. It is safe to assume that he and his supporters want someone who belongs to their hardline faction to be the next Supreme Leader. It is also safe to assume that members of the other fundamentalist factions (i.e., reformist and expedient) want someone from their faction to be the next Supreme Leader. This has further exacerbated intra-elite struggles for power. Khamenei has allowed members of reformist and expedient factions to run for the presidency, Majles, Assembly of Experts, and other positions. Many members of the hardline factions are not as inclusive as Khamenei and may use the powers of the Office of Supreme Leader to purge other factions. There is a high likelihood that there will be violence among fundamentalists after Khamenei's death.[14]

One of the few hardliners who had support among reformist and expedient members of the fundamentalist oligarchy was Gen. Qassem Soleimani.[15] Gen. Sol-

B1%D8%B3%D8%AA%D8%A7%D8%B1%DB%8C-%D8%AA%D9%87%D8%B1%D8%A7%D9%86-%
D9%85%D8%A7%D9%87%D8%A7%D9%86%D9%87-%DB%B5%DB%B0%DB%B0-%D9%BE%D8%B1%
D8%B3%D8%AA%D8%A7%D8%B1-%D8%A8%D9%87-%D8%AF%D9%84%DB%8C%D9%84-%D8%AD
%D9%82%D9%88%D9%82-%D9%BE%D8%A7%DB%8C%DB%8C%D9%86-%D8%A7%D8%B2-%D8%
A7%DB%8C%D8%B1%D8%A7%D9%86-%D9%85%D9%87%D8%A7%D8%AC%D8%B1%D8%AA-%
D9%85%DB%8C%E2%80%8C%DA%A9%D9%86%D9%86%D8%AF, also available at https://melliun.
org/iran/257437.
11 Ibid.
12 Esfandiari, "Iran," op. cit.
13 Khazani, "Just When They're Needed Most," op. cit.
14 Masoud Kazemzadeh, "Post-Khamenei Iran and American National Interests," *The Hill* (July 11, 2016), http://thehill.com/blogs/pundits-blog/foreign-policy/287175-post-khamenei-iran-and-american-national-interests.
15 Mohsen Ghaemmagham, *"Ghassem Soleimani—Dar Khedmat Nezam Estebdad Mazhabi Va Vali Faqih"* [Ghassem Soleimani—In Service of the System of Religious Dictatorship and Fundamentalist Regime] (January 19, 2020), Melliun, https://melliun.org/iran/223359.

eimani was, perhaps, the only hardliner who could have appealed to expedient and reformist fundamentalists to give a new hardline Supreme Leader a chance. The U.S. killing of Gen. Soleimani on January 3, 2020 eliminated the one major figure that might have been able to bring some calm and reassurance to various members of the ruling fundamentalist oligarchy.

The regime in general, and the IRGC in particular, had spent massive efforts in creating a political persona for Soleimani in the previous 15 years. Soleimani was portrayed as the "superman" who protected Iran's national interests and expanded Iran's power over neighboring countries. Since the early 2000s, he was kept assiduously out of Iran's domestic repressive policies and its intra-elite factional fights in public, although he was closely involved with domestic repression.[16] Soleimani was publicly portrayed as above politics and factions and as protector of Iran. But why did the regime do that? In my opinion, the IRGC had done this in order to create a person who could save the regime in its time of existential crisis. For example, if there was to be a war with the U.S., or in case of upheaval due to the passing of the Supreme Leader, Soleimani could play the role of the "savior" of the country. There is no one within the fundamentalist oligarchy that could play that role today.

The regime's propaganda was partially successful. Virtually all the supporters of the fundamentalist regime (reformists, expedients, and hardliners), as well as some non-fundamentalists supported Soleimani, as was demonstrated by the large-scale mourning of his death in January 2020. However, the lack of full success of the propaganda was demonstrated by the protesters during the protests in January 2020, when, after January 11, Soleimani banners that the regime had placed in various locations were burned and torn down.[17] Slogans chanted were not only against the Su-

---

16 In 1999, Soleimani was among a group of 24 high-ranking IRGC generals who wrote a confidential letter to then-President Mohammad Khatami threatening that if he did not crush the student protests, they would intervene themselves. The letter was leaked to the press and published to further embarrass Khatami. Supreme Leader Khamenei promoted these signatories in subsequent years. The letter was considered to be a veiled threat to carry out a coup by hardline IRGC generals. A translation of the letter is available at https://web.archive.org/web/20121012133424/http://www.iranian.com/News/1999/July/irgc.html.

17 VOA, *"Moatarezan Dar Tehran Bilbord Qassem Soleimani Ra Atesh Zadand"* [Protesters in Tehran Set Ablaze Qassem Soleimani's Billboards] (January 12, 2020), https://ir.voanews.com/episode/mtrdan-dr-thran-bylbwrd-qasm-slymany-ra-atsh-zdnd-235040; and VOA, *"Pareh Kardan Bannerhay Tablighati Qassem Soleimani Tavasot Mardom Dar Tehran"* [Tearing Down of Propaganda Banners for Qassem Soleimani by the People of Tehran] (January 12, 2020), https://ir.voanews.com/episode/iran-235050.

preme Leader and the IRGC but also called Soleimani a murderer.[18] Many protesters chanted that the IRGC and *Basij* are the equivalent of ISIS.[19] Moreover, many of the slogans were against all forms of dictatorship, whether fundamentalist or monarchist.[20]

The third anniversary of Soleimani's death occurred during the mass protests on January 3, 2023. Protesters throughout Iran began demolishing and burning Soleimani statuettes and banners.[21] The failure of the fundamentalist regime's propaganda demonstrates the political maturity and sophistication of the Iranian people who, despite massive amounts of propaganda, were not fooled by the fundamentalist regime. The regime buttressed its propaganda with repression against any disrespect toward Soleimani. For example, opponents of the regime began using the term "cutlet" to satirize the death of Soleimani with "Qassem cutlet" graffiti. The regime arrested Navab Ebrahimi, a celebrity chef and Instagram influencer with about 2.7 million followers, and closed down his restaurant because he placed a video on how to cook a Persian cutlet on the anniversary of Soleimani's death.[22]

4.3 Economic Crisis

The greater the financial resources and political legitimacy provided to the fundamentalist regime, the higher the likelihood that the fundamentalist regime may

---

18 VOA, "*Koshteh Nadadim Keh Sazesh Konim, Rahbar Ghatel Ro Setayesh Konim*" [We Did Not Have Deaths in Order to Compromise, and Praise the Murderer Supreme Leader] (January 13, 2020), https://ir.voanews.com/episode/kshth-ndadym-kh-sazsh-knym-rhbr-qatl-rw-staysh-knym-shar-hzaran-mtrd-nfr-dr-thran-235018; and VOA, "*Soleimani Ghatel-e Rahbaresh Ham Ghatel-e*" [Soleimani is a Murderer, His Leader is a Murderer], YouTube (January 11, 2020), https://www.youtube.com/watch?v=1bl6ITEoStQ&app=desktop.

19 VOA, "*Basiji Sepahi, Daesh Ma Shomae*" [Basij and IRGC You are Our ISIS] (January 13, 2020), https://ir.voanews.com/episode/bsyjy-spahy-dash-ma-shmayy-shar-mrdm-mtrd-dr-mshhd-235013.

20 VOA, "*Marg Bar Setamgar Cheh Shah Basheh Cheh Rahbar*" [Death to the Oppressor, Whether Shah or Supreme Leader] (January 13, 2020), https://ir.voanews.com/episode/iran-protest-sunday-235014. The slogans against monarchy were due to chants in favor of monarchists in other demonstrations. Monarchists usually chant "*Reza Shah Roohat Shad*" [Reza Shah, Your Soul Be Happy]. The pro-democracy protesters like the slogans "*Esteghlal, Azadi, Jomhuri Irani*" [Independence, Freedom, Iranian Republic] and "*Na Sharghi, Na Gharbi, Jomhuri Irani*" [Neither East, Nor West, Iranian Republic].

21 Iran International, "News" (January 5, 2023), https://www.youtube.com/watch?v=Hv6lth_7idM.

22 *The Guardian*, "Iran Arrests Celebrity Chef in Crackdown on Protests: Detainment of Navab Ebrahimi is Speculated to be Linked to Post about Cutlets, a Possible Taunt over General's Death" (January 5, 2023), https://www.theguardian.com/world/2023/jan/05/iran-arrests-celebrity-chef-in-crackdown-on-protests.

continue to muddle through. The greater the economic and political sanctions imposed on the fundamentalist regime, the higher the likelihood of regime collapse.

The pressures from the Trump administration, particularly the economic sanctions, have greatly undermined the regime's economic stability.[23] The nuclear accord, known as the Joint Comprehensive Plan of Action (JCPOA), was reached between the fundamentalist regime and P5+1 (five permanent members of the U.N. Security Council and Germany) on July 14, 2015. President Donald Trump withdrew from the JCPOA on May 8, 2018.

According to President Rouhani, the sanctions cost the government about $214 billion in revenues between May 2018 and August 2020.[24] According to Rouhani, Iran received about $120 billion from the sale of oil in 2011. Due to U.S. sanctions, Rouhani says that Iran only received about $20 billion in 2019.[25] According to Eshagh Jahangiri, First Deputy President, Iran's income from the sale of oil declined from about $100 billion (the year is not clear) to about $8 billion in the previous Iranian calendar year (March 20, 2019 to March 20, 2020).[26] Both Rouhani and Jahangiri are referring to Iran's sale of oil in 2019, but provide different figures.[27] Probably, Jahangiri is referring to the "legal" sale of Iran's oil, whereas Rouhani might be referring to both "legal" and "secret" sales of Iran's oil.[28] According to Majid Reza Hariri, the Chairman of the Iran–China Chamber of Commerce, before sanctions Iran used to sell about $120 billion dollars of oil annually during the

---

23 Behrang Tajdin, *"Eghtesad Iran Beh Ravayat Panj Nemoodar Dar Panjomin Salgard Barjam"* [Iran's Economy According to Five Charts on the Fifth Anniversary of the JCPOA], BBC Persian (July 13, 2020), https://www.bbc.com/persian/business-53381573.

24 Ibid.

25 Radio Farda, "Iran's Oil Revenue Dropped to Less Than $20 Billion, Rouhani Says" (September 14, 2020), https://en.radiofarda.com/a/30838504.html.

26 Radio Farda, "Rouhani Says Sanctions Cost Government 900 Trillian Rials in Revenues" (August 26, 2020), https://en.radiofarda.com/a/rouhani-says-sanctions-cost-government-900-trillion-rials-in-revenues/30803859.html.

27 The Iranian government does not always provide official figures. And when they do, different government entities provide contradictory data. For example, both the Central Bank of Iran and the Statistical Center of Iran are part of the President's administration and the President appoints their Chairmen. These two entities (whose Chairmen are appointed by President Rouhani and work for him) have provided different figures for Iran's GDP. Therefore, scholars and other observers usually rely upon the speeches and interviews of officials for various data. See Fereydoon Khavand, "Interview," Radio Farda (October 6, 2020), https://www.radiofarda.com/a/30876747.html.

28 In order to avoid U.S. sanctions, Iran has developed extensive secret trade networks whereby Iranian oil tankers secretly download their oil at night to other oil tankers, which then sell it usually to Chinese companies. Iran provides huge discounts, and the Chinese government ignores such trades. The interlocuters (Iranians and non-Iranians) make many millions of dollars by providing such services.

good years. Iran's non-oil exports in 2018 brought about $40 billion. Because of the sanctions, the non-oil exports brought about $30 billion in 2020. Hariri attributes the decline to the U.S. sanctions and Covid-19.[29]

For the following two years after the JCPOA, Iran's GDP went up by about 17%. Since Trump's election, Iran's GDP has shrunk by about 20%.[30] In 2019, Iran's GDP declined by over 8%.[31] This was the third year in a row (2017, 2018, and 2019) that Iran's GDP had declined. According to official regime data, per capita annual income declined by about 35% from 2011 to 2019.[32]

According to the IMF, by 2018 Iran's net debt was less than $118 billion. The IMF projected that this figure would rise to about $258 billion by the end of 2020. This figure is about 44% of Iran's GDP, according to the IMF. According to the IMF report, the annual state budget deficit for 2020 will be around $58 billion. Moreover, large amounts of Iran's foreign reserves are not accessible due to the U.S. sanctions. According to the IMF, in 2018 Iran had access to about $122 billion of its foreign reserves. By October 2020, about $8.8 billion was accessible to the Iranian government from its money outside Iran.[33]

According to the Iranian government, the inflation rate, which had gone down to less than 10% by 2015, had gone up again to over 40% by 2020.[34] The Statistical Center of Iran, which works directly under the government, has officially announced that the inflation rate is around 26%.[35] Even the official state news agency ILNA, that is close to President Rouhani, casts doubt on the accuracy of the data. According to an economist that ILNA has interviewed, the real inflation rate was over 60% in September 2020.[36]

29 ILNA, *"Rais Otagh Bazargani Iran Va Chin Dar Goftego Ba ILNA"* [Interview with the Chairman of the Iran–China Chamber of Commerce] (October 4, 2020), https://www.ilna.news/fa/tiny/news-977917.
30 Tajdin, *"Eghtesad Iran,"* op. cit.
31 Jamshid Asadi and Mehdi Jamali, *"Gozar Az Eghtesad Nezam Valaee Beh Eghtesad Bazzar Bonyad: Naghsh 'Bazzar Azad'"* [Transition from the Fundamentalist Regime Economy to Market Orientated Economy: The Role of 'Free Markets'], Iran-Emrooz (July 22, 2020), http://www.iran-emrooz.net/index.php/politic/more/85222/.
32 Ibid.
33 All the figures in this paragraph are from a report by the IMF released on October 19, 2020. See Radio Farda, "Iran's Net Debt, 44% of Its GDP, IMF Says" (October 20, 2020), https://en.radiofarda.com/a/iran-s-net-debt-44-of-its-gdp-imf-says/30903332.html.
34 Ibid.
35 ILNA, *"Ehsan Soltani Dar Goftogo Ba ILNA: Tavarom Vaghe-e Balay 60 Darsad Ast"* [Interview with Ehsan Soltani: Real Inflation is Over 60 Percent] (September 20, 2020), www.ilna.news/fa/tiny/news-970141.
36 Ibid.

Looking at the market exchange rate of Iran's national currency, the rial, would be a better way to capture the decline of Iran's economy. The rial has been in gradual decline since the fundamentalists came to power in 1979. Since Trump's withdrawal from the JCPOA, the rial has suffered historical declines, usually right after the U.S. announced more pressure. In 1978, one U.S. dollar was about 70 rials. In 2015, after the JCPOA, the rial was stable at around 30,000 rials to one dollar. After Trump's withdrawal from the JCPOA, on May 8, 2018, one dollar reached 70,000 rials.[37] On May 10, 2018, one dollar reached about 80,000 rials. With the Trump administration's policy of "Maximum Pressure" restricting the fundamentalist regime's access to world markets, on July 19, 2020 one U.S. dollar was about 260,000 rials.[38] This was the lowest value for the rial in history until then. The Central Bank of Iran injected about 1 billion dollars into the currency exchange market during July and August in order to prop up the value of the rial, which brought the exchange rate to 210,000 rials to one dollar. However, the rial fluctuated thereafter, reaching a low point on September 9, when it traded at over 250,000 rials to one dollar.[39] On September 14, 2020, the rial reached another historic low at 269,500 rials to a dollar. On September 20, 2020, on the eve of the U.S. announcement that it would carry out the U.N. sanctions that the JCPOA had suspended (although U.S. allies the U.K., France, and Germany officially stated that the suspension of the U.N. sanctions would continue), the rial dropped to its then lowest level against the dollar, trading at around 273,000.[40] Right after Trump's speech at the U.N. General Assembly, the rial dropped to its lowest level again on September 23, 2020, trading at about 281,000 rials to one dollar.[41] By September 26, the rial had dropped further, trading around 293,000 rials to a dollar.[42] On October 1, 2020, the rial again established an-

37 Radio Farda, "Iranian Currency Roils As Trump Decision Looms" (May 8, 2018), https://en.ra diofarda.com/a/iran-currency-drops-ahead-of-trump-nuclear-announcement/29214907.html.

38 Radio Farda, "Iran's Rial Hits New Historic Low Against US Dollar, Other Currencies" (July 5, 2020), https://en.radiofarda.com/a/iran-rial-hits-new-historic-low-against-us-dollar-other-currencies/ 30706985.html; and Radio Farda, "Devaluation of Iran's Currency Accelerates With Dollar Hitting 260,000 Rials" (July 19, 2020), https://en.radiofarda.com/a/devaluation-of-iran-s-currency-accel erates-with-dollar-hitting-260-000-rials/30735734.html.

39 Radio Farda, "Dollar Soars to Near Record Level in Iran" (September 9, 2020), https://en.radio farda.com/a/dollar-soars-to-near-record-level-in-iran-/30829462.html.

40 Radio Farda, "*Nerkh Dollar Va Tala Dar Iran Record Dobareh Zad*" [The Price of Dollar and Gold in Iran Hit Another Record] (September 20, 2020), https://www.radiofarda.com/a/30848568.html.

41 Radio Zamaneh, "*Dollar Az Marz 28 Hezar Tooman Oboor Kard*" [Dollar Crossed the 28,000 Toman Border] (September 23, 2020), https://www.radiozamaneh.com/539959.

42 Radio Farda, "*Dollar Beh Kanal 30 Hezar Toman Nazdiktar Shod*" [Dollar Got Closer to 30,000 Toman] (September 26, 2020), https://www.radiofarda.com/a/30859135.html.

other low record. One dollar was traded for 300,000 rials.[43] According to Radio Farda, between February 1979 and October 1, 2020, the value of the dollar went up by 4,285 times to the rial.[44] On October 8, 2020, the U.S. Secretary of the Treasury, Steven Mnuchin, announced sanctions on 18 financial institutions in Iran.[45] On October 11, 2020, the rial dropped, exchanging for 317,000 rials to one dollar. On October 12, the Chairman of the CBI, Abdol-Nasser Hemmati, announced that in order to support the value of the rial, the CBI would inject $50 million daily.[46] On October 14, one dollar was sold for 318,500 rials.[47] On October 15, one dollar was sold for 322,000 rials.[48] On October 20, 2020, however, the value of the dollar all of a sudden dropped by more than 30,000 rials.[49] One of the main financial dailies in Tehran, *Donya-e Eghtesad*, gave the reason as "many foreign exchange and gold coin traders were worried about the U.S. election and were afraid to hold onto their dollars and thus there were many sellers in the market."[50] Dr. Fereydoon Khavand, one of the most prominent Iranian economists, explained that although the primary reason for the reduction of the value of the rial was the structural maladies of the economy and the U.S. sanctions, and particularly the Trump administration's "Maximum Pressure" campaign, there was also a short-term psychological element. Only two weeks before the November 3 elections in the U.S., many thought that Joe Biden might win and he might ease the sanctions on the fundamentalist regime. In that case, the fundamentalist regime would be able to sell oil and the regime's foreign exchange would drastically rise, and thus the value of the rial would also rise. That concern, according to many observers, was the primary reason for selling off dollars and the rise in the rial's value on October 19 and 20.[51] With Biden's victory, the price of the

---

43 Radio Farda, "*Sekkeh Az Marz 15 Million Gozasht; Dollar 30 Hezar Toman Shod*" [Gold Coin Crossed the 15 Million Rial Border; Dollar Became 30,000 Toman] (October 1, 2020), https://www.radiofarda.com/a/30868839.html.

44 Ibid.

45 Radio Farda, "Washington Blacklists Iran's Entire Financial Sector" (October 8, 2020), https://en.radiofarda.com/a/washington-blacklists-iran-s-entire-financial-sector/30883130.html.

46 Radio Farda, "*Gheymat Dollar Az 32 Hezar Toman Gozasht*" [The Price of Dollar Crossed 32 Thousand Toman] (October 15, 2020), https://www.radiofarda.com/a/dollar-Iran/30894913.html.

47 My monitoring of the prices at the website https://bonbast.com/ on October 14, 2020. This is one of the most reliable sites on exchange rates for the rial.

48 Radio Farda, "*Gheymat Dollar Az 32 Hezar Toman Gozasht*" [The Price of Dollar Crossed 32 Thousand Toman] (October 15, 2020), https://www.radiofarda.com/a/dollar-Iran/30894913.html.

49 Radio Farda, "*Kahesh Bish-Az 3 Hezar Tomani Gheymat Dollar Dar Bazaar Arz Tehran*" [Reduction of More Than 3,000 Toman of Dollar's Value at Tehran's Foreign Exchange Market] (October 20, 2020), https://www.radiofarda.com/a/30902739.html.

50 Ibid.

51 Fereydoon Khavand, "*Bazaar Arz Iran Taht-e Taasir Entekhabat Amrika*" [Iran's Foreign Exchange Market Under the Impact of the American Elections], Radio Farda (October 19, 2020),

dollar and gold declined by about 20% in a matter of days. By November 7, the dollar was exchanged for less than 230,000 rials.[52] On November 8, the U.S. Secretary of State announced that the U.S. would impose a flood of new sanctions on Iran (until the Trump administration left the White House). It was said that Israel and several Arab countries would cooperate closely to make these sanctions more effective. Within hours, the value of the rial declined again and was exchanged at round 270,000 rials to the dollar by November 9, 2020.[53] By mid-December 2020, the value of the rial was more or less the same. President Biden drastically changed U.S. policy toward the fundamentalist regime. Due to the Biden policy, the fundamentalist regime was able to increase oil exports, thus providing the economy with dollars. The value of the rial rose and remained stable at around 200,000 rials to a dollar between January and October 2021.

It has been the policy of the CBI to inject dollars into the market in order to stem the decline of the rial's value. With drastic decline of the amount of dollars in the hands of the regime (from sale of oil, petrochemicals, and other exports), the CBI is less and less able to support the value of the rial. This has greatly contributed to the hyper-inflation since 2018.

The decline in the sale of oil (and other exports) causes budget deficits. The government then has had to borrow from the CBI. The CBI has pursued three policies to provide money to the government. First, it has printed rials to finance the budget deficit. Second, it has made what the CBI calls *"naghdinegi shebha pool sepordeh modat-dar"* [semi-liquidity "demand deposits" or "time deposits"] in various banks. Third, it has borrowed from banks.

In February 2021, after years of printing money, finally the Chairman of the CBI publicly admitted that the CBI had been doing precisely what the critical economists had been saying for years. Abdol-Nasser Hemmati made the public admis-

---

https://www.radiofarda.com/a/30901565.html. Some believe that due to pressure from President Rouhani, the CBI had to inject about $50 million daily and that might have also had some influence on the market.

52 Deutsche Welle, *"Piroozi Biden Va Taasir An Bar Kahesh Bahayeh Dollar Va Talla Dar Iran"* [Biden's Victory and Its Effect on the Reduction of Prices of Dollar and Gold] (November 8, 2020), https://www.dw.com/fa-ir/%D9%BE%DB%8C%D8%B1%D9%88%D8%B2%DB%8C-%D8%A8%D8%A7%DB%8C%D8%AF%D9%86-%D9%88-%D8%AA%D8%A7%D8%AB%DB%8C%D8%B1-%D8%A2%D9%86-%D8%A8%D8%B1-%DA%A9%D8%A7%D9%87%D8%B4-%D8%A8%D9%87%D8%A7%DB%8C-%D8%AF%D9%84%D8%A7%D8%B1-%D9%88-%D8%B7%D9%84%D8%A7-%D8%AF%D8%B1-%D8%A7%DB%8C%D8%B1%D8%A7%D9%86/a-55535683.

53 Radio Farda, *"Navasan-e Gheymat Dollar Dar Ashofteh Bazaar Iran"* [The Fluctuations of the Price of Dollar in Iran's Chaotic Market] (November 9, 2020), https://www.radiofarda.com/a/30938959.html.

sion that the regime had no other way to make the payments but to print money.[54] According to a report by the CBI in February 2021, due to printing money, the number of rials in circulation in November 2020 was 70% higher than the number in circulation in November 2019.[55] And the number of rials in circulation in November 2020 was 2.5 times the number in circulation in November 2018.[56] The same CBI report states that the government's debt to domestic banks rose by 36% over the previous year (November 2019) and by 74% over November 2018. According to the IMF, the total debt of the Iranian government in 2020 was around $260 billion, which is about 40% of Iran's GDP. The IMF states that the Iranian government's total debt more than doubled over the previous two years. The foreign debt of the Iranian government is a little more than $9 billion.[57] The CBI report puts the annual inflation rate at 30.5% in November 2020.[58] According to the IMF, Iran's annual inflation rate in 2020 was the sixth highest in the world; the highest being Venezuela, Zimbabwe, Sudan, Lebanon, and Suriname.[59]

The injection of massive amounts of liquidity into the market without proportionate increase in production and services produces inflation. The injection of massive amounts of rials into the market has produced inflation in Iran. As the value of the rial declines and the value of the dollar increases, the price of imports increases, which further increases inflation. In order to protect the value of their savings and income, the people convert their rials to dollars and gold (coins, jewelry, bullion). Thus, the price of food, autos, rent, homes, and land increases while incomes and savings decline in real purchasing power. The prices of the dollar and gold as well as anecdotal evidence seem to indicate that the data the regime announces on inflation and unemployment rates are false and underestimate the real decline in Iran's economy.

The Covid-19 pandemic in 2020 made the economic situation worse. Also the decline in the price of oil due to the global economic decline further reduced the regime's oil income by October 2020.

---

54 Radio Farda, *"Rais Kol-e Bank Markazi: Baray Taamin Manabeh Rahi Joz Chaap Eskenas Nadarim"* [Chairman of the Central Bank: We Have No Other Way But to Print Money to Make Payouts] (February 3, 2021), https://www.radiofarda.com/a/31083483.html.

55 Radio Farda, *"Owjgiri Naghdinegi Va Bedehi Dowlat Iran Beh Bank-ha Dar 9 Mah Aval 99"* [Rise of Liquidity and Iran's Government Debt to the Banks in the First 9 Months of the Year 1399] (February 6, 2021), https://www.radiofarda.com/a/31089592.html.

56 Ibid.

57 Ibid.

58 Ibid.

59 Ibid.

It is necessary to add that the economy under the fundamentalist regime has not been a "normal" economic system. There is very little true private sector.[60] Since capturing power in 1979, much of the economy has been owned and controlled by fundamentalist Shia clerics and fundamentalist lay. Initially through outright expropriation, they accumulated vast wealth. Then through utilizing extra legal means, force, and political connections, the top officials obtained the coveted monopolistic licenses to import various products, get around custom duties, and the like. Peter Waldman of the *Wall Street Journal* called the system "clergy capitalism" in a front-page article in 1992.[61] Paul Klebnikov of *Forbes* magazine has called the regime's rulers "millionaire mullahs."[62] Elaine Sciliano of the *New York Times* has referred to the elites as being like "Mafia families."[63]

The bulk of the economy is under the control of fundamentalist entities such as the *"Setad Farman Ejraee Imam"* [Headquarters for the Execution of Imam Khomeini's Order], *"Bonyad"* [foundations], the IRGC, and religious shrines (as well as the state). According to a study by Reuters, Ayatollah Khamenei directly controls the *Setad*, which has assets worth over $94 billion.[64] *Bonyads* are also under the control of the Supreme Leader. According to one source, *bonyads* control somewhere between 10 and 20% of Iran's GDP.[65] One such *bonyad* is the *"Bonyad Moztazafin"* (the Foundation of the Deprived), which has assets worth over $10 billion.[66] The IRGC is believed to control over 40% of the economy. Its biggest economic holding is *Khatam al-Anbia*. To these, one might add religious shrines that after the revolution came under the direct control of the regime. The biggest such shrine is *"Astan Qods Razavi"* [Eight Shia Imam Reza Holy Shrine] in Mashhad. The *Astan Qods Razavi* is one of Iran's largest economic conglomerates. Its real estate assets alone are estimated to be worth between $15 billion and $20 billion.[67] It is believed (although hard to verify) that four entities— *Setad*, the IRGC's

60 Asadi and Jamali, *"Gozar Az Eghtesad,"* op. cit.

61 Peter Waldman, "Clergy Capitalism: Mullahs Keep Control of Iran's Economy with an Iron Hand," *The Wall Street Journal* (May 8, 1992), pp. 1, 16.

62 Paul Klebnikov, "Millionaire Mullahs," *Forbes* (July 20, 2003), https://www.forbes.com/global/2003/0721/024.html#54378f504108.

63 Elaine Sciliano, "Interview," PBS (April 17, 2002), https://www.pbs.org/wgbh/pages/frontline/shows/tehran/interviews/sciolino.html.

64 Steve Stecklow, Babak Dehghanpisheh, and Yeganeh Torbati, "Reuters Investigates: Assets of the Ayatollah," Reuters (November 11, 2013), https://www.reuters.com/investigates/iran/#article/part1.

65 Klebnikov, "Millionaire Mullahs," op. cit.

66 Ibid.; and Waldman, "Clergy Capitalism," op. cit.

67 Abdolreza Ahmadi, *"Astan Qods Razavi: Dowlat Penhan Tofangdar"* [Imam Reza Holy Shrine: Government in the Shadow with Guns], Independent Persian (December 15, 2019), https://www.independentpersian.com/node/32851/%D8%A2%D8%B3%D8%AA%D8%A7%D9%86-%D9%82%D8%AF

Khatam al-Anbia, Bonyad Mostazafin, and the *Astan Qods Razavi*—own about 60 % of Iran's economy. These entities do not pay taxes, and the Majles and the government have no oversight rights of them. They operate at the pleasure of the Supreme Leader. These businesses hire those who prove loyal to the regime. For lack of a better term, I call this group, fundamentalist *nomenklatura.* In addition to these fundamentalist businesses, the state apparatus itself (before and after the revolution) owns vast economic entities, including oil and natural gas.

Iran possesses enormous oil and natural gas reserves, which provide the regime with vast amounts of resources. Iran contains the fourth largest known crude oil reserves and the second largest natural gas reserves in the world. Iran is number one in the world in terms of total value of its crude oil and natural gas reserves (known reserves at current prices). The income from the sale of oil and natural gas goes directly to the hands of the government. This vast income makes the regime in Iran highly autonomous from the social classes in society. Therefore, those countries and companies that purchase oil and gas from the regime ruling Iran provide the fundamentalist regime the resources that enable it to dominate the Iranian people. In other words, by purchasing oil from the Islamic Republic, these countries and companies are interfering in the internal political struggles in Iran in favor of the fundamentalists and against the people who oppose them. The vast oil and gas income allows the regime to pay for its vast coercive apparatuses, keep the fundamentalist *nomenklatura* happy, fund the state apparatuses, co-opt non-fundamentalists, and provide subsidies for some goods and services (e.g., fuel, electricity, and bread) to buy social submission.

The income from the sale of oil and gas, ranging between $40 billion to about $120 billion annually, has kept the "clerical capitalist system" afloat despite the many structural flaws and weaknesses of the fundamentalist economic system.[68] The economic sanctions simply took out the annual injection of billions of dollars that kept the system muddling along.

The fundamentalist regime's ideological foreign policy of spending billions of dollars for its wars in Iraq, Syria, Yemen, Lebanon, and elsewhere not only takes

---

%D8%B3-%D8%B1%D8%B6%D9%88%DB%8C%D8%9B-%D8%AF%D9%88%D9%84%D8%AA-%D9% BE%D9%86%D9%87%D8%A7%D9%86-%D8%AA%D9%81%D9%86%DA%AF%D8%AF%D8%A7%D8% B1, provides the figure of $20 billion. Jamshid Asadi, *"Astan Qods Razavi: Daraeehay Pichideh, Hesabrasi Naroshan"* [Imam Reza Holy Shrine: Complex Assets, Unclear Transparency], Radio Farda (February 24, 2019), https://www.radiofarda.com/a/commentary-on-Iran-powerful-religious-institute-astan-qods-razavi/29787445.html, provides the figure of $15 billion.

68 Iran's annual income from oil, natural gas, and petrochemicals depends on global prices and how much Iran is able to export. In 2011, under President Mahmoud Ahmadinejad, the government's income from the sale of oil reached the record level of around $120 billion.

money from investments in Iran, but also creates tensions with regional and world powers, and deprives the people of normal and prosperous lives like others in the region.[69] For example, in 2019 the GDP per capita in Iran was $5,219. Corresponding figures for the following countries were: Lebanon $8,257; Turkey $10,862; Oman $14,982; Saudi Arabia $20,028; Bahrain $22,579; Kuwait $27,359; UAE $37,622; and Qatar $59,324.[70] Opposition to the fundamentalist regime's regional policies is often expressed by large segments of the population. For example, one of the most common slogans of the protesters in recent years has been *"Na Ghazeh, Na Lobnan, Janam Fadayh Iran"* [Neither Gaza, Nor Lebanon, My Life for Iran]. Another slogan is *"Sorieh Ra Raha Kon, Fekri Be Hale Ma Kon"* [Leave Syria Alone, Do Something for Us].

The fundamentalist regime has suffered great setbacks in its policy in Syria since 2018 due to successful Israeli military operations.[71] Saudi Arabia has waged a successful diplomatic campaign condemning and isolating the fundamentalist regime in both the Arab League and the Organization of Islamic Cooperation.[72] In August and September 2020, the United Arab Emirates and Bahrain established normal relations with Israel under the auspices of the United States. Soon after, Sudan and Morocco established normal relations with Israel. Common security concerns over the fundamentalist regime ruling Iran motivated these Arab regimes and Israel to establish friendly relations. The fundamentalist regime has made public threats against the leadership of both the UAE and Bahrain.[73]

---

69 Mansour Farhang, *"Malikholiah Sodor Enghelab Va Chalesh 'Gheire Khodiha'"* [Melancholy of the Export of the Revolution and "Non-fundamentalists"], Iran Emrooz (September 12, 2020), http://www.iran-emrooz.net/index.php/politic/more/85845/.

70 World Bank, "National Accounts Data, GDP Per Capita" (2019), https://data.worldbank.org/indicator/NY.GDP.PCAP.CD.

71 Reuters, "Israel's Outgoing Defence Minister Says Iran Starting to Withdraw from Syria" (May 18, 2020), https://www.reuters.com/article/us-israel-iran-syria/israels-outgoing-defence-minister-says-iran-starting-to-withdraw-from-syria-idUSKBN22U2MU.

72 Reuters, "Arab League Labels Hezbollah Terrorist Organization" (March 11, 2016), https://www.reuters.com/article/us-mideast-crisis-arabs/arab-league-labels-hezbollah-terrorist-organization-idUSKCN0WD239; and Middle East Monitor, "Saudi Arabia Blocked Iran from Participating in OIC Meeting, Says Ministry" (February 3, 2020), https://www.middleeastmonitor.com/20200203-saudi-arabia-blocked-iran-from-participating-in-oic-meeting-says-ministry/.

73 Radio Farda, "Iran's Khamenei Says U.A.E. 'Betrayed' Islamic World With Israel Normalization Deal" (September 1, 2020), https://en.radiofarda.com/a/iran-s-khamenei-says-u-a-e-betrayed-islamic-world-with-israel-normalization-deal/30814699.html; Radio Farda, "Iran Condemns Bahrain Deal With Israel" (September 12, 2020), https://en.radiofarda.com/a/iran-condemns-bahrain-deal-with-israel/30834978.html; and Radio Farda, "IRGC Threatens Bahrain with Tough Revenge" (September 14, 2020), https://en.radiofarda.com/a/30838530.html.

Chapter 5
Woman, Life, Freedom, the 2022–2023 Mass Protests

On September 13, 2022, Mahsa Amini and her younger brother walked out of the subway station in Tehran. Mahsa was arrested by the Morality Police for not wearing her hijab properly. She was in police custody for about two hours. According to other women in custody, Mahsa was beaten by the police. Mahsa was taken from the police station to a hospital a few blocks away. When she arrived at the hospital, Mahsa was brain-dead. She was pronounced dead on September 16. After the news of the event was published by a brave female journalist, people gathered at the hospital. Mahsa Amini's murder in the custody of the Morality Police became the spark that triggered the explosion. The brave resistance by her mother, father, and younger brother to regime threats and demands, and their courageous determination to bury Mahsa in their small town and hold a public funeral on September 17, served as the trigger for the mass protests. Next came the brave actions of her relatives and the people of Saghez, her hometown. Saghez is a small town in the Eastern Azerbaijan province whose population comprises mostly Sunni Kurds.

Less than two weeks away from celebrating her 23rd birthday, Mahsa was on her trip to Tehran. Mahsa became every woman, perhaps because she was not an activist.[1] Like millions of women in Iran, she was minding her own business when she was suddenly plucked for what the Morality Police considered insufficient hijab. Few hours later, she was taken to a hospital. She was pronounced dead a few days later. Why did Mahsa's death spark such widespread protests all over Iran? In this chapter, I argue that her death was the last straw that broke the proverbial camel's back. If the last straw is the 100th, this means that we have to understand the 99 straws that came before in order to understand the trigger that the 100th straw would be.

---

[1] Mahsa Amini's parents wanted to name their daughter "Zhina" but because that is a Kurdish name, the fundamentalist regime official responsible for registering births ordered them to choose a Persian name for her. At home she was called Zhina.

https://doi.org/10.1515/9783111280288-007

5.1 The Straws Before the Final Straw that Broke the Camel's Back

In the previous chapters, I explained the history and causes of the major protests. In this chapter, I discuss those factors that directly led to the protests in 2022. As demonstrated throughout this book, the fundamentalist regime has always been terribly repressive. However, there have been increases and decreases of levels of repression in one or more areas (e. g., women's hijab, censorship of newspapers, book, and movies, civil society organizations, opposition groups, ethno-sectarian minorities). After 1997, when the reformist and expedient members of the fundamentalist oligarchy held the presidency there were often reductions in repression in some areas.

After Ebrahim Raisi assumed office in August 2021, the regime drastically increased repression on all fronts. Increase of repression had begun earlier, but due to Rouhani's presidency, there was no uniform regime action. To attract votes, Rouhani had promised to stand up to the hardline elements. Therefore, he owed his social base to, at a minimum, not cooperating with extreme harsh repression. However, increased repression was a reality. At the same time, the regime, including segments that were under the control of the Rouhani government, was engaging in harsh repression. This was evident not only during the violent repressions during the mass protests of December 2017–January 2018 and November 2019, but also regime repression during various small protests.

The disappointment with Rouhani's government led to a massive boycott of the June 2021 election and allowed Raisi to easily become President. As soon as Raisi was inaugurated in August, there was a drastic increase in repression. The Ministry of the Interior is responsible for appointing provincial governors and city governors. These officials are responsible for security in provinces and cities, and coordinate repression by regime elements that are under the control of the Supreme Leader such as police, IRGC, IRGC-Intelligence Organization, *Basij*, plain-clothes forces, and Morality Police. The Ministry of Intelligence is constitutionally under the control of the President but in reality works under the control of both the President and the Supreme Leader. The officials and offices of the Ministry of Intelligence in each province and city also work under the coordination provided by provincial governors and city governors.

By and large Rouhani had appointed technocrats with university degrees as provincial and city governors. Raisi appointed mostly high-ranking IRGC officers to these crucial offices. The appointment of IRGC Gen. Ahmad Vahidi is a prime example. Vahidi is the former Head of the IRGC-Qods Force and the person responsible for the terrorist bombing of AMIA, the Jewish center in Buenos Aires on July 18, 1994, which caused the deaths of 85 people and injured over 200. The posture of the new appointments by the Ministry of the Interior is unmistakably militaristic. The obvious message to the population was that under a uniform hardline regime, there will be more extreme hardline conservative policies and that they will be harshly and violently enforced.

Repression of human rights lawyers increased with the jailing of prominent lawyers such as Nasrin Sotoudeh and Narges Mohammadi. Many prominent independent and pro-democracy leaders of civil society organizations (e.g., teachers' associations, labor organizations, retired people's associations, "*mal-bakhtegan*," women's groups, and university students) that had been harassed and jailed periodically, all of a sudden were dragged into courts and prisons.[2] The regime began with executing a large number of prisoners who had been in jail for many years for drug smuggling or armed robbery and had been given death sentences, but their sentences had not been carried out.

During this period, the regime also used violence in Khuzestan and Isfahan provinces to repress those protesting lack of drinking water as well as Isfahan farmers who were not given their water rights.[3] When a high-rise under construction by a regime insider in Abadan collapsed on May 23, 2022 and killed at least 41, the regime sent large numbers of police and anti-riot forces to violently suppress the protesters who were peacefully protesting and complaining about collaboration of officials and the builder against the technical recommendation of the safety official.[4]

5.2 Women's Oppression Under the Fundamentalist Regime

Fundamentalists are by far the most misogynist and patriarchal group within Iran's political groups.[5] As soon as Khomeini came to power, he and his supporters imposed terribly misogynist policies. By 1979, Iranian women were university pro-

---

2 The term "*mal-bakhtegan*" refers to people who lost their money in financial institutions and the stock market. Both then-President Rouhani and Supreme Leader Khamenei had publicly encouraged the people to invest in these institutions, which promised high returns on their investments.
3 Mohammad Salami, "The Water Crisis and the Decline of Legitimacy in Iran," Trends Research and Advisory (October 6, 2022), https://trendsresearch.org/insight/the-water-crisis-and-decline-of-legitimacy-in-iran/.
4 Associated Press, "Death Toll From Iran Building Collapse Rises to 41" (June 5, 2022), https://www.voanews.com/a/death-toll-in-iran-building-collapse-rises/6604340.html.
5 Parvin Paidar, *Women and the Political Process in Twentieth Century Iran* (Cambridge: Cambridge University Press, 1995); Shirin Ebadi and Azadeh Moaveni, *Iran Awakening: One Woman's Journey to Reclaim Her Life and Country* (New York: Random House, 2007); and Kazemzadeh, *Islamic Fundamentalism*, op cit.

fessors, students, physicians, nurses, schoolteachers, lawyers, civil servants, even members of the parliament and cabinets. Therefore, it was not easy for the fundamentalists to impose their patriarchal policies without incurring major costs. The fundamentalists' policies elicit responses from women and opposition groups. When in March 1979, Khomeini ordered all women to wear hijab, there were massive protests by tens of thousands of women. Political parties and major figures, although opposed to the compulsory hijab, tended to place opposition to the fundamentalists' misogynist policies such as dismissal of females from paid employment, university education, and custody of children at the top of their agenda.

For the fundamentalists, hijab served several objectives. First, for fundamentalists' interpretation of Islam, women had to wear hijab as a religious duty. Second, hijab served as the obvious and glaring symbol of the fundamentalists' successful domination of the polity. Due to major costs, the fundamentalists were willing to retreat on several parts of their misogynist policies such as women's access to most university majors, civil service employment, even to membership in the Majles and cabinet. The fundamentalists were even willing to use loopholes and make changes in women's rights in custody of children in divorce against the Shia version of Sharia. The hijab was a major issue that the fundamentalists were not willing to abandon, although they were willing to tolerate less draconian versions of it. Hijab, then, came to serve as the symbol of women's acceptance of, or at least acquiescence to, fundamentalist rule. For the conservative social base of the fundamentalist regime, including both male and female, the imposition of the hijab became the public symbol of their power, domination, and satisfaction of their ideological domination.

5.3 The Emergence of Prominent Female Leaders

Since 2000, many Iranian women have assumed roles as national leaders. I will mention several, that, in my opinion, have played truly major roles.

5.3.1 Shirin Ebadi

Shirin Ebadi is the 2003 Iranian Nobel Peace laureate. She was a judge before the revolution. After the revolution, she was dismissed from being a judge because, according to the fundamentalist interpretation of Shia Islam, females lack the ability to be judges. She became a secretary in the same court where she had served as the presiding judge, where she had to teach the Shia clergy judge how to conduct the court. She founded the Defenders of Human Rights Center, which concentrated on women's and children's rights, and provided pro bono defense of political prisoners. Due to threats to her life after she was awarded the Nobel Peace prize, she had to leave Iran. From exile, she has continued her work on human rights, despite threats against her.

5.3.2 Nasrin Sotoudeh

A prominent human rights lawyer, Ms. Sotoudeh was among the main founders of the Defenders of Human Rights Center. Like Ebadi, Sotoudeh has been an admirer of Dr. Mossadegh and close to the pro-democracy Iran National Front. Ms. Sotoudeh has been repeatedly sent to prison merely for defending political prisoners and women's rights activists. She has remained in Iran despite maltreatment of her, her husband, and her children. Sotoudeh's brave activities have made her an iconic figure among vast swathes of the population that oppose dictatorship. Her intellect, erudition, bravery, and decency have made her the favorite choice to become the first President of Iran if there is a transition to democracy. During the 2022 protests, she was a political prisoner.

5.3.3 Narges Mohammadi

Ms. Mohammadi is another human rights lawyer. Ms. Mohammadi was Deputy President of the Defenders of Human Rights Center. She managed the center after Ebadi was forced to leave Iran. Articulate and brave, she has defended political prisoners and has been sent to jail merely for doing so. During the 2022 protests, she was a political prisoner. Her supportive husband is Taghi Rahmani, who is also a prominent pro-democracy activist. Mr. Rahmani is part of the Melli-Mazhabi group. In order to protect their two children from maltreatment, Mr. Rahmani and their children have left Iran and live in France.

5.3.4 Parastoo Forouhar

Ms. Forouhar is the daughter of Dariush Forouhar and Parvaneh Eskandari. Forouhar and Eskandari were the leaders of the Iran Nation Party, one of the constituent parties of the Iran National Front, and close friends of Dr. Mossadegh. Agents of the Ministry of Intelligence murdered them in November 1998.[6] Parastoo Forouhar showed great courage in persistently following up on the murders, demanding truth as well as organizing annual commemoration of the murders. Although she lives in Germany, she has traveled to Tehran virtually every year to organize the commemorations, despite death threats and harassment by the fundamentalist coercive apparatuses.

5.3.5 Darya Safai

By 2005, many young women also wanted to have the right to enjoy sports and enter stadiums to watch sports. A movement emerged among many young women demanding to enter stadiums. Virtually all political parties and feminist leaders ignored that demand. There were few exceptions. A major exception was Ms. Darya Safai. After leaving Iran, she began a lonely campaign of going around the globe and holding a banner demanding the right for Iranian women to enter their stadiums. Safai's persistent, courageous efforts produced results. FIFA forced the regime to allow women to enter soccer stadiums and watch games. Safai is a dentist. She was elected to Belgium's parliament.

5.3.6 Masih Alinejad

By 2015, another major leader had emerged. Her name is Masih Alinejad. Born into a poor family in a village, she became a reporter inside Iran and supportive of reformist policies and politicians. She currently resides in New York. She began several public campaigns for women inside Iran. She got her own program on VOA. The program has become hugely popular among young people and women. Alinejad began a campaign she called "White Wednesdays," where women in Iran would take off their hijab, video themselves, and send the videos to her. Alinejad broadcast these videos to millions of people inside Iran. Then, she came up with a campaign of women holding their hijab on a stick in a public place and waving it defiantly. Several brave women did so. They were arrested and assaulted by the regime.[7] Several received prison sentences of 20 years. The first such woman, Vida Movahedi, escaped Iran and currently lives in Canada. Many women who had been harassed and humiliated by the Morality Police responded to Alinejad's

---

6 Kazemzadeh, *The Iran National Front,* op cit.
7 See Alinejad's website at https://www.mystealthyfreedom.org/topics/news/white-wednesdays/.

calls. Alinejad popularized public opposition and protest against hijab, an issue neglected by political parties, feminists, and women's rights activists until September 2022.

The fundamentalist regime recognized Alinejad's threat very early. The regime began a major propaganda campaign to silence her. In one case, the regime's television station falsely reported that she had been raped in front of her son. In another case, it brought her sister to publicly condemn her. The regime's attempts to force her parents and brother to condemn her did not work. In another case, the regime attempted to lure her to Turkey to kidnap her by having her parents tell her to go to Turkey for a reunion. The regime's attempt failed when her brother revealed the trap to Ms. Alinejad, for which he was sent to prison, where he remains as of this writing. The FBI foiled an attempt by the IRGC to kidnap Alinejad and take her to Iran. Another law enforcement agency arrested a man outside her home that was there to assassinate her.[8] None of these attempts silenced Alinejad. But they made her more famous and popular among vast sectors of the Iranian population, particularly young women who came to consider Ms. Alinejad their voice, inspiration, spokeswoman, and leader.

5.3.7 Sepideh Gholian

Ms. Gholian was born in Dezful, a medium-sized city in the northern part of Khuzestan province in southwest Iran, a province which contains much of Iran's oil and gas fields with many refineries and factories. Although a university student, she was a truly brave human rights activist concentrating on labor issues. Despite repeated arrests, maltreatment, and threats, Gholian remained defiant and courageously spoke against dictatorship. Gholian lives in Iran and during the protests was in jail for her human rights and labor rights activities. She became a symbol of resistance to dictatorship, which undermined the regime's atmosphere of fear and intimidation. Gholian's bravery became an example that was emulated repeatedly during the protests.[9]

---

8 Rachel Pannett, "Man with Assault Rifle Arrested Near Iranian American Writer's Brooklyn Home," *The Washington Post* (August 1, 2022), https://www.washingtonpost.com/nation/2022/08/01/iran-journalist-masih-alinejad-ak47-brooklyn/.

9 Masih Alinejad, "Sepideh Gholian is Exposing Abuse in Iranian Prisons," *The Washington Post* (October 14, 2021), https://www.washingtonpost.com/opinions/2021/10/14/26-year-old-woman-is-exposing-abuse-iranian-prisons/.

5.3.8 Atena Daemi

Ms. Daemi is a brave prominent human rights activist. She was born in 1988. She was arrested in November 2016 for her human rights activities and sentenced to seven years in jail. She was released in January 2022. She was held in solitary confinement for long periods in order to break her.[10] She played a major role during the 2022 mass protests, making public statements on social media and elsewhere supporting the protests and criticizing entities that support the fundamentalist regime.[11]

5.3.9 Faezeh Hashemi Rafsanjani

Unlike the other female leaders mentioned above, Ms. Rafsanjani comes from inside the fundamentalist regime. Her father, Ayatollah Ali Akbar Hashemi Rafsanjani, was one of the founders of the regime and one of its top leaders. Ms. Rafsanjani was elected to the Majles and was regarded as a reformist. She was sent to prison for her criticisms of the regime. She has been outspoken and brave. Some of her comments are intra-regime criticisms, that is, as a regime insider expressing worries and recommending policies to save the regime. However, she has increasingly been expressing serious criticism of the regime. After the protests began in mid-September 2022, the regime arrested her and put her in jail. Ms. Rafsanjani represents a faction of the regime that believes the regime will collapse sooner or later. Therefore, Ms. Rafsanjani could play a role in leading a faction of the fundamentalist oligarchy to leave the regime and side with the opposition. Ms. Rafsanjani is not alone in that role. There are other members of the fundamentalist oligarchy, such as Mir-Hussein Moussavi, that may also play that role.

5.4 Brilliant Women as Role Models

The women profiled above are only the most famous cases. There have been many more women who, through their actions and activities, have inspired millions of Iranian women to look at them as role models, to realize that they do not have

---

10 United for Iran, "Atena Daemi" (September 2020), https://united4iran.org/wp-content/uploads/Atena-Daemi-Fact-Pattern-and-Legal-Analysis-September-2020.pdf.
11 Yaghoub Fazeli, "Iran Rights Activists Spurn Iranian-American Group NIAC as Regime 'Lobby,'" AlArabiya News (October 19, 2022), https://english.alarabiya.net/News/middle-east/2022/10/19/Iran-rights-activists-spurn-Iranian-American-council-NIAC-as-scarlet-letter-.

to submit to the fundamentalist regime's ideology of submission, that they deserve better conditions and to feel confident that they could and should fight for their rights. Among such figures one may mention Ladan Boroumand, Roya Boroumand, Shadi Sadr, and Raha Bahreini. The two Boroumand sisters have founded the Abdorrahman Boroumand Center for Human Rights in Iran, named after their father, who was assassinated by the fundamentalist regime in France in 1991. They have been documenting the regime's human rights violations and assassinations abroad.[12] Ms. Sadr is a lawyer and human rights activist and founder of Justice for Iran, which has been organizing tribunals on the regime's crimes against humanity.[13] Raha Bahreini is a researcher on Iran for Amnesty International. She frequently appears on satellite television programs. She is young, articulate, erudite, compassionate, and honest.

5.5 Courage Under Repression by Men

Large numbers of men have continued to publicly stand up to the regime despite repeated arrests, torture, and maltreatment. One prominent example is Mr. Hashem Khastar. Mr. Khastar has been a high school teacher and leader of a teachers' association. Despite repeated prison sentences, he has refused to be intimidated into silence. A supporter of Dr. Mossadegh and the INF, he and his supportive wife have continued their brave resistance.

Keyvan Samimi is one of Iran's most prominent dissidents and journalists. He was born in Abadan in 1949. He has been a political prisoner under both the Shah's dictatorship and the fundamentalist regime. One of his brothers was executed by the Shah and another by the fundamentalist regime. He is a supporter of Dr. Mossadegh and close to *Melli-Mazhabi* [Religious-Nationalist] group.[14] He has been a brave public intellectual, publishing articles critical of dictatorship and in support of freedom and democracy despite constant pressures and incarceration.

Another courageous person was Navid Afkari, a wrestling champion who had participated in the mass protests in 2019. He was executed for what pro-democracy activists consider to be trumped up charges of murder. Afkari was severely tortured, and he refused to recant his opposition to the regime.

---

12 See their website at https://www.iranrights.org/. Dr. Abdorrahman Boroumand was a prominent leader of the INF until late 1978, when he and Dr. Bakhtiar split from the INF.
13 The organization's website is at https://justice4iran.org/.
14 Radio Free Europe/Radio Liberty, "Iranian Journalist Samimi Released From Prison" (January 1, 2023), https://www.rferl.org/a/iran-journalist-samimi-freed/32203118.html.

Still another prominent brave pro-democracy activist is Majid Tavakoli, a student from the University of Tehran. Despite maltreatment and prison, Mr. Tavakoli remained defiant and continued to express his opposition and criticisms of the regime. During the 2022 protests he was a political prisoner.

There is also Hussein Ronaghi. He had been jailed and tortured before the 2022 protests began. After they began, he refused to be silent and supported the protests. He was arrested and the torturers broke both his legs to force him into public confessions.

A dissident rapper, Toomaj Salehi, has made very popular rap songs encouraging resistance to the regime. He has been arrested several times for his songs. He was very active in encouraging the people to participate in the mass protests. He was arrested on October 29 or 30.[15]

Several other men outside Iran have played major roles in undermining the regime: Hassan Dai, Ruhollah Zam, Ali Javanmardi, Dr. Hamid Akbari, Dr. Hamed Esmaeilion, Dr. Kamran Matin, and Mehdi Nakhl-Ahmadi.

Mr. Dai is a pro-democracy and human rights activist. He emerged publicly around 2007–2008 by publishing scathing articles against the fundamentalist regime as well as individuals and groups he considered to be pro-IRI lobbyists, and those promoting and funding appeasement of the fundamentalist regime.[16] The National Iranian American Council (NIAC), a group regarded by many Iranian and American observers as a lobby for the fundamentalist regime, sued him for defamation, a tactic that the group has used to intimidate others into silence (i. e., not to call it a lobby group for the Iranian government).[17] Not only was Dai not intimidated into silence, but he was also able to defeat the lawsuit.[18] The court ordered NIAC to pay $183,480.09 to Mr. Dai. NIAC appealed the court's decision, and the appellate court upheld the decision of the district court and strongly criticized Mr. Trita Parsi (founder and then-President of NIAC) for various actions.[19] In my opinion, the case made Mr. Dai a hero to many opponents of the fun-

---

15 Iran International, "Islamic Republic's Security Forces Arrest Dissident Rapper" (October 30, 2022), https://www.iranintl.com/en/202210306648.

16 See Dai's group website at http://iranian-americans.com/about/.

17 Eli Lake, "Exclusive: Iran Advocacy Group Said to Skirt Lobby Rules," *The Washington Times* (November 13, 2009), https://www.washingtontimes.com/news/2009/nov/13/exclusive-did-iranian-advocacy-group-violate-laws/.

18 Masoud Kazemzadeh, "On the Lawsuit 'Trita Parsi and NIAC v. Hassan Daieoleslam,'" Iranian.com (September 15, 2012), http://iranian.com/main/blog/masoud-kazemzadeh/lawsuit-trita-parsi-and-niac-v-hassan-daieoleslam-0.html.

19 Armin Rosen, "America's Most Prominent Group Advocating Engagement with Iran was Hit with a Rough Court Decision," *Business Insider* (March 5, 2015), https://www.businessinsider.com/

damentalist regime for his willingness to stand up to the regime and a group regarded by large numbers of Iranian Americans as its lobby in the United States.[20]
Since then, Dai has appeared on numerous satellite TV programs providing his
analysis of the fundamentalist regime and supporters of the regime in the West.
Until around 2017, Dai was among few public intellectuals in the U.S. that publicly
advocated the replacement of the fundamentalist regime with democracy. Since
2017–2018, Dai's views have become widespread inside and outside Iran. Dai
has published more research on the fundamentalist regime's networks of lobbyists, influencers, and supporters than any other person or group. He is very articulate and brave. Dai is very popular among Iranians who oppose the regime inside
and outside Iran.

Mr. Zam was the son of a clerical leader of the fundamentalist regime. He became a journalist and critic of the regime. He left Iran and went to France. Zam
had many connections to many members of the fundamentalist intelligence agencies. These members of the intelligence agencies trusted Zam and gave him top secret intelligence about other high-ranking members of the fundamentalist oligarchy in order to undermine their rivals within the regime. The Ministry of
Intelligence was able to deceive Zam and convince him to go to Iraq for a meeting
with Grand Ayatollah Ali Sistani. The regime then kidnapped Zam, took him to
Iran, tortured him, broadcast his confessions, and then executed him.[21]

Mr. Javanmardi is a prominent journalist who was working for the VOA. In addition to his reporting from Iraqi Kurdistan for the VOA, Javanmardi began broadcasting his own news and analysis on his site and various TV programs. Javanmardi's commentaries became popular because he is very intelligent and articulate
and intimately familiar with Iranian politics. He was forced to leave the VOA. Javanmardi, who is Kurdish, advocates a free, democratic, and unified Iran that
would respect the civil rights of all groups. The fundamentalist regime had been
portraying Kurds as secessionist and communist. Javanmardi's very popular programs undermined the regime's propaganda. The regime have made several attempts to assassinate Javanmardi, who lives in Iraqi Kurdistan and Washington,
D.C.

Dr. Hamid Akbari is Dean of the School of Business at Carroll University in
Wisconsin, United States. He has been one of the most active pro-democracy think-

---

americas-most-prominent-group-advocating-engagement-with-iran-was-hit-with-a-rough-court-deci
sion-2015-3.

20 Kazemzadeh, "On the Lawsuit," op cit.

21 Amnesty International, "Iran: Execution of Journalist Rouhollah Zam a 'Deadly Blow' to Freedom of Expression" (December 12, 2020), https://www.amnesty.org/en/latest/press-release/2020/12/
iran-execution-of-journalist-rouhollah-zam-a-deadly-blow-to-freedom-of-expression/.

ers and activists in the past 30 years. His tireless work organizing conferences and giving talks on democracy paved the way for the "democratic discourse" to replace the "reforming within the fundamentalist regime" discourse that had dominated intellectual debates before 2017.

Dr. Esmaeilion is a dentist and author of several books of short stories and novels. He was not a public figure until the IRGC shot down the Ukrainian passenger airplane over the skies of Tehran on January 8, 2020. Esmaeilion is the founder of the Association of Victims of Flight PS752.[22] Esmaeilion, whose wife and daughter were on the plane, has emerged as an articulate spokesman for the families of the victims. The organization was highly effective in pressuring various governments to investigate and publicize how the IRGC shot down the passenger airplane. Moreover, he has expressed solidarity with all other victims of the fundamentalist regime and has successfully organized and mobilized support for protests in Canada and elsewhere against the regime's brutality and dictatorship. He has played a major role organizing support and solidarity with the 2022 mass protests inside and outside Iran. He was responsible for organizing a march on October 1 at Richmond Hill, Canada that over 50,000 people attended and a march on October 22 in Berlin, Germany that over 80,000 people attended.[23]

Dr. Kamran Matin is a Senior Lecturer in International Relations at the University of Sussex.[24] Dr. Matin has been a frequent commentator and analyst at Iran International satellite TV, appearing about five times a week. He is brilliant and articulate. He is also a Kurd. The fundamentalist regime has been demonizing Kurds as secessionist, violent, and communist. Although Dr. Matin is a Marxist, he advocates political freedom, human rights, and civil rights. His views and analysis are fair and sophisticated. He advocates a unified Iran with freedom for all Iranians. Millions of Iranians who have been watching Dr. Matin's analysis for several years have seen for themselves the utter falsity of the fundamentalist regime's racist propaganda against the Iranian Kurds.

The fundamentalist regime has been portraying various ethno-sectarian groups in Iran as secessionists that pose a major threat to other Iranians; and thus, its massive oppressive measures are the only way to protect the territorial integrity of Iran. The appearances of several Iranian scholars and commentators

---

22 See the group's website at https://www.ps752justice.com/.

23 Isaac Callan, "More Than 50k Attend Richmond Hill, Ont. Protest against Iranian Government," *Global News* (October 1, 2022), https://globalnews.ca/news/9169782/richmond-hill-iran-protest/; and Leon Malherbe and Paris Hafezi, "Tens of Thousands March in Berlin in Support of Iran Protests," Reuters (October 22, 2022), https://www.reuters.com/world/middle-east/irans-guards-warn-cleric-over-agitating-restive-southeast-2022-10-22/.

24 Dr. Matin's faculty webpage is at https://profiles.sussex.ac.uk/p138207-kamran-matin.

from these ethno-sectarian groups on various satellite TV programs broadcast to millions of Iranians for several years have undermined the fundamentalist regime propaganda.[25]

The fundamentalist regime has been demonizing the Iranian Balochis as Sunni extremists, violent and secessionist. The most prominent Baloch intellectuals and political leaders, however, are very moderate, democratic, and highly supportive of Iran. Among them are Mehdi Nakhl-Ahmadi, Ebrahim Ahrari, Dr. Reza Hussein Bor, and Fariba Baloch. Nakhl-Ahmadi is a sophisticated pro-democracy Baloch analyst and commentator. He has given many interviews and analyses on various TV programs. Ahrari is one of the anchors and producers at the Kalame television program. Dr. Hussein Bor is a monarchist, although a very atypical one. He works closely with republicans and advocates of ethnic rights. Ms. Fariba Baloch is a human rights advocate. The appearances of these sophisticated, moderate, and democratic intellectuals, highly supportive of Iranian territorial integrity, on satellite television programs have eviscerated more than 40 years of the fundamentalist regime's propaganda, demonization, and ethno-sectarian bigotry against Iranian Balochis.

5.6 2019 – 2022: The Worst Years for Fundamentalist Intelligence Agencies and Military Apparatuses

On November 27, 2020, Mossad, Israel's foreign intelligence agency, assassinated Mohsen Fakhrizadeh, the father of the fundamentalist regime's clandestine nuclear weapons program. He had over a dozen bodyguards when he was assassinated. This was neither the first nor the last incident in Mossad's highly successful campaign of assassinations and sabotage of the regime's nuclear personnel and facilities. Between 2012 and 2014, Mossad carried out half a dozen assassinations of top regime officials directly involved in the fundamentalists' clandestine nuclear weapons program. Under pressure from the Obama administration, which was involved in negotiations with the regime, the Israelis had to put an abrupt end to their assassinations. With a green light from the Trump administration, the Israelis carried out a highly effective campaign of sabotage of nuclear facilities and assassinations of nuclear officials as well as IRGC-Qods force personnel tasked with retaliation against Israelis such as assassinations of Israeli tourists and officials in Turkey. Mossad's infiltrators inside the regime's intelligence entities also told Mos-

---

25 On the role of satellite TV, and particularly Iran International TV see below.

sad about many attempts by the regime to carry out terrorist actions in Europe and the U.S., which were thus foiled due to Mossad's intelligence.

On August 7, 2020, Mossad assassinated Abdullah Ahmed Abdullah. Abdullah was residing in Tehran and was considered al Qaeda's number two leader, after Ayman al-Zawahiri. Abdullah was one of the founding members of al Qaeda and the mastermind of the bombings of U.S. embassies in Kenya and Tanzania, which killed 224 people on August 7, 1998.[26] The fundamentalist regime has denied that it had provided safe haven to Abdullah, a terribly embarrassing fact, and claimed (falsely) that Abdullah had been a Lebanese history professor. The fundamentalist regime has allowed large numbers of al Qaeda operatives to move about freely in Iran, raise money, and plan operations as long as they target Saudis and the Americans. Mossad had caried out this assassination for the United States.

On January 31, 2018, Mossad agents broke into a warehouse in Turghoozabad, a village outside of Tehran, and seized half a ton of Iran's secret nuclear documents, including 50,000 pages and 163 compact disks of files. After the July 2015 nuclear deal with world powers, the regime had decided to store its nuclear secrets in that place rather than provide them to the International Atomic Energy Agency (IAEA).[27] Some of the secrets, for example, included details of the regime's clandestine nuclear weapons program, including facilities where enriched uranium was stored, and nuclear tests conducted. The regime's Foreign Minister, Mohammad Javad Zarif, and the Deputy Foreign Minister, Abbas Araghchi, denied the existence of that warehouse and ridiculed the Israeli announcement made by Prime Minister Netanyahu. Araghchi and Zarif claimed that the Israelis were lying in order to influence the upcoming decision by Donald Trump whether to stay with or leave the nuclear deal.[28] Subsequent investigations by the IAEA and other experts vindicated the authenticity of the archives.[29] The investigation by the IAEA of the infor-

---

26 Adam Goldman, Eric Schmitt, Farnaz Fassihi, and Ronen Bergman, "Al Qaeda's Number 2, Accused in U.S. Embassy Attacks, Killed in Iran," *The New York Times* (November 13, 2020, updated September 14, 2021), https://www.nytimes.com/2020/11/13/world/middleeast/al-masri-abdullah-qaeda-dead.html.

27 *Haaretz*, "How the Mossad Broke Into an Iranian Facility and Stole Half a Ton of Nuclear Files" (July 16, 2018), https://www.haaretz.com/israel-news/2018-07-16/ty-article/how-the-mossad-broke-into-an-iranian-facility-and-stole-nuclear-files/0000017f-db07-d856-a37f-ffc7b14c0000.

28 *Times of Israel*, "Iran Dismisses Netanyahu's Nuclear Exposé as 'Childish' and 'Ridiculous,'" (April 30, 2018), https://www.timesofisrael.com/iran-dismisses-netanyahus-nuclear-expose-as-childish-and-ridiculous/.

29 David Albright and Sarah Burkhard, "Highlights of *Iran's Perilous Pursuit of Nuclear Weapons*," (August 25, 2021), https://isis-online.org/uploads/isis-reports/documents/Highlights_of_Irans_Perilous_Pursuit_of_Nuclear_Weapons_August_25%2C_2021.pdf; and Aaron Arnold et al., *The Iran Nuclear Archive* (Cambridge, MA: Belfer Center for Science and International Affairs, Harvard Universi-

mation revealed from the archives found traces of enriched uranium in three un-declared secret sites and natural uranium in one undeclared site.[30] These sites are Turghoozabad, Abadeh, Varamin, and Marivan. The fundamentalist regime has not provided any scientifically plausible response to the IAEA for the existence of traces of uranium at these sites.

Another embarrassing operation was Mossad's apprehension and interroga-tion of two IRGC-Qods Force officials inside Iran, taping of their confessions, and then their release. One such operation led to the foiling of the fundamentalist regime's plan to assassinate an Israeli in Turkey, an American General in Germa-ny, and a journalist in a third country. When the IRGC-Intelligence Organization sent a large group to Istanbul to assassinate any Israeli tourist they could find, as well as a former Israeli ambassador on vacation in Istanbul, Mossad's intelli-gence was shared with Turkish officials, who apprehended the group of IRGC as-sassins. In apparent retaliation, on May 25, 2022, Mossad assassinated Col. Sayad Khodayee, who was the Deputy Head of the IRGC-Intelligence Organization respon-sible for clandestine operations abroad. Khodayee was tasked with planning and carrying out the assassinations of Israelis in Istanbul.[31]

In addition to Mossad's highly successful operations inside Iran, the Israeli Air Force has carried out over 1,000 operations in Syria, killing large numbers of mili-tary personnel from the IRGC, IRGC-Qods Force, Lebanese Hezbollah, and IRI's rad-ical Shia proxies there, and destroying military bases and hardware.[32]

Since 1979, the fundamentalist regime had created an image of the IRGC, IRGC-Qods Force, IRGC-Intelligence Organization, and the Ministry of Intelligence as all-knowing, all-powerful, highly competent, brutal, and fearsome entities. Members of these entities were recruited from among the most extreme, ideological, and loyal fundamentalists. The fundamentalist regime had wanted to sow fear among its opponents. The operations by Mossad and the Israeli military vaporized the image the fundamentalist regime had worked so hard to propagate and incul-

ty, April 2019), https://www.belfercenter.org/sites/default/files/files/publication/The%20Iran%20Nu clear%20Archive_0.pdf.

30 BBC, "IAEA Urges Iran to Explain Uranium Particles at Undeclared Sites" (June 7, 2021), https:// www.bbc.com/news/world-middle-east-57386296.

31 Farnaz Fassihi and Ronen Bergman, "Israel Tells U.S. It Killed Iranian Officer, Official Says," *The New York Times* (May 25, 2022), https://www.nytimes.com/2022/05/25/world/middleeast/iran-israel-killing-khodayee.html.

32 Aljazeera, "Major Destruction after Israel Targets Missile Facility in Syria" (August 28, 2022), https://www.aljazeera.com/news/2022/8/28/israel-targeted-missile-facility-in-syria-war-monitor; Su-leiman Al-Khalidi, "Israeli Strikes Hit Iranian Targets Near Russian Mediterranean Base," Reuters (August 14, 2022), https://www.reuters.com/world/middle-east/syrian-state-media-says-israel-targets-coastal-province-tartous-2022-08-14/.

cate. The situation had gotten so bad that on June 23, 2022 it was announced that the regime had dismissed Hussein Taeb, the Head of the IRGC-Intelligence Organization, widely regarded as the third most powerful figure in Iran after Supreme Leader Khamenei and his influential son Mojtaba Khamenei.[33] Taeb was a trusted man for Khamenei and the man who had been close to Mojtaba and believed that he would work hard to maneuver to make Mojtaba the next Supreme Leader after his father's demise. Taeb's dismissal was a shock to the system. By August 2022, the Iranian people were making jokes about the intelligence and coercive apparatuses of the fundamentalist regime.

5.7 Celebrities Speak Up

Until mid-2021, with very few exceptional cases, celebrities were silent. By and large, the bulk of celebrities cozied up to those in power and were handsomely rewarded with astronomical financial rewards. Some celebrities publicly supported reformist and expedient members of the oligarchy during elections: a safe path which allowed both access to regime largesse and popular support. In 2021 a new phenomenon emerged: celebrities bravely standing up to the regime and willing to incur the violent wrath of the regime. Iranians revere their top athletes and singers, as well as movie directors, actors, and actresses.

First and foremost was Ali Karimi, one of Iran's most beloved soccer superstars, former captain of Iran's national soccer team and Persepolis (one of Iran's top soccer teams). Karimi first showed his political leanings in 2008 when he wore green armbands during the mass protests in a public show of solidarity with the Green Movement and the masses on the streets. He also endorsed Hassan Rouhani for the presidency. By 2021, he had retired from professional soccer. Karimi spoke out after the IRGC used two missiles to attack and down a Ukrainian passenger airplane taking off from Tehran's international airport, killing all 176 people onboard. Among the victims were a son and daughter of a former Deputy Minister of Health. The former official and his wife revealed that a high-ranking IRGC official gave them their condolences and told them that if the IRGC had not downed the airplane then there would have been a war between the U.S. and Iran and 10 million Iranians would have died. On January 8, 2020, the regime had fired 12 ballistic missiles at an American airbase in Iraq in retaliation against

---

33 Reuters, "Iran Replaces Powerful Chief of Guards' Intelligence Unit–State TV" (June 23, 2022), https://www.reuters.com/world/middle-east/iran-dismisses-taeb-head-revolutionary-guards-intelligence-unit-state-tv-2022-06-23/.

the U.S. killing of IRGC-Qods Force Head Qassem Soleimani. The regime wanted to look tough in front of its supporters in Iran and the region but was afraid of the American response. Therefore, it downed the passenger airplane to create a diversion that would draw sympathy. The regime wanted the people to think that either the U.S. hit the airplane, or that it fell due to mechanical problems. The regime harshly repressed the families of the victims of the Ukrainian passenger plane. In that milieu, Karimi spoke out and defended the rights of the families. This was in January 2020 and Rouhani was still President; conditions, although gradually becoming worse, had not yet reached their peak of repression. After August 2021, there were a number of protests against the high prices and water shortage in Khuzestan and Isfahan provinces. Karimi courageously condemned the regime's violent repression of unarmed peaceful protesters. By September 2022, Karimi was living in Dubai and relatively safe from regime violence. So, when Mahsa Amini was killed, Karimi spoke out courageously and strongly condemned the regime, fully siding with Mahsa's family and the protesters on the streets. As the most beloved soccer superstar of his generation, Karimi was admired and loved by millions of ordinary Iranians who did not like the regime but would not take any action against it. Karimi not only provided inspiration and support to the people, but he also called for protests and even told them what to do and what not to do. Karimi compared the protests in 2022 with the protests against the Shah's dictatorship, thus providing great legitimacy to the people and placing the regime as the tyrannical oppressor of the people. Regime officials publicly called for the arrest and punishment of Karimi until they found out that he was in Dubai. Regime officials called for seizure of his assets. Then the regime publicly confiscated his house in Tehran. The people in soccer stadiums wore Karimi's jersey, shouted his name, called him their hero and leader. Other top athletes publicly sided with Karimi, such as Karim Bagheri, the former captain of Iran's national soccer team; Rasool Khadem, Iran's Olympic gold medal wresting champion and former Head of the Iran National Wresting Federation; and Ali Dai, former top star of the national soccer team.

Beginning in 2021, Voria Ghafouri, a top player in Iran's national soccer team and the captain of Esteghlal, one of the top soccer teams in Iran, began publicly criticizing the regime and supporting the people. He was expelled from the national team and his contract with Esteghlal was not renewed. Ghafouri knew full well that his public criticisms would bring harsh punishments, but nevertheless he courageously sided with the people on several cases. People shouted his name during games that he was allowed to play as well as during games that he was not allowed to play.

The brave public positions of Karimi and Ghafouri, as well as the support given them by other athletes and the public appreciation and support they received, made many other athletes who had either been silent or even supportive of various fundamentalist officials to publicly distance themselves from the regime and support the people. Sardar Azmoun, a member of the national soccer team, is a prime example of this. Ali Dai is another example of such figures. Ghafouri was arrested on November 24, 2022, after he made harsh criticisms of the regime and the national soccer team. He was released after public furor.

Movie directors, actors, and actresses are hugely popular with average Iranians. The regime monitors those in the film industry very closely. The regime bans any director, actor, or actress that is critical of the regime. The regime also rewards those who support the regime with funds and permits. Therefore, because they require permits to make movies as well as to act in them, those in the film industry keep their views to themselves. Many who oppose the regime have chosen to leave Iran. In 2021, something new occurred. Jafar Panahi and Mohammad Rasoulof organized a public statement entitled "Put Your Rifles Down," which was signed by over 100 directors, actors, and actresses that asked those in the coercive apparatuses not to shoot the unarmed protesters after the regime shot and killed many unarmed protesters in Abadan, Ahvaz, and Isfahan. The regime arrested Panahi and Rasoulof, and threatened other signatories that if they did not withdraw their signatures they would be banned from movies and/or arrested by the regime. It was not clear whether they would be intimidated into silence or not. In September 2022, in reaction to the murder of Mahsa Amini, many in the film industry made the decision to stand up to the regime and re-issue their earlier statement asking the coercive apparatuses to put their rifles down and not to shoot unarmed peacefully protesting citizens.

After the revolution many top singers left Iran. Although many were socially conscious and opposed both the Shah's dictatorship and the fundamentalist regime, they tended not to be overtly political. For the first time in 2022 many such singers took unprecedented positions and publicly called for active protests against the regime. One such figure was Dariush Eghbali, one of Iran's most beloved singers since the early 1970s. He publicly called for Iranians inside and outside Iran to participate in protests against the regime. Others included Faramarz Aslani and Googoosh.

5.8 The Role of Satellite Television and Social Media

During the 1977–1979 revolutionary process, Iranians used several entities to organize and mobilize the masses. The opposition groups used copy machines to copy their *"elamieh"* [statement, declaration] calling for protests. These one-page calls were distributed by sympathizers in universities, bazaars, workplaces, schools, and mosques. Ayatollah Khomeini, who was residing in Najaf, Iraq, also tape recorded his fiery speeches, and his supporters smuggled them into Iran, and through mosques and seminaries spread them to his followers throughout the country. What was highly crucial was that BBC Persian radio made the decision to broadcast Khomeini's messages on an almost daily basis after Khomeini went to Paris, France, directly into the homes of millions of Iranians. This allowed Khomeini to have direct access to millions of Iranians on an almost daily basis. Whatever Khomeini said was broadcast by BBC Persian radio as news.

The Iranian people had been using social media such as Facebook and Twitter to communicate and organize protests between 2009 and 2020. By 2020, other social media such as Instagram, WhatsApp, and Telegram were also used extensively to organize protests. The role that BBC Persian played in the 1979 revolution is being played by Iran International satellite television.

5.8.1 Iran International Television

Iran International is a 24-hour satellite television station, which broadcasts about 6 – 8 hours of live television programs and then rebroadcasts them the rest of the day.[34] Its main studios are in London and Washington, D.C. It began operations in 2017 and emerged as the top satellite television station among Iranians inside and outside Iran. It has recruited some of the best journalists from BBC Persian, Voice of America, and Radio Farda. During the 2022 mass protests, Iran International had 24-hour coverage. Iran International has also been able to hire exceptional journalists and commentators. Its news programs are highly professional and reliable. Its commentaries are highly sophisticated and scholarly. Its commentators and guests include those pro-democracy and the anti-democratic opposition (e. g., monarchists, PMOI, communists), as well as supporters of the fundamentalist regime. Many pro-democracy leaders have criticized Iran International for not interviewing their spokespersons while providing extensive coverage to the anti-democratic monarchists.

Iran International has played a truly unique role in Iranian politics since 2020. Many officials inside the regime who oppose either some policies or the whole regime send the regime's secret documents to Iran International. Hackers who gain access to the regime's ministries, agencies, prisons, surveillance cameras, and other sites provide Iran International the data and tapes. The journalists at Iran

---

34 Its website is at https://www.iranintl.com/. Its YouTube page is at https://www.youtube.com/c/IRANINTL.

International also have done large numbers of exceptional investigative reports exposing financial corruption by regime officials and their relatives.

Iran International regularly features Iran's top scholars such as Dr. Kamran Matin, Dr. Mansour Farhang, Dr. Touraj Atabaki, and Dr. Afshin Shahi, to name just a few. During the mass protests, Iran International brought more top scholars of Iran to analyze the political situation, such as Dr. Nayereh Tohidi, Iran's top feminist sociologist; Faraj Sarkohi, Iran's top socialist literary critic and one of Iran's most influential socialist public intellectuals; and Dr. Majid Mohammadi, Iran's most respected neo-conservative sociologist.[35] Iran International regularly features Farzin Nadimi, Iran's top expert on Iran's military doctrine. Iran International has Iran's top journalists and commentators such as Mehdi Mahdavi Azad, Jamshid Barzegar, and Kambiz Ghafoori, who regularly present truly sophisticated analyses of the political situation.

As soon as Mahsa Amini was killed, Iran International began providing 24-hour special coverage of the protests. Thus, Iran International became the best source of accurate reporting and analysis of Iranian politics. The persistent exposure of regime cruelties and hypocrisies by Iran International have greatly undermined regime propaganda and legitimacy. The constant access that Iran International provided opposition groups and commentators further galvanized opposition and gave hope to the Iranian people.

Iran International's coverage of the collapse of the high-rise in Abadan, and various protests in Isfahan and Ahvaz was both professional and emotional. The coverage factually demonstrated the utter lack of basic competence of the regime's officials as well as their utter lack of care for human lives. The commentaries, then, showed the human costs that such regime policies have caused the Iranian people. The coverage of Sepideh Reshno's cruel treatment by the IRGC caused great outrage among vast numbers of viewers. The coverage of the regime's foreign policies clearly showed how the regime repeatedly undermined Iran's national interests for the sake of promoting the regime's ideological beliefs.

Iran International's coverage of Mahsa Amini was truly exceptional. Within hours, Iran International's honest investigations exposed the lies of the regime again and again. When hackers gained access to CT scans of Mahsa's head and torso, Iran International brought in top Iranian physicians who clearly explained that the regime was lying, and that the CT scan clearly showed that her skull was fractured due to being struck by hard objects. Iran International brought in commentators who asked the people to show their opposition to what the regime had

---

35 Tohidi's faculty webpage is at https://www.csun.edu/humanities/gender-womens-studies/nayer eh-tohidi.

done to Mahsa. Iran International broadcast calls by various figures to protest the regime's oppressive and violent actions.

Iran International broadcast videos sent by people inside Iran to millions of its viewers. It broadcast the views of athletes, movie directors, and political activists, as well as various government officials around the world and non-Iranian celebrities. Pink Floyd, the progressive British rock group, is hugely popular among Iranians, and Iran International repeatedly broadcast its interview with Roger Waters (co-founder and -composer of the group), who strongly condemned the regime's repression and sided with the Iranian people. Iran International also mentioned the support and solidarity of Justine Bieber, Dua Lipa, and Yungblud. To many of the protesters, who are between 15 and 30, support from these popular international artists is heartwarming and further encourages them to struggle for their freedom.

Iran International did great service to the cause of non-violent methods of struggle by interviewing Iran's top scholar of non-violence, Dr. Amaar Maleki (Political Science Professor at Tilburg University in the Netherlands) and Arash Aramesh (a top scholar of international law and national security). Aramesh argued what actions would harm the cause of non-violence and how Iranian Americans could best influence their senators and representatives.

The fundamentalist regime and its supporters have been attacking Iran International and trying to silence it. On November 7, 2022, Iran International released a statement about specific threats to two of its journalists by the IRGC that the Metropolitan Police in London had shared with it. The statement read:

> Iran International, the independent UK-based Farsi-language news channel is shocked and deeply concerned by the credible threats to life its journalists have received from the IRGC.
>
> Two of our British-Iranian journalists have, in recent days, been notified of an increase in the threats to them. The Metropolitan Police have now formally notified both journalists that these threats represent an imminent, credible and significant risk to their lives and those of their families. Other members of our staff have also been informed directly by the Metropolitan Police of separate threats.
>
> Our journalists are subject to abuse 24/7 on social media. But these threats to life of British-Iranian journalists working in the UK mark a significant and dangerous escalation of a state-sponsored campaign to intimidate Iranian journalists working abroad. These lethal threats to British citizens on British soil come after several weeks of warnings from the IRGC and Iranian government about the work of a free and uncensored Farsi-language media working in London.[36]

---

36 Iran International, "Statement on Formal Threats to the Life of Journalists on UK Soil" (November 7, 2022), https://www.iranintl.com/en/202211076450.

Supreme Leader Khamenei has called the 2022 mass protests a "hybrid war" organized by the U.S., the U.K., Israel, and Saudi Arabia. The official website of the Supreme Leader published a long interview with the Minister of Intelligence, Hojatolislam Val Moslemin Esmail Khatib, on November 10, 2022.[37] Khatib said:

> In addition to the control of satellite networks by intelligence agencies, there are numerous reports of the activities of various counter-revolutionary groups in the media, which carry out their activities under the direction of hostile intelligence agencies. The most significant of these has been the direct intervention of the United States in coordinating some counter-revolutionary terrorist groups with the Iran International network, which in practice has formed the International Terrorist Organization. In some cases, the Zionist regime has also communicated with and guided some members of terrorist groups. ...
>
> According to the statements of the Leader of the Revolution, the US, England, and Saudi Arabia played an obvious role in fueling the recent unrest in the country. What plans do the security agencies and Ministry of Intelligence have to compensate for these attempts being made to disrupt security? ...
>
> As for the US regime, in addition to all the hostilities, damages and blows that it has directly and indirectly inflicted upon the Iranian nation, this terrorist regime is the official murderer of the great leader of the Resistance, Martyr Lieutenant General Haj Qasem Soleimani. The position of the US is declining in facing a strong Iran. I say with certainty and decisively that the United States is not capable of a face-to-face military war with us. Therefore, it either joins up with a terrorist group and officially carry [sic] out assassinations [and of course receives a crushing, clear, appropriate, military response in return] or it goes behind the scenes and engages in hybrid warfare, soft warfare and starts provoking others. It has always received responses in these cases and it will continue to receive the same.
>
> As for England, their case as a country that takes the approach of a wily old fox that has never stopped its troublemaking against the Islamic Republic of Iran is different. Currently, the media in England is seeking to create and spread riots in Iran. Both in the past and in the present, their media outlets have stepped beyond the field of directing riots and are seeking to organize malicious movements and acts of terrorism inside the country. These are actions that England has taken. In the past, Iran has repeatedly been a prevention to acts of terrorism against European countries. However, England and a number of European countries have not stopped their hostilities against the Islamic Republic of Iran. Without a doubt, unlike England, we will never support acts of terrorism and the creation of insecurity in other countries. However, we also have no obligation to prevent insecurity in these countries either. Therefore, England will pay for the actions it has taken to try to make the great country of Iran insecure.
>
> Unfortunately, the British government, which operates the BBC and Iran International satellite stations with its support and within its media framework, has taken on a terrorist role today. And this means they are crossing the red line of the Islamic Republic of Iran's security. I would like to state here that the Iran International satellite network is recognized by

---

37 Esmail Khatib, "Interview with the Website of the Supreme Leader" (November 10, 2022), https://english.khamenei.ir/news/9277/Minister-of-Intelligence-analysis-of-recent-hybrid-war-against.

Iran's security agency as a terrorist organization. Its operatives and affiliates will be pursued by the Ministry of Intelligence. And from now on, any kind of connection with this terrorist organization will be considered to be tantamount to entering into terrorism and a threat to the national security of the Islamic Republic of Iran.[38]

London Metropolitan Police stationed armored police vehicles outside the offices of Iran International on November 19, 2022, after Scotland Yard and MI5 discovered threats to the television station by the Iranian government.[39] According to MI5, between January and November 2022, British law enforcement officials foiled at least 10 attempts by the Iranian government to kidnap or kill British citizens, Iranian dissidents, and journalists in the U.K.[40]

The fundamentalist regime had earlier designated the German government's official broadcasting agency, Deutsche Welle Farsi and German newspaper *Bild* as terrorist.[41] It has long been the policy of the fundamentalist regime to designate any entity that criticizes it or publishes critical reports about the regime as terrorist.

5.8.2 Voice of America Television and Radio Farda

Although Iran International TV Has played the bigger role during the 2022 mass protests, one should also emphasize the great roles that the VOA and Radio Farda have been playing for about 40 years in undermining the fundamentalist regime's monopoly of news and analysis, as well as providing objective news and sophisticated analyses. VOA and Radio Farda are broadcasting outlets of the U.S. government. Their missions are to provide objective news and sound analyses, which they usually do. During the past several years and particularly during the 2022–2023 mass protests, several of their journalists have provided excellent programs and analyses. At VOA, one may mention Mehdi Falahati and Siamak Dehghanpour. The producers at VOA, such as Hooman Bakhtiar, have done a truly excellent job inviting some of Iran's top scholars to present their analyses to millions of Irani-

---

38 Ibid.

39 Iran International, "UK Police Positions Armed Vehicles Outside Iran International Building," (November 19, 2022), https://www.iranintl.com/en/202211198849.

40 Iran International, "MI5 Names Iran as Major Security Threat for UK" (November 17, 2022), https://www.iranintl.com/en/202211176309.

41 Deutsche Welle, "Tehran Sanctions DW Farsi for Coverage of Iran Protests" (October 26, 2022), https://www.dw.com/en/iran-sanctions-dw-farsi-for-coverage-of-protests/a-63562810.

ans. At Radio Farda, one may mention Ms. Fahimeh Khezr-Heidari for her excellent reporting.

5.9 The Final Straw

From June 2021, the regime drastically increased not only what constituted proper hijab but also drastically increased violent treatment of women. Before August 2021, as long as a woman had covered much of her hair, it was tolerated. But after August 2021, extremely violent measures were used to more strictly enforce the more draconian version of the hijab law. Before Raisi, the Morality Police would verbally warn women and as soon as they complied would let them leave. After Raisi, the Morality Police would arrest women and drag them into police vans, take them to police stations, and issue hefty fines. The Morality Police (composed of both female and male officers) would use extreme violence against women, publicly beat them up, and force them into police vans. Dozens of videos of these arrests and women's resistance were posted on social media and broadcast on Iran International.

Before Raisi it was uncommon to witness regular fundamentalist women go around and order women to adhere to the more extreme version of hijab. Since Raisi, all of a sudden many videos were posted on social media of fundamentalist women clad in black chador ordering and threatening women (who already had hijab) that their hijab was not sufficient and that they should cover more.

On July 16, 2022, two women in the female section of a bus approached a woman and warned her and videoed her and told her that they were going to give the video to the IRGC. That woman and many other women on the bus resisted the two fundamentalist women and forced them out of the bus. Within hours the woman who had refused to comply was arrested by the IRGC: she was severely tortured to gain a public confession, then the confession was broadcast on state television. The woman, Sepideh Reshno, appeared on television, with her face bruised and purple, in full hijab, confessing. Right after her tortured confession Ms. Reshno was taken to the emergency room and treated for internal bleeding and injuries due to severe beatings and torture.[42]

---

42 Rosie Swash, "Arrests and TV Confessions as Iran Cracks Down on Women's 'Improper' Clothing," *The Guardian* (August 23, 2022), https://www.theguardian.com/global-development/2022/aug/23/arrests-and-tv-confessions-as-iran-cracks-down-on-women-improper-clothing-hijab; and Iran International, "Detained Hijab Protester Beaten Into 'Forced Confessions'" (August 5, 2022), https://www.iranintl.com/en/202208052017.

Many feminists and human rights activists believe that many women have been killed by the Morality Police and buried, and their families threatened into silence. However, Niloufar Hamedi, a brave female journalist, was able to go to the hospital, document, take photos, and write reports on the case of Ms. Mahsa Amini.[43] And, just as significantly, Mahsa's parents refused to remain silent and ignored the threats from the officials, and talked with Ms. Hamedi. Hamedi had earlier reported on Ms. Sepideh Reshno as well. Ms. Hamedi was arrested for reporting the case of Ms. Amini and charged with crimes of photographing and publishing an article for the paper, *Shargh Daily*, that she worked for. The punishment for the crime of reporting could be execution.

5.10 Chronology of the 2022–2023 Mass Protests

For 43 years, the fundamentalist regime had demonized Sunni Kurds as secessionist, anti-Iranian, violent, dangerous, and communist. During Mahsa's public funeral, the people of Saghez utterly vaporized 43 years of propaganda and demonization. Videos of the funeral showed the grieving of Mahsa's loved ones, from her parents, brother, uncles, and aunts. There was not a single call for secession, not a single utterance against Iranians, or Shias, or calls for communism. Most women at the funeral took off their hijab in protest against the murder of Mahsa.

Someone wrote the slogan *"Zan, Zendegi, Azadi"* [Woman, Life, Freedom] and the mourners began shouting this slogan. The slogan had its origins in the PKK, a radical leftist guerrilla group from the Kurdish population of Turkey and had spread to the Iraqi Kurdish region. Kurdish women from Turkey, Iraq, Syria, and Iran had joined various armed groups and had fought bravely against ISIS. The slogan has been embraced by large segments of the Iranian population. This slogan perhaps has a different meaning for the Iranian people than the original meaning of the PKK.

The Iranian people, who have been reeling from 43 years of ultra-misogynist and oppressive rule, condemn the oppression of women. Mahsa could have been any (non-fundamentalist) Iranian woman. To non-fundamentalist women, Mahsa was them. To non-fundamentalist men, Mahsa could have been their sister, mother, wife, or daughter. The people opposed the utter lack of concern for human life under the fundamentalist regime. By "life" the people mean "normal life" like

---

43 *Shargh Daily*, "Niloufar Hamedi, Khabarnegar Shargh Bazdasht Shod" [Niloufar Hamedi, Shargh's Reporter Was Arrested] (September 22, 2022), https://www.sharghdaily.com/fa/tiny/news-856872.

all other people in this world: to pursue what makes them happy. They want to smile, dance, walk in the park holding the hands of loved ones, party with the opposite sex, enjoy public water fights in a park, all activities that are banned and severely punished by the fundamentalist regime. For over 120 years, a substantial segment of the Iranian population has been struggling for *"Azadi"* [freedom]. The demand for freedoms of speech, the press, and political parties were violently repressed by the monarchists and fundamentalists. In recent years the demand for freedom has been embraced by large swathes of the people. Thus, the call for *"Azadi"* resonated with virtually all Iranians (except fundamentalists, monarchists, and Stalinists).

The public reactions among Iranian women and men were immediate and strong. Iranian women grieved publicly, and their anger erupted in mass protests. The fundamentalist regime has imposed a grotesquely oppressive rule on the Iranian people. The murder of Mahsa Amini by the Morality Police triggered an emotional response among non-fundamentalist Iranians, who form the overwhelming majority of the population. The collective lumps in their throats that had been simmering for many years burst into tears. And their silent anger that had been smoldering beneath the surface for these years erupted into protests. After enduring years of discrimination and humiliation by the ultra-reactionary totalitarian theocratic regime, vast swathes of the population have had enough of living on their knees as slaves and have chosen to stand up, fight back, and live and die as free women and men.

The regime responded with massive violence. The regime arrested thousands of protesters, particularly those who acted as leaders. In one infamous case, Nika Shakarami, a 16-year-old female, was arrested during the protests. Her last text to her mother said that the security forces were following her, and she was escaping from them. The police returned her body to her parents 10 days later.[44] The regime broadcast reports on state TV reporting that Nika had committed suicide on September 30 by falling from the fifth floor of a building. The regime then stole the corpse from the family and buried it in a distant village. The regime arrested and tortured Nika's uncle and aunt and forced them to make false confessions on television and threatened to do the same to her grieving mother as well. A CNN investigative report studied 50 videos of September 30 protests in Tehran and spoke to six witnesses that had seen Nika that night. According to the CNN investigation and the videos, Nika had taken a leading role in the September 30 pro-

---

[44] Martin Chulov, "Mother Says Police Beat Daughter to Death in Iranian Protests," *The Guardian* (October 8, 2022), https://www.theguardian.com/world/2022/oct/08/mother-says-police-beat-daughter-to-death-in-iranian-protests.

tests and thrown stones at the coercive apparatuses, and was then trying to leave the scene while being chased by the coercive apparatuses. She was finally cornered and caught and taken into custody. The coroner's report stated that she died due to her head being in contact with a hard object. The CNN investigation with the videos clearly proved that the regime had lied all along.[45]

It appears that picking, arresting, and torturing the individuals that the regime considered to be leaders was a main tactic of the coercive apparatuses. The regime then spread false stories claiming that those it had murdered had died due to suicide, or underlying conditions unrelated to the protests or the regime's coercive apparatuses' actions.

In another tactic, the regime simply massacred the protesters, a tactic that it had used during the November 2019 protests. This occurred in Zahedan on September 30, 2022. After Friday prayers, the worshipers marched toward the police station. The police chief was reported to have raped a 15-year-old girl in custody, a practice that has been done by the coercive apparatuses since 1981 to create an atmosphere of fear among the population and the dissidents. Subsequently the report of the rape of the 15-year-old girl was substantiated and the regime began arresting Balochis who reported the case. According to Amnesty International's investigations, the coercive apparatuses gunned down the protesters, killing 66 unarmed protesters. Another 16 people were killed shortly afterwards as protests spread.[46]

On Friday October 28, after Friday prayers, the people of Zahedan went on a peaceful protest march to condemn the massacre of September 30. The regime killed four of the protesters and wounded many. Among the main slogans were: "Woman, Life, Freedom," "Death to the Dictator," and *"Az Tehran Ta Zahedan, Janam Faday Iran"* [From Tehran to Zahedan, My Life for Iran]. The fundamentalist regime had attempted for over 40 years to portray the Sunni Balochi population as Sunni extremists who are anti-Iranian, and supportive of secession. The peaceful protests calling for freedom and unity of all Iranians undermined 40 years of propaganda and demonization. The Iranian protesters throughout Iran condemned the regime's violence against the people of Zahedan and shouted slogans such as *"Zahedan Cheshm Va Cheragh Iran"* [Zahedan is Eyes and Light of Iran].

---

45 Gianluca Mezzofiore, Katie Polgese, and Adam Pourahmadi, "What Really Happened to Nika Shahkarami? Witnesses to Her Final Hours Cast Doubt on Iran's Story," CNN (October 27, 2022), https://www.cnn.com/2022/10/27/middleeast/iran-nika-shahkarami-investigation-intl-cmd/index.html.
46 Amnesty International, "Iran: At Least 83 Balochi Protesters and Bystanders Killed in Bloody Crackdown" (October 6, 2022), https://www.amnesty.org/en/latest/news/2022/10/iran-at-least-82-ba luchi-protesters-and-bystanders-killed-in-bloody-crackdown/.

Again, on Friday November 4, the Baloch people went on peaceful protests in Baloch-majority cities. In the small city of Khash, the coercive apparatuses killed at least 16 protesters. The highest-ranking Sunni Baloch cleric, Mowlavi Abdol-Hamid, gave a sermon on November 4 to tens of thousands of worshipers. He said: "We do not have Sunni and Shia in Iran, we do not have ethnic groups in Iran, we are all Iranians, we are all one for Iran."[47]

In Iranian culture, people gather at the gravesite of a loved one 40 days after the burying of the loved one to commemorate his or her life. The gathering is called *"Chehelom"* [Fortieth]. The regime threatened the family of Mahsa to make them announce that they would not be holding Mahsa's *Chehelom.* The family refused the regime's threats. The coercive apparatuses showed up in force to prevent the gathering of the people for Mahsa's *Chehelom* at her gravesite in Saghez. Film footage of the crowds shows massive participation. Some estimates indicate that somewhere between 80,000 and 100,000 people went to Saghez to participate in Mahsa's *Chehelom.* Mahsa's mother posted a brief message thanking the Iranian people. She explicitly referred to Mahsa as *"Dokhtar Iran"* [Daughter of Iran] and added that her death brought together people from all regions and ethnic groups from Iran to support Mahsa and grieve for her. Mahsa's mother's words are politically greatly significant. She did not refer to Mahsa as daughter of Kurdistan but daughter of Iran, and moreover she wrote that all ethnic groups were together for the struggle. Her message is a nightmare for the fundamentalist regime whose strategy was to demonize the protest as secessionist, Sunni, communist, and anti-Iranian.

Another tactic that the fundamentalist regime has used to intimidate the people into submission is rape of male and female protesters. On November 21, 2022, CNN published an investigative report on this tactic during the 2022 mass protests.[48] The fundamentalist regime has used this tactic extensively since 1980.[49]

Iranians in the diaspora also have played major roles in supporting the mass protests in various ways. They have organized mass protests that have informed the people and political leaders around the globe of the true nature of the fundamentalist dictatorship. Thanks to these actions, many have reassessed their policies from those that assist the fundamentalist regime to those that side with the Iranian people. For example, on October 1, 2022, more than 50,000 people participated

---

47 Iran International, "News" (November 4, 2022), https://www.iranintl.com/202211041399.

48 CNN, "How Iran's Security Forces Use Rape to Quell Protests: Covert Testimonies Reveal Sexual Assaults on Male and Female Activists as a Women-Led Uprising Spreads" (November 21, 2022), https://www.cnn.com/interactive/2022/11/middleeast/iran-protests-sexual-assault/.

49 Kazemzadeh, *Islamic Fundamentalism,* op cit.

in marches in Richmond Hill, Ontario, Canada, and about 80,000 people participated in marches in Berlin, Germany.[50]

The 2022 mass protests have continued almost non-stop. There have been more activities on certain days and less on others. The *Chehelom* of Mahsa witnessed a major increase in protests despite the regime's threats and preparations to stop the commemorations in various cities. An unexpected increase in protest activities occurred on November 3. Protests occurred in more cities and more people participated in protests. Moreover, there was a major difference in the attitudes of the protesters. In previous protests, there were only a handful of cases where the people attacked the coercive apparatuses. On November 3, there were many cases where the people fought back against the coercive apparatuses, took their weapons from them, and then used the weapons against the coercive apparatuses. Several members of the coercive apparatuses were injured, and the regime evacuated them with helicopters.[51] There are also videos of helicopters that appear to show them used to attack the protesters with "objects and tear gas."[52] Even seasoned observers who were reporting the change in the behavior did not know the reasons for the major change.[53]

Several events occurred on previous days that might have caused the surge in protests and the increased assertiveness of the protesters. On October 30, IRGC Supreme Commander, Gen. Hussein Salami made his infamous threat declaring that "as of today all protests will cease."[54] On November 1, Khamenei made his most threatening speech until then. On November 2, the U.N. held a public hearing on the Iran protests where Javed Rahman, the U.N. Special Rapporteur on Iran's human rights violations, gave a strong speech condemning the fundamentalist regime for the extreme use of violence against unarmed protesters, including killing dozens of children as young as 12. According to Rahman, the regime has killed at

---

50 Isaac Callan, "More than 50k Attend Richmond Hill, Ont. Protest against Iranian Government," *Global News* (October 1, 2022), https://globalnews.ca/news/9169782/richmond-hill-iran-protest/; and Leon Malherbe and Paris Hafezi, "Tens of Thousands March in Berlin in Support of Iran Protests," Reuters (October 22, 2022), https://www.reuters.com/world/middle-east/irans-guards-warn-cleric-over-agitating-restive-southeast-2022-10-22/.

51 Iran International, "News" (November), https://www.iranintl.com/202211031228.

52 Ibid.

53 Iran International, "News Report" (November 3, 2022), https://www.youtube.com/watch?v=qEo0hh4k6i4&t=1s.

54 IRNA, *"Emrooz, Rooze Payan Eghteshashat Ast"* [Today, is the Last Day of the Riots] (October 30, 2022), https://www.irna.ir/news/84925031/%D8%B3%D8%B1%D8%AF%D8%A7%D8%B1-%D8%B3%D9%84%D8%A7%D9%85%DB%8C-%D8%A7%D9%85%D8%B1%D9%88%D8%B2-%D8%B2-%D9%BE%D8%A7%DB%8C%D8%A7%D9%86-%D8%A7%D8%BA%D8%AA%D8%B4%D8%A7%D8%B4%D8%A7%D8%AA-%D8%A7%D8%B3%D8%AA.

least 277 protesters and arrested over 14,000 people, including human rights activists, lawyers, students, and journalists. That speech was followed by two very strong and effective speeches by Shirin Ebadi and Ms. Nazanin Boniadi. With the exceptions of ambassadors from China and Russia, all other ambassadors from the U.N. Security Council strongly supported the protests by the Iranian people. The words from the ambassador from Albania, who was one of the two ambassadors sponsoring the meeting, were particularly heartwarming. He said that Albania also suffered from a terrible totalitarian dictatorship. But the people resisted and fought until their country became free. That if the Iranian people continued their protests, they too would become free.[55] And during the previous days, more and more people, and commentators inside and outside Iran, began referring to the mass protests as revolution and revolutionary uprisings.

It appears that for the first time, many people have come to believe that it is possible to overthrow the regime; therefore, the risks are worth their efforts. In other words, as the protests continue, it shows that the regime is unable to crush the protests; therefore, the regime looks weak, which in turn changes the calculations of many to the benefit of the people. Also, as more world leaders publicly side with the people and condemn the fundamentalist regime, more people in Iran come to believe that their efforts are worth the risks. As the likelihood of regime collapse increases, more people join the protests.

It is clear that the overwhelming majority of the Iranian people oppose the regime, but most are not willing to risk their lives, liberties, wealth, and jobs by joining the protests. Political scientists call this the free-rider problem. Most people in Iran want to live in a democracy but are not willing to pay with their lives and liberties to get it. They hope that others will risk their lives. Once the fundamentalist regime has been overthrown, then we will witness that tens of millions will come to the streets to celebrate the overthrow of the fundamentalist regime and the establishment of democracy.

There are also large numbers of individuals who are opportunists who simply side with whomever is in power. In Iran they are called *"Hezb Baad"* [Party of the Wind]. These individuals have no ideology or partisan attachments or principles. Their primary motivation is connection to power for personal financial gain. These opportunistic individuals leave the regime as soon as they come to believe that the regime might collapse.

Unlike the previous mass protests, the 2022 protests look more and more like a revolution that might overthrow the regime. The longer the protests continue and

---

55 The video of the U.N. Security Council's informal meeting is available at https://media.un.org/en/asset/k11/k119xlbgct.

the stronger the global support for the Iranian people, the weaker the fundamentalist regime will become. Once it appears that the overthrow is highly likely, the collapse will come very fast.

The fundamentalist regime appears to be very concerned about being overthrown. Many believe that the regime's missile and drone attacks on the headquarters of several Iranian Kurdish groups (e. g., Democratic Party of Iranian Kurdistan and Komala) in the Iraqi Kurdish region are carried out by the regime in order to divert attention from the mass protests. The regime also sent the military to attack and occupy the Kurdish-majority city of Mahabad on November 20, 2022.[56] Many believe that the fundamentalist regime is deliberately attempting to provoke the Iranian Kurdish parties to retaliate and use armed struggle to defend themselves and the Iranian Kurds from the terribly violent attacks by the fundamentalist regime.[57]

A major factor that would increase the likelihood of success of the movement to overthrow the regime would be increased divisions among the fundamentalist elites and major segments of the fundamentalist elites breaking away from the regime and siding with the opposition. On February 4, 2023, Mir-Hussein Moussavi released a statement announcing that he now opposes the fundamentalist regime and the fundamentalist constitution.[58] Moussavi is one of the top leaders of the fundamentalist regime and one of the top two leaders of the reformist faction of the oligarchy. Moussavi's support for a referendum and free elections for a constituent assembly to write a new constitution based on democracy and human rights is highly significant. Moussavi enjoys great support among the social base of the fundamentalist regime, including among the rank-and-file members of the IRGC and Ministry of Intelligence. It is highly likely that Moussavi would chisel away a segment of the fundamentalist base and bring them to the democratic opposition. Moussavi's decision greatly increases the likelihood of regime collapse and greatly increases the likelihood of success of the democratic opposition.

A major piece of evidence that the 2022 mass protests have drastically increased internal divisions may have surfaced on March 19, 2023. A secret document was provided to Iran International and Iran Wire. It is not clear whether the docu-

---

56 Iran International, "Islamic Republic Steps Up Military Crackdown in Kurdish Cities" (November 20, 2022), https://www.iranintl.com/en/202211207781; and Iran International, "Islamic Republic Deploys Military to Quash Protests in Kurdish City" (November 21, 2022), https://www.iranintl.com/en/202211206594.

57 Iran International, "Islamic Republic Intensifying Attacks on Kurdish Targets in Iran and Iraq" (November 21, 2022), https://www.iranintl.com/en/202211215732.

58 Maryam Sinaee, "Former Iran PM Turned Opposition Has Believers and Critics," Iran International (February 8, 2023), https://www.iranintl.com/en/202302071911.

ment was leaked by a member of the fundamentalist oligarchy or hacked by a spy agency. If the document is genuine, it is one of the most significant secret documents from the IRI that has become public. According to the document, there was a secret meeting on January 3, 2023, on the anniversary of Gen. Soleimani's death, between high-ranking military and intelligence officials and Khamenei. The secret document was written by someone at the Supreme Leader's Office and is a summary of the minutes of the meeting. The officials talked for about two hours. Then, Khamenei talked briefly. The document is 44 pages long.[59]

According to the document, 45 high officials, including 32 generals and admirals, 8 colonels, and 5 clerics (who were top security and intelligence officials) spoke during the meeting. Among them were: Gen. Hussein Salami, the Head of the IRGC; Gen. Esmail Qaani Akbarnejad, the Head of the IRGC-Qods Force; Gen. Gholam-Ali Rashid, the Head of Khatam al-Anbia Unified Command and former Deputy-Head of the General Command of the Armed Forces of the IRI; Admiral Ali-Reza Tangsiri, Head of the IRGC-Navy; Gen. Mohammad Hussein Nejat, Deputy Head of the Sarallah Command (the IRGC unit responsible for the security of Tehran); Gen. Amir Ali Hajizadeh, the Head of the IRGC Aerospace Force; Admiral Ali Shamkhani, current Secretary of the Supreme National Security Council, former Minister of Defense and former Head of IRGC-Navy, and one of the top promoters of acquisition of nuclear weapons; and Gen. Mohammad Kazemi, Head of the IRGC-Intelligence Organization. Most of the other generals and colonels are combatant commanders in various provinces and cities. The clerics include: Hojatolislam Mahmoud Mohammadi Shahroodi, the Head of *Basij* Clergy, the hardline clerics and seminary students; Hojatolislam Abdollah Haji-Sadeghi, the Representative of the Supreme Leader at the IRGC; Hojatolislam Ali Saeedi Shahroodi, former Representative of the Supreme Leader at the IRGC and current Head of the Political-Ideological Bureau of the Supreme Commander; Hojatolislam Esmail Khatib, Minister of Intelligence; and Hojatolislam Ali-Asghar Hejazi, the Head of the Security and Political Bureau of the Office of the Supreme Leader.

According to hardline Hojatolislam Mohammadi Shahroodi, "more than 5,000 *Basiji* seminary students have abandoned their studies. ... They have ideological problems with the [fundamentalist] regime, many insult the Supreme Leader." According to Hojatolislam Abdollah Haji-Sadeghi, "many high-ranking clerical teach-

---

59 The document in Persian is at https://static.prod.iranwire.com/pdfcomponent/Final_pcSv.pdf#view=fitH. Also see Iran Wire, "Exclusive: IRGC Commanders Warn Khamenei About Implosion" (March 19, 2023), https://iranwire.com/en/politics/114906-exclusive-irgc-commanders-warn-khamenei-about-implosion/; and Maryam Sinaee, "Leaked Document Reveals Loss of Loyalty, Insubordination in IRGC," Iran International (March 20, 2023), https://www.iranintl.com/en/202303192652.

ers at the seminaries insult the Supreme Leader." Haji-Sadeghi added that it is true that there has been substantial abandonment of the fundamentalist regime among the coercive apparatuses, including fights among the forces. Haji-Sadeghi said that there are about 600,000 members of the coercive apparatuses. That not supporting the regime does not mean that they will fight against the regime. Haji-Sadeghi said that various reports indicate that from 12 % to 68 % of the members of the coercive apparatuses have abandoned the regime. Haji-Sadeghi said that they could rely upon a little more than 50 % of the members of the coercive apparatuses to support the regime. According to Hojatolislam Khatib, there have been about 20,000 members of the coercive apparatuses that have had issues that the Ministry of Intelligence had to investigate and send reports to other entities about them. Khatib added that the youth are showing great courage in confronting the coercive apparatuses.[60]

According to Col. Ehsan Khorshidi, many of his soldiers are sympathetic to the protesters. Some stole food from the IRGC facility and distributed it among the poor in the city of Karaj. Col. Khorshidi added that many of the IRGC members have their own family members among the protesters. He said that: "This morning at least six of my IRGC members came to me and asked that I intervene and release their family members who have been arrested during the protests." Gen. Rahim Noee-Eghdam reported that many of his Qods Force troops in Syria have problems with both economic issues and ideological issues: "Many have been selling our intelligence to Israel which it uses to trap and kill our forces."[61] Gen. Hussein Hekmatian Raz said that his troops included many ethnic groups who fight bravely against foreign forces but refuse to fight against the protesters and have disobeyed orders to suppress the people. Gen. Rashid said that there have been several major disobediences by the troops, including three occasions that a group planned to use artillery to bomb various places in Tehran including the Residence of the Supreme Leader. Gen. Ghodratollah Karimian said that his troops have fought bravely against foreign forces, but they will not shoot at women and poor people who lack food. There is a difference between rioters and protesters, and his troops will not shoot at protesters. Gen. Nejat said that half of the members of the coercive apparatuses want to leave the forces. Gen. Mahmoud Chahar-baghi said that one of his top commanders in Syria left the battlefield and came back to Tehran because his wife had been arrested by the IRGC during the protests and is in Evin prison. Gen. Kazemi, the Head of the IRGC Intelligence Organization, said that there are about 4 million youth between 14 and 18 years of age who strongly

---

60 Ibid. All direct words cited are my translation.
61 Ibid. All direct words cited are my translation.

oppose the regime and show courage in their fight against the regime. Gen. Kazemi added that in cities up to 55% of the people stood up to the coercive apparatuses and that in certain neighborhoods up to 79% of the people stood up to the coercive apparatuses.[62]

Khamenei then spoke and ordered increase in salaries for the members of the coercive apparatuses. Shortly thereafter, the budget for the coercive apparatuses was increased by 52%. Members of the *Basij* were exempt from income taxes as well as ever paying for utilities such as water, electricity, gas, and the like. He also ordered the judiciary to be lenient toward family members of the coercive apparatuses who had been arrested during the protests. He also said that those members of the coercive apparatuses who had disobeyed orders to suppress the protesters should be won back by increasing their salaries.[63]

On February 14, 2023, a charter was published by 20 of Iran's most prominent and active civil society organizations and syndicates resisting the fundamentalist regime.[64] These 20 organizations included two teachers' syndicates, nine workers' unions, two university student groups, one high school student group, two women's organizations, three pensioners' groups, and one human rights organization. All these groups are independent of the state and represent people in their areas of vocation. These grassroots organizations have been organizing their constituents in the previous years to protest the policies of the regime. Many of their leaders and members have been arrested, incarcerated, and tortured by the regime. The text of the charter is clearly social democratic and against the dictatorships of the fundamentalist regime and the Pahlavi regime.

Within hours of the publication of this charter, Iran's main pro-democracy and progressive parties and organizations published their full support of the charter and the civil society organizations behind it. These parties include the Iran National Front-Organizations Abroad, Iran National Front-Europe, the Left Party of Iran (LPI), United Republicans of Iran, and Solidarity of Iranian Republicans.[65] The Iran National Front is Iran's main, oldest, and largest pro-democracy political party and is a coalition of liberal democrats and social democrats. The LPI is the largest leftist party of Iran. The United Republicans of Iran and the Solidarity of Iranian Repub-

---

62 Ibid.

63 Iran Wire, "Exclusive: IRGC Commanders Warn Khamenei About Implosion" (March 19, 2023).

64 *"Manshoor Motalebat Tashakolhay Mostaghel Senfi Va Madani Iran"* [Charter of Demands of the Independent Organizations of Civil Society and Syndicates of Iran] (February 2023), https://www.iran-emrooz.net/index.php/news1/more/106294/.

65 *"Bayaniyeh Jamee Az Sazemanha Va Ahzab Jomhurikhah Va Secular Democrat"* [Statement of a Group of Republican and Secular Democratic Organizations and Parties] (February 16, 2023), https://melliun.org/iran/352267.

licans are the two main organizations of democratic republicans. These parties constitute Iran's main pro-democracy coalition.[66] The LPI had been working closely with the INF in order to create a broad-based pro-democracy coalition. On March 9, 2023, these five democratic republican parties and groups announced the formation of their coalition.[67] These five groups had been closely working with each other for the previous five years. This coalition has the potential to attract other forces, such as the 20 civil society organizations. If it is able to do so, it will become the main alternative to the fundamentalist regime and guarantee that the post-fundamentalist Iran will be a democracy.

5.11 Characteristics

There is widespread consensus among observers inside Iran that the objective of the 2022 mass protests is to overthrow the regime. Leaders and top members of all fundamentalist factions (hardline, expedient, reformist) have opposed the mass protests.[68] By and large, hardliners have strongly condemned the protests, while expedients and reformists have condemned the protests or remained silent or made suggestions on how to save the system through reform. Khamenei has publicly characterized the mass protests as a hybrid war orchestrated by the U.S., Britain, Israel, and Saudi Arabia, with the objective to overthrow the fundamentalist regime. Former President Mohammad Khatami has also expressed opposition to the 2022 mass protests, as he did with the mass protests during 2017 and 2019. In his Instagram account, Khatami wrote: "overthrow is neither possible nor desirable; however, with the continuation of the current situation, every moment will increase the condition for social collapse."[69] Obviously, for members of the fundamentalist oligarchy overthrow of their regime is not desirable. However, for the opponents of the fundamentalist dictatorship, the replacement of the fundamentalist dictatorship with secular democracy is highly desirable. Not only the democratic opposition considers democracy preferable to the fundamentalist dictatorship, but also the non-democratic opposition considers democracy to be more desirable than the fundamentalist regime. The only groups in Iran that do not consider the replacement of the fundamentalist regime to be desirable are supporters

66 Kazemzadeh, *The Iran National Front,* op cit.
67 See the announcement at https://melliun.org/iran/355228.
68 There are only a handful of exceptions, such as Mir-Hussein Moussavi and Faezeh Hashemi Rafsanjani.
69 Mohammad Khatami (November 14, 2022) https://www.instagram.com/p/Ck7-Ru9sdgd/?utm_source=ig_embed&ig_rid=ba244963-52c6-4f2b-9804-af1daf4170b5.

of the fundamentalist dictatorship, which include all three main fundamentalist factions.

Outside Iran, however, the supporters of the fundamentalist regime portray the 2022 mass protests (as well as the mass protests of 2017–2018 and 2019) as reforms within the system. In other words, the supporters of the fundamentalist regime, including non-Iranian promoters of appeasement of the fundamentalist regime, argue that the objective of the mass protests is not overthrow, or revolution. The supporters of the fundamentalist regime and the non-Iranian pro-appeasement individuals argue that the objective of the 2022 mass protests is merely to change the law on compulsory hijab.

The best research that debunks the falsehoods of the supporters of the fundamentalist regime has been published by the Tony Blair Institute for Global Change.[70] Cooperating with the Group for Analyzing and Measuring Attitudes in Iran (GAMAAN), the most reliable public opinion research institute on the attitudes of the Iranian people, the study convincingly demonstrates that the overwhelming majority of the Iranian people oppose the fundamentalist regime and have been struggling to change the regime to a democratic secular political system.[71] According to this study:

> **Young people are not the only group who oppose the compulsory hijab.** Polling found that 78 per cent of respondents aged between 20 and 29, 68 per cent between 30 and 49, and 74 per cent aged over 50 are against the mandatory imposition of the hijab.
>
> **Men support Iranian women and stand against the mandatory imposition of the hijab.** Through polling Iranians, we found that 71 per cent of men and 74 per cent of women disagree with the mandatory imposition of the hijab.
>
> **Iranian society has experienced mass secularisation, which cuts across Iran's rural–urban divide.** Only 26 per cent of urban Iranians pray five times a day while 33 per cent of rural Iranians follow the same Islamic prescription. Similarly, only 28 per cent of rural Iranians and 21 per cent of urban Iranians believe in the practice of wearing the hijab. …
>
> **Protests against the compulsory hijab are about regime change.** Of those who are against the compulsory hijab, 84 per cent also want to live in a secular state. As a secular state is impossible under the Islamic Republic, this is indicative of the demand for regime change among the people.[72]

---

70 Kasra Aarabi and Jemima Shelley, "Protests and Polling Insights From the Streets of Iran: How Removal of the Hijab Became a Symbol of Regime Change" (November 22, 2022), https://institute.global/policy/protests-and-polling-insights-streets-iran-how-removal-hijab-became-symbol-regime-change.

71 GAMAAN's website is at https://gamaan.org/.

72 Aarabi and Shelley, "Protests and Polling Insights," op. cit.

GAMAAN conducted a comprehensive survey of Iranians inside and outside Iran between December 21 and 31, 2022.[73] According to this survey:

> In response to the question "Islamic Republic: Yes or No?" 81% of respondents inside the country responded "No" to the Islamic Republic, 15% responded "Yes," and 4% were not sure. Of the Iranian respondents abroad, 99% responded "No," opting against the Islamic Republic.
>
> Those who answered "No" to the Islamic Republic or "I do not know" in the question on a referendum about the Islamic Republic were asked a follow-up question about their preferred democratic and secular alternative regime type. Of those, 28% inside Iran and 32% outside Iran would prefer a presidential republic, 12% inside Iran and 29% outside Iran would prefer a parliamentary republic regime type, and 22% inside Iran and 25% outside Iran would prefer a constitutional monarchy.
>
> Regarding the nationwide protests of the past months, 80% of those inside the country support the protests; 67% believe the protests will succeed, while 14% think they will not succeed. Around 15% of the population inside the country oppose the protests. Respondents outside the country overwhelmingly support the protests; of these, 90% think they will succeed, and only 9% think they will not succeed.
>
> In response to a question about their political orientations, 60% of respondents inside the country describe themselves as proponents for regime change as a precondition for any meaningful change; 16% are proponents of a structural transformation and transition away from the Islamic Republic; 11% are proponents of the principles of the Islamic Revolution and the Supreme Leader; 6% are proponents of gradual reforms within the framework of the Islamic Republic; and 6% don't identify with any of these political orientations. In comparison with GAMAAN's previous surveys, after the 2022 nationwide protests the percentage of those who support regime change increased by 20%.[74]

According to the December 2022 GAMAAN survey, about 15% of Iranians inside Iran support the fundamentalist regime and only about 1% of Iranians outside Iran support the fundamentalist regime. About 11% of the population inside Iran support Khamenei and the hardline faction while between 4 and 6% of the population support the reformist faction; all the fundamentalist factions constituting about 15% of the population. About 81% of Iranians inside Iran oppose the fundamentalist regime, and about 4% were not sure. About 99% of Iranians outside Iran oppose the fundamentalist regime. Of the 85% of Iranians inside Iran who oppose the regime or are not sure, a total of 40% support a democratic republican form of regime for the post-fundamentalist system while 22% support monarchy.

---

73 Ammar Maleki and Pooyan Tamimi Arab, "Iranians' Attitudes Toward the 2022 Nationwide Protests," GAMAAN (February 4, 2023), https://gamaan.org/wp-content/uploads/2023/02/GAMAAN-Protests-Survey-English-Report-Final.pdf.
74 Ibid., p. 1.

Of the 99 % of Iranians outside Iran who oppose the regime, about 61 % support a republican form of system while 25 % support monarchy.

One of the most reliable sources for collection of data on the 2022 protests is the Human Rights Activists News Agency (HRANA), which includes the work of all the major Iranian human rights organizations.[75] According to HRANA, between September 17 and November 20, 2022, the regime killed at least 419 protesters, including at least 60 children under 18 years of age, and arrested at least 17,451 people, including at least 540 university students. According to HRANA, protests occurred in 155 cities and 142 universities.[76]

In mid-November, the hacktivist group Black Reward was able to gain access to files of the Fars News Agency, which is the IRGC's media arm and staffed by many intelligence officers from the IRGC-Intelligence Organization. The Black Reward shared the files with Iran International. In one file, the Deputy Commander of the *Basij*, IRGC Gen. Qassem Qoreishi, was speaking with hardline media managers associated with the IRGC discussing the mass protests for about two and half hours.[77] Iran International has made available the audio file as well as Persian and English excerpts of the talk and discussion between Gen. Qoreishi and the media managers. One of the main topics of discussion is the morale of the coercive apparatuses. They express worries that the coercive apparatuses are exhausted, unhappy, and their confidence shaken. The report states:

> It is also revealed in the file that Supreme Leader Ali Khamenei has complained about the silence of the members of the Expediency Council regarding the protests. According to one of the speakers, Khamenei in his meeting with Police Chief Hossein Ashtari has warned that "You must not lose your confidence." The managers of the state-affiliated media have also demanded a pay raise for special police forces, warning, "There is no good news about police forces. They are exhausted and so unhappy, especially after the events happened [sic] in Sistan and Baluchestan."[78]

The Black Reward hackers also gained access to a 123-page top-secret report on the 2022 mass protests that the Fars News Agency had prepared for IRGC Gen. Hussein

---

75 Its website is at https://www.hra-news.org/. The website's English-language page is at https:// www.en-hrana.org/.
76 See a summary of HRANA's report (November 21, 2022) at https://melliun.org/iran/340164. HRANA posts its daily count on its Telegram social media. See https://t.me/hranews/75723.
77 Iran International, "Hacked Audio File Reveals Concern About Failure to Stop Iran Unrest" (November 28, 2022), https://www.iranintl.com/en/202211282012.
78 Ibid.

Salami, the Head of the IRGC.[79] The top-secret report was completed on November 24, 2022. The report was made solely for Gen. Salami and was not submitted to any other official. According to this secret report, the regime has arrested over 30,000 protesters, including 115 members of the coercive apparatuses for their support for the people. Although not presenting a number, the report states that the number of deaths of protesters has been several times that of the deaths of the 2019 mass protests. It is significant that the internal secret numbers of the regime for those killed and incarcerated have been much higher than those published by civil society sources. It is also significant that the regime's publicly stated numbers are vastly less than the numbers the regime includes in its secret documents. According to the report, about 600,000 people had participated in the mass protests. The report also cites several polls taken by various fundamentalist entities (e. g., the Ministry of the Interior). According to one poll cited, 84 % of the respondents said that the mass protests will have positive ramifications. About 70 % of the respondents said that they would not participate in pro-regime rallies. According to the report, the biggest victory for the opposition is that the people's fears of the coercive apparatuses have evaporated.

Although the protests since 1981 share many characteristics, each set of protests has also had its unique features. The following characteristics distinguish the 2022–2023 protests from earlier protests.

5.11.1 Women's Revolution

Large numbers of women participated in these protests. Moreover, women took leadership roles in these protests. Men strongly supported women in these protests. In other words, while women were asking for their rights, men stood shoulder to shoulder with them supporting equal rights for women.

5.11.2 Widespread Participation by Young Women

For the first time since 1981, large numbers of female high school students participated in these protests. The protests coincided with the opening of schools in Iran, which open on September 23. The sheer numbers and their courage had not been seen since 1981. High school teachers had been protesting for better pay during the

---

79 Iran International has posted the secret report (November 24, 2022) at https://issuu.com/ira nintl/docs/b29_2_1.

previous year and they called upon their students to support the protests after Mahsa's murder, which might have played a role, but that role was minor. Young females have enthusiastically participated in the 2022 protests. The regime has violently attacked female high schools and arrested large numbers of students and sent them to mental institutions. Despite extremely violent attacks by the regime, the continued brave resistance of young high school female students is one of the major surprises of the 2022 mass protests.

The fundamentalist regime has had a program to brainwash children from kindergarten to high school through textbooks, ideological lectures, songs, and the like. The widespread participation of young females and males in the 2022 mass protests clearly shows that the regime's brainwashing programs failed badly.[80] According to IRGC Adm. Ali Fadavi, Deputy Commander of the IRGC, the average age of those arrested during the mass protests is 15 years of age.[81] The coercive apparatuses have attacked high schools and rounded up large numbers of students and sent them to mental institutions to teach them to conform to the fundamentalist rules.[82]

There are many reasons why the fundamentalist regime's intense brainwashing programs at schools failed. One, a major reason is the overall failure of the fundamentalist regime, as discussed earlier in this book. Two, many non-fundamentalist parents teach their children values in contradiction to the fundamentalist values. Three, because of the internet and social media, students have access to information, values, and lifestyles that they find contrary to and far more attractive than the reactionary and oppressive ideology of the fundamentalist regime. Four, many teachers and administrators in schools from 1st to 12th grades actually love to teach students rather than to indoctrinate them in fundamentalist dogma. Students tend to respect such teachers who truly care for them and respect them rather than the fundamentalist apparatchiks and enforcers at schools.[83]

80 Nadeem Ebrahim, "Iran Faces Dilemma as Children Join Protests in 'Unprecedented' Phenomenon," CNN (October 17, 2022), https://www.cnn.com/2022/10/17/middleeast/iran-school-children-protests-mime-intl/index.html.
81 Ibid.
82 Ibid.
83 Iran International, "Special Coverage of the Protests" (October 19, 2022), https://www.youtube.com/watch?v=UyIQzC_kA_Q.

5.11.3 Youth's Revolution

For the first time, young people have participated in very large numbers. The regime has also systematically targeted the youth.[84] The regime's coercive apparatuses shoot children in the head and heart to kill them. By November 21, the regime had killed at least 60 children under 18years of age. The youngest is Kian Pirfalak, a nine-year-old boy killed by the regime in the city of Izeh in Khuzestan province.[85]

5.11.4 Ethno-sectarian Minorities as Pillars of a Pluralistic Iran

Men and women from all ethnic groups participated in these protests. In some earlier protests only people from Persian provinces were protesting, for example, while the others tended to remain silent, or protests were occurring in Kurdistan or Baluchistan and other ethnic-majority provinces were silent. The fundamentalist regime has pursued a policy of sowing fear and hatred among various ethno-sectarian groups and presenting its (despotic) rule as necessary for preserving the territorial integrity of Iran. In the 2022 mass protests, protesters in Khuzestan province shouted slogans in Azerbaijani to send their solidarity to the people of Azerbaijan when the regime was using extremely violent repression. And the people in Azerbaijan shouted slogans in Kurdish to show their solidarity with the people in Kurdish regions. And the Kurds shouted slogans in Persian to support people in Persian-majority provinces and Balochis in the Balochi regions. In the 2022 mass protests, the Iranian people explicitly rejected the fundamentalist regime's ideology of hatred and division.

The fact that the 2022 mass protests have been explicitly inclusive of all ethno-sectarian groups in Iran is significant. The slogans have been consciously for freedom and democracy for Iran. Not a single call for secession has been made, no racist slogan has been shouted. This has great significance for the success of the mass protests. The fundamentalist regime had relied upon the fear of the population of secession, civil war, and bloodshed to both justify its repression and convince the population to submit to its dictatorship. The fundamentalist regime's Shia fundamentalist constitution, laws, and policies explicitly discriminate against the non-Shia population. The regime has pursued terribly bigoted propaganda against Iran's ethno-sectarian minorities such as Kurds, Balochis, Turkomans, and Arabs

84 Iran International, "News" (November 20, 2022), https://www.iranintl.com/202211217863.
85 Babak Dehghanpisheh, "The Killing of a 9-Year-Old Boy Further Ignites Iran's Anti-government Protests," *The Washington Post* (November 18, 2022), https://www.washingtonpost.com/world/2022/11/18/iran-protests-izeh-kian-pirfalak/.

in conjunction with its violent suppression and oppression of these minorities. The 2022 mass protests demand freedom, democracy, and secularism for all Iranians. This movement totally removes any notions of ethno-sectarian identity and considers all Iranians equal before the law. It demands human rights, civil liberties, and democratic rights for all Iranians. Moreover, the demands are modern, secular, feminist, democratic, and pluralistic.

This movement reflects a seismic shift in Iranian politics. There have been ethnic parties among some ethnic groups in Iran that were based on ethnic demands. For example, the Democratic Party of Iranian Kurdistan (DPIK) made demands for autonomy right after the revolution. Around 2000–2001, the DPIK modified that position and began demanding *"federalism bar asas meliyat"* [federalism on the basis of nationality] in Iran. To many, such demands appear more like confederation than federal systems in the U.S. or Germany. Moreover, many fear that such demands may lead to civil war and secession. In 2022 sentiments and politics have changed greatly. The ethnic-nationalist demands were based on several assumptions. One, most Kurds in Iran want to have a Kurdish autonomous region. Two, non-Kurds discriminate against Kurds. Three, Kurds in Iran have more in common with Kurds in Iraq, Turkey, and Syria so that a great Kurdish state encompassing all Kurds in the Middle East is both feasible and desirable.

Although the DPIK has great support among the Kurds, most Kurds in Iran do not support it. The Kurds constitute about 8–10% of Iran's population and about 40–45% of Iranian Kurds are Shia. The dominant sentiment of Shia Kurds has always been for Iran and against secession. The Shia Kurdish regions have always been strongholds of the Iran National Front, which advocates democracy for Iran and full legal equality for all Iranians. For example, the number one leader of the INF was Dr. Karim Sanjabi (between 1977 and the 1990s), who was elected to the Majles from Kermanshah, whose population is primarily Shia Kurd. The same is true for Dr. Ali Ardalan.[86] Moreover, many Sunni Kurds have also been members and leaders of the INF. For example, Dr. Ali Mehrasa, the mayor of Saghez after the revolution, has been a top leader of the INF. The same is true for Hormoz Chamanara.

To the shock and horror of many Iranian Kurds, some Kurds in Iraq, Turkey, and Syria have good relations with the fundamentalist regime that has been oppressing and brutalizing Iranian Kurds. For example, the Patriotic Union of Kurdistan, the second largest party among Iraqi Kurds, has had close relations with the fundamentalist regime, receiving funds and weapons from the IRI, and has had close collaboration with the IRGC. The largest party among Kurds in Turkey has

---

86 Kazemzadeh, *The Iran National Front*, op. cit., p. 45.

been the PKK, a far-left militant party. The PKK has had a long and strange relationship with the fundamentalist regime. When the IRI has had bad relations with the government of Turkey, the IRI has provided funds and weapons to the PKK and has allowed it to use Iranian territory to carry out violent attacks on Turkey. The PKK has collaborated closely with the IRGC in cornering and violently attacking the DPIK. However, when the IRI has had good relations with the Turkish government, then the PKK has allowed PJAK (its Iranian Kurdish affiliate) to carry out attacks against the Iranian government inside Iran. PJAK has refused to cooperate with other Iranian Kurdish groups.

It appears to me that the vast majority of the Iranian Kurds have come to view Iran as their true home, particularly in recent years. Furthermore, they have come to realize that there have not been serious conflicts between the Iranian Kurds and other ethnic groups in Iran. Rather, the violent conflicts have been instigated by the Pahlavi regime (Reza Shah and Mohammad Reza Shah) and the fundamentalist regime, regimes that have also oppressed and brutalized all other ethnic groups in Iran including Persians.

In sum, the secessionist sentiments among Iranian Kurds have been diminishing drastically in recent years. The deep grieving, outpouring of emotion, and reactions of all Iranian ethno-sectarian groups for Mahsa's death have cemented the emotional bonds between Iranian Kurds and the rest of the population. The Iranian Kurds saw the outrage, uprisings, struggles, and mass protests by all Iranians. These reactions proved the love and unity that all other ethno-sectarian groups in Iran have for Iranian Kurds. It appears to me that the vast majority of the Iranian Kurds want to be part of a free and democratic Iran where all citizens are equal before the law and there would be no ethnic or sectarian discrimination. Under such popular sentiments, the DPIK may change its demands and embrace a unitary system in Iran with decentralization whereby people would in democratic elections choose their provincial governors and mayors. Such a position would pave the way for a broad-based alliance between national political parties and ethnic-based parties, which would not only expedite the overthrow of the fundamentalist regime but also virtually guarantee the establishment of democracy in the post-fundamentalist Iran.

There are historical reasons for optimism that the DPIK may evolve in this direction. When the revolution occurred in 1977–1979, the DPIK was a conventional pro-Moscow Communist Party working closely with the Tudeh Party. However, under the able leadership of Dr. Abdul Rahman Qassemlou, its long-time Secretary-General, the DPIK gradually moved away from being a Stalinist party to Eurocommunist, then democratic socialist, and finally a social democratic party.[87] As of March 2023, the DPIK refers to Iranian Kurds (and other ethnic minorities in Iran) as *"mellat"* [nation] and not *"ghom"* [ethnic group]. This is politically significant and sensitive. A nation is associated with a state of its own, whereas many ethnic groups coexist in one state. To consider Kurds in Iran an ethnic group, means that one calls Iran its nation and that one supports a unified Iran. Whereas to consider Kurds in Iran (and Balochis, Turkmans, Azerbaijanis, Arabs) a nation may mean that each of these groups may secede. And as of March 2023, the DPIK has not modified its demand for a "federalism based on nationalities."

We observe an interesting evolution in the Komala Party of Iranian Kurdistan, the second largest ethnic party among Sunni Kurds. Under the leadership of Abdullah Mohtadi, the Komala, which was an extremist Maoist party in 1979, has abandoned extremism and dictatorship and has embraced social democracy. Whereas in 1979–1985, there were armed clashes between DPIK and Komala, today the two parties work closely together.[88] In January and February 2023, Mohtadi began working closely with Reza Pahlavi and others attempting to organize an alternative to the fundamentalist regime. In early March 2023, Mohtadi began using the term *"ghom"* rather than *"mellat"* for Kurds in Iran.[89]

5.11.5 From Small Towns and Rural Areas to Large Cities

People from small towns, medium-sized cities, and large cities participated in these protests. In the 2009–2010 protests, although millions were participating, the protests tended to occur in the five largest cities.

5.11.6 Multi-class Mass Participation

The protests occurred among the working classes, lower middle classes, middle classes, and upper middle classes. In 2009–2010, the protests largely came from middle classes in large cities. In the protests during 2018 and November 2019, the overwhelming majority of the protesters were from the working classes. The middle classes were conspicuous by their absence between 2017 and 2019. The 2022 mass protests have truly been multi-class protests.

---

87 The party's website is at https://pdki.org/english/.
88 The party's website is at https://www.komalainternational.org/.
89 See his views at Iran International, *"Chashmandaz"* (March 11, 2023), https://www.youtube.com/watch?v=pzTKvruDLjE.

Workers in the oil refineries and petrochemical industries participated in the 2022 mass protests. This category had not participated in mass protests since the 1979 revolution. Significantly, the workers did not go on strike for personal financial benefit; rather, they said they were going to strike to express solidarity with the mass protesters and put pressure on the fundamentalist regime's coercive apparatuses to stop using violence against the people. Workers in other areas have had major strikes since 1979 and some of them began strikes in solidarity with the mass protesters and the oil and petrochemical workers. A major example is the workers in the Haft-Tapeh Sugar Cane Company in Khuzestan province, Iran's largest sugar cane agrobusiness enterprise. Esmail Bakhshi, the leader of the workers at the Haft-Tapeh company, said that the primary reason that the workers were protesting was to express their solidarity with the mass protesters and the workers in the oil industry.[90]

By late November, workers and employees from several major industries were also on strike; some made explicit political demands while others made only economic demands. Among these were a steel mill in Isfahan, aluminum factory in Fars, diesel factory in Qazvin, and one of only two syringe factories in Iran.[91]

Keepers of small shops in the traditional bazaars in several cities (e. g., Mashhad, Tehran) also participated in the 2022 mass protests. With a few minor exceptions, the bazaar shop keepers had not participated in mass protests since the 1979 revolution. The only places that had witnessed participation of shop keepers in protests between 1979 and 2022 had been in Kurdish areas. According to hardline media managers associated with the IRGC, on November 15 the strikes by shop keepers were highly successful. According to these sources: "In the meeting, state media managers say 22 provinces were the scene of strikes on November 15, adding that around 70 to 100 percent of markets and bazaars were shut down on that day. Based on the file, most of the closures were in [the] capital Tehran and in some cities almost 100 percent of the shops and businesses were closed."[92]

For the first time since 1981, university professors have joined the protest movement. Before 1981, Iranian university professors (along with their students) had been at the forefront of all liberal and progressive movements in Iran. This

90 Iran International, *"Tadavom Eatesab Kargaran Peymani Palayeshgaha Va Tajamoe Karkonan Sherkat Neishekar Haft-Tapeh Dar Rooz Seshanbeh"* [The Continuation of the Strikes by Contract Workers at Refineries and Assembling of Employees of Haft-Tapeh Sugarcane Company on Tuesday] (October 18, 2022), https://www.iranintl.com/202210182107.
91 Iran International, "News" (November 23, 2022), https://www.iranintl.com/en/202211231359.
92 Iran International, "Hacked Audio File Reveals Concern About Failure to Stop Iran Unrest" (November 28, 2022), https://www.iranintl.com/en/202211282012.

was particularly the case during Dr. Mossadegh's government (1951–1953), when professors and students were one of the main pillars of the pro-democracy movement and the Iran National Front (1960–1963).[93] In the 1970s and 1980s, university professors tended to be liberal while university students tended to join more radical groups (usually on the far-left communist or far-right Islamist). From 1981, university professors kept their views private because they were worried about being fired or arrested by the intelligence agencies. For the first time since 1981, during the 2022 protests university professors supported their students and condemned the repression of the regime.

Historically, large numbers of physicians in Iran have been strong supporters of democracy, modernity, personal freedoms, civil liberties, and civil rights. The Physicians' Organization of the INF is one of its strongest groups, and early on it published a statement supporting the mass protests. The fundamentalist regime had engaged in several activities that particularly angered and enraged physicians. For example, the regime was using ambulances to surreptitiously take its coercive apparatuses into areas under the control of the protesters and then they would arrest protest leaders and take them in the ambulances to prison. This illegal use of ambulances greatly upset the physicians. The regime also barged into emergency rooms to arrest injured protesters who were being given medical care. The regime has also forced the physicians at the coroners' offices to write false reports on the deaths of the protesters and dissidents, a practice that physicians find despicable, and which undermines their credibility and honor.

In October physicians gathered in major cities such as Mashhad, Shiraz, Tehran, and Isfahan in major protests.[94] They shouted anti-dictatorship slogans and supported the mass protests. Some of the slogans included: "*Azadi Azadi*" [Freedom Freedom], "*Kurdistan, Zahedan, Cheshm Va Cheragh Iran*" [Kurdistan and Zahedan, Eyes and Lights of Iran], "*Az Shiraz Ta Kurdistan, Iran Shodeh Ghabrestan*" [From Shiraz to Kurdistan, Iran Has Become a Graveyard], "*Hokomat Bacheh-kosh, Nemikhahim Namikhahim*" [We Do Not Want a Regime That Murders Children], and "*Marg Bar Dictator*" [Death to the Dictator].[95] In Tehran on October 26, 2022, the regime used guns with pellets to shoot the physicians, beat them up with batons, arrested many of them, and used tear gas against the rest. According to Dr. Hussein Moussavian, who was present at the protest, there were about 3,000

---

93 Kazemzadeh, *The Iran National Front*, op. cit.
94 Iran International, "*Ba Vojod Hamleh Beh Tajamo Shiraz, Pezeshkan Baray Tajamo Dar Tehran Va Isfahan Farakhan Dadand*" [Although the Gathering Was Attacked in Shiraz, Physicians Called for Meetings in Tehran and Isfahan] (October 24, 2022), https://www.iranintl.com/202210240128.
95 Ibid.

physicians at the protest.[96] One female surgeon physician, Dr. Parisa Bahmani, was killed, and many others suffered serious injuries.[97] The people joined the beleaguered and stunned physicians and pushed back the coercive apparatuses. On October 27, 2022, in Isfahan, the regime roughed up physicians and arrested them.

Such use of violence against physicians has no precedence in Iran. The Shah's regime also feared physicians, but its methods were very different. The Shah's regime usually sent its coercive apparatuses to the clinic or house of dissident physicians, took them to the interrogation place, threatened them, and then let them leave when they agreed to cease political activities.

5.11.7 Monarchists Vs. Democrats

Iranian people and politics are very fragmented and polarized. The opposition to the fundamentalist regime includes many groups. One major divide is between the monarchists who want the return of the Pahlavi regime and those who want to establish a democratic secular republic. The democratic forces include the secular liberal democrats and social democrats of the Iran National Front, various republicans, and *Melli-Mazhabi* [nationalist religious] groups, as well as former communists who have abandoned their support for dictatorship and embraced a secular democratic republican system.[98] In addition to the pro-democracy groups, there are other non-democratic opposition groups that also oppose the monarchists, such as the PMOI and communist groups. There are also ethnic parties whose positions are not clear.

Unlike the protests during 2017–2018 and 2019, where some shouted slogans in support of the monarchy, in the 2022 protests there were virtually no such slogans by the protesters in Iran. During the 2017–2018 and November 2019 protests some (a minority of the protesters) shouted slogans such as *"Reza Shah, Rouhat Shad"* [Reza Shah, Bless Your Soul] and a handful *"Javid Shah"* [Long Live the King]. Both the causes and consequences of this phenomenon are of great significance.

---

96 Hussein Moussavian, "Interview with Radio Farda" (October 27, 2022), https://www.radiofarda. com/a/32102030.html. Dr. Moussavian is the number one leader of the INF.

97 Iran International, *"Etesab Pezeshkan Dar Shahrhay Mokhtalef Dar Eteraz Beh Koshteh Shodan Yek Pezeshk Dar Hamleh Mamouran"* [Physicians Go on Strike in Various Cities in Protest of the Killing of One Physician by the Authorities] (October 29, 2022), https://www.iranintl.com/ 202210291552.

98 For an analysis of the conflicts between the INF and the monarchists, as well as brief discussions of other pro-democracy and progressive groups, see Kazemzadeh, *The Iran National Front,* op. cit.

The 2017–2018 and November 2019 protests were primarily over economic issues. Some people made a simple comparison between the terrible economic conditions and the economic conditions before the revolution. There is no doubt that the fundamentalists have badly managed the economy and the Iranian people have been suffering under the utter lack of economic competence of the fundamentalist regime. The economic situation before the revolution was much better for virtually all classes, including the working classes. And when the fundamentalist coercive apparatuses came to violently suppress the protesters, many shouted the slogan "Reza Shah, Bless Your Soul." Since 1979, the fundamentalists have consistently and emotionally attacked Reza Shah for his violent suppression of clerics as well as expelling the Shia clerics from control of education and the judiciary, two lucrative and powerful positions they held. The slogan praising Reza Shah reflects the emotional hope of large segments of the population of a strong violent man standing up to the fundamentalists and violently putting them down and repressing them.

The 2022 protests began with the fundamentalist police beating a Sunni Kurdish woman to death over her hijab. Reza Shah had ordered his police to use batons and beat up women who were wearing hijab and violently take off their hijab. There exists a clear similarity between Reza Shah and the fundamentalist regime: both used violence against women to impose the regime's view of what women should wear. Both Reza Shah and the fundamentalist regime deny women the right to choose whether to wear hijab or not. Both Reza Shah and the fundamentalists use police violence to force women to submit to their orders about women's clothing. Another major demand of the 2022 protests is freedom. There existed no freedoms of thought, expression, the press, political parties, or elections under the two Pahlavi kings and the fundamentalist regime. By the word "*azadi*" [freedom] the people are demanding both freedom and democracy. Both the fundamentalist regime and the two Pahlavi kings were terribly dictatorial and repressive. Unlike the (bulk of the) Iranian people, who want freedom and democracy, the monarchists praise the terribly tyrannical rule of the two Pahlavi kings.

The 2022 protests explicitly condemn discrimination against various ethnic minorities and fully support equal rights for all Iranians. Both Reza Shah Pahlavi and Mohammad Reza Pahlavi terribly discriminated against ethnic minorities and harshly and violently repressed ethnic minorities. A major segment of the monarchists publicly express violent Persian chauvinist views that many Iranians consider reprehensible. A mass movement that advocates equal rights for all ethnic groups could not logically embrace chauvinist programs.

On June 3, 2022, Reza Pahlavi gave a press conference, and he presented himself as the spokesman of the opposition and condemned all the other opposition groups.[99] There were strong reactions by almost all other major opposition groups. The Iran National Front, the main and largest pro-democracy political party, along with several other parties issued a strong statement categorically condemning Mr. Pahlavi. They stated that Mr. Pahlavi is the leader of the monarchists, he is not the leader of the opposition.[100] Several far-left parties issued a joint statement strongly condemning Mr. Pahlavi as well. Several Kurdish and Baloch ethnic parties also issued statements condemning Mr. Pahlavi, who referred to various ethnic groups as *"ghabayel va ashayer"* [tribes and clans].[101]

Until March 2022, non-monarchist opposition groups had, by and large, ignored Mr. Pahlavi and the monarchists. Due to the pro-monarchist slogans that were shouted during the 2017–2018 and 2019 protests, it became clear that Mr. Pahlavi and his supporters were pouncing to declare Mr. Pahlavi the sole leader and spokesman for the opposition. Many monarchists were publicly threatening various opposition groups with punishment for their opposition to monarchy in 1979, as well as for their current activities if these activities were not under the leadership of monarchists. Some major monarchists were publicly arguing that after the overthrow of the fundamentalist regime it was necessary to have a period of authoritarianism to last about 10 years, so that law and order could be created, and good economic systems re-established for the prosperity of the country. In August 2022, former empress Farah Pahlavi gave an interview with Italian publication *Libero*, where she claimed that the people want the monarchy to come back and that, if so, she is ready to go back and re-establish the Pahlavi monarchy, Reza Pahlavi would be king, and that his daughter, Noor, would become his successor.[102] Ms. Farah Pahlavi's words provoked strong reactions and were ridiculed and condemned by many people inside and outside Iran.

---

99 Iran International, "Iran's Exiled Prince Calls for Coordinated Front Against Islamic Republic" (June 3, 2022), https://www.iranintl.com/en/202206030892.
100 *"Bayanieh Moshtarak 6 Sazeman Democrat Va Jomhurikah"* [Joint Statement of 6 Democratic and Republican Organizations] (June 9, 2022), https://melliun.org/iran/317844.
101 The technical term used by scholars as well as most political parties and groups to refer to various such groups in Iran is *"ghom"* [ethnic group] or *"ghomiyat"* [ethnicity]. Several ethnic parties usually use the term *"mellat"* [nation] and *"melliyat"* [nationality] to refer to their group. Clearly, Reza Pahlavi's use of the terms "tribe" and "clan" was insulting. It is not clear whether Mr. Pahlavi was ignorant of the debates on this crucial issue or purposefully wanted to insult such minority groups.
102 Iran International, "Exiled Queen Says Ready to Return Home After Iran Is Free" (August 17, 2022), https://www.iranintl.com/en/202208176071.

The words of Mr. Reza Pahlavi and Ms. Farah Pahlavi came across as arrogant and condescending. For many years, both publicly and privately, monarchists have been asking and pressing Reza Pahlavi to take the role of leader, galvanize the people, overthrow the fundamentalist regime, and re-establish the Pahlavi monarchy. When Mr. Pahlavi did what his supporters had been asking him to do, there was widespread strong condemnation by the non-monarchist segments of the population and opposition groups that form the overwhelming majority of the population.

Numerous comments in the comments sections of online media contain vulgar insults and personal attacks by the monarchists. Although many well-known monarchist personalities use such language, less extreme monarchists claim that the bulk of such venomous comments are by the fundamentalist cyber army to make the monarchists look dictatorial, violent, and intolerant. Some believe that the fundamentalist regime wants to frighten the people with the possibility of the return of the Pahlavi dictatorship, so that its agents, acting as *agents provocateurs*, have pretended to be monarchists, and shouted pro-monarchy slogans during the protests in order to discredit them and cause many pro-democracy segments of the population not to join the protests. There is no doubt that a large minority of the Iranian population supports the return of the Pahlavi dictatorship. There is also no doubt that many monarchists hold the portraits of Reza Shah, Mohamad Reza Shah, and Reza Pahlavi during their protests outside Iran and publicly shout slogans for the return of the Pahlavi monarchy. Therefore, it is plausible that monarchists inside Iran would also shout monarchist slogans. Although it is plausible that the fundamentalist regime has been engaging in operations pretending to be monarchists to make the monarchists look bad and to undermine support from the people for the protests, actual evidence that such operations have occurred was very thin.

The situation changed drastically by mid-January 2023. In early January 2023, in a gathering in Izeh, several monarchists held signs in support of the monarchy. One sign said: *"Marg Bar Seh Fased: Mullah, Chapi, Mojahed: Javid Shah"* [Death to the Three Bad: Clergy, Leftist, Members of the PMOI: Long Live the King]. Violent and genocidal threats, slogans, and views are very common among the monarchists. What was uncommon was that Ms. Yassemin Pahlavi, the wife of Reza Pahlavi, the claimant to the throne and the leader of the monarchists, re-tweeted the tweet containing the slogan in an unmistakable sign of support.[103] On January 8, in a protest march in London organized by non-monarchists, the monarchists arrived

---

103 The *Independent Persian* paper, which tends to be supportive of the Pahlavi monarchists, posted the re-tweet at https://twitter.com/indypersian/status/1611166819360075777.

and began chanting this slogan. The monarchists also had a new slogan: *"Harki Nageh Javid Shah, Ajnabieh"* [Whoever Does Not Say Long Live the Shah, is a Non-Iranian].[104] From then on pro-democracy forces, including liberal democrats, social democrats, and leftists, began more vigorously and publicly criticizing the monarchists. The pro-democracy forces condemn the monarchists' slogans as further signs of the brutal and violent dictatorial politics and policies of the monarchists.

Most opposition groups had ignored the monarchists because they consider the main enemy to be the fundamentalist regime although many monarchists had constantly attacked various opposition groups in the past 40 years. By early February 2023, it was clear that the monarchists and Mr. Reza Pahlavi want to impose Reza Pahlavi's leadership on the opposition. This caused a huge backlash against the monarchists and tremendously escalated the conflicts between the monarchists and all other opposition groups. On the streets of Iran and abroad, new slogans were shouted: *"Marg Bar Setam-gar, Cheh Shah Basheh Cheh Rahbar"* [Death to the Oppressor, Whether it is the Shah or the Supreme Leader]; *"Na Shah, Na Rahbar, Democracy, Barabari"* [No King, No Supreme Leader, Democracy, Equality]; *"Na Shah Mikhahim Na Akhund, Laanat Beh Har Do-ta Shoon"* [We Neither Want a King Nor a Supreme Leader, Curse Upon Both of Them].

The conflicts between the monarchists and other opposition groups reached new heights and vitriol after photos of Parviz Sabeti were published by his daughter attending a rally in either Los Angeles or Miami on February 11, 2023.[105] Mr. Sabeti is one of the most despised figures of the Pahlavi regime. He was Deputy Director of SAVAK and one of the most extreme, violent, and dishonest officials of the Pahlavi dictatorship. The worst abuses of human rights during the Shah's dictatorship occurred under the leadership of Mr. Sabeti. For example, between 1970 and 1976 about 80% of all the people incarcerated by SAVAK were university students whose sole crime was possession of banned books.[106] Many such students were severely tortured during this period.

---

104 The word *"ajnabi"* has a negative connotation and means "foreigner" or "stranger." It is used the way the term "Un-American" is used in the United States to refer to enemies of the people.
105 Golnaz Esfandiari, "'Hands Are Stained With Blood': Iranians Outraged After Shah-Era Secret-Police Official Attends U.S. Rally," Radio Free Europe/Radio Liberty (February 15, 2023), https://www.rferl.org/a/iran-sabeti-us-protest-savak/32271395.html.
106 For example, Mehdi Fatahpour, who was a political prisoner in the 1970s. He was arrested for protesting while he was a university student. He was tortured by SAVAK. According to Fatahpour, about 80% of those incarcerated by SAVAK were there for the sole crime of possession of banned books. See https://www.youtube.com/watch?v=0ugbjK8ol4o.

Mr. Sabeti also targeted leaders and members of the INF, who were non-violent secular liberals and social democrats who were asking the Shah to respect the 1906 constitution. The Shah sent about 300 SAVAK agents in plain clothes to beat up INF members when they had gathered at a private garden called Bagh Golzar in Karvansarae Sangi on the outskirts of Tehran on November 22, 1977. SAVAK agents broke the windows of the building and severely damaged about 300 autos of the attendees in the parking lot. About 30 were seriously injured and were taken to hospitals. SAVAK agents broke Abdul-Karim Anvari's hip and knee, broke Shapour Bakhtiar's arm, and bludgeoned Dariush Forouhar's head.[107] After President Carter praised the Shah profusely on December 31, 1977, at the New Year's Eve party in Niavaran Palace in Tehran,[108] the Shah's campaign of terror against the INF became more violent. On April 8, 1978, SAVAK bombed the homes and offices of Dr. Karim Sanjabi, Dariush Forouhar, and Mahmoud Manian, as well as several close to the INF such as Mehdi Bazargan.[109] SAVAK also bombed the homes and offices of other liberals and social democrats close to the INF, such as Dr. Matin-Daftari, Dr. Hassan Nazih, Dr. Abdol-Karim Lahiji, and Moghadam Maraghei.[110]

According to Ervand Abrahamian, one of the most prominent historians of Iran, from 1971 SAVAK's tortures became far worse. Abrahamian writes:

> Brute force was supplemented with the bastinado; sleep deprivation; extensive solitary confinement; glaring searchlights; standing in one place for hours on end; nail extractions; snakes (favored for use with women); electrical shocks with cattle prods, often into the rectum; cigarette burns; sitting on hot grills; acid dripped into nostrils; near-drownings; mock executions; and an electric chair with a large metal mask to muffle screams while amplifying

107 Abdul-Karim Anvari, *Talash Baray Esteghlal: Khaterat Siasi* [Struggle for Independence: Political Memoirs] (London: Self-Publication, 2015), pp. 173–174. Anvari's injuries were so severe that even today, after 42 years, he has to walk with crutches.
108 Andrew Glass, "Carter Lauds Shah of Iran, Dec. 31, 1977," Politico (December 30, 2018), https://www.politico.com/story/2018/12/30/this-day-in-politics-december-31-1077103.
109 Abdol Hussein Azarang, *"Jebhe Melli Iran, Bozorgtarain Eatelaf Nirohayeh Siasi Iran Dat Tarikh Moaser Iran Ta Pish Az Enghelab Islami 1357"* [Iran National Front, the Largest Coalition of Political Forces in Iran's Contemporary History Until the Islamic Revolution of 1979], *Encyclopaedia Islamica* (no date). https://web.archive.org/web/20150318064343/http://www.encyclopaediaislamica.com/madkhal2.php?sid=4503.
110 Ervand Abrahamian, *Iran Between Two Revolutions*, (Princeton: Princeton University Press, 1982), p. 508. Also see Hassan Nazih, "Interview," Harvard University, Iranian Oral History Project, Paris (April 3, 1984), https://curiosity.lib.harvard.edu/iranian-oral-history-project/catalog/32-nazih__hassan01. All these individuals had been strong supporters of Dr. Mossadegh and had been a member of or close associate of the INF.

them for the victim. ... Prisoners were also humiliated by being raped, urinated on, and forced to stand naked.[111]

SAVAK under Sabeti's leadership also engaged in severe torture for the sole purpose of forcing public confessions on television. Among those that were so tortured was Dr. Gholam-Hussein Saedi, Iran's foremost playwright. Dr. Saedi was a psychiatrist and a social democrat. According to Abrahamian:

> Sa'edi did not speak of his own prison experiences until 1984—when in Paris dying from cirrhosis of the liver. There he revealed for the first time how he had been kidnapped, taken to Evin, and subjected to days of "nightmarish tortures"—all for the purpose of extracting an "interview." He reported, "I kept pleading that if they had any charges against me they should try me in court. They kept retorting that they were interested not in a trial but in a television interview." The interrogator admitted that he wanted Sa'edi to be publicly humiliated because mere imprisonment would make him into a public hero—a mistake made with previous writers. Sa'edi mentions in passing that his body still bore the marks of these tortures.[112]

SAVAK also engaged in the murder of opponents of the Pahlavi dictatorship. In one case, on April 19, 1975, under the leadership of Mr. Sabeti, SAVAK agents murdered nine political prisoners claiming that they were escaping Evin prison. The prisoners were the top leaders of two leftist guerrilla organizations that had been given prison sentences. After the revolution, SAVAK agents who carried out the murders testified on their role. According to these testimonies, the order to kill the political prisoners had come from the Shah and Sabeti organized the murders.[113]

SAVAK also threatened non-political persons. For example, Mr. Sabeti himself interrogated Behrouz Vossoughi, one of Iran's top actors in the 1970s. Not only was Vossoughi non-political but he had close relations with the royal court. After he played the leading role in *Gavaznha* [The Deer], he was interrogated by Sabeti. According to Vossoughi, Sabeti told him that if he accepted a role in another movie like that "one night returning from a party at 12 or 2 [a.m.] when no one is around, he would be hit by a truck and crushed to the wall. A bottle of alcoholic drink would be put in his car. The next morning [the mass circulation dailies] *Kayhan* and *Etellaat* would report that the previous night he died in an accident driving drunk."[114]

---

111 Ervand Abrahamian, *Tortured Confessions: Prisons and Public Recantations in Modern Iran* (Berkeley: University of California Press, 1999), p. 106.
112 Ibid., pp. 118–119.
113 Ibid., pp. 107–108.
114 See Behrouz Vossoughi's recollections at https://www.youtube.com/watch?v=2NSzqqj5V9Y.

Pro-democracy, human rights, and leftist activists consider Mr. Sabeti to have committed large-scale murder and torture and want him to be tried for crimes against humanity, while monarchists consider him a hero.[115] Hundreds of victims of SAVAK torture under the leadership of Sabeti have signed petitions to organize efforts to bring Sabeti to trial for crimes against humanity, including murders and tortures.[116]

Some monarchists say that those who opposed the Shah were terrorists and that SAVAK had to undermine and eliminate them. They say that Mr. Sabeti was right to use violence against all those who opposed the Shah. Many monarchists further add that the Shah and SAVAK did not use enough violence against the opponents of the Shah and that the Shah and SAVAK were too lenient. They say that after they come to power again, they will punish all those who opposed the Shah. Some monarchists say that Mr. Sabeti should be given a high-level position after the overthrow of the fundamentalist regime. Some monarchists, including Mr. Sabeti, deny that SAVAK used torture, and describe the testimonies and evidence of torture by SAVAK as lies and propaganda.[117]

Within days of Sabeti's appearance at the February 11, 2023 protest, monarchists were hoisting large portraits of Sabeti alongside those of Reza Pahlavi in their rallies. For example, on February 19, 2023, in a protest in Munich, monarchists held a portrait of Sabeti with the caption *"Kaboos Terrorist-hay Ayandeh"* [Nightmare of Future Terrorists].[118]

Mr. Pahlavi has refused to explicitly condemn Parviz Sabeti or his supporters for hoisting Sabeti's photos. Mr. Sabeti's photos were posted on social media by his daughter, Dr. Pardis Sabeti, a Professor at Harvard University. Pardis Sabeti is a

115 For example, see the views of Iran's highly respected experts such as human rights lawyer Pegah Bani-Hashem, sociologist and human rights activist Dr. Kazem Kardavani, and progressive human rights and transitional justice activist Ladan Bazargan at VOA, *"Sezaye Shekanje-garan Va Naghesan Hoghogh Bashar Chist?"* [What are Punishments for Torturers and Violators of Human Rights?] (February 20, 2023), https://www.youtube.com/watch?v=zn4yOHub3R0.
116 Radio Zamaneh, *"Asghar Izadi: Parviz Sabeti Kesi Ast Keh Shekanjeh Rah Beh Nezamyafteh Va Beh Maharat Tabdil Kard"* [Asghar Izadi: Parviz Sabeti is the Person Who Made Torture Institutionalized and an Expertise] (March 1, 2023) https://melliun.org/iran/354076; and see the petition at https://www.daadkhast.org/petition/258887.
117 See monarchists' views at https://www.youtube.com/watch?v=QS6FAc217TM, https://www.youtube.com/watch?v=o-m3VKVOXQc, https://www.youtube.com/watch?v=GZKsE9Qgoew, and https://www.youtube.com/watch?v=0ugbjK8ol4o.
118 Hossein Daei Alislam, "Posters of Parviz Sabeti at Pahlavi Rally," National Council of Resistance of Iran (February 19, 2023), https://www.ncr-iran.org/en/news/iran-resistance/demonizing-mek/posters-of-parviz-sabeti-at-pahlavi-rally-scaring-off-tehran-or-dissent-thereof/.

member of the Advisory Council of NUFDI, which is a monarchist lobby organization in Washington, D.C.[119]

A reporter from Radio France International directly asked Pahlavi about Mr. Sabeti.[120] Pahlavi avoided a direct response and did not even mention Sabeti's name. Rather, he made general remarks condemning anyone who undermines unity and insults others. And, adding insult to injury, he directly blamed the fundamentalist regime's cyber element for purposefully using this controversy to sow divisions. The case was very clear. Sabeti shows up in a protest organized by Pahlavi's supporters, Sabeti's daughter posts photos of Sabeti on social media, monarchists hoist Sabeti's photos in the monarchist rallies, and there are strong condemnations by pro-democracy and progressive groups and the actual torture victims of SAVAK. There is no moral equivalency in this case. There is no moral equivalency between those who direct torture and murder and those who condemn these. To condemn those who order torture and murder is not to insult and sow division. Pahlavi refused to condemn Sabeti, the notorious man responsible for the torture of thousands of people, including innocent high school and university students for merely possession of books. All Mr. Pahlavi had to do was to say something to the effect that he condemns Parvis Sabeti for the gross violations of human rights of dissidents, for grotesque tortures and murders that he committed, and that he condemns his father's dictatorship for authorizing Sabeti to carry out such atrocities.

As of this writing, I have not seen NUFDI, or any other monarchist organization, publicly condemn Mr. Sabeti. The monarchists have either been highly supportive of Parviz Sabeti or silent on his crimes. This is yet another indication that not only are the monarchists unrepentant of their crimes against humanity and brutal dictatorship but remain highly supportive of the man who orchestrated those cruel and barbaric tortures under the Shah tyranny.

---

119 NUFDI, "Pardis Sabeti Joins Advisory Council" (November 1, 2022), https://nufdiran.org/pardis-sabeti-joins-advisory-council/.

120 Radio France International, *"Vakonesh Reza Pahlavi Beh Ekhtelafha Bar Sar Parviz Sabeti: Az Havadaran Fahash Va Nefaghankan Faseleh Migiram"* [Reaction of Reza Pahlavi to the Events Over Parviz Sabeti: I Distance Myself from Supporters who Insult and Create Divisions] (February 23, 2023), https://www.rfi.fr/fa/%D8%A7%DB%8C%D8%B1%D8%A7%D9%86/20230222-%D9%88%D8%A7%DA%A9%D9%86%D8%B4-%D8%B1%D8%B6%D8%A7-%D9%BE%D9%87%D9%84%D9%88%DB%8C-%D8%A8%D9%87-%D8%A7%D8%AE%D8%AA%D9%84%D8%A7%D9%81-%D9%87%D8%A7-%D8%A8%D8%B1-%D8%B3%D8%B1-%D8%AD%D8%B6%D9%88%D8%B1-%D9%BE%D8%B1%D9%88%DB%8C%D8%B2-%D8%AB%D8%A7%D8%A8%D8%AA%DB%8C-%D8%AF%D8%B1-%D8%AA%D8%B8%D8%A7%D9%87%D8%B1%D8%A7%D8%AA-%D8%AC%D9%85%D9%87%D9%88%D8%B1%DB%8C-%D8%A7%D8%B3%D9%84%D8%A7%D9%85%DB%8C-%D8%AA%D9%81%D8%B1%D9%82%D9%87-%D8%A7%D9%81%DA%A9%D9%86%DB%8C-%D9%85%DB%8C-%DA%A9%D9%86%D8%AF.

Mr. Sabeti is not the only terribly violent monarchist that the monarchists praise. Many monarchists also consider Mr. Shaaban Jaafari, better known as Shaaban *Bi-Mokh* [Shaaban the Brainless], to be their national hero. Mr. Jaafari was leader of a violent gang that beat up others. He was part of a conspiracy to murder Dr. Mossadegh in 1953. He made an assassination attempt on the life of Dr. Hussein Fatemi after the coup and knifed him several times, but Dr. Fatemi survived the assassination attempt.

Mr. Reza Pahlavi claims that he supports a democratic constitutional monarchy. However, the overwhelming majority of the pro-democracy forces do not trust Mr. Pahlavi. Moreover, the pro-democracy forces do not trust the majority of the monarchists. There is little doubt that a large minority of the population supports the re-imposition of the Pahlavi monarchy and Mr. Reza Pahlavi. It is also clear that most of the monarchists are terribly dictatorial and violent. The INF and other major pro-democracy and progressive forces consider the monarchists to constitute a major obstacle to the establishment of democracy in Iran after the overthrow of the fundamentalist regime. It is painfully obvious that the existence of a major anti-democratic force in the opposition harms the movement to fight against the fundamentalist regime. The pro-democracy forces believe, with good reason, that the monarchists and Reza Pahlavi want to establish their dictatorship. The democratic forces believe it would be unwise to cooperate with a terribly dictatorial group. Considering the fact that both Pahlavi kings were extremely dictatorial and that the overwhelming majority of the monarchists strongly admire these tyrants, makes any cooperation with the monarchists hard for democrats. The INF as well as most other pro-democracy and progressive forces believe that the two Pahlavi kings were enemies of freedom, democracy, independence, human rights, popular sovereignty, and national sovereignty of the Iranian people. Therefore, when Reza Pahlavi and the monarchists praise these dictators and hold up their portraits, the pro-democracy forces conclude that the current monarchists continue those policies.[121]

The position of monarch is an unelected, life-term, and inherited position, which makes it an anti-democratic position. A political system that contains a monarch could be a democracy only if the monarch has no real political power. A political system is democratic to the extent that the people through their elected representatives in a parliament have the power of government. To the extent that a monarch has power, to that extent that system is non-democratic. A constitutional monarchy is democratic not because of the monarchy, but despite it. In other words, monarch is an anti-democratic position, whose powers have to be con-

---

121 Kazemzadeh, *The Iran National Front*, op. cit.

tained through various mechanisms (e. g., parliaments, free press, courts, political parties, political culture) for a political system to be democratic. Constitutional monarchies in Europe were the result of many centuries of political struggles where gradually the people were able to force the monarch to concede power to the people. It would be utter folly, in a country that lacks a monarch, to re-create that anti-democratic position, and then attempt to create mechanisms to contain that anti-democratic position and its powers. For analogy, in a body that contains a deadly virus, we would want to come up with a mechanism to contain the effect of that virus. However, it is utter folly for a body that lacks that deadly virus, to first introduce that virus and then attempt to contain the harmful effect of that virus by attempting to create various mechanisms.

The fundamentalist regime has been so oppressive and brutal that many Iranians want regime change at any cost. They know that the monarchists will be dictatorial, but they think that the situation would be far less bad than life under the fundamentalist regime. Many also know that the Pahlavi kings were puppets of the British and the United States. They also believe that Reza Pahlavi would also be a puppet of the United States. The fundamentalist regime has been so oppressive that many Iranians support a forceful regime change to life under the fundamentalist tyranny. Thus, many prefer an American military invasion and Pahlavi dictatorship to living under the rule of the fundamentalist regime. For many, if there are only two options, living under the fundamentalist regime or forceful regime change and monarchical dictatorship, they would choose Pahlavi dictatorship.

Pro-democracy forces (e. g., the INF), most other democrats, and progressives oppose the fundamentalist regime. They also oppose the re-establishment of the Pahlavi dictatorship. The INF has explicitly stated that it opposes the return of the monarchy, that it regards the monarchists as dictatorial, and that it will not cooperate with Reza Pahlavi. This position is shared by other major pro-democracy groups such as United Republicans of Iran and Solidarity of Iranian Republicans and the Left Party of Iran, which is the largest leftist party of Iran. All the major leftist groups strongly oppose the monarchists and consider them fascist. The Secretary-General of the DPIK, Mostafa Hejri, said in an interview with BBC Persian on February 21, 2023, that the DPIK "is absolutely not prepared to cooperate with Reza Pahlavi."[122] The PMOI has also explicitly condemned the monarchists as a dictatorial group that it would never work with.

All the above opposition groups and parties consider the monarchists to be extremely tyrannical. They believe that the fundamentalist regime is weak and on its way to being overthrown sooner or later. They believe that the monarchists want to

---

122 See the comments of Hejri, https://twitter.com/KavehGhoreishi/status/1627664618465161219.

re-establish their brutal fascistic dictatorship. They believe that if the monarchists succeed, then Iran will suffer from another 50 years or more of brutal tyranny. These opposition groups do not want to replace one form of dictatorship with another form of dictatorship. By March 2023, the opposition to monarchists was so intense that during the mass protests on March 23, 2023, the main slogan was *"Marg Bar Setam-gar, Cheh Shah Basheh, Cheh Rahbar"* [Death to the Tyrant, Whether the Shah or the Supreme Leader].[123]

GAMAAN's survey of Iranians inside and outside Iran clearly shows the primary dilemma of the opposition to the fundamentalist regime. Although 40% of Iranians outside Iran who oppose the fundamentalist regime support a democratic secular republican form of government, only 22% support monarchy; and while 61% of Iranians outside Iran support a democratic secular republican political system only 25% support monarchy.

Mr. Reza Pahlavi is the single most popular figure among all those who oppose the regime. Mr. Pahlavi's popularity is primarily due to astronomical funds spent to promote him. He was born as Crown Prince in October 1960. The Shah's regime spent great amounts of funds and efforts promoting him as the next king until the regime fell in 1979. Since 1979, the monarchist groups and media have spent virtually all their funds and energy promoting him and attacking other opposition groups. For many years, the CIA provided huge funds and efforts promoting Mr. Pahlavi. It is widely believed that the governments of Saudi Arabia and Israel have been providing enormous funds to monarchist groups and satellite television stations that support the monarchists. Despite 62 years of massive investments of funds and energy, only a minority of Iranians support the return of the monarchy. This clearly shows that the Iranian people are too smart and sophisticated to be brainwashed and manipulated by the monarchist propaganda. Although the funds spent on Mr. Pahlavi have been a thousand times those spent on the democratic secular republicans, the overwhelming majority of the Iranian people support democracy and oppose monarchy. The massive efforts and propaganda have made Mr. Pahlavi popular among certain segments of the population despite Mr. Pahlavi's lack of leadership abilities. Ironically, the more assistance is provided to Mr. Pahlavi and the monarchists, the more intense opposition of pro-democracy forces and the progressives to the monarchists has become, further dividing and weakening the opposition to the fundamentalist regime, and thus benefiting the fundamentalist regime.

---

123 See the videos, photos, and commentaries from Radio Farda and Iran Wire, re-published at Melliun (March 3, 2023) https://melliun.org/iran/354285. Also see https://www.radiofarda.com/a/32042577.html and https://iranwire.com/fa/news-1/114389.

The tragedy of Iranian politics is that while most Iranians want democracy, the democratic forces have not been able to produce a leader with wide support while the dictatorial opposition possesses one figure that enjoys the support of a substantial segment of the population. Although the GAMAAN survey found that Mr. Pahlavi is the most popular figure, that constitutes a minority. The majority of the Iranian people want a secular democratic republic.[124]

Monarchists are extremely intolerant and aggressive against anyone who is not monarchist. Since at least 1984, I have observed on numerous occasions monarchists disrupt, threaten, and use violence against liberals, democrats, and leftists in protests in Los Angeles. On many occasions, the Los Angeles police had to intervene and take them away. The monarchists even disrupted the speech of Masih Alinejad, a close collaborator of Reza Pahlavi, while giving a speech at a rally on February 20, 2023, in Brussels, Belgium. The monarchists kept shouting: *"Masih, Begoo Javid Shah"* [Masih, Say Long Live the Shah].[125] This case clearly shows that even before they have power, the monarchists in Europe want to impose their views on an ally that is not a monarchist. For the pro-democracy forces, this case clearly shows that the monarchists have become even more intolerant and violent than they were before 1979.

Monarchists have been attempting to convince Western audiences by saying that they wish to establish a constitutional monarchy similar to those in Britain and Western Europe. Their actual behavior, however, shows that they remain as dictatorial as when they ruled Iran between 1926 and 1979.

5.11.8 Slogans of the Protesters

The slogans of the 2022 protests are unmistakably for freedom and democracy. The most common slogans have been: *"Marg Bar Dictator"* [Death to the Dictator], *"Marg Bar Khamenei"* [Death to Khamenei], *"Marg Bar Asl Velayat Faqih"* [Death to the Principle of Rule of the High-Ranking Shia Clergy], and *"Zendani Siasi Azad Bayad Gardad"* [Political Prisoners Have to Be Freed], slogans that have been used for many years in previous protests. The unique slogan of the 2022 protests has been: *"Zan, Zendegi, Azadi"* [Woman, Life, Freedom], which became the

---

124 Ammar Maleki, "Iranians' Attitudes Towards Political Systems," GAMAAN (2022), https://gamaan.org/wp-content/uploads/2022/03/GAMAAN-Political-Systems-Survey-2022-English-Final.pdf, p. 12, figure 6. This survey was conducted February 17–27, 2022.
125 BBC Persian, *"Dar Opposisioun Padeshahikhah Cheh Migozarad?"* [What is Going on in the Monarchist Opposition?] (March 8, 2023), https://www.youtube.com/watch?v=iqx-BPdW2Js.

most frequently used slogan. Also, one of the most frequently used slogans has been *"Azadi Azadi Azadi"* [Freedom Freedom Freedom].

Other slogans include: *"Toop Tofang Feshfesheh, Basiji Bayad Gom Besheh"* [... *Basiji* Should Get Lost]; *"Akhund Bayad Gom Besheh"* [Shia Clerics Should Get Lost]; *"Jomhuri Islami Nemikhahim"* [We Do Not Want the Islamic Republic]; *"Mijangim, Mimirim, Iran Ro Pas Migirim"* [We Will Fight, We Will Die, We Will Get Iran Back]; *"Emsal Sal Khoneh, Seyyed Ali Sarnegoneh"* [This Year is the Year of Bloodshed, Khamenei Will Be Overthrown]; and *"Natarsid Natarsid, Maa Hameh Ba Ham Hastim"* [Do Not Be Afraid, We Are All In This Together]. University students use the slogans *"Daneshjoo Mimerad, Zelat Nemipazirad"* [Students Will Die, But Will Not Submit to Humiliating Oppression] and *"Daneshjoo Zendani Azad Bayad Gardad"* [Incarcerated Students Should Be Released]. Protesters also shout *"bisharaf"* [lacking honor] at the fundamentalist coercive apparatuses when they attack the protesters.

For the first time on October 27, 2022, during the 40th day commemoration of the death of Nika Shakarami, who was beaten to death around the head by the IRGC, the mourners shouted the slogan: *"Marg Bar Sepahi"* [Death to the IRGC]. The regime not only had murdered Nika but broadcast news that she had committed suicide by falling from a fifth floor building. The video of this 16-year-old high school student had captured the hearts of the people. And the regime pressures on her family to deny the fact that she was participating in the protests when she was arrested were considered most odious. Within hours, the slogan "Death to the IRGC" and *"Marg Bar Basiji"* [Death to *Basiji*] were shouted in protests throughout Iran.

There have also been slogans calling for *"Jomhuri Irani"* [Iranian Republic], which is used in contradiction to the fundamentalist regime title of *"Jomhuri Islami"* [Islamic Republic]. By this slogan, the people express their demand for the replacement of the fundamentalist regime with a democratic secular republic form of government.

In interviews, many protesters say that they are outraged by the utter lack of respect for their dignity by the fundamentalist regime. The Iranian people want respect for their basic human dignity. For 43 years, their basic human rights have been violated by a backward, reactionary regime. They believe that a backward regime is simply not compatible with a dignified life in the 21st century. They want a political system that simply respects them as human beings. The vast majority of the population has come to the conclusion that the only way to gain a normal life, a dignified life, would be to replace the fundamentalist regime with a secular democratic political system. And many are willing to risk their life and liberty to gain freedom for the people. Slogans that reflect this are: *"Na Roosari, Na Toosari, Azadi, Barabari"* [No to Headscarf, No to Hit on the Head, Freedom, Equality] and *"Daneshjoo Mimirad, Zellat Nemipazirad"* [Students Will Die, But Will Not Accept Living With Humiliation].[126]

Another slogan shouted by women usually right after the slogan "Woman, Life, Freedom" is *"Mard, Mihan, Abadi"* [Man, Country, Prosperity]. By this slogan, women are expressing their support of men who support women's equality and freedom. The Iranian feminist movement is not anti-men; rather, it wants a system of equality, freedom, and dignity for all. By using the term *"mihan"* [country], they support the modern attachment to Iran rather than the pre-modern attachment of the fundamentalists to Shia Islamic *Ummah*. By the term *"abadi"* they want a modern economic system that would provide them what they see in advanced prosperous countries.

In late October, a new slogan emerged. Apparently in a university in Shiraz, a fundamentalist woman and a fundamentalist man attacked a protesting female student and called her *"harzeh"* [lewd, whore]. She yelled back *"Hiz Tuee, Harzeh Tuee, Zan-e Azadeh Manam"* [You are Lewd, You are Whore, I am a Woman Who Fights for the People's Liberation and Freedom].[127] By November 2, this slogan had spread all over Iran and it became one of the most popular slogans.

Shervin Hajipour's song "For" has become the 2022 mass protest movement's anthem, sung by the people at universities, high schools, factory yards, balconies, rooftops, and on the streets.[128] Hajipour had collected the lyrics from tweets by young protesters during the first few days of the protests. Right away, Hajipour was arrested by the regime and charged with "propaganda against the system" for making this song. The lyrics of his song are:

> For dancing in the streets
> For the fear [from the Morality Police] when kissing [in public]
> For my sister, your sister, our sisters
> For changing fossilized brains
> For the shame of lacking money
> For the yearnings for a normal life
> For the kid who gets into garbage dumps for food, and his or her dreams
> For this economy ordered by decrees from above
> For this polluted air
> For Valiasr Street and its old trees

---

126 One of the main slogans of the fundamentalists since 1979 has been *"Ya Roosari, Ya Toosari"* [Either Headscarf or Hit on the Head]. And fundamentalists would actually beat up women who did not cover their head.

127 Translations of the Persian words *"harzeh,"* *"hiz,"* and *"zan-e azadeh"* to English are not easy. My translations of these terms attempt to covey the spirit and true meanings of these terms rather than the literal translations that a dictionary would convey.

128 The song is at https://www.youtube.com/watch?v=z8xXiqyfBg0.

For Pirooz [cheetah cub] and his possible extinction
For the forbidden and innocent dogs [that the regime kills]
For the endless tears

For the imagery that should never happen again [grieving of Hamed Esmaeilion after the downing of the Ukrainian passenger airplane by IRGC missiles which killed all 176 onboard including his wife and daughter]

For faces with smiles
For students, for future
For this compulsory heaven [life under the fundamentalist regime]
For our brilliant students in jails
For Afghan children [refugees in Iran]
For all these "for"s with no repeats
For all [the regime's] worthless slogans
For the wreckage of collapsing houses [in Abadan]
For feeling tranquility
For the sunrise after long nights
For pills for anxiousness and insomnia
For man, homeland, prosperity
For the girl who wished to be a boy [to attend a soccer game or ride a bicycle]
For woman, life, freedom
For freedom
For freedom
For freedom

Chapter 6
Conclusion: Regime Survival or Regime Collapse

In this book, I have discussed 10 major mass protests since 1981. In various chapters, I described major mass protests and causes of those protests. In this concluding chapter, I will discuss the causes and consequences of the mass protests since 1981.

The 1977–1979 Iranian revolution was a truly massive broad-based revolution against the monarchy. The revolution was initially organized by liberal democrats and social democrats of the INF and various socialist and communist groups. Islamic fundamentalists soon joined and were able to assume the leadership of the revolution by September 1978. By February 1979, when the Shah's regime fell, although Khomeini was the clear leader of the revolution, the pro-democracy forces (INF, Liberation Movement of Iran), PMOI, communists, and others were present and played major roles in the revolution.

The assumption was that, after the revolution, all these major non-fundamentalist forces would be free to exist, organize, and run for parliament and other offices and, if they won, they would be able to assume the offices they had won. The major reason Khomeini was allowed to become the leader of the revolution and not just the leader of the Islamic forces was because in France (between November 1978 and February 1979) Khomeini explicitly promised that he would not accept any position of power, would go to the shrine city of Qom and return to his studies at the seminary, that Shia clerics would not become President, that all groups including even Marxists would be free to express their views.

Khomeini lied. He later said that he engaged in *"taghieh"* [lying] and *"khodeh"* [deception]. Khomeini did have substantial support, perhaps somewhere between 35 and 40 % of the population. Khomeini did not want to share power (and the ability to make laws and policies that political power provides). Khomeini soon established an ultra-reactionary totalitarian regime. In order to accomplish his goal, Khomeini and his supporters had to defeat liberals, socialists, communists, non-fundamentalist Islamists (liberal Islamists, socialist Islamists, and communist Islamists), and ethnic parties. By July 1981, Khomeini and his fundamentalist supporters had done precisely that.

Although defeated, the bulk of the opposition groups continued to exist clandestinely inside Iran and openly outside Iran. The fundamentalist regime's campaign of assassinations of Iranian dissidents outside Iran, mostly in Europe, that murdered about 450 dissidents did not succeed in intimidating the opposition into silence.

https://doi.org/10.1515/9783111280288-008

Today, Iranian liberals and social democrats of the INF are stronger than they have been since 1979. Various non-fundamentalist Islamists such as *Melli-Mazhabi* groups have abandoned Islamism (mixing of religion and the state) and have embraced secularism. The PMOI continues to exist despite tens of thousands of its members and sympathizers being executed and killed. Today, ethnic parties continue to exist and remain strong. Today, communists are very weak compared with 1979–1981. The largest leftist party today is the Left Party of Iran, which has embraced democracy and pluralism and has been working closely with liberal democrats and social democrats of the INF.[1]

Perhaps more significantly, the civil society in Iran has been able to survive the violent totalitarian project of the fundamentalist regime to crush the civil society and instead create a fundamentalist mass society. Women, workers, nurses, physicians, civil servants, journalists, teachers, professors, university students, have refused to embrace fundamentalist ideology and conform to its dress codes and behavior. The fundamentalist project of combining mass executions, mass violence, and mass brainwashing to create a new subservient fundamentalist population has completely and totally failed.

The seeds of the mass protests were contained in Khomeini's totalitarian project. Khomeini and his fundamentalist supporters wanted to violently impose an ultra-reactionary totalitarian system on a society that had become too modern to succumb to his ultra-reactionary and traditional ways. Despite brainwashing from kindergarten to university, propaganda from state monopoly of radio and television to regime control in virtually all offices and workplaces, the Iranian people have shown amazing resilience to the fundamentalist project to create a fundamentalist mass society.

There are many reasons why the fundamentalist project has failed. One obvious reason is that the fundamentalists were a minority of the population and the majority, although not unified and dispersed among several ideological, political, class, and ethnic categories, nevertheless possessed enough resources and abilities to successfully resist the fundamentalist project.

Khomeini stated: "Yes, we are reactionaries. You are intellectuals. You intellectuals want us not to return to 1,400 years ago. You are afraid that if we train our youth like 1,400 years ago that with their small population, they wiped out two large empires [the Persian Empire and Byzantine Empire]."[2] Khomeini ordered the closing of universities for about two years and purging of professors and stu-

---

1 Kazemzadeh, *The Iran National Front*, op. cit.
2 Ruhollah Khomeini, *Aghshar Ejtemaee Az Didgah Imam Khomeini* [Social Strata from the Perspective of Imam Khomeini], http://www.imam-khomeini.ir/fa/c78_123770/.

dents who were liberal, Marxist, secular, or feminist. The fundamentalists call the purge of the universities, "Islamic Cultural Revolution." Despite massive repression and Islamization, the universities have remained bastions of resistance to the fundamentalist regime. The fundamentalists have realized that they cannot close universities because the country needs their graduates. Therefore, the regime has had to allow the existence of universities but monitor its students and faculty and manage them through a mix of threats, rewards, and repression.

One reason may be that the culture of the fundamentalists was very different from the culture of vast swathes of the population. The fundamentalists come from particular segments of the population that were highly traditional and religious. Religious rituals rather than pre-Islamic cultural practices animated them. For example, the majority of the Iranian population love and celebrate *Nowruz* (the Persian New Year) and *Chaharshanbeh Souri* (the last Wednesday of the year, when the people jump over small fires and go door to door and get sweets). Fundamentalists consider these hugely popular celebrations as pre-Islamic and thus anti-Islamic.

The Iranian people have been struggling to establish freedom and democracy at least since 1900. Successes include the Constitutional Revolution 1905–1911, the constitution of 1906, and the lukewarm democracy until about 1925. Iran again enjoyed lukewarm democracy between 1941 and 1951. Most significantly, Iran enjoyed a real democracy between 1951 and August 1953 during the government of Dr. Mossadegh. The 1977–1979 revolution also ushered in a brief respite from dictatorship until Khomeini and his supporters snuffed out that period of relative freedom. The 120 years of political struggles against dictatorships have provided the Iranian culture and people with a reservoir of tools for struggle against dictatorship. In other words, the achievements of the Constitutional Revolution (1905–1911), the pro-democracy government (1951–1953), and the 1977–1979 revolution have endowed the Iranian people with historical memories that have undermined the fundamentalists from imposing their totalitarian fascistic project.

Although both Reza Shah Pahlavi (1926–1941) and Mohammad Reza Shah Pahlavi (1953–1979) were brutal one-man tyrannies, they nevertheless held sham elections and sham parliaments to create illusions of popular legitimacy. Although virtually everyone knew the utter fakeness of the elections under Reza Shah and Mohammad Reza Shah, holding fake elections and fake parliaments showed the Iranian people that a democratic alternative was possible.

Although ideologically, Khomeini and his fundamentalist followers considered the true legitimate form of government to be *"Velayat Faqih"* [rule by the high-ranking Shia cleric], under the massive influence of democratic history in Iran, they had to create a façade of a popular vote. Therefore, the fundamentalists created fundamentalist-only elections whereby only trusted members of the fundamentalist oligarchy were allowed to participate in various elections by the Council of Guardians. These pseudo-elections and pseudo-parliaments show the public the gigantic gap between fundamentalist tyranny and democratic legitimacy.

The Constitutional Revolution and the Mossadegh period have created democratic historical memories that haunt the dictatorships of both the Pahlavi monarchs and the fundamentalists. Since 1905, the Iranian people have used mass protests, economic boycotts, and strikes to resist and fight against the ruling dictatorships.

The utter lack of competence of the fundamentalists to create an economy that would provide jobs and stable prices has pushed vast numbers of non-political people who wish nothing more than a simple life into opposition. The fundamentalist regime's ideology has robbed the vast majority of the population from enjoying a normal life: to laugh, to dance, to attend parties with the opposite sex, to kiss, to be what one wants. The fundamentalist regime's foreign policy of aggressive bellicose warmongering spends billions of dollars that could be better spent in Iran providing jobs, opportunities, universities, health care, environment, housing, and the like.

Satellite televisions, internet, and social media have allowed the Iranian people windows into how the rest of the world lives, not only in Europe and North America but also even in neighboring countries such as Turkey, the UAE, Georgia, and Bahrain. Iranians in diaspora have been hugely successful. There are about 8 million Iranians who live outside Iran. The people inside Iran look at their relatives who live in Europe, the U.S., and Canada and compare the oppressive and suffocating lives they have in Iran and want a system that would provide them the prosperous and free lives that their relatives have outside Iran. Iranians in diaspora have demonstrated their love for Iran and their intense opposition to the tyrannical regime ruling it. They came out in massive numbers to support their relatives inside Iran who struggle for freedom.

In sum, the fundamentalist project is incompatible with what the vast majority of the Iranian people want. The fundamentalists were a sizeable minority of the population that was able to impose its rule through deception and mass violence. The fundamentalists have failed to brainwash the population. The fundamentalist regime has lost its legitimacy and authority. It rules through utter naked coercion. The mass protests are the result of the Iranian people going to the streets to show their opposition to a violent totalitarian dictatorship. The fundamentalist regime knows full well that the overwhelming majority of the Iranian people oppose their rule.

Since early 1979, the fundamentalists have invested heavily in their coercive apparatuses. Every country has limited resources. The more legitimate a political system is, the less the political leaders have to invest in coercive apparatuses and more on economic, infrastructural, and educational entities. Because of lack of political legitimacy among the vast majority of the population, the fundamentalist regime has created truly grotesquely large security apparatuses such as the IRGC, *Basij*, Ministry of Intelligence, IRGC-Intelligence Organization, Morality Police, and the so-called *Yegan Vijej:* extremely large anti-riot special forces. These gargantuan investments in security forces have deprived the system of the funds to invest in the economic infrastructure of the country. This strategic decision by the funda-mentalist regime has further undermined the economic well-being of the popula-tion and further increased the need for more investments in security apparatuses —a dynamic that has been going on since 1979. The failures of the brainwashing and propaganda have further forced the regime to increase its investments in ap-paratuses of repression.

As long as the various factions of the ruling oligarchy (hardliners, reformists, and expedients) were peacefully maneuvering for power behind the scenes, they could successfully repress dissent. Since the 2010 protests, pro-democracy student activists, women's rights activists, teachers, and labor union activists have contin-ued their resistance to the regime despite beatings, imprisonment, torture, and deaths while in custody. The eight years of Ahmadinejad's presidency witnessed increased political repression, harsher enforcement of restrictions on women (es-pecially the compulsory hijab), and increased censorship of cultural productions. The increasing intra-elite tensions spun out of control during the 2009 presidential elections. Rouhani's eight years of presidency, however, ameliorated some of the intra-elite tensions. The crisis of succession to the position of Supreme Leader has drastically increased intra-elite tensions among the three main factions. Per-haps as significant have been tensions among various hardline individuals and fac-tions within the hardline camp who have been jockeying for position for when Khamenei leaves the scene. The mass protests in 2018 and 2019 brought the work-ing classes and the poor into mass protests which had been relatively uncommon.

Today, in 2023, large segments of the Iranian population crave democracy and freedom and want to be part of the modern world. The government pursues re-pressive and dictatorial policies domestically, and confrontational policies in for-eign affairs. Many hardline factions are extremely hostile to the U.S. and pursue extremist and hostile policies toward Israel as well as many Arab states.

The 1979 revolution began in June 1977 and culminated in the overthrow of the monarchy in February 1979. The revolutionary process took about one year and eight months. If the political paralysis continues, and is accompanied by a more severe economic downturn, this could bring larger segments of the working classes into open opposition. If general strikes are successful, the regime would face the real possibility of instability and collapse. The 2022–2023 mass protests are the cul-mination of the struggles of various social classes since the 1979–1981 struggles.

If the analysis in this book is correct, the nature of the conflict makes compromise extremely difficult because the demands of each side would mean the crushing of the wishes of the other side. The fundamentalist regime suffers from a crisis of legitimacy. The crisis of succession leaves little room for compromise among various fundamentalist political leaders because the fundamentalist constitution grants the position of Supreme Leader extraordinary powers. The fundamentalist regime could rely upon a small fraction of the population for support. The economic situation is bad and prospects for major changes are dim. The vast majority of the population wants fundamental change such as the replacement of the fundamentalist dictatorship with a secular democracy.

By 2022–2023, the vast majority of Iranians intensely despised the fundamentalist regime and anything associated with it. For example, when on January 19, 2023, the European Parliament voted to consider the IRGC a terrorist organization, the people inside Iran celebrated that decision by setting off fireworks and waving the E.U. flag.[3] Even more telling, during the 2022 World Cup, when the U.S. national soccer team defeated Iran's national team, the Iranian people inside and outside Iran widely celebrated the defeat of the Iranian team. This was an unprecedented phenomenon because until 2022 the Iranian people considered the national team to constitute a national team. But because of the fundamentalist regime's propaganda portraying the team as signifying the Islamic Republic of Iran, then the people chose to oppose it.

The regime is at a precipice. There is a very high likelihood of regime collapse. The decisions by various domestic and international players could either assist the fundamentalists to stabilize the situation and consolidate their power or assist the Iranian people who oppose the regime to overthrow the regime. This revolutionary process may take a few weeks or a few years. This book has attempted to describe the process of how we got here and where Iran is going, and what decisions by which actors may influence the outcome.

6.1 The Election of Ebrahim Raisi to the Presidency: Hardline Solution to Crises or the Final Nail in the Coffin?

The hardliners orchestrated the election on June 18, 2021, to make certain that Ebrahim Raisi would become President. Raisi is one of the more extreme members

---

3 Iran International, "Iranians Rejoice Europe's Move Against IRGC As Regime Vents Anger," (January 20, 2023), https://www.iranintl.com/en/202301200927.

of the hardline faction. Raisi was born on December 14, 1960.[4] His father was a mid-ranking cleric. He attended only six years of primary school. Then he began attending seminaries. When the revolution occurred in 1979, he was 18 years old. He began working with the fundamentalists after the revolution. Raisi held a series of positions in the judiciary from revolutionary prosecutor to judge. He was responsible for the execution of thousands. He was a member of the so-called Death Board in Tehran and Karaj during the Second Reign of Terror in August–September 1988, when about 5,000 political prisoners were summarily mass executed. The Death Boards consisted of three individuals who would ask several questions and then decide whether the political prisoner would live or be executed. On Saturday June 19, 2021, when the regime announced that Raisi had won the election to the presidency, Amnesty International and Human Rights Watch called for probes for crimes against humanity committed by Raisi.[5]

By August 2021, the hardline faction controlled all levers of power in Iran: Supreme Leader, President, Majles, Council of Guardians, Assembly of Experts, Council for Expediency of the System, and the IRGC. This not only cemented hardline control of the regime in the short term but also eliminated the likelihood of a non-hardline candidate becoming the next Supreme Leader after Khamenei dies in the long term.

The expulsion of reformist and expedient factions from the top positions of power and the monopolization of power in the hands of hardliners has advantages and disadvantages for the fundamentalist regime, both domestically and internationally. The marginalization of reformists and expedients eliminates the hope of many inside Iran that gradual and small changes are possible. This would benefit the opposition (e.g., democratic opposition) that wants to replace the ruling fundamentalist regime with another form of political system (e.g., democracy). When another uprising such as those that occurred in 2017 and 2019 occurrs, the likelihood of more people going to the streets and joining the uprising increases. Ebrahim Raisi's presidency indicates that Khamenei and hardliners have reached the conclusion that they fear mass uprisings and believe the best way to keep power is through brute force.

Raisi's presidency also makes it harder for the U.S. and Europeans to make concessions to the fundamentalist regime. One of the main arguments for the appeasement of the fundamentalist regime has been that, by doing so, the U.S. and E.U. would increase the power of the reformists and moderates (expedients) within

---

4 Raisi's biography is on his website: https://raisi.ir/page/biography.

5 Reuters, "Rights Groups Call for Probe into Iran's Raisi for Crimes against Humanity" (June 19, 2021), https://www.reuters.com/world/middle-east/amnesty-calls-investigation-into-irans-raisi-crimes-against-humanity-2021-06-19/.

the fundamentalist regime. The presidencies of Khatami and Rouhani had made those arguments plausible for many. Raisi's presidency would undermine the plausibility of such arguments.

The INF had called for a boycott of this election, as it had all the elections since 1980, with only two exceptions. (The INF had called the people to vote for Mohammad Khatami for reelection to the presidency in 2001 and for reformists for the Majles elections in 1998.) The INF argued that the people have moved on from choosing between "bad" (i.e., reformists, expedients, or less extremist hardliners) and "worse" (i.e., hardliners or more extreme hardliners). The INF believes that the Iranian people deserve freedom, democracy, and human rights. The INF advocates changing the current dictatorship to a democracy. By participating and voting, one would be providing legitimacy to the fundamentalist regime. Therefore, the INF called for a boycott of the elections.[6]

6.2 Policy Ramifications

Scholars, like other people, use analogies to clarify a complex subject to better illustrate it in simple terms. The best analogy I can think of to describe the situation in Iran since early 1979 when Khomeini showed his intention to create a fundamentalist regime is a tug of war. On the one side is the fundamentalist regime, its supporters, and those who lobby for its benefit. On the other side are the Iranian people who oppose the fundamentalist regime and the opposition groups. In the past 43 years, more and more segments of the population have left the side of the regime and have either joined the people, left the country, or simply become apolitical.

In this tug of war between the fundamentalist regime and its opponents, others may choose to engage in activities or advocate policies that benefit the regime, or the opponents of the regime, or remain neutral.

Those countries and companies that purchase oil, natural gas, and petrochemicals from the regime ruling Iran, provide the fundamentalist regime the resources that enable it to dominate the Iranian people. In other words, by purchasing oil from the Islamic Republic, these countries and companies are interfering in the internal political struggles in Iran in favor of the fundamentalists and against the people who oppose them. The vast oil and gas income allows the regime to

---

6 Jebhe Melli Iran, *"Mellat Iran Az Entekhab Bein Bad Va Badtar Oboor Kardeh Ast"* [The Iranian Nation Has Moved On From Choosing Between Bad and Worse] (April 7, 2021), https://melliun.org/iran/257087. Also see Hussein Moussavian, "Interview," Iran National Front-Organizations Abroad TV, Channel One (June 20, 2021), https://www.youtube.com/watch?v=XflRlCIejVk.

pay for its vast coercive apparatuses, keep the fundamentalist *nomenklatura* happy, fund the state apparatuses, co-opt non-fundamentalists, and provide subsidies for some goods and services (e.g., fuel, electricity, and bread) to buy social submission.

6.2.1 Pro-IRI Lobby Groups and Individuals

There are groups and individuals in the West that lobby and promote policies that benefit the fundamentalist regime in this tug of war. These pro-IRI groups and individuals attempt to influence the governments in the U.S., Canada, the U.K., and E.U. countries as well as think-tanks, journalists, and academics in these countries.

One main group considered by many observers to promote the interests of the fundamentalist regime is the National Iranian American Council.[7] NIAC claims that it is not a lobby for the fundamentalist regime. Many opponents of the fundamentalist regime believe that NIAC makes that claim in order to deceive the people. Many opponents of the fundamentalist regime agree with the presiding judge at the lawsuit, who wrote:

> That Parsi occasionally made statements reflecting a balanced, shared blame approach is not inconsistent with the idea that he was first and foremost an advocate for the regime. Given the other evidence defendant amassed to support his views, the Court sees no "actual malice" in defendant's decision to disregard occasional contrary statements and assume that they were made largely to burnish Parsi and NIAC's image in the United States. **After all,** any moderately intelligent agent for the Iranian regime would not want to be seen as unremittingly pro-regime, given the regime's reputation in the United States.[8]

From the very beginning, NIAC's strategy was to camouflage its primary objective of removing sanctions on the fundamentalist regime with issues such as human rights or civil rights of Iranian Americans in order to create a human face for

---

7 Eli Lake, "Exclusive: Iran Advocacy Group Said to Skirt Lobby Rules," *Washington Times* (November 13, 2009), https://www.washingtontimes.com/news/2009/nov/13/exclusive-did-iranian-advocacy-group-violate-laws/; Iranian American Forum, http://iranian-americans.com/; Lee Smith, "Meet the Iran Lobby," Hudson Institute (September 1, 2015), https://www.hudson.org/national-security-defense/meet-the-iran-lobby; Kaveh Shahrooz, "*Labigari Jomhuri Islami*" [Islamic Republic Lobbying], Iran International (October 25, 2022), https://www.youtube.com/watch?v=UwZl6O-gsN4. For an excellent documentary on NIAC see Iran International, "On NIAC" (2021), https://www.youtube.com/watch?v=zBBa7qfHyUk. For NIAC's response see https://www.youtube.com/watch?v=ck8dDxL8lC0. NIAC's website is at https://www.niacouncil.org/.
8 The court's decision is available at https://ecf.dcd.uscourts.gov/cgi-bin/show_public_doc?2008cv0705-189, p. 12. Trita Parsi was the founder and President of NIAC.

its activities. In one of NIAC's main secret emails preparing the founding of NIAC, Trita Parsi wrote:

> Although the mission of the proposed lobby should be to improve relations between the US and Iran and open up opportunities for trade, the initial targets should be less controversial issues such as visas and racial profiling/discrimination. Since the lobby will be spared from creating a grassroots network of its own, the initial focus on non-controversial issues will only serve to establish credibility within the community, and not massive support (which would necessitate the complete avoidance of issues such as US–Iran relations).

> Furthermore, it would be a wise strategy to mainly target Iranian-American businessmen for financial support. This group has both a higher propensity to support the lobby's mission and it is also in a better position to underwrite the expenses of the lobby. Nonetheless, despite its predominantly business oriented constituency, it is essential that the lobby creates a "human face" for its aims and goals. AIPAC successfully painted the opponents of the Iran Libya Sanctions Act as "greedy businessmen who had no scruples when it came to doing business with terrorist regimes." The oil companies failed to characterize their campaign with "human concern for the well-being of innocent Iranians stuck with a dictatorial regime" or "support for the poor mid-Western family father who lost his job due to the sanctions." The human element is essential both when it comes to attracting support among Iranian-Americans and when it comes to winning the debate and the votes on the Hill.[9]

Trita Parsi opposed designating the IRGC as terrorist and placing it on the U.S. State Department's Foreign Terrorist Organizations list. From the beginning, opponents of the fundamentalist regime argued that NIAC was engaged in activities that benefited the fundamentalist regime.[10] Astute Iranians, such as Hassan Dai and many others, were not deceived by NIAC's tactics and fought to reveal that the actual intention of NIAC was to lift sanctions against the fundamentalist regime. NIAC sued Mr. Dai for defamation for saying that NIAC was working to benefit the fundamentalist regime. Not only was Mr. Dai not intimidated into silence, but he was also able to defeat the lawsuit.[11] The court ordered NIAC to pay $183,480.09 to Mr. Dai. NIAC appealed the court's decision, and the appellate court upheld the decision of the district court and strongly criticized Parsi for various actions.[12]

---

9 Trita Pari email on October 10, 2002, http://iranian-americans.com/wp-content/doc/Towards-creation-lobby.pdf. This email was revealed as part of the discovery process in the lawsuit between Hassan Dai and Trita Parsi.

10 Hassan Dai, "How Trita Parsi and NIAC Advance Iran's Agenda," Tablet (July 1, 2017), http://iranian-americans.com/how-trita-parsi-and-niac-advance-irans-agenda/.

11 Masoud Kazemzadeh, "On the Lawsuit 'Trita Parsi and NIAC v. Hassan Daieoleslam,'" Iranian.com (September 15, 2012), http://iranian.com/main/blog/masoud-kazemzadeh/lawsuit-trita-parsi-and-niac-v-hassan-daieoleslam-0.html.

12 Rosen, "America's Most Prominent Group," op. cit.

The opponents of the fundamentalist regime inside Iran also publicly criticize and condemn the groups and policies promoted by pro-IRI groups. For example, Ms. Atena Daemi wrote the following tweet:

NIAC = DIRTY

NIAC is not representative of the Iranian people but is the representative and lobby of the Islamic Republic [of Iran] in the West. It is clear that the people do not want the Islamic Republic and whatever NIAC says and whoever NIAC introduces is for the preservation and survival of the Islamic Republic and is like laundering blood.[13]

Opponents of the fundamentalist regime outside Iran have been highly critical of NIAC. For example, Ms. Ebadi, Iran's 2003 Nobel Peace Prize laureate told Eli Lake that she regrets participating in an event with NIAC in 2011. Ebadi said: "When I analyzed what they say and do … I realized what they say is closer to what the government says than what the people want."[14]

After the 2022 mass protests, many Iranians in the U.S. and elsewhere increased their criticisms and condemnation of NIAC. Many former supporters of NIAC also distanced themselves from NIAC. There have also been calls for the abolition of NIAC.[15]

First and foremost, the pro-IRI groups and individuals promote the removal of economic sanctions against the fundamentalist regime. They usually have as allies the major businesses in their countries that wish to remove the sanctions so that they can engage in lucrative trade relations with Iran.

Second, in order to remove sanctions and/or prevent new sanctions, the pro-IRI groups and individuals have to influence the political environment so that it will be more hospitable to, or at least less critical of, the fundamentalist regime. The pro-IRI groups and individuals argue that the majority of the Iranian people support the fundamentalist regime. They argue that reforms within the fundamentalist regime are possible. The pro-IRI groups and individuals try to obfuscate the utterly dictatorial system of the regime by arguing that the system in Iran contains a democratic element and a theocratic (religious or Islamic) element. The pro-IRI groups and individuals portray the reformist and expedient factions of the funda-

---

13 See her tweet at https://twitter.com/AtenaDaemi/status/1582110148759126016.

14 Eli Lake, "Iran's Nobel Laureate Is Done With Reform. She Wants Regime Change," Bloomberg (April 5, 2018), https://www.bloomberg.com/opinion/articles/2018-04-05/shirin-ebadi-is-done-trying-to-reform-iran-she-wants-regime-change.

15 For an excellent report on this by VOA's Siamak Dehghanpour, which includes an interview with NIAC's President, see VOA, *"Goftegoo-e Chaleshi Siamak Dehghanpour Ba Jamal Abdi, Rais NIAC"* [Challenging Interview by Siamak Dehghanpour with Jamal Abdi, President of NIAC] (November 8, 2022), https://www.youtube.com/watch?v=XS-_sS0Ucc&t=3s.

mentalist oligarchy as democratic and liberal. They hide the anti-democratic actions and speeches of the reformist and expedient members of the fundamentalist regime. They argue that the West should pursue policies that would guarantee the safety of the fundamentalist regime, so that the Supreme Leader would allow gradual reforms within the system.

Third, the pro-IRI groups and individuals viciously attack various opposition groups and dissidents (e.g., Masih Alinejad, Shirin Ebadi) and echo the regime's propaganda against the opponents of the regime. They criticize and attack rivals and foes of the regime (e.g., the U.S., the U.K., Saudi Arabia, Israel).

Fourth, the pro-IRI groups and individuals oppose the overthrow of the regime. When they are explicitly asked publicly whether they support the regime or they support regime change, they avoid answering the question by claiming that their position has "nuance." Of course, any thoughtful person respects nuance and complexity rather than coarseness and oversimplification. In my opinion, the pro-IRI groups and individuals use the term "nuance" as an Orwellian doublespeak in order to hide their sympathies for the IRI and not for providing actual nuanced and precise analyses of the situation in Iran.

Fifth, the pro-IRI groups and individuals also engage in deception and misleading of Western audiences by portraying the mass protests as "reforms within the system" rather than demands and struggles for "overthrow of the regime." It is one thing to say that one prefers reforms and a very different thing to portray a mass movement for overthrow as mere reforms within the system. As this book has clearly demonstrated, the demands and slogans of the protests, with the exception of the 2009 protests, have been explicitly for the overthrow of the regime. The Iranian people obviously know about the demands for overthrow of the regime; therefore, no group has portrayed the mass protests as reform. However, the supporters of the fundamentalist regime have been, with some success, deceiving Western audiences and governments by portraying the mass protests as mere reforms or dismissing them as marginal attempts by marginal groups. There are also excellent studies that debunk the falsehoods of the pro-IRI propaganda and present objective and truthful analysis. One of the best such studies has been published by the Tony Blair Institute for Global Change.[16]

The pro-IRI groups and individuals argue that if the fundamentalist regime were to be overthrown, the results would be far worse than the current situation domestically (such as civil war or the break-up of Iran) and internationally. The

---

16 Kasra Aarabi and Jemima Shelley, "Protests and Polling Insights From the Streets of Iran: How Removal of the Hijab Became a Symbol of Regime Change," Tony Blair Institute for Global Change (November 22, 2022), https://institute.global/policy/protests-and-polling-insights-streets-iran-how-removal-hijab-became-symbol-regime-change.

pro-IRI groups and individuals oppose designating the IRGC as a terrorist group. The fundamentalists have obviously engaged in many terrorist activities.

Sixth, when American and British journalists and policymakers criticize the fundamentalist regime's attacking of their embassies and taking hostage or killing their citizens, fundamentalists and the pro-IRI groups and individuals bring up the 1953 coup by the CIA and MI6 against Mossadegh's government. In my opinion, their pat responses are deliberate distortion and deception. Rather than condemning the fundamentalists' terrorism and violence, they say that these actions are retaliation for the 1953 coup against Mossadegh's government. The fundamentalists and the pro-IRI groups and individuals ignore or hide the fact that Ayatollah Khomeini, Islamic fundamentalists (e. g., Fadaian Islam), and right-wing Islamic clerics (e. g., Ayatollah Behbahani, Ayatollah Taghi Falsafi) supported and constituted major groups that were mobilized by the CIA coup against Mossadegh.[17] Moreover, in 1981 Khomeini declared not only the Iran National Front as apostate but also its founder Mossadegh as apostate, and thus should be killed.[18] Khomeini and his supporters were supporters of the Shah until June 1963 when the Shah, under pressure from the Kennedy administration, enacted land reform and female franchise. The reason Khomeini opposed the Shah and the U.S. was not due to the 1953 coup but due to the 1963 reforms.[19] To put it another way, the fundamentalists opposed Mossadegh, made an assassination attempt on Dr. Hussein Fatemi (Mossadegh's Foreign Minister), had plans to assassinate Mossadegh himself, collaborated with the CIA coup, declared Mossadegh and his political party (INF) apostate, and have oppressed and brutalized members of Mossadegh's party (INF) to this very day. Fundamentalists oppose democracy and nationalism, that Mossadegh and the INF represent.[20] Khomeini's ideology and policy positions have their roots in Sheikh Fazlollah Nouri and the *Fadaian Islam.* Nouri was the highest-ranking Shia cleric during the Constitutional Revolution, who opposed and condemned the constitution and supported the rule of Sharia as the law of the land. Nouri was executed by the constitutionalists in 1909. The *Fadaian Islam* was founded in 1946 and had engaged in many assassinations before August 1953. The dictatorship, violence, terrorism, bellicosity, and warmongering of the fundamentalists has to do with their own ideology and actions that have to be criticized and condemned by those who believe in democracy. The Shia fundamentalists' extremism, violence, and terrorism pre-date the 1953 coup; therefore, Shia fundamentalist terrorism could not be attributed to the 1953 coup.

---

17 Kazemzadeh, *The Iran National Front*, op. cit, pp. 10–18.
18 Ibid., pp. 45–46.
19 Ibid., pp. 28–29.
20 Ibid.

The 1953 coup was orchestrated by the CIA and MI6, and organized and mobilized the Shah, Shia fundamentalists, and right-wing Islamic forces. The coup should be criticized and condemned by those who support democracy, Iranian sovereignty, and the national interests of Iran. The INF, whose government was overthrown by the 1953 coup, has consistently opposed and condemned terrorism, dictatorship, and jingoism. The INF advocates democracy, peace, and amity with all the countries in the world, including the U.S., the U.K., and Iran's neighbors. The INF was the only political party in Iran that condemned the taking over of the American Embassy and holding of American diplomats as hostages for 444 days by the fundamentalists.[21] Western journalists and policymakers, who are ignorant of the actual facts, have been easily fooled by the fundamentalists and the pro-IRI groups and individuals. In other words, rather than condemn the IRI for its terrorism, the fundamentalists and the pro-IRI groups and individuals deceive the gullible critics of the fundamentalist regime.

The pro-IRI groups hide, ignore, or deemphasize the facts of collaboration between the IRI and al Qaeda and the Taliban; and when they do, they tend to blame the U.S. for the IRI's policies. They exaggerate the role that the IRI played against ISIS, al Qaeda, and the Taliban at certain junctures. As the bin Laden documents captured by the U.S. from the bin Laden compound and recently declassified by the Office of the Director of National Intelligence illustrate, the regime in Iran has provided a great deal of assistance to al Qaeda, including safe passage of funds, operatives, and weapons.[22] As long as al Qaeda was attacking American and Saudi targets, Tehran was assisting them. Although officially Iran is an ally of the government of Afghanistan, Tehran has been covertly providing money, weapons, and training to the Sunni fundamentalist Taliban in Afghanistan as well as providing safe haven for their commanders inside Iran.[23] The goal has been to kill American troops and force the United States out of the region.[24]

Seventh, the pro-IRI groups and individuals ignore warmongering and bellicose policies of the fundamentalist regime and usually blame any conflict on the IRI's foes (e.g., the U.S., Israel, Saudi Arabia). In other words, while the fundamentalist regime is engaging in war, they tend to remain silent, but when others want

---

21 Ibid.

22 Alma Keshavarz, "Iran: al-Qaeda's 'Main Artery for Funds, Personnel and Communications.' The Recently Released Osama bin Laden Letters," *Small Wars Journal* (March 10, 2016), http:// smallwarsjournal.com/jrnl/art/iran-al-qaeda%E2%80%99s-%E2%80%9Cmain-artery-for-funds-per sonnel-and-communication%E2%80%9D-the-recently-released-o.

23 Carlotta Gall, "In Afghanistan U.S. Exits, and Iran Comes In," *The New York Times* (August 5, 2017).

24 Ibid.

to stand up to the fundamentalists then the pro-IRI side criticizes the opponents of the IRI as warmongers, and themselves and the IRI as wanting peace. The pro-IRI groups and individuals almost always refuse to publicly use the term "terrorist" for the regime.

Because the IRI has a bad reputation among Western countries and the vast Iranian diaspora, the pro-IRI groups and individuals hide their true sympathies and portray themselves as neutral or even hostile to the fundamentalist regime and pretend to be pursuing diplomacy and peace. The opponents of the fundamentalist regime strongly oppose these pro-IRI groups, individuals, and lobbyists.[25] The pro-IRI groups and lobbyists claim that they are not supporters and lobbyists for the IRI and that they are realists and have nuance. The conflict and tensions inside Iran between the fundamentalist regime and protesters are echoed outside Iran as conflicts between the opponents of the fundamentalist regime and the groups that promote appeasement of the fundamentalist regime.

When the democratic governments in the West invite and accept the policy proposals of the pro-IRI groups and lobbyists, the opponents of the fundamentalist regime inside and outside Iran regard these actions as tantamount to the governments in the West spitting in their faces. The opponents of the fundamentalist regime oppose appeasement of the fundamentalist regime and policies that benefit the fundamentalist regime. When the Western democracies accept and pursue policies that benefit the fundamentalist regime (and their supporters outside Iran), they assist the fundamentalist side in the tug of war. When the Western democracies pursue policies that harm the fundamentalist regime, they assist the Iranian people who oppose the fundamentalist regime in the tug of war.

6.2.2 The Obama Presidency: Costs of Appeasement

Between 2009 and 2015, the Obama administration engaged in policies that greatly benefited the fundamentalist regime and terribly harmed the Iranian people, both symbolically and materially. When protesters on the streets of Iran were saying *"Obama, Ya Ba Onaa Ya Ba Ma"* [Obama Either with Them (the fundamentalists)

---

25 Iran International, *"Tajamo Motarezan NIAC Dar Moghabel Maghar In Sazeman"* [Protest of Opponents of NIAC in Front of its Office] (July 19, 2019), https://www.youtube.com/watch?v=xbMOvZk_P3Y. Also see Farzaneh Roostaee, *"Yek Khanevadeh NIAC Baray Toof Va Laanat Chahar Fasl"* [One NIAC Family for Four Seasons of Condemnation and Spit] (October 19, 2022), https://www.youtube.com/watch?v=A3bDbY1UE1o; and Majid Mohammadi, *"NIAC Darad Jonbesh Mahsai Ra Midozdad"* [NIAC Is Stealing the Movement Inspired By Mahsa], Gooya News (October 18, 2022), https://news.gooya.com/2022/10/post-69411.php.

or With Us (the people)], President Obama's silence was painful and heartbreaking, which demoralized the people and assisted the fundamentalist regime. President Obama sent four secret messages to Khamenei telling him that he respected him and his regime. President Obama also sent public messages stating that he respected the Islamic Republic. President Obama also engaged in secret negotiations with Khamenei's envoy that resulted in the JCPOA in July 2015, which allowed the fundamentalist regime to sell oil and natural gas and get hundreds of billions of dollars. With those hundreds of billions of dollars, Khamenei was able to substantially increase the budget for his coercive apparatuses, which means that he hired more members for the IRGC, *Basij*, IRGC-Intelligence Organization, and Ministry of Intelligence: the very persons who engaged in mass arrests, torture (including rape of male and female political prisoners), and murder of protesters. Khamenei was also able then to increase assistance to violent extremist groups such as Lebanese Hezbollah, Houthis, Iraqi Shia terrorist groups, Palestinian Islamic Jihad, and Hamas.

6.2.3 The Biden Presidency: Respite or Reprieve?

If the economic, military, and diplomatic pressures continue, there is a high likelihood of regime collapse in Iran, as occurred in Eastern Europe, the Soviet Union, and the apartheid regime in South Africa.

The Obama policy of rapprochement with the fundamentalist regime provided the regime a great deal of legitimacy and financial benefits (from the sale of oil). Obama's policy thus prolonged the fundamentalist dictatorship's rule. The Trump policy of "Maximum Pressure" imposed strong sanctions on the fundamentalist regime and greatly undermined the regime's economic situation and political stability. Trump's policy began by leaving the JCPOA in May 2018. The pressure policy was in effect only between May 2018 and January 2021. When the Biden administration took office in January 2021, the fundamentalist regime was in a highly precarious economic and political situation. The regime's economy was in a shambles, its influence in Iraq and Syria greatly reduced, and politically it was under great pressure. Biden's election has been a huge psychological boost to the fundamentalist regime.

The U.S. policy toward the fundamentalist regime would have great influence on the prolongation of dictatorship or the emergence of democracy in Iran. If the Biden administration were to continue Trump's pressure policy on the fundamentalist regime, the likelihood of regime survival would be very low and the likelihood of regime collapse and transition to democracy high. If the Biden administration were to return to Obama policies of appeasement, the likelihood of fundamentalist regime survival would be high, and the likelihood of transition to democracy would be much lower.

After January 2021, the fundamentalist regime witnessed huge reductions of pressure from the United States. During this period, the Biden administration was pursuing a policy of enticing the fundamentalist regime to return to the JCPOA via suspending many sanctions and lax enforcement of many others. Therefore, the fundamentalist regime was able to export more oil (and other goods and services) and the economic situation became more stable between January 2021 and late November 2021. It is believed that the fundamentalist regime was able to export over 1 million barrels of oil per day, the bulk of it illegally to China at huge discounts via smugglers and secret third parties. At the height of Trump's pressures, such oil exports had declined to about 100,000 barrels per day. Due to Biden's policies, the value of the rial rose against the dollar until late October 2021. For this period the value of rial was stable at around 200,000 rials to a dollar.

Despite the Biden administration's appeasement policies, the fundamentalist regime since Raisi's inauguration has pursued more aggressive policies toward the U.S. and in the negotiations on the return to JCPOA restrictions on its nuclear policies. Several Biden administration officials made threats that the U.S. would increase sanctions again if the fundamentalist regime continued its aggressive policies. These threats were not taken seriously by fundamentalist officials. The Biden administration's withdrawal from Afghanistan and handing of it to the Taliban indicated to the fundamentalist regime that the Biden administration was leaving the Middle East and was afraid to pay the price of opposing fundamentalist forces.

The JCPOA negotiations between November 29 and December 3, 2021 failed because of the unrealistic positions of the fundamentalist regime. On December 5, the value of the rial plunged. On December 5, 2021, one dollar was traded at 304,500 rials.[26] On December 6, the rial dropped for the third day in a row, exchanging for 310,400 rials to a dollar.[27] It remains to be seen whether the Biden administration will continue its appeasement policies or change to a confrontational posture toward the fundamentalist regime.

---

26 VOA, "*Paslarzehay Binatijeh Mandan Mozakerat Vean, Arzesh Rial Iran Beh 'Paentarin Had Dar Tarikh' Resid*" [The Aftershocks of Failure of the Vienna Talks: The Value of the Iranian Rial Reached "Its Lowest Point in History"] (December 5, 2021), https://ir.voanews.com/a/iran-rials-jcpoa-talks/6340254.html.

27 Radio Farda, "*Nerkh Dollar Az 31 Hezar Tooman Obor Kard; Sooghot 25 Darsadi Arzesh Rial Dar 100 Rooz Dowlat Raisi*" [Price of a Dollar Crossed the 31 Thousand Tooman; 25 Percent Fall of the Value of Rial During the 100 Days of Raisi's Government] (December 6, 2021), https://www.radiofarda.com/a/iran-dollar-rise-raeisi/31596216.html. One tooman is 10 rials.

As of this writing in March 2023, the Biden administration has continued its policy of not seriously enforcing sanctions on the IRI's sale of oil, petrochemicals, and other products. By early 2023, the fundamentalist regime was exporting between 1.1 million and 1.3 million barrels of oil per day.[28]

6.2.4 China, Russia, and the E.U.

China and Russia consider democracy an ideological threat to their authoritarian systems. A transition to democracy in Iran would not benefit China and Russia. Not surprisingly, therefore, they have provided support to the fundamentalist regime.

European democracies have pursued friendly economic, diplomatic, and political relations with the ruling fundamentalist dictatorship in Iran, as they did with the Pahlavi dictatorship. This is (perhaps) surprising considering that the fundamentalist regime has numerous times conducted terrorist activities on European soil (U.K., Germany, France, Austria, Italy, Bulgaria, Poland, the Netherlands, Belgium, Sweden, Spain, and Switzerland).[29] These terrorist activities include bombings, assassinations, and kidnappings. Several of the agents of the regime have been arrested, convicted, and jailed. Some assassins have been simply let go; for example, in Austria for the assassinations of Dr. Qassemlou and two of his lieutenants. Some were exchanged for European citizens jailed in Iran: for example, by France for the assassination of Dr. Bakhtiar. Many terrorist activities have been foiled by European intelligence and security agencies, such as the attempt to bomb the annual meeting of the PMOI in France in 2018.[30] The fundamentalist regime uses terrorism as a major tool of statecraft in its foreign policy.[31]

Before 2012, many believed that the European governments' friendly relations with the fundamentalist regime were due to lucrative trade relations. After 2012,

---

28 Iran International, "Biden Administration Showing 'Weakness On Iran': US Senator" (March 23, 2023), https://www.iranintl.com/en/202303239547; Iran International, "Iran Claims Oil Exports Surpass 1.3 Million Barrels Per day" (March 23, 2023), https://www.iranintl.com/en/202303235409.

29 U.S. Government, Department of State, *Outlaw Regime: A Chronicle of Iran's Destructive Activities* (Washington, D.C., 2018), https://www.state.gov/wp-content/uploads/2018/12/Iran-Report.pdf, p. 15; Radio Farda, *"Gozaresh Jadid: Jomhuri Islami 'Dast Kam 540 Irani' Ra Dar Kharej Az Keshvar Koshteh Ya Rebodeh Ast"* [New Report: The Islamic Republic Has Murdered or Kidnapped "At Least 540 Iranians" Outside the Country] (July 28, 2021), https://www.radiofarda.com/a/boroumand-foundation-we-has-identified-more-than-540-iranians-whose-murder-or-kidnapping-is-attributed-to-the-islamic-republic-of-iran/31380796.html; and Iran International, *"Emrooz"* [Today] (July 28, 2021), https://www.youtube.com/watch?v=eVj_ajlNSW4.

30 Ibid.

31 Masoud Kazemzadeh, *The Grand Strategy of the Islamic Republic of Iran* (forthcoming).

many believe that these friendly relations have been due to Europeans' fears about the massive numbers of refugees pouring into their countries that revolution or regime change might produce. Or perhaps, foreign policies of European governments are formulated on Realist grounds and their pronouncements about democracy and human rights have been little more than window dressing.

The year 2022 witnessed a shift in Europe's policies toward the fundamentalist regime. A combination of the mass protests in Iran, the massive demonstrations by Iranians in Europe against the fundamentalist regime, and the IRI's military support for Russia in its invasion of Ukraine appears to have shown many European governments the utter unpopularity of the fundamentalist regime and its likely overthrow. Until August 2022, the policy of the European countries toward the fundamentalist regime was total appeasement. Since early 2023, it appears that some shifts are occurring. As of January 2023, the changes appear to be mostly symbolic and rhetorical and there exists little substantive change.

It appears that in the United States, public discussion on foreign policy pays far more attention to concerns for democracy and human rights than it does in Europe. It is true that human rights and democracy have been used expediently and applied selectively. However, it may also be true that under certain conditions and for some administrations in the United States concerns for democracy and human rights play a role in the formulation of foreign policy.[32] We have observed major changes in American foreign policy toward the fundamentalist regime.[33] Ebrahim Raisi's presidency will have no effect on the foreign policies of China and Russia. The effects of Raisi's presidency on the Biden administration and Europeans are not clear.

6.3 Conclusion

Iran is in a pre-revolutionary situation. On the one side is the fundamentalist regime and its supporters. On the other side is the Iranian people who oppose the regime. The mass protests discussed in this book describe various episodes of struggle between the two sides. Like a tug of war, the two sides pull in their favor. Actions of various domestic and global actors will have determining effects on the result.

---

32 Kazemzadeh, *Iran's Foreign Policy*, op. cit.
33 Masoud Kazemzadeh, *U.S.–Iran Confrontation: Alternative Scenarios and Consequences* (forthcoming).

Of course, the reality is more complex than this analogy. On the fundamentalist side there are hardline elements that want to use repression to suppress the people. There are also reformist and expedient elements within the fundamentalist oligarchy that believe that the regime has to provide concessions to the people if the regime is to survive. They include Mohammad Khatami, Hassan Khomeini, Hassan Rouhani, and Ali-Akbar Nategh-Nouri. There are also elements that argue that the regime has to cede power. They include Mir-Hussein Moussavi and perhaps Faezeh Hashemi Rafsanjani.

For the opposition, there are the pro-democracy coalition, Reza Pahlavi and his allies, the PMOI, communists, and ethnic parties. Each of these "alternatives" has its strengths and weaknesses. The pro-democracy coalition includes the INF and the LPI.

The group around Reza Pahlavi has the best connections to world leaders and substantial funds. It includes well-known individuals but lacks organization. Much of the Persian-language media is dominated by supporters of Reza Pahlavi. It suffers from domination by a group with a terribly dictatorial past and present. It remains to be seen whether the non-monarchist elements in this group will remain with Reza Pahlavi or they will break with the group.

The PMOI possesses highly organized and disciplined members and supporters as well as huge funds. However, it lacks large support from the population. It could not win elections but could play a variety of roles. Ethnic parties have small numbers. However, due to oppression and discrimination by the regime, strong solidarities exist among ethno-sectarian minorities. It remains to be seen whether these ethno-sectarian parties will be able to reach compromises with the national alternatives.

There are several far-left communist organizations. Their numbers are too small to be of major influence. They could, under certain circumstances, act as spoilers for other major alternatives.

6.3.1 Possible Outcomes of the Mass Protests

Scholars, government officials, and think-tank fellows prepare for various political events by analyzing various policies, their potential political outcomes, and consequences.[34] In my previous publications, I have applied this framework for the case of Iran for several phenomena.[35]

---

34 Graham T. Allison, "Conceptual Models and the Cuban Missile Crisis," *American Political Sci-*

6.3.1.1 Hardline Policies and Outcomes

Khamenei and his hardline faction have used repression as their solution to the mass protests and the crisis. The logic of their policy is clear. They control the coercive apparatuses, the state apparatuses, and the huge natural resources of Iran. They constitute a minority and possess an ideology that is opposed by the overwhelming majority of the population. The only way they could hold power and pursue their ideological goals is to use massive repression and dictatorship. Any reduction of repression would reduce costs of opposition to the regime and allow mass mobilization of the people against the regime. Considering the fact that they have committed horrendous crimes against humanity against the Iranian people as well as international terrorism, they would face trials in Iran and outside Iran.

I see five possible outcomes of the hardline policy: (1) successful crushing of the protests; (2) unsuccessful crushing of the protests; (3) successful repression and policy reversal; (4) regime collapse after Khamenei dies; (5) nuclear panacea.

6.3.1.1.1 Successful Crushing of the Mass Protests

The mass repression will succeed in crushing the people into submission. In the short term, this scenario is the most likely outcome. However, because all the causes of the discontent and all the main causes of the crises remain, history tells us that we will witness mass protests again and again. This means a long period of mass protests and violent repression of the people. If other countries buy oil from the regime, the fundamentalist regime will be able to continue this struggle.

6.3.1.1.2 Unsuccessful Crushing of the Mass Protests

The mass repression will not succeed if other countries do not buy oil from the regime. In this case the regime will run out of funds to keep the economy afloat and its coercive apparatuses and supporters on side.. Economic collapse and political collapse become likely.

---

ence Review, Vol. 63, No. 3 (September 1969); and Graham Allison and Philip Zelikow, *Essence of Decision: Explaining the Cuban Missile Crisis,* 2nd edition (New York: Longman, 1999).
35 Masoud Kazemzadeh, "U.S.–Iran Confrontation in the Post-NIE World: An Analysis of Alternative Policy Options," *Comparative Strategy,* Vol. 28, No. 1 (2009), pp. 37–59; Masoud Kazemzadeh, "Five Possible Outcomes Following the Mass Protests in Iran," Radio Farda (February 6, 2018), https://en.radiofarda.com/a/iran-unrest-scenarios-war-revolution-uprising/29023446.html; and Masoud Kazemzadeh, "Post-Khamenei Iran and American National Interests," *The Hill* (July 11, 2016), http://thehill.com/blogs/pundits-blog/foreign-policy/287175-post-khamenei-iran-and-american-national-interests.

6.3.1.1.3 Successful Repression and Policy Reversal

Khamenei could use mass repression to suppress the mass protests. Then, he could pursue a number of policies that had contributed to the crises. For example, Khamenei could order Raisi to re-enter the JCPOA or negotiate a new version of it that in exchange for nuclear reversals, the U.S. and the E.U. suspend or abolish sanctions. The regime could also reach secret or public *modus vivendi* with the U.S., Saudi Arabia, and Israel without resolving underlying issues of conflicts. The premise of this scenario is that by making concessions to foreign actors, the fundamentalist regime would be able to gain funds to keep its coercive apparatuses and social base happy and provide enough economic benefits to various segments of society that would buy the regime their submission. This scenario might have a high likelihood of success in the medium term. The Biden administration and the E.U. have given mere lip service to human rights and democracy in Iran, and have been eager to reach an agreement with the fundamentalist regime. Khamenei could have chosen this path, but as of March 2023, he has decided not to choose this path despite pleas and offers of major concessions and appeasement by the Biden administration and the E.U.[36]

To many scholars and Western observers this option appears to make great sense for Khamenei to pursue. One has to explain why Khamenei has not done so, as of March 2023. By adopting such policy reversals, Khamenei would be admitting that hardline policies were harmful for the fundamentalist regime and that the policies that have been advocated by reformist and expedient factions of the fundamentalist oligarchy were better for the fundamentalist regime. Such policy reversal would have adverse effects on the balance of power among the factions in the fundamentalist oligarchy, increasing the power of the reformists and expedients and reducing the power of the hardline factions. Moreover, this would greatly undermine the prospects for hardliners to capture the presidency and the position of Supreme Leader after Khamenei dies. It would also greatly reduce the likelihood of Khamenei's son, Mojtaba, becoming the next Supreme Leader after Khamenei's death.

A criticism of this outcome is that the fundamentalist regime will use this policy to avoid collapse and, in a few years, when it feels secure, it will return to its bellicose and aggressive foreign policies such as a nuclear weapons program, regional aggression, and international terrorism.

There have been major conflicts between the supporters and opponents of the fundamentalist regime to influence the policies of Western democracies. Such conflicts would drastically increase if Khamenei were to choose this policy. The sup-

---

36 This scenario was articulated by Penny L. Watson.

porters of the fundamentalist regime will lobby Western countries to suspend sanctions on the fundamentalist regime in order to entice Khamenei to return to the JCPOA, arguing that the best way to prevent the IRI from completing its nuclear weapons program is to provide it with extensive concessions. Some of the very same individuals who make this argument used to argue that the IRI did not have a nuclear weapons program; that concerns about the IRI's nuclear weapons program were an unnecessary crisis and that sanctions were imposed on the IRI because the IRI had an independent foreign policy.

The opponents of the fundamentalist regime argue that in previous agreements, the fundamentalist regime lied to European countries and the U.S., and continued its clandestine nuclear weapons program. The opponents of the fundamentalist regime have the actual history of the fundamentalist regime to substantiate their position. For example, Hassan Rouhani, who was the chief nuclear negotiator, has provided great detail on how he lied to and deceived his EU3 (France, UK, and Germany) counterparts in order to continue the work on the nuclear program.[37] There is no reason to believe that it will not lie again and fool Western countries yet again, as it has on many occasions.[38] By suspending sanctions, the West will prolong the rule of the fundamentalists, and sooner or later, the fundamentalists will, thus, complete their nuclear weapons construction.

6.3.1.1.4 Nuclear Panacea

In 2023, the IRI has become a threshold state. This means that the regime has mastered all the necessary technologies and fissile materials for the assembly of a nuclear bomb but has not taken the final step of putting them into an actual bomb. The fundamentalist regime has well over 100 billion dollars plus the opportunity costs of its clandestine nuclear program. One should ask what the advantages and consequences are of taking the final step for Khamenei and the IRGC. Possession of nuclear weapons would make the regime secure from its foreign and domestic opponents. Khamenei would not have to worry about military attacks from the U.S.

---

37 Masoud Kazemzadeh, *Iran's Foreign Policy*, op. cit., pp. 42–44.
38 Masoud Kazemzadeh, "Explaining the Obama Administration Overlooking Iran's Cheating on the Nuke Deal," *Small Wars Journal* (August 18, 2016), http://smallwarsjournal.com/blog/explaining-the-obama-administration-overlooking-iran%E2%80%99s-cheating-on-the-nuke-deal; David Albright and Sarah Burkhard, "Highlights of *Iran's Perilous Pursuit of Nuclear Weapons*" (August 25, 2021), https://isis-online.org/uploads/isis-reports/documents/Highlights_of_Irans_Perilous_Pursuit_of_Nuclear_Weapons_August_25%2C_2021.pdf; and Arnold Aaron et al., *The Iran Nuclear Archive*. Belfer Center for Science and International Affairs, Harvard University (April 2019), https://www.belfercenter.org/sites/default/files/files/publication/The%20Iran%20Nuclear%20Archive_0.pdf.

or Israel. Khamenei and his supporters would claim that Khamenei was so wise that he was able to fool the West by engaging in *"khodeh"* (deception) and complete the IRI's nuclear weapons program. This would clearly increase the prestige of the regime among its supporters in Iran and outside Iran. Khamenei might also believe that he could use that accomplishment to demand abolition of the sanctions against the regime. He could threaten the U.S. that if sanctions were not lifted, he would close the Straits of Hormuz or attack oil fields of neighboring countries, or even invade Kuwait or the oil-rich Eastern Province of Saudi Arabia.

To Western analysts, such a view seems irrational considering the fact that the U.S. possesses over 6,000 nuclear weapons and the IRI would possess only a handful. However, from the perspective of Khamenei and the IRGC, the Biden administration left Afghanistan to the Taliban rather than stay and fight. Also, the Obama administration wanted to leave both Iraq and Afghanistan rather than stay and fight.

In sum, a clandestine breakout appears to be a highly desirable policy option for Khamenei and the IRGC. If Khamenei decides to pursue this policy and he succeeds in keeping it secret before making the announcement of a nuclear test, then he assumes that this policy would guarantee the survival of the fundamentalist regime and secure the regime for his son Mojtaba. The fear that such a breakout would be detected by foreign powers and of military attacks by the U.S. or Israel are probably the reasons Khamenei has not ordered taking the final step.[39]

One has to ask whether the U.S. under President Biden possesses a deterrent effect. The answer is, in all likelihood, negative. One also has to ask would a hawkish Republican President have a deterrent power. The answer is, in all likelihood, yes. Therefore, it logically follows that Khamenei would order a breakout under President Biden and not risk military confrontation with the U.S. under a Republican President. In other words, if Biden wins the 2024 election, Khamenei might order the breakout before or after the American election, but if a Republican were to win that election, Khamenei will order the breakout before the presidential inauguration.[40]

The remaining concerns for Khamenei would be whether or not the breakout would be detected, what the Israeli response might be, whether or not the IRI could hide some nuclear bombs, and how to retaliate against Israel. The outcome might range from conventional war to nuclear exchange between the IRI and Israel.

---

39 Kazemzadeh, "U.S.–Iran Confrontation in the Post-NIE World," op. cit..
40 Kazemzadeh, *U.S.–Iran Confrontation*, op. cit.

This is the worst-case scenario for the West, Iran's neighbors, and the Iranian people. However, this might be considered the best-case scenario for Khamenei and his son Mojtaba if the regime is able to keep the breakout secret.

6.3.1.1.5 Regime Collapse after Khamenei Dies

Khamenei was born in 1939. In 2023, he is 84 years old and not in great health. Khamenei has been able to keep the regime alive and control various entities such as the IRGC. As of this writing, no other person appears to be able to do what Khamenei has been doing. The position of Supreme Leader is given enormous powers by the fundamentalist constitution. Therefore, in all likelihood, after Khamenei dies there will be intense bloody struggles among members of the fundamentalist oligarchy for the capture of that position. The violent fights will include not only opposing factions but will also take place within factions. There is no consensus even among hardline factions for the person who should succeed Khamenei. The mass protests and the crises have greatly weakened the fundamentalist regime. Thus, there is a very high likelihood that the fundamentalist regime would collapse after the bloody intra-fundamentalist fights in the aftermath of Khamenei's death.

6.3.1.2 Reformist Policy

Many leaders of the reformist and expedient factions of the fundamentalist oligarchy, as well as many members of the hardline faction, believe that repression alone will not succeed in the long term. These include Khatami and Hassan Khomeini from the reformist faction, Rouhani from the expedient faction, and Nategh-Nouri from the hardline faction. They believe that the regime should make concessions to the people, such as reduction of repression and reduction of harsh enforcement of hijab, make concessions to the E.U. on the JCPOA, détente with Saudi Arabia, and suspend hostile rhetoric against the U.S. and Israel. They could enact these policies if one of them were allowed to become President or Supreme Leader after Khamenei's death. Khamenei opposes reduction of repression because that policy would reduce the costs of resistance, which in turn would allow millions of people to join the protests and overthrow the fundamentalist regime. These policies would have the same outcome if they were pursued by a Reformist Supreme Leader after Khamenei's death as well. In other words, what occurred in the former Soviet Union and communist regimes in Eastern Europe would occur in Iran if there were a reduction of repression.

Some top reformist leaders such as Mir-Hussein Moussavi and Abolfazl Ghadyani have reached the above conclusion and have argued that the fundamentalist regime has to accept free elections and leave power. If more members of the fundamentalist oligarchy reach this conclusion and follow the leadership of Moussavi, then this will increase the likelihood of regime collapse and transition to democracy in Iran.

6.3.1.3 Reza Pahlavi and the Monarchists

Although Mr. Pahlavi and his monarchist supporters constitute a minority among the population, they possess vast resources. For example, the monarchists dominate the satellite television programs, which is the main way of mass communication with millions of people inside Iran. Reza Pahlavi and his monarchist supporters have been attempting to impose his leadership on the opposition and reimpose the Pahlavi monarchy in Iran. Mr. Pahlavi, however, suffers from several factors seriously undermining the efforts to impose him as the leader of the opposition. Pahlavi lacks a serious political party or organization that would mobilize his supporters, despite enormous funds that have been available to Mr. Pahlavi and his supporters.

Because of the horrendous record of the fundamentalist regime, there is a nostalgia for the Pahlavi period among many average Iranians. Of course, politically sophisticated Iranians, who have been supportive of democracy, civil rights, civil liberties, human rights, or leftist politics, do not suffer from such nostalgia. Hence, we observe intense conflicts between the monarchists and pro-democracy parties. The conflicts between the monarchists and those on the left and among ethnic parties are even more intense.

The INF, the main Iranian pro-democracy party, has four major criticisms of the Shah. First, the Shah was a puppet of the British and the United States. For example, he collaborated with MI6 and the CIA and overthrew the government of Dr. Mossadegh that had nationalized Iran's oil, then gave Iran's oil to a consortium of oil companies. These companies controlled Iran's oil until the 1979 revolution, and it was Mehdi Bazargan's provisional government in 1979 that took *de facto* control of Iranian oil. The oil companies sued Iran at the International Court at the Hague and the Court ruled in favor of Iran and against the oil companies. Basically, in exchange for protecting their colonial interests, the U.K. and the U.S. supported the Shah's dictatorship. In other words, rather than defending the national interests of Iran and the interests of the Iranian people, the Shah was a puppet who was serving the interests of foreign powers. Second, there were no freedoms of speech, the press, assembly, or political parties. Third, the Shah's regime was a one-man tyranny. Even the monarchist officials were not allowed to criticize the Shah. Fourth, the Shah engaged in horrendous human rights violations, including severe torture and murders and executions.[41]

---

41 Kazemzadeh, *The Iran National Front*, op. cit., pp. 8–29, 121–127.

What is politically significant is that monarchists are more violent, intolerant, and dictatorial than they were in 1979. Therefore, other major opposition parties strongly oppose Reza Pahlavi and the monarchists. They consider the monarchists a threat to the movement to overthrow the fundamentalist regime. They also believe that if Reza Pahlavi and the monarchists were able to come to power, they would engage in brutal repression of liberal democrats, social democrats, liberal nationalists, liberal Islamists,[42] Marxists, the PMOI, and ethnic parties.

If Reza Pahlavi and the monarchists were able to come to power, then a long bloody civil war is a certainty. The reason is that in the vacuum that would occur after the overthrow of the fundamentalist regime and before the monarchists could re-establish their SAVAK and coercive apparatuses, all other forces would arm themselves and engage in armed struggle to defeat the monarchists.

6.3.1.4 The Iranian Democrats and the Transition to Democracy

The democratic forces wish to establish a secular democratic republic after the overthrow or collapse of the fundamentalist regime. The Iran National Front is the largest and oldest pro-democracy coalition in Iran and is one of the main groups among the pro-democracy forces. The Left Party of Iran is the largest Iranian leftist party and is in a coalition with the INF. Two major democratic republican groups are also part of this coalition. Their vision of a democratic secular republic is Iran's best hope for democracy. If the pro-democracy coalition is able to gain support from civil society organizations and Mir-Hussein Moussavi, it would have the best option to lead the movement against the fundamentalist regime and transition to democracy. The pro-democracy coalition possesses strong parties but lacks one charismatic leader who would be able to galvanize the population. It also lacks contacts with democratic governments around the globe. It lacks funds, in large part, because it does not solicit funds from foreign governments.

The supporters of the PMOI and the far-left groups are too few to be able to gain the leadership of the mass protests or to come to power after the overthrow or collapse of the fundamentalist regime. The PMOI and the far left are not only strongly against the fundamentalist regime, but they are also intensely against the monarchists and will certainly pick up arms and fight against the monarchists in the aftermath of the overthrow of the fundamentalist regime. The same is also true of many ethnic parties and organizations. Unlike the fundamentalists and monarchists, who have repressed, tortured, and executed the members and supporters of the PMOI, far left, and ethnic parties, the INF has had a history of de-

---

42 Under the term "liberal Islamists" I include members and supporters of the Liberation Movement of Iran, the *Melli-Mazhabi* group, and the late Dr. Abol-Hassan Bani Sadr.

fending their political rights and human rights. In a democratic Iran, members of these parties will have the right to run for election to the parliament and national and local offices and, if they win, to serve as members of the parliament and cabinets as well as mayors and provisional governors. Therefore, such parties have no incentive to act as spoilers in the aftermath of the overthrow or collapse of the fundamentalist regime if the pro-democracy coalition is considered the leader of the opposition.

6.3.2 Policy Ramifications for Democratic Countries

The U.S., Canada, Britain, Australia, New Zealand, Japan, South Korea, and the E.U. could take action that would undermine the fundamentalist regime and thus enable and empower the Iranian people who oppose the regime. The expressions of support from democratic and progressive groups and leaders have been heartwarming for the Iranian people who oppose the regime. These expressions of solidarity increase the self-confidence of those engaging in mass protests. Such global expressions of support also have an impact on the fundamentalist regime and their supporters. These expressions of support increase the costs of repression. Therefore, the fundamentalist leaders and members of the coercive apparatuses become more reluctant to use massive violence. The stronger such verbal support, the more it increases the will of the people and their willingness to continue the struggle. These words of solidarity show the people that their sacrifices are not in vain and that they are heard and that there are costs to the regime and that they might succeed in their struggles.

Actual policies that undermine the regime would have great benefit for the people. The political, diplomatic, and economic sanctions on the apartheid regime in South Africa may be used as a model. Universal sanctions on the sale of oil, natural gas, and petrochemicals and strict enforcement of them would be highly effective. The Biden administration has drastically reduced the enforcement of sanctions on the fundamentalist regime to sell oil and retrieve the funds. Under the Trump administration, the IRI sale of oil was reduced to about 150,000 barrels of oil per day and the regime had trouble retrieving its money. Under the Biden administration, the IRI has been able to increase its oil sales to over 1.5 million barrels of oil per day and has been able to retrieve the proceeds of those sales. Had the Biden administration continued the Trump policy of strict enforcement of the sanctions, then the fundamentalist regime would have lacked the funds that it has had since January 2021.

Other policies that would undermine the fundamentalist regime include expelling it from certain international organizations such as the United Nations Commission on the Status of Women, UNESCO, and the like. The democratic countries could close the IRI's embassies and cultural centers, or at least expel the regime's ambassadors. The democracies could withdraw their ambassadors from Tehran. The democratic countries could designate the IRGC as terrorist. It is not clear why the E.U. has not done so when the fundamentalist regime has used the IRGC and Ministry of Intelligence to assassinate so many dissidents on European soil and many of its terrorist plots have been foiled by various intelligence agencies. The democratic countries could also place the Lebanese Hezbollah, which is the Lebanese proxy of the fundamentalist regime, on their terrorist list. Democratic countries could freeze the assets of the fundamentalist regime and return them to Iran after free elections where Iran would elect the true representatives of the Iranian people. The mass demonstrations show that the vast majority of the Iranian people regard the fundamentalist regime as illegitimate and have been willing to risk their lives to overthrow it. The assets belong to the Iranian people; the regime has taken them from the people and used such assets to oppress them.

Not only have many opponents of the fundamentalist regime been publicly calling for measures against the fundamentalist regime, but we have surveys of the Iranian people that widely support such calls. For example, according to GAMAAN's survey conducted on December 21–31, 2022:

> Also, 73% inside the country believe that Western countries should defend the protestors' rights by seriously pressuring the Iranian government. Of the Iranian respondents outside the country, 96% support this view. In contrast, around 19% of respondents inside the country think that Western powers should not intervene, as the protests are an internal matter.
>
> A majority of 70% agree with Western governments proscribing the Islamic Revolutionary Guard Corps (IRGC) as a terrorist organization, expelling the ambassadors of the Islamic Republic, allowing international foreign intervention to protect protestors, sanctioning officials who played a role in suppressing the protests, and seizing Iran's property and assets to cut the government's access to them. Moreover, 66% think that Western governments should support civil leaders and engage with opposition activists and groups. Around 62% agree with ending negotiations to revive the joint nuclear deal (JCPOA), while 6% disagree with ending the negotiations.[43]

In addition to policies that would undermine the regime, expressions of solidarity by political, intellectual, and cultural figures around the globe would, on the one hand, increase the confidence of the protesters and opponents of the regime, and, on the other hand, increase the cost of repression to the fundamentalist regime.

---

43 Ammar Maleki and Pooyan Tamimi Arab, "Iranians' Attitudes Toward the 2022 Nationwide Protests," GAMAAN (February 4, 2023), https://gamaan.org/wp-content/uploads/2023/02/GAMAAN-Protests-Survey-English-Report-Final.pdf.

For example, the strong public support from Hillary Clinton had great effect on the struggles between the people and the regime. However, the actions and the words of the U.S. Special Representative for Iran, Robert Malley, had a deleterious effect on the morale of the pro-democracy forces and positive effect on the morale of the fundamentalist regime and its supporters.

If the economy deteriorated further or the international pressures increased further, we might witness the tipping point whereby the regime could collapse. We do not know when the tipping point will occur, or if it will occur. What is clear, however, is that for the first time since 1981, the regime is extremely weak and subject to collapse. Decisions by various actors, including international actors, could have a determining impact on the outcome.

Although collapse of the fundamentalist regime is highly likely, it is not certain. Individuals and groups have agency and free will. Whether the fundamentalist regime collapses or survives will be the result of the actions of various domestic and global actors. This book has attempted to show what actions and policies would lead to which result.

Bibliography

Aarabi, Kasra, and Jemima Shelley. "Protests and Polling Insights From the Streets of Iran: How Removal of the Hijab Became a Symbol of Regime Change," Tony Blair Institute for Global Change, (November 22, 2022), https://institute.global/policy/protests-and-polling-insights-streets-iran-how-removal-hijab-became-symbol-regime-change.

Abrahamian, Ervand. *Iran Between Two Revolutions*. Princeton: Princeton University Press, 1982.

Abrahamian, Ervand. *Tortured Confessions: Prisons and Public Recantations in Modern Iran*. Berkeley: University of California Press, 1999.

AFP, "Internet down in Iran ahead of planned protests," (December 5, 2009) http://news.yahoo.com/s/afp/20091205/wl_mideast_afp/iranpoliticsinternet_20091205174520.

AFP, "'Thugs' vandalized apartment of Iran's Karroubi," (March 15, 2010), http://www.google.com/hostednews/afp/article/ALeqM5inF2uzaSRQ8lXw6r7p_uLL45hW3 A.

Afshari, Reza. *Human Rights in Iran: The Abuse of Cultural Relativism*. Philadelphia: University of Pennsylvania Press, 2001.

Aftab News, "*Goft O Goo Ba Maqam Bolandpayeh Amniyati, Shakhsi Bedon Naam Va Aks*" [Discussions With a High Level Security Official, A Person With No Name and Photo], (April 20, 2010), http://aftabnews.ir/vdcjvheh.uqeaxzsffu.html.

Ahmadi, Abdolreza. "*Astan Qods Razavi: Dowlat Penhan Tofangdar*" [Imam Reza Holy Shrine: Government in the Shadow with Guns], Independent Persian, (December 15, 2019), https://www.independentpersian.com/node/32851/%D8%A2%D8%B3%D8%AA%D8%A7%D9%86-%D9%82%D8%AF%D8%B3-%D8%B1%D8%B6%D9%88%DB%8C%D8%9B-%D8%AF%D9%88%D9%84%D8%AA-%D9%BE%D9%86%D9%87%D8%A7%D9%86-%D8%AA%D9%81%D9%86%DA%AF%D8%AF%D8%A7%D8%B1.

Ahmadi Khorasani, Noushin. "Interview," Madreseh Feministi [Feminist School] reposted at Iran Emrooz (May 25, 2010) http://www.iran-emrooz.net/index.php?/politic2/more/21973/.

Akhbar Rooz, "*Porsesh Daneshjuyan Az Kandiaday Jebhe Mosherekat: Koshtar Sal-e 67, Mir Hussein Javab Bedeh!*" [Students' Questions of the Candidate of the Participation Front: The Massacre of the Year 1988, Mir Hussein Provide an Answer!], (May 5, 2009) http://akhbar-rooz.com/news.jsp?essayId=20689.

Alamdari, Kazem. "*Neshanei Digar Az Shekast Estrategic Jumhuri Islami*" [Another Indication of the Strategic Defeat of the Islamic Republic], Iran Emrooz, (February 16, 2010) http://www.iran-emrooz.net/index.php?/politic/more/21088/.

Al-Arabiya, "*Taeb Baradar Moaven Sepah Az Bi-Khatari Dastgiri Rafsanjani Sokhan Goft; Baradar Movaen Sepah Pesar Hashemi Ra Beh Rah Andazi Khaneh Fesad Moteham Kard*" [Taeb the Brother of the IRGC Deputy Remarked on the Lack of danger in Arresting Hashemi; Brother of IRGC Deputy Accused Hashemi's Son of Organizing A House of Prostitution], (November 25, 2009), http://www.alarabiya.net/articles/2009/11/25/92341.html#.

Alavi, Nasrin. "This Magic Green Bracelet: Ayatollah Khomeini's Grandsons Supporting the Reformers?" *New Internationalist*, January 2010, http://www.newint.org/features/web-exclusive/2010/01/20/magic-green-bracelet/.

Albright, David, and Sarah Burkhard. "Highlights of *Iran's Perilous Pursuit of Nuclear Weapons*," (August 25, 2021), https://isis-online.org/uploads/isis-reports/documents/Highlights_of_Irans_Perilous_Pursuit_of_Nuclear_Weapons_August_25%2C_2021.pdf.

Alfoneh, Ali. "How Intertwined Are the Revolutionary Guards in Iran's Economy?," American Enterprise Institute, Outlook Series, No. 3, (October 2007), http://www.aei.org/outlook/26991.

Alfoneh, Ali. "More bloodshed, harsher repression in Iran's protests," The Arab Weekly, (August 12, 2019), https://thearabweekly.com/more-bloodshed-harsher-repression-irans-protests.

Alinejad, Masih. "Sepideh Gholian is Exposing abuse in Iranian prisons," *The Washington Post*, (October 14, 2021), https://www.washingtonpost.com/opinions/2021/10/14/26-year-old-woman-is-exposing-abuse-iranian-prisons/.

Al Jazeera, "Iran blocks opposition protests," (February 11, 2010) http://english.aljazeera.net/news/middleeast/2010/02/20102117332284608.html.

Aljazeera, "Major destruction after Israel targets missile facility in Syria," (August 28, 2022), https://www.aljazeera.com/news/2022/8/28/israel-targeted-missile-facility-in-syria-war-monitor.

Al-Khalidi, Suleiman. "Israeli strikes hit Iranian targets near Russian Mediterranean base," Reuters (August 14, 2022), https://www.reuters.com/world/middle-east/syrian-state-media-says-israel-targets-coastal-province-tartous-2022-08-14/.

Allison, Graham T. "Conceptual Models and the Cuban Missile Crisis," *American Political Science Review*, vol. 63, no. 3 (September 1969).

Allison, Graham T., and Philip Zelikow, *Essence of Decision: Explaining the Cuban Missile Crisis*, 2nd edition (New York: Longman, 1999).

Amir Kabir University Students News, "*Gozaresh Bazdasht Daneshjooyan Tey Aban Mah; Bazdasht 60 Daneshjoo Dar Yek Mah*" [Report on the Arrests of Students During the Month of Aban: Arrests of 60 Students in One Month], (November 4, 2009) http://www.autnews.es/node/4364.

Amir Kabir University Students News, "*Ehzar-e Nazdik Beh 100 Daneshjoy Daneshgah Azad Ahwaz*" [Arraignments of Close to 100 Students of the Free University of Ahwaz], (November 4, 2009), http://www.autnews.es/node/4375.

Amnesty International, *Blood-soaked Secrets: Why Iran's 1988 Prison Massacres Are Ongoing Crimes Against Humanity* (London: 2017), https://www.amnesty.org/download/Documents/MDE1394212018ENGLISH.PDF.

Amnesty International, "Iran: Top government officials distorted the truth about 1988 prison massacres," (December 12, 2018), https://www.amnesty.org/en/latest/press-release/2018/12/iran-top-government-officials-distorted-the-truth-about-1988-prison-massacres/.

Amnesty International, "Iran: Execution of journalist Rouhollah Zam a 'deadly blow' to freedom of expression," (December 12, 2020), https://www.amnesty.org/en/latest/press-release/2020/12/iran-execution-of-journalist-rouhollah-zam-a-deadly-blow-to-freedom-of-expression/.

Amnesty International, "Iran: At least 83 Balochi protesters and bystanders killed in bloody crackdown," (October 6, 2022), https://www.amnesty.org/en/latest/news/2022/10/iran-at-least-82-baluchi-protesters-and-bystanders-killed-in-bloody-crackdown/.

Amuzegar, Jahangir. "The Rial Problem," *Foreign Policy* web edition, (February 11, 2010) http://www.foreignpolicy.com/articles/2010/02/11/the_rial_problem.

Anvari, Abdul-Karim. *Talash Baray Esteghlal: Khaterat Siasi* [Struggle for Independence: Political Memoirs]. London: Self-Publication, 2015. https://melliun.org/v/wp-content/uploads/2020/08/talash-baraye-esteghlal.pdf.

Aqai, Samnak. "*Gozareshi Az Bargozari Rooze Kargar Dar Keshvar: Kargaran Amandand*" [A Report on the Participation on the Workers Day in the Country: Workers Came], Rooz Online, (May 2, 2010) www.roozonline.com/persian/news/newsitem/article/2010/may/02//-0583b70fa8.html.

Arani, Sharif. "Iran: From the Shah's Dictatorship to Khomeini's Demagogic Theocracy," *Dissent*, No. 27 (Winter 1980), pp. 9–26.

Arasteh, Yalda. *"Hoshdar Sepah Dar Astaneh Khordad: Cheh Kasi Saran Eslahat Ra Terror Mikonad?"* [The Warning of the IRGC Approaching Anniversary of June: Who Assassinates the Reformist Leaders?], JARAS, (May 10, 2010), http://www.rahesabz.net/story/15184/.

Arjomand, Said Amir. *The Turban for the Crown: The Islamic Revolution in Iran.* Oxford and New York: Oxford University Pres, 1988.

Arnold, Aaron, et al., *The Iran Nuclear Archive.* Belfer Center for Science and International Affairs, Harvard University, (April 2019), https://www.belfercenter.org/sites/default/files/files/publication/The%20Iran%20Nuclear%20Archive_0.pdf.

Aryan, Hossein. "Falling Price of Oil Compounds Iranian President's Problems," Radio Free Europe/Radio Liberty, (October 29, 2008) http://www.rferl.org/content/By_Hossein_Aryan/1336169.html.

Asadi, Jamshid. *"Astan Qods Razavi: Daraeehay Pichideh, Hesabrasi Naroshan"* [Imam Reza Holy Shrine: Complex Assets, Unclear Transparency], Radio Farda, (February 24, 2019), https://www.radiofarda.com/a/commentary-on-Iran-powerful-religious-institute-astan-qods-razavi/29787445.html.

Asadi, Jamshid, and Mehdi Jamali, *"Gozar Az Eghtesad Nezam Valaee Beh Eghtesad Bazzar Bonyad: Naghsh 'Bazzar Azad',"* [Transition from the Fundamentalist Regime Economy to Market Orientated Economy: The Role of 'Free Markets'], Iran-Emrooz, (July 22, 2020), http://www.iran-emrooz.net/index.php/politic/more/85222/.

Associated Press, "4000 arrests in Iran reform protests," (June 12, 2003), https://www.cbsnews.com/news/4000-arrests-in-iran-reform-protests/.

Associated Press, "Iranian cleric calls for shooting Israeli FM," re-published in *The International Herald Tribune*, (January 17, 2009), http://www.iht.com/articles/ap/2009/01/17/news/ML-Iran-Israel.php.

Associated Press, "Death Toll From Iran Building Collapse Rises to 41," (June 5, 2022), https://www.voanews.com/a/death-toll-in-iran-building-collapse-rises/6604340.html.

Assoudeh, Eliot. "Shia Phoenix: Is Iran's Islamic Republic a Variety of Political Religion?" *The Journal for Interdisciplinary Middle Eastern Studies*, Vol. 4 (2019), pp. 57–95.

Azarang, Abdol Hussein. *"Jebhe Melli Iran, Bozorgtarain Eatelaf Nirohayeh Siasi Iran Dat Tarikh Moaser Iran Ta Pish Az Enghelab Islami 1357"* [Iran National Front, the Largest Coalition of Political Forces in Iran's Contemporary History Until the Islamic Revolution of 1979], *Encyclopaedia Islamica* (no date). https://web.archive.org/web/20150318064343/http://www.encyclopaediaislamica.com/madkhal2.php?sid=4503.

Bakeri, *"Pedar Jaan Jayat Inja Aslan Khali Nist"* [Dear Father Your Place Is Not Here], Kaleme, (May 18, 2010), http://www.kaleme.com/1389/02/28/klm-19784.

Bastani, Hussein. *"Eteham: Khabar Gereftan Az 'Molaqathay Khososi Imam'"* [Accusation: Getting News of 'Khomeini's Private Meetings'], BBC Persian, (March 7, 2010) http://www.bbc.co.uk/persian/iran/2010/03/100307_l39_khanevadeh_khomeini_vataneemrooz.shtml.

Bastani, Hussein. *"Aya Rahbar Iran Az Hamleh Beh Hassan Khomeini Razi Bood?"* [Did The Supreme Leader of Iran Consent to the Attack on Hassan Khomeini?], BBC Persian, (June 7, 2010) http://www.bbc.co.uk/persian/iran/2010/06/100607_l39_hassankhomeini_rahbar.shtml.

Batou, Jean. "Maxime Rodinson Was a Revolutionary Historian of the Muslim World," Jacobin, (January 31, 2021), https://www.jacobinmag.com/2021/01/maxime-rodinson-islam-middle-east.

"Bayaniyeh Jamee Az Sazemanha Va Ahzab Jomhurikhah Va Secular Democrat" [Statement of a Group of Republican and Secular Democratic Organizations and Parties], (February 16, 2023), https://melliun.org/iran/352267.

"Bayanieh Moshtarak 6 Sazeman Democrat Va Jomhurikah" [Joint Statement of 6 Democratic and Republican Organizations], (June 9, 2022), https://melliun.org/iran/317844.

BBC, "Six days that shook Iran," (July 11, 2000), http://news.bbc.co.uk/2/hi/middle_east/828696.stm.

BBC, "IAEA urges Iran to explain uranium particles at undeclared sites," (June 7, 2021), https://www.bbc.com/news/world-middle-east-57386296.

BBC Persian, "*Ayatollah Montazeri Naghshe Pour-Mohammadi Dar Edamhay Sal 67 Ra Taeed Kard*" [Ayatollah Montazeri Confirmed the Role of Pour-Mohammadi in the Executions of the Year 1998], (December 16, 2005), http://www.bbc.co.uk/persian/iran/story/2005/12/051216_mf_si_hrw.shtml.

BBC Persian, "*Taasis Bonyad Jahani Holocast Dar Tehran*" [Establishment of the Global Foundation of the Holocaust in Tehran], (December 14, 2006), www.bbc.co.uk/persian/iran/story/2006/12/061214_mf_holocaust.shtml.

BBC Persian, "*Zendeginameh Namzadha: Mir-Hussein Mousavi*" [Biography of the Candidates: Mir-Hussein Mousavi], (May 21, 2009) http://www.bbc.co.uk/persian/iran/2009/05/090521_og_ir88_mosavi.shtml.

BBC Persian, "Tehran Students Protest on Campus," (September 28, 2009) http://news.bbc.co.uk/2/hi/middle_east/8279193.stm.

BBC Persian, "*Khatami: Ma Mikhahim Rahbari, Rahbar Hameh Mardom Bashad*" [We Want the Leadership, to Be the Leader of All the People], (February 1, 2010) http://www.bbc.co.uk/persian/lg/iran/2010/02/100201_l10_ir88_khatami_khamenei.shtml.

BBC Persian, "*Enteqad Mousavi Va Karrubi Az 'Mosadereh' Rahpeymaii 22 Bahman*" [Criticisms of Mousavi and Karrubi of 'Usurpation' of the February 11 Rally], (February 18, 2010) http://www.bbc.co.uk/persian/iran/2010/02/100218_l10_mousavi_karubi_22bahman.shtml.

BBC Persian, "*Jame'eh Rouhaniyat Mobarez Az Rafsanjani Hemayat Mikonad*" [The Society of Combatant Clergy Supports Rafsanjani], (March 7, 2010) http://www.bbc.co.uk/persian/lg/iran/2010/03/100307_l39_rafsanjani_salek.shtml.

BBC Persian, "*Pasokh Eqtesad-danan Majles Iran Beh Ahmadinejad*" [The Response of the Economists in Iran's Majles to Ahmadinejad], (March 20, 2010) http://www.bbc.co.uk/persian/lg/iran/2010/03/100320_l10_ahmadinejad_subsidies_tavakoli_naderan_mesbahi_reax.shtml.

BBC Persian, "*Mahkomiyat Dobareh Moaven Siasi Daftar Rais Jomhur Iran Beh Tahamol Zendan*" [Sentencing of the Political Deputy of the Office of the President of Iran to Prison, Again], (April 20, 2010) http://www.bbc.co.uk/persian/iran/2010/04/100420_l10_behdad_hosseinkhan_sentenced.shtml.

BBC Persian, "*Jologiri Az Barpaee Ghorfeh Asar Ayatollah Beheshti Dar Namayeshgah Ketab Tehran*" [Preventing The Publisher of the Publication of Ayatollah Beheshti Holding Its Booth At the Tehran Book Faire], (May 5, 2010), http://www.bbc.co.uk/persian/lg/iran/2010/05/100505_l07_iran89_politics_bookfair89_beheshti.shtml.

BBC Persian, "*Ali Mottahari: Agar Osolgarayan Ekhrajam Konanad, Ferakciuni Jadid Tashkil Midaham*" [Ali Mottahari: If the Hard-liners Expel Me, I Will Create A New Faction], (June 8, 2010) http://www.bbc.co.uk/persian/iran/2010/06/100608_l07_iran89_motahari_parliament.shtml.

BBC Persian, "*Entesharat Nokat Tazeh Dar Mored Ayatollah Khamenei*" [The Publication of New Things About Ayatollah Khamenei], (June 11, 2010), http://www.bbc.co.uk/persian/iran/2010/06/100611_l10_rafsanjani_mohajerani_khamenei_disclosure.shtml.

BBC Persian, "*Dar Opposisioun Padeshahikhah Cheh Migozarad?*" [What is Going on in the Monarchist Opposition?], (March 8, 2023), https://www.youtube.com/watch?v=iqx-BPdW2Js.

Borger, Julian. "Mojtaba Khamenei: gatekeeper to Iran's supreme leader," *The Guardian*, (June 22, 2009) http://www.guardian.co.uk/world/2009/jun/22/mojtaba-khamenei-iran-protest.

Borger, Julian. "Khamenei's son takes control of Iran's anti-protest militia," *The Guardian*, (July 8, 2009) http://www.guardian.co.uk/world/2009/jul/08/khamenei-son-controls-iran-militia.

Boroujerdi, Mehrzad. "Iran's Potato Revolution," *Foreign Policy* Web Exclusive, (May 2009), available at: http://www.foreignpolicy.com/story/cms.php?story_id=4921.

Callan, Isaac. "More than 50k attend Richmond Hill, Ont. Protest against Iranian government," *Global News*, (October 1, 2022), https://globalnews.ca/news/9169782/richmond-hill-iran-protest/.

Chulov, Martin. "Mother says police beat daughter to death in Iranian protests," *The Guardian*, (October 8, 2022), https://www.theguardian.com/world/2022/oct/08/mother-says-police-beat-daughter-to-death-in-iranian-protests.

CNN, "How Iran's security forces use rape to quell protests: Covert testimonies reveal sexual assaults on male and female activists as a women-led uprising spreads," (November 21, 2022), https://www.cnn.com/interactive/2022/11/middleeast/iran-protests-sexual-assault/.

Cowell, Alan, and Michael Slackman, "Iran Controls Protests and Defies West on Nuclear Fuel," *The New York Times*, (February 11, 2010) http://www.nytimes.com/2010/02/12/world/middleeast/12iran.html?hp.

Croft, Adrian. "Britain has frozen $1.6 billion in Iranian assets," Reuters, (June 18, 2009), http://www.reuters.com/article/idUSTRE55H5Z620090618.

Daei Alislam, Hossein. "Posters of Parviz Sabeti at Pahlavi Rally" National Council of Resistance of Iran, (February 19, 2023), https://www.ncr-iran.org/en/news/iran-resistance/demonizing-mek/posters-of-parviz-sabeti-at-pahlavi-rally-scaring-off-tehran-or-dissent-thereof/.

Daemi, Atena, https://twitter.com/AtenaDaemi/status/1582110148759126016.

Dai, Hassan. "How Trita Parsi and NIAC Advance Iran's Agenda," Tablet, (July 1, 2017), http://iranian-americans.com/how-trita-parsi-and-niac-advance-irans-agenda/.

Dareini, Ali Akbar. "Iranian hardliner call opposition leader US agent," Associated Press, (July 4, 2009), http://news.yahoo.com/s/ap/20090704/ap_on_re_mi_ea/ml_iran_election.

Dareini, Ali Akbar. "Iran student protests bring out tens of thousands," Associated Press, (December 7, 2009) http://news.yahoo.com/s/ap/20091207/ap_on_re_mi_ea/ml_iran/print.

Dareini, Ali Akbar, and Lee Keath, "Iran election dispute escalates to new phase," Associated Press, (July 20, 2009).

Daragahi, Borzou. "Iran Students Carry on Protests," *The Los Angeles Times*, (November 3, 2009) http://www.latimes.com/news/nationworld/world/la-fg-iran-protests3-2009nov03,0,1803055,print.story.

Daragahi, Borzou. "Iran's supreme leader tells militias not to meddle," *The Los Angeles Times*, (January 10, 2010) http://www.latimes.com/news/nation-and-world/la-fg-iran-khamenei10-2010jan10,0,5472926.story.

Daragahi, Borzou, and Ramin Mostaghim, "Iranian protesters galvanized by sermon," *The Los Angeles Times*, (July 18, 2009).

Daragahi, Borzou, and Ramin Mostaghim, "Tehran protesters clash with Iranian security forces," *The Los Angeles Times*, (December 25, 2009).

Daragahi, Borzou, and Ramin Mostaghim, "Pro-government demonstrators overshadow opposition in Iran," *The Los Angeles Times*, (February 12, 2010).

Dehghanpisheh, Babak. "The killing of a 9-year-old boy further ignites Iran's anti-government protests," *The Washington Post*, (November 18, 2022), https://www.washingtonpost.com/world/2022/11/18/iran-protests-izeh-kian-pirfalak/.

Deutsche Welle, *"Defaa Rais Setad Kole Nirohay Mosalah Az Ahmadinejad"* [The Chairman of the Joint Chiefs of Staff Defends Ahmadinejad], (August 19, 2007), www.dw-world.de/popups/popup_printcontent/0,,2744095,00.html.

Deutsche Welle, *"Tadarok Marasem Haftom Ayatollah Montazeri"* [Preparation for the Ceremonies for the Seventh of Ayatollah Montazeri], (December 25, 2009) http://www.dw-world.de/dw/article/0,,5056115,00.html?maca=per-rss-per_politik-4076-xml-mrss.

Deutsche Welle, *"Defaa Rais Majles Az Faaliyathay Eqtesadi Sepah"* [The Speaker of the Majles Defends the Economic Activities of the IRGC], (May 13, 2010), http://www.dw-world.de/popups/popup_printcontent/0,,5568997,00.html.

Deutsche Welle, *"Peyda Va Penhan Daftar Ayatollah Khamenei"* [Hidden and Open Aspects of the Office of Ayatollah Khamenei], (July 23, 2010) http://www.dw-world.de/dw/article/0,,5832999,00.html?maca=per-rss-per_politik-4076-xml-mrss.

Deutsche Welle, *"Azan Farmandeh Kol Sepah Beh Vojod 'Pasdaran Hami Fetneh'"* [Admission of the Commander-in-Chief of the IRGC About the Existence of 'IRGC Officials Who Support the Sedition'], (July 25, 2010), http://www.dw-world.de/dw/article/0,,5835486,00.html?maca=per-rss-per_politik-4076-xml-mrss.

Deutsche Welle, *"Barkenari Va Ebqa Dobareh Vazir Etelaat Iran dar Yek Rooz"* [Dismissal and Reinstatement of the Minister of Intelligence of Iran in One Day], (April 17, 2011) http://www.dw-world.de/dw/article/0,,6505906,00.html?maca=per-rss-per-all-1491-rdf.

Deutsche Welle, *"Negarani Do Rouhani Nezami Az Mahar Jonbesh Eaterazi"* [Worries of Two Clerics in the Armed Forces About Containing the Protest Movement], (April 19, 2011) http://www.dw-world.de/dw/article/0,,6507336,00.html?maca=per-rss-per-all-1491-rdf.

Deutsche Welle, *"'Fetneh Nofozihay Dowlati' Dar Azl Moslehi"* ['Sedition of Those Who Have Infiltrated the Government' in the Dismissal of Moslehi], (April 19, 2011) http://www.dw-world.de/dw/article/0,,15001857,00.html?maca=per-rss-per-all-1491-rdf.

Deutsche Welle, "Tehran sanctions DW Farsi for coverage of Iran protests," (October 26, 2022), https://www.dw.com/en/iran-sanctions-dw-farsi-for-coverage-of-protests/a-63562810.

Deutsche Welle, *"Piroozi Biden Va Taasir An Bar Kahesh Bahayeh Dollar Va Talla Dar Iran"* [Biden's Victory and Its Effect on the Reduction of Prices of Dollar and Gold], (November 8, 2020), https://www.dw.com/fa-ir/%D9%BE%DB%8C%D8%B1%D9%88%D8%B2%DB%8C-%D8%A8%D8%A7%DB%8C%D8%AF%D9%86-%D9%88-%D8%AA%D8%A7%D8%AB%DB%8C%D8%B1-%D8%A2%D9%86-%D8%A8%D8%B1-%DA%A9%D8%A7%D9%87%D8%B4-%D8%A8%D9%87%D8%A7%DB%8C-%D8%AF%D9%84%D8%A7%D8%B1-%D9%88-%D8%B7%D9%84%D8%A7-%D8%AF%D8%B1-%D8%A7%DB%8C%D8%B1%D8%A7%D9%86/a-55535683.

Ebadi, Shirin, and Azadeh Moaveni, *Iran Awakening: One Woman's Journey to Reclaim Her Life and Country.* New York: Random House, 2007.

Ebrahim, Nadeem. "Iran faces dilemma as children join protests in 'unprecedented' phenomenon," CNN, (October 17, 2022) https://www.cnn.com/2022/10/17/middleeast/iran-school-children-protests-mime-intl/index.html.

The Economist, "Showing who's the boss: Iran's hard men purge opponents and line their pockets," (August 27, 2009), http://www.economist.com/world/middle-east/displaystory.cfm?story_id=14327633&source=login_payBarrier.

The Economist, "Iran's foreign minister: Thank you and good bye," (December 16, 2010) http://www.economist.com/node/17733215.

Erdbrink, Thomas. "Iranian Details Alleged Fraud: Mousavi Is Also Accused of Treason," *The Washington Post*, (July 5, 2009), http://www.washingtonpost.com/wp-dyn/content/article/2009/07/04/AR2009070402685.html?hpid=topnews.

Erdbrink, Thomas. "Protesters Clash With Police in Iran: Demonstrators Endure Batons, Tear Gas As They Try to Mark 1999 Unrest," *The Washington Post*, (July 10, 2009).

Esfandiari, Golnaz. "Iran: Coping With The World's Highest Rate of Brain Drain," Radio Farda, (March 8, 2004), https://www.rferl.org/a/1051803.html.

Esfandiari, Golnaz. "'Death to Obama' Chants In Iran," Radio Free Europe/Radio Liberty, (April 9, 2009) http://www.rferl.org/content/Death_To_Obama_Chants_In_Iran/1605628.html.

Esfandiari, Golnaz. "Reformers Hope Iran's 'Silent Voters' Will Be Heard in June," Radio Free Europe/Radio Liberty, (May 28, 2009) http://www.rferl.org/content/Reformers_Hope_Irans_Silent_Voters_Will_Be_Heard_In_June/1741914.html.

Esfandiari, Golnaz. "Supreme Leader Stokes Fears Of New Cultural Revolution In Iran," Radio Free Europe/Radio Liberty, (September 3, 2009) www.rferl.org/content/Fears_Of_A_New_Cultural_Revolution_In_Iran/1814207.html.

Esfandiari, Golnaz. "Iran's Campuses On Edge As University Doors Open," Radio Free Europe/Radio Liberty, (September 23, 2009) www.rferl.org/content/Irans_Campuses_On_Edge_As_University_Doors_Open/1829627.html.

Esfandiari, Golnaz. "Protesters, Police Clash In Tehran On Anniversary of U.S. Embassy Takeover," Radio Free Europe/Radio Liberty, (November 4, 2009) http://www.rferl.org/content/Protesters_Security_Forces_Clash_In_Tehran_On_Anniversary_Of_US_Embassy_Takeover_/1869186.html?page=1#relatedInfoContainer.

Esfandiari, Golnaz. "'Hands Are Stained With Blood': Iranians Outraged After Shah-Era Secret-Police Official Attends U.S. Rally," Radio Free Europe Radio Liberty, (February 15, 2023), https://www.rferl.org/a/iran-sabeti-us-protest-savak/32271395.html.

Etemadi, Nasser. *"Chera Mardom Iran Ebrahim Raisi Va Ozaeh Keshvareshan Ra Shabih Eichmann Va Alman Nazi Midanand?"* [Why the Iranian People Consider Ebrahim Raisi and the Condition of Their Country to Be Similar to Eichmann and Nazi Germany?], Radio France International, (August 6, 2021), https://www.rfi.fr/fa/%D8%A7%DB%8C%D8%B1%D8%A7%D9%86/20210806-%DA%86%D8%B1%D8%A7-%D9%85%D8%B1%D8%AF%D9%85-%D8%A7%DB%8C%D8%B1%D8%A7%D9%86-%D8%A7%D8%A8%D8%B1%D8%A7%D9%87%DB%8C%D9%85-%D8%B1%D8%A6%DB%8C%D8%B3%DB%8C-%D9%88-%D8%A7%D9%88%D8%B6%D8%A7%D8%B9-%DA%A9%D8%B4%D9%88%D8%B1%D8%B4%D8%A7%D9%86-%D8%B1%D8%A7-%D8%B4%D8%A8%DB%8C%D9%87-%D8%A2%DB%8C%D8%B4%D9%85%D9%86-%D9%88-%D8%A2%D9%84%D9%85%D8%A7%D9%86-%D9%86%D8%A7%D8%B2%DB%8C-%D9%85%DB%8C-%D8%AF%D8%A7%D9%86%D9%86%D8%AF.

Etezadosaltaneh, Nozhan. "Rafsanjani's Legacy: The Father of Neoliberalism in Iran," International Policy Digest, (January 12, 2017), https://intpolicydigest.org/rafsanjani-s-legacy-father-neoliberalism-iran/.

Fadavi, IRGC Gen. Ali. *"Sardar Fadavi: 'Sepah Pasdaran Enghelab Islami' Hich Kalamee Dar Edameh Khod Nadarad Hatta Iran"* [Gen. Fadavi: "The Islamic Revolutionary Guards Corps" Does Not Have Any Words After its Title, Even Iran], Bahar News, (April 22, 2018), https://www.baharnews.ir/news/148310/%D8%B3%D8%B1%D8%AF%D8%A7%D8%B1-%D9%81%D8%AF%D9%88%DB%8C-%D8%B3%D9%BE%D8%A7%D9%87-%D9%BE%D8%A7%D8%B3%D8%AF%D8%A7%D8%B1%D8%A7%D9%86-%D8%A7%D9%86%D9%82%D9%84%D8%A7%D8%A8-%D8%A7%D8%B3%D9%84%D8%A7%D9%85%DB%8C-%D9%87%DB%8C%DA%86-%DA%A9%D9%84%D9%85%

D9%87-%D8%A7%DB%8C-%D8%A7%D8%AF%D8%A7%D9%85%D9%87-%D8%AE%D9%88%D8%
AF-%D9%86%D8%AF%D8%B1%D8%AF-%D8%AD%D8%AA%DB%8C-%D8%A7%DB%8C%
D8%B1%D8%A7%D9%86.

Faramarzi, Scheherzade. "Iran cracks down on dissent in universities," Associated Press, (December 4, 2009) http://news.yahoo.com/s/ap/20091204/ap_on_re_mi_ea/ml_iran_university_crackdown.

Farhang, Mansour. *"Malikholiah Sodor Enghelab Va Chalesh 'Gheire Khodiha'"* [Melancholy of the Export of the Revolution and "non-fundamentalists"], Iran Emrooz, (September 12, 2020), http://www.iran-emrooz.net/index.php/politic/more/85845/.

Fars News Agency, *"Rahpemai Zede Zeihonisti Pas az Marasem Namza Jomeh Tehran"* [Anti-Zionist Rally After The Friday Prayer Ceremonies], (January 16, 2009) http://www1.farsnews.com/imgrep.php?nn=8710270933.

Fars News Agency, *"Tajamo Daneshjooyan Tehrani Moghabel Laneh Jasoosi Sabeq Amrica Aghaz Shod"* [Gathering of Students from Tehran began in Front of the Former Den of Spies], (April 9, 2009) http://www.farsnews.com/newstext.php?nn=8801200232.

Fars News Agency, *"Tajamo Daneshjoyan dar Salrooz Ghate Rabeteh Iran va Amrica"* [Gathering of Students on the Anniversary of the Breaking of Relations between Iran and America], (April 9, 2009) http://www.farsnews.net/imgrep.php?nn=8801200623.

Fars News Agency, *"Rahbar Moazam Enqelab Islami Dar Azimtarin Namaz Jomeh Tehran"* [The Great Leader of the Islamic Revolution at the Greatest Friday Prayer in Tehran], (June 19, 2009) http://www.farsnews.net/newstext.php?nn=8803290701.

Fars News Agency, *"Dar Nameii Khatab Beh Ayatollah Yazdi Soorat Gereft; Hemayat 306 Ostaad Howzeh Az Mavazeh Ayatollah Yazdi Dar Ertebat Baa Hashemi"* [In a Letter Addressed to Ayatollah Yazdi That Occurred; Support of 306 Seminary Teachers of the Positions of Ayatollah Yazdi in Regard to Hashemi], (July 22, 2009) http://www.farsnews.net/newstext.php?nn=8804310610.

Fars News Agency, *"Refrandom 50 Million Nafari Mardom Iran Jahan Ra Mabhoot Khod Kard"* [A Referendum of 50 Million Persons of the Iranian People Amazed the World], (February 11, 2010) http://www.farsnews.com/newstext.php?nn=8811220307.

Fars News Agency, *"Sarlashkar Jafaari: Farmandehan Sepah Baray Ayandeh Enqelab Khod Ra Amadeh Konand"* [Gen. Jafaari: Commanders of the IRGC Should Prepare for the Future of the Revolution], (May 26, 2010), http://www.farsnews.com/newstext.php?nn=8903051665.

Fars News Agency, *"Chera Barkhi Sardaran Dar Barabar Fetneh-hay Akhir Mozea Roshani Nemigirand?"* [Why Some High-Ranking Officers Do Not Take Clear Position on the Recent Sedition?], (May 31, 2010) http://www.farsnews.com/newstext.php?nn=8903070179.

Fars News Agency, *"Sarlashkar Jafaari Dar Hamayesh Morabiyan Amadegi Defaii"* [Gen. Jafaar in the Seminar for Coaches of Defense Readiness], (July 24, 2010) http://www.farsnews.com/newstext.php?nn=8905020568.

Fars News Agency, *"Rais Sazeman Basij Mostazafin Khabar Dad: Ehdas 7,000 Paygah Moqavemat Basij Dar Sal Jari"* [The Commander of the Basij Presented The News: 7,000 Basij Resistance Bases Will Be Constructed This Year], (July 29, 2010) http://www.farsnews.net/newstext.php?nn=8905061538.

Fassihi, Farnaz. "Iran Protesters Defy Clampdown," *The Wall Street Journal*, (July 10, 2009).

Fassihi, Farnaz. "Inside the Iranian Crackdown," *The Wall Street Journal*, (July 13, 2009).

Fassihi, Farnaz, and Ronen Bergman. "Israel Tells U.S. It Killed Iranian Officer, Official Says," *The New York Times*, (May 25, 2022), https://www.nytimes.com/2022/05/25/world/middleeast/iran-israel-killing-khodayee.html.

Fathi, Nazila. "Tehran Protesters Defy Ban and Clash With Police," *The New York Times*, (December 27, 2009).

Fathi, Nazila. "Iran, With Opposition Protests Continuing, Executes More Prisoners," *The New York Times*, (February 2, 2010).

Fathi, Nazila. "6 More Iranian Activists Reported Arrested," *The New York Times*, (March 3, 2010).

Fattahi, Kambiz. *"Payam Mahramaneh Ayatollah Khomeini Beh Dowlat Kennedy"* [The Secret Message from Ayatollah Khomeini to the Kennedy Administration], BBC Persian, (June 1, 2016), https://www.bbc.com/persian/iran/2016/06/160601_kf_khomeini_carter_kennedy.

Fazeli, Yaghoub. "Iran rights activists spurn Iranian-American group NIAC as regime 'lobby'," AlArabiya News, (October 19, 2022), https://english.alarabiya.net/News/middle-east/2022/10/19/Iran-rights-activists-spurn-Iranian-American-council-NIAC-as-scarlet-letter-.

Feminist School, *"Qate'nameh Payani 'Jam'i Az Faalan Jonbesh Zanan Dar Gerdhamai Sabz Beh Monasebat 8 Mars' Va Gozaresh Tasviri Az Marasem In Rooz"* [The Declaration of 'A Group of Women's Movement Activists for the Green Meeting For March 8' And A Photo Report of the Ceremonies of This Day], (March 8, 2010) http://iranfemschool.net/spip.php?article4425.

Financial Tribune, "Brian Drain Continues in Iran," (November 9, 2016), https://financialtribune.com/articles/people/53254/brain-drain-continues.

Fletcher, Martin. "Iran crushes opposition protests with violence," *Times* online edition, (February 11, 2010) http://www.timesonline.co.uk/tol/news/world/middle_east/article7023684.ece.

Fletcher, Martin. "Iranian regime ships in support for anniversary celebrations," *Times* online, (February 12, 2010) http://www.timesonline.co.uk/tol/news/world/middle_east/article7024206.ece.

Forozanfar, "Interview," Khodnevis, (April 8, 2011), http://www.khodnevis.org/persian/%D8%B1%D8%B3%D8%A7%D9%86%D9%87%E2%80%8C%D9%87%D8%A7%DB%8C-%D8%AE%D9%88%D8%AF%D9%85%D8%A7%D9%86%DB%8C/%D8%B3%DB%8C%D8%A7%D8%B3%D8%AA/12119--فروزانفر %""مجتبی-خامنهای-عوضشده-هادی-خامنهای-ریاکار-است.html.

Fromm, Erich. *Escape from Freedom*. NY: Farrar & Rinehart, 1941.

Gall, Carlotta. "In Afghanistan U.S. Exits, and Iran Comes In," *The New York Times*, August 5, 2017.

Ghaemmagham, Mohsen. *"Ghassem Soleimani – Dar Khedmat Nezam Estebdad Mazhabi Va Vali Faghih"* [Ghassem Soleimani – In Service of the System of Religious Dictatorship and Fundamentalist Regime], (January 19, 2020), Melliun, https://melliun.org/iran/223359.

Ghafari, Mahan. *"Marg O Mir Aban 98: Moamae Chand Hezar Nafari Keh Ezafeand?"* [Deaths of November 2019: The Puzzle of Several Thousand Additional Deaths?], Radio Farda, (May 28, 2021), https://www.radiofarda.com/a/commentary-on-death-toll-report-of-november-2019/31276714.html.

Ghafari, Mahan, Alireza Kadivar, and Aris Katzourakis. "Excess deaths associated with the Iranian COVID-19 epidemic: A province-level analysis," *International Journal of Infectious Diseases*, Vol. 107, (June 2021), pp. 101–115, https://www.sciencedirect.com/science/article/pii/S120197122100326X.

Gharib, Ali. *Istad-e Bar Arman* [Standing on Principles], (2006) https://www.enghelabe-eslami.com/pdf/Gharib-Istade-bar-Arman.pdf?fbclid=IwAR2UjiHF0eHH03iyfTbTH6G81gZ8xdnfy6GcJnAHNXEm10wUZ-Iv2knFhAU.

Ghoghnoos, Bijan. *"Aya 'Jomhuri Velayat Faghih' Regimi Fashisti Ast?"* [Is the "Rule of Shia Cleric Republic" a Fascist Regime?], Iran Emrooz, (January 31, 2021), http://www.iran-emrooz.net/index.php/politic/more/87667/.

Glass, Andrew. "Carter lauds shah of Iran, Dec. 31, 1977," Politico, (December 30, 2018), https://www.politico.com/story/2018/12/30/this-day-in-politics-december-31-1077103.

Goldman, Adam, Eric Schmitt, Farnaz Fassihi, and Ronen Bergman. "Al Qaeda's Number 2, Accused in U.S. Embassy Attacks, Killed in Iran," The New York Times, (November 13, 2020, updated September 14, 2021), https://www.nytimes.com/2020/11/13/world/middleeast/al-masri-abdullah-qaeda-dead.html.

Golshiri, Ghazal. "L'incroyable succès d'Hannah Arendt en Iran," Le Monde, (August 6, 2021), https://www.lemonde.fr/series-d-ete/article/2021/08/06/l-incroyable-succes-d-hannah-arendt-en-iran_6090745_3451060.html.

Gooya News, "Aaks-hay Mahvareh Google Az Jamiyat 22 Bahman + Esteqrar Otobus-hay Dowlati" [The Photos of Google's Satellites From the Population on February 11 + Placement of Government's Buses], (February 12, 2010) http://news.gooya.com/didaniha/archives/2010/02/100390.php.

Griffin, Roger. editor, Fascism. Oxford: Oxford University Press, 1995.

The Guardian, "Iran arrests celebrity chef in crackdown on protests: Detainment of Navab Ebrahimi is speculated to be linked to post about cutlets, a possible taunt over general's death," (January 5, 2023), https://www.theguardian.com/world/2023/jan/05/iran-arrests-celebrity-chef-in-crackdown-on-protests.

Haaretz, "How the Mossad Broke Into an Iranian Facility and Stole Half a Ton of Nuclear Files," (July 16, 2018), https://www.haaretz.com/israel-news/2018-07-16/ty-article/how-the-mossad-broke-into-an-iranian-facility-and-stole-nuclear-files/0000017f-db07-d856-a37f-ffc7b14c0000.

Hajipour, Shervin. "Barayeh" [For], (September 2022), https://www.youtube.com/watch?v=z8xXiqyfBg0.

Hajjarian, Saeed. "Television Roundtable Hajjarian, Atrianfar, and Shariati," broadcast from Evin Prison on IRIB (Islamic Republic of Iran Broadcasting), Channel One, (September 22, 2009), large excerpts available at: http://www.farsnews.com/newstext.php?nn=8806311665.

Halliday, Fred. "The Iranian Revolution and Its Implications," New Left Review, No. 166 (November/December 1987).

Hashemi Rafsanjani, Ali Akbar., "Hashemi: 22 Bahman Motealeq Beh Hameh Vafadarain Nezam Ast" [Hashemi: February 11 belongs to All Faithful to the System], Parcham, (February 10, 2010) http://www.parcham.ir/vdcd.j052yt0kxa26y.html.

Hashemi Rafsanjani, Ali Akbar., "Hoshdar Hashemi: Mardom Va Masoulan Movazeb Bashand" [Hashemi's Warning: The People and the Officials Should be Careful], Farda News, (February 10, 2010) http://www.fardanews.com/fa/pages/?cid=103370.

HRANA, "Report," (November 21, 2022) https://melliun.org/iran/340164.

Human Rights Watch, "Ministers of Murder: Iran's New Security Cabinet," (December 2005) http://hrw.org/backgrounder/mena/iran1205/.

ILNA, "Rahbari Mikhahad Sahneh Kheili Dagh Nashavad Va Kasi Asib Nabinad" [The Supreme Leader Does Not Want to See the Situation Heated Up, and Anyone Is Harmed], (February 23, 2010) http://www.ilna.ir/newsText.aspx?ID=109649.

ILNA, "Sarmayehha Mizbani Irani Ra Doost Nadarand: Kahesh Shadid Sarmayeh-Gozari Khareji Iran Az Sal 2002 ta 2008" [Investments Do Not Like Iranian Hosts: Severe Reductions in Foreign Investments In Iran Between 2002 And 2008], (June 6, 2010) http://www.ilna.ir/newsText.aspx?ID=127547.

ILNA, "Dar 5 Sal Gozashteh 340 Millianrd Dollar Daramad Nafti Kasb Shodeh Ast" [During the Past 5 Years Oil Income Has Been 340 Billion Dollars], (June 9, 2010) http://www.ilna.ir/newsText.aspx?ID=128346.

ILNA, *"Ehsan Soltani Dar Goftogo Ba ILNA: Tavarom Vaghe-e Balay 60 Darsad Ast"* [Interview with Ehsan Soltani: Real Inflation is Over 60 Percent], (September 20, 2020), www.ilna.news/fa/tiny/news-970141.

ILNA, *"Rais Otagh Bazargani Iran Va Chin Dar Goftego Ba ILNA"* [Interview with the Chairman of the Iran-China Chamber of Commerce], (October 4, 2020), https://www.ilna.news/fa/tiny/news-977917.

Imami Kashani, Ayatollah Mohammad. *"Edameyeh Enteqadha Az Tadris Olum Ensani Gharbi Dar Iran"* [The Continuation of Criticisms on Teaching the Western Humanities and Social Sciences in Iran], BBC Persian, (September 4, 2009) http://www.bbc.co.uk/persian/iran/2009/09/090904_op_ememikashani-azghadi_humanities.shtml.

International Campaign for Human Rights in Iran, "Crackdown on Students Ahead of National Student Day," (November 24, 2009), http://www.iranhumanrights.org/2009/11/crackdownstudent day/.

International Monetary Fund, "Islamic Republic of Iran and the IMF," (April 16, 2011) http://www.imf.org/external/country/irn/index.htm part of International Monetary Fund, "World Economic Outlook," (April 16, 2011), http://www.imf.org/external/pubs/ft/weo/2011/01/index.htm.

Iran Emrooz, *"Hamleh Beh Hashemi Az Tribune Majles"* [Attack on Hashemi from the Majles's Tribune], (January 7, 2010) http://www.iran-emrooz.net/index.php?/news2/20543/.

Iran Emrooz, *"Hamleh Beh Karrubi, Khatami, Mousavi va Rahnavard, Jahat Jologiri Az Hozoor Anha Dar Tazahorat Mardom"* [Attacks on Karrubi, Khatami, Mousavi, and Rahnavard In Order to Prevent Them from Participating in the People's Protests], (February 11, 2010) http://www.iran-emrooz.net/index.php?/news2/21038/.

Iran Emrooz, *"Mohammad Atrianfar: Hamchenan Moataghedam Keh Mahmoud Ahmadinejad Baramadeh Az Aray Omumi Mardom Naboodeh Va Az Nazar Orfi Rais Jomhur Boodan Oo Mahal Tardid Ast"* [Atrianfar: I Still Believe that Mahmoud Ahmadinejad Did Not Get The Vote of the People And From the Perspective of the Common Law There is Doubt that He Can Be Regarded the President], (June 23, 2006) www.iran-emrooz.net/index.php?/news2/print/9000/.

Iran Human Rights Documentation Center, *Deadly Fatwa: Iran's 1988 Prison Massacre* (February 5, 2011), https://iranhrdc.org/deadly-fatwa-irans-1988-prison-massacre/.

Iran International, *"Tajamo Motarezan NIAC Dar Moghabel Maghar In Sazeman"* [Protest of Opponents of NIAC in Front of its Office], (July 19, 2019), https://www.youtube.com/watch?v=xbMOvZk_P3Y.

Iran International, "On NIAC," (2021) https://www.youtube.com/watch?v=zBBa7qfHyUk.

Iran International, *"Nezam Parastari Tehran: Mahaneh 500 Parastar Be Dalil Hoghogh Paeen Az Iran Mohajerat Mikonand"* [Tehran Nurses Organization: Every Month 500 Nurses Emigrate From Iran Due to Low Wages], (April 11, 2021), https://iranintl.com/%D8%AA%D8%A7%D8%B2%D9%87-%DA%86%D9%87-%D8%AE%D8%A8%D8%B1/%D9%86%D8%B8%D8%A7%D9%85-%D9%BE%D8%B1%D8%B3%D8%AA%D8%A7%D8%B1%DB%8C-%D8%AA%D9%87%D8%B1%D8%A7%D9%86-%D9%85%D8%A7%D9%87%D8%A7%D9%86%D9%87-%DB%B5%DB%B0%DB%B0-%D9%BE%D8%B1%D8%B3%D8%AA%D8%A7%D8%B1-%D8%A8%D9%87-%D8%AF%D9%84%DB%8C%D9%84-%D8%AD%D9%82%D9%88%D9%82-%D9%BE%D8%A7%DB%8C%DB%8C%D9%86-%D8%A7%D8%B2-%D8%A7%DB%8C%D8%B1%D8%A7%D9%86-%D9%85%D9%87%D8%A7%D8%AC%D8%B1%D8%AA-%D9%85%DB%8C%E2%80%8C%DA%A9%D9%86%D9%86%D8%AF, also available at https://melliun.org/iran/257437.

Iran International, *"Vakonesh Magham Dowlati Beh Koshtar Aban Mah"* [Reaction of the Government Official to the Massacre of November 2019], (April 24, 2021), https://www.youtube.com/watch?v=FiNvX16SF1M._

Iran International, "Iran's Exiled Prince Calls for Coordinated Front Against Islamic Republic," (June 3, 2022), https://www.iranintl.com/en/202206030892.

Iran International, *"Emrooz"* [Today], (July 28, 2021), https://www.youtube.com/watch?v=eVj_ajlNSW4.

Iran International, "Detained Hijab Protester Beaten Into 'Forced Confessions'," (August 5, 2022), https://www.iranintl.com/en/202208052017.

Iran International, "Exiled Queen Says Ready To Return Home After Iran Is Free," (August 17, 2022), https://www.iranintl.com/en/202208176071.

Iran International, *"Tadavom Eatesab Kargaran Peymani Palayeshgaha Va Tajamoe Karkonan Sherkat Neishekar Haft-Tapeh Dar Rooz Seshanbeh"* [The Continuation of the Strikes by Contract Workers at Refineries and Assembling of Employees of Haft-Tapeh Sugarcane Company on Tuesday], (October 18, 2022), https://www.iranintl.com/202210182107.

Iran International, Special Coverage of the Protests, (October 19, 2022), https://www.youtube.com/watch?v=UyIQzC_kA_Q.

Iran International, *"Ba Vojod Hamleh Beh Tajamo Shiraz, Pezeshkan Baray Tajamo Dar Tehran Va Isfahan Farakhan Dadand"* [Although the Gathering Was Attacked in Shiraz, Physicians Called for Meetings in Tehran and Isfahan], (October 24, 2022), https://www.iranintl.com/202210240128.

Iran International, *"Etesab Pezeshkan Dar Shahrhay Mokhtalef Dar Eteraz Beh Koshteh Shodan Yek Pezeshk Dar Hamleh Mamouran"* [Physicians Go on Strike in Various Cities In Protest to the Killing of One Physician By the Authorities], (October 29, 2022), https://www.iranintl.com/202210291552.

Iran International, "Islamic Republic's Security Forces Arrest Dissident Rapper," (October 30, 2022), https://www.iranintl.com/en/202210306648.

Iran International, "News," (November 3, 2022), https://www.iranintl.com/202211031228.

Iran International, "News Report," (November 3, 2022), https://www.youtube.com/watch?v=qEo0hh4k6i4&t=1s.

Iran International, "News," (November 4, 2022), https://www.iranintl.com/202211041399.

Iran International, "Statement On Formal Threats To The Life Of Journalists On UK Soil," (November 7, 2022), https://www.iranintl.com/en/202211076450.

Iran International, "MI5 Names Iran As Major Security Threat For UK," (November 17, 2022), https://www.iranintl.com/en/202211176309.

Iran International, "UK Police Positions Armed Vehicles Outside Iran International Building," (November 19, 2022), https://www.iranintl.com/en/202211198849.

Iran International, "Islamic Republic Steps Up Military Crackdown In Kurdish Cities," (November 20, 2022), https://www.iranintl.com/en/202211207781.

Iran International, News, (November 20, 2022), https://www.iranintl.com/202211217863.

Iran International, "Islamic Republic Deploys Military To Quash Protests In Kurdish City," (November 21, 2022), https://www.iranintl.com/en/202211206594.

Iran International, "Islamic Republic Intensifying Attacks On Kurdish Targets In Iran And Iraq," (November 21, 2022), https://www.iranintl.com/en/202211215732.

Iran International, "News," (November 23, 2022), https://www.iranintl.com/en/202211231359.

Iran International has posted the secret report (November 24, 2022) at https://issuu.com/iranintl/docs/b29_2_1_.

Iran International, "Hacked Audio File Reveals Concern About Failure To Stop Iran Unrest," (November 28, 2022), https://www.iranintl.com/en/202211282012.

Iran International, "News," (January 5, 2023), https://www.youtube.com/watch?v=Hv6lth_7idM.

Iran International, "Iranians Rejoice Europe's Move Against IRGC As Regime Vents Anger," (January 20, 2023), https://www.iranintl.com/en/202301200927.

Iran International, *"Chashmandaz,"* (March 11, 2023), https://www.youtube.com/watch?v=pzTKvruDLjE.

Iran International, "Biden Administration Showing 'Weakness On Iran': US Senator," (March 23, 2023), https://www.iranintl.com/en/202303239547.

Iran International, "Iran Claims Oil Exports Surpass 1.3 Million Barrels Per day," (March 23, 2023), https://www.iranintl.com/en/202303235409.

Iran National Front-Abroad, *"Ahdaf Va Rahkarhay Jonbesh Melli Iranian"* [Goals and Plans of the Nationalist Movement of Iranians], (August 18, 2009) http://www.iranazad.info/jebhehkharej/jkh09/08/27mordad.htm.

Iran Press News, *"Shoar-e 'Marg bar Obama' dar Tazahorat Tehran"* [The Slogan of "Death to Obama" at Demonstrations in Tehran], (April 9, 2009) http://www.iranpressnews.com/source/057215.htm.

Iran Wire, "Exclusive: IRGC Commanders Warn Khamenei About Implosion," (March 19, 2023), https://iranwire.com/en/politics/114906-exclusive-irgc-commanders-warn-khamenei-about-implosion/.

IRGC Constitution, http://www.tooba-ir.org/_Book/BookFehrest.asp?BookID=225&ParentID=61149.

IRGC Laws, Rules, and Bylaws http://www.tooba-ir.org/_Book/bookfehrest.asp?Bookid=225.

IRGC, *"Razmandegan Bedon-e Marz Ra Behtar Beshnasid: Niroyeh Qods Sepah Chegoneh Shekl Gereft?"* [Get to Know Better the Fighters Without Borders: How Was the Qods Force Formed?], Fars News Agency (January 25, 2020), https://www.farsnews.ir/news/13981105000470/.

IRGC, *"'Razmandegan Bedon-e Marz' Dar Meydan Razm: Niroyeh Qods Dar Kodam Jang-ha Hozoor Yaft?"* ["Fighters Without Borders" on the Battlefield: Qods Force Was Present in Which Wars?], Fars News Agency (January 26, 2020), https://www.farsnews.ir/news/13981106000522/.

IRNA, *"Khatami Namzadi Khod Ra Rasman Ealam Kard"* [Khatami Officially Announced His Candidacy], (February 8, 2009) http://www5.irna.ir/View/FullStory/?NewsId=346045.

IRNA, *"Jashn Piroozi Mellat: 'Ahmadi Bot Shekan, Bot-e Bozorg Ro Beshkan"* [The Great Celebration of the Nation: Ahmadinejad the Idol Smasher, Smash the Bog Idol], (June 14, 2009), http://www.irna.ir/View/FullStory/?NewsId=546770.

IRNA, *"Sokhanan Rais Jumhur Dar Meidan Vali Asr Tehran"* [The Speech of the President in Vali Asr Square Tehran], (June 14, 2009), http://www.irna.ir/View/FullStory/?NewsId=546894.

IRNA, *"Nokhostin Sokhanan Pas Az Piroozi Dar Entekhabat Riyasat Jumhuri; Ahmadinejad: Dorani Jadid Dar Tarikh Mellat Iran Aghaz Shod"* [The First Speech After the Victory in the Presidential Elections; Ahmadinajed: A New Era Has Begun in the History of the Iranian Nation], (June 14, 2009) http://www.irna.ir/View/FullStory/?NewsId=545489.

IRNA, *"Emrooz, Rooze Payan Eghteshashat Ast"* [Today, is the Last Day of the Riots], (October 30, 2022), https://www.irna.ir/news/84925031/%D8%B3%D8%B1%D8%AF%D8%A7%D8%B1-%D8%B3%D9%84%D8%A7%D9%85%DB%8C-%D8%A7%D9%85%D8%B1%D9%88%D8%B2-%D8%B1%D9%88%D8%B2-%D9%BE%D8%A7%DB%8C%D8%A7%D9%86-%D8%A7%D8%BA%D8%AA%D8%B4%D8%A7%D8%B4%D8%A7%D8%AA-%D8%A7%D8%B3%D8%AA

Islamic Republic of Iran, "Constitution," https://www.constituteproject.org/constitution/Iran_1989.pdf?lang=en.

Islamic Republic of Iran, Ministry of Interior, Boushehr, *"Ayatollah Jennati: Saran-e Fetneh Dar Sadad Tazief Rahbari Va Velayat Faqih Boodand"* [Ayatollah Jennati: The Leaders of the Sedition Sought to Undermine the Supreme Leader and the Rule of the Cleric], Ministry of Interior, Boushehr Province, April 15, 2010, http://www.ost-boushehr.ir/fa/pages/?cid=1183.

ISNA, *"Sarnevesht Daneshjooyan Eshghalkonandeh Sefarat America"* [What Became of the Students Occupying the American Embassy], (November 3, 2016), https://www.isna.ir/news/95081309267.

ISNA, *"Monadi: 900 Ostad Dar Sal 98 Az Iran Kharej Shodand"* [Mondai: 900 Professors Left Iran in the Year 2019–2020], (March 6, 2021), https://www.isna.ir/news/99121612250.

Jahan News, *"Ranzgoshaee Az Yek Tasliyat"* [Decoding The Secret of Expressing Condolences], (May 13, 2010) http://www.jahannews.com/vdcfcmdyxw6dyta.igiw.html.

Jannati, Ayatollah Ahmad. Channel 1, Iranian TV, and placed at MEMRI site: http://www.memritv.org/clip/en/1986.htm?auth=ea4d243656d2616d0cd5788ad984764f.

JARAS, *"Karrubi: Dar Entekhabat Taghalob Shodeh va Mohkam Bar Harf Khod Estadeam"* [Karrubi: There Have Been Cheating in the Election and I Stand Strong on My Position], (January 25, 2010) http://www.rahesabz.net/story/8684/.

JARAS, *"Mir-Hussein Mousavi Va Mehdi Karrubi Eadamhay Akhir Ra Mahkoom Kardand"* [Mir-Hussein Mousavi and Mehdi Karrubi Condemned the Recent Executions], (January 30, 2010) http://www.rahesabz.net/story/9089/.

JARAS, *"22 Bahman Zabz- Reza Khatami Va Zahra Eshraqi Azad Shodand"* [Green February 11: Reza Khatami and Zahra Eshraqi Were Released], (February 11, 2010), http://www.rahesabz.net/story/10023/.

JARAS, *"Elham: Hashemi Rafsanjani Tabe' Rahbari Nabood"* [Elham: Hashemi Rafsanjani Was Not Submitting to the Leader], (March 24, 2010) http://www.rahesabz.net/story/12630.

JARAS, *"Bazneshastegi 250 Sardar Pasdar Hami Mir Hussein Mousavi"* [The Retiring of 250 IRGC Commanders Who Supported Mir Hussein Mousavi], (July 26, 2010), http://www.rahesabz.net/story/20243/.

Jebhe Melli Iran, *"Mellat Iran Az Entekhab Bein Bad Va Badtar Oboor Kardeh Ast"* [The Iranian Nation Has Moved On From Choosing Between Bad and Worse], (April 7, 2021), https://melliun.org/iran/257087.

Kakavandi, Abbas. "Interview," *Resalat*, (August 6, 2002), excerpts in Farsi available at http://www.iran-emrooz.de/yaddasht/bagerz810516.html (August 10, 2006).

Kaleme, *"Eateraf Zoulnour Beh natavani jaryan Eqtedar-Gara Az Sazemandehi Janiyat"* [Admission of Zoulnour to Not Being Able to Gather Popular Support by the Hard-Liners], (April 18, 2011) http://www.kaleme.com/1390/01/29/klm-55429/.

Kaleme Political Group, *"Tavafoq Na-Neveshteh Oposisioun Zede Enqelab Va Halqeh Mahfeli Qatl-hay Zanjirei"* [The Unwritten Agreement between the Counter-Revolutionary Opposition and the Private Circle of Chain Murders], Kaleme, (March 15, 2010), http://www.kaleme.com/1388/12/24/klm-14326.

Kamrava, Mehran. "National Security Debates in Iran: Factionalism and Lost Opportunities," *Middle East Policy*, vol. 24, no. 2 (Summer 2007), pp. 84–100.

Karrubi, Mehdi. *"Bayaniyeh Mohem Mehdi Karrubi Dar Mored Ekhtiyarat Velayat Faqih"* [The Significant Statement of Mehdi Karrubi on the Powers of the Supreme Leader], Saham News, (June 20, 2010) http://www.sahamnews.org/?p=4091. An English translation of parts of Karrubi's statement is available at http://www.zamaaneh.com/enzam/2010/06/opposition-leader-critici-2.html.

Karrubi, Mehdi. *"Rahkarhay Mehdi Karrubi Jahat Khoroj Az Bohran"* [Mehdi Karrubi's Solution for Exiting the Crisis], Iran Emrooz, (January 11, 2010) http://news.iran-emrooz.net/index.php?/news1/20604.

Karrubi, Mehdi. "Speech," *"Avalin Sokhanrani Karrubi Pas Az 11 Sal"* [The First Speech by Karrubi After 11 Years], Ensaf News, (October 5, 2021), http://www.ensafnews.com/312263/%D8%A7%D9%88%

D9%84%DB%8C%D9%86-%D8%B3%D8%AE%D9%86%D8%B1%D8%A7%D9%86%DB%8C-%DA%
A9%D8%B1%D9%88%D8%A8%DB%8C-%D9%BE%D8%B3-%D8%A7%D8%B2-%DB%B1%DB%B1-%
D8%B3%D8%A7%D9%84-%D8%B9%DB%8C%D9%88%D8%A8-%D9%86/.

Kashmiripour, Behzad. "*Afzayesh Varedat; Rah Mahar Tavvarom?*" [Increasing Imports; The Way to Contain Inflation?], Deutsche Welle, (June 14, 2008) http://www.dw-world.de/dw/article/0,,3412457,00.html.

Kashmiripour, Behzad. "*Karnameh Saderat Va Varedat Iran Dar Sal 1387*" [Imports and Exports Results of Iran in the Year 1387], Deutsche Welle, (April 12, 2009) http://www.dw-world.de/dw/article/0,,4171924,00.html.

Kayhan, "*Ma'muriyat-e niru-ye qods towse'eh-ye enghelab-e eslami dar jahan ast*" [The Quds Force's Mission is to Expand the Islamic Revolution Throughout the World], (October 2, 2014), http://kayhan.ir/fa/news/24370.

Kazemzadeh, Masoud. "Teaching the Politics of Islamic Fundamentalism," *PS: Political Science and Politics*, Vol. 31, No. 1 (1998), pp. 52 – 59.

Kazemzadeh, Masoud. *Islamic Fundamentalism, Feminism, and Gender Inequality in Iran Under Khomeini.* Lanham, MD: University Press of America, 2002.

Kazemzadeh, Masoud. "The Perils and Costs of a Grand Bargain with the Islamic Republic of Iran," *American Foreign Policy Interests*, vol. 29, no. 5 (September-October 2007), pp. 301 – 327.

Kazemzadeh, Masoud. "Opposition Groups," in Mehran Kamrava and Manochehr Dorraj, eds., *Iran Today: An Encyclopedia of Life in the Islamic Republic.* Vol. II. Westport, Connecticut: Greenwood Press, 2008, pp. 363 – 367.

Kazemzadeh, Masoud. "U.S.-Iran Confrontation in the Post-NIE World: An Analysis of Alternative Policy Options." *Comparative Strategy*, vol. 28, no. 1, (2009), pp. 37 – 59.

Kazemzadeh, Masoud. "On the Lawsuit 'Trita Parsi and NIAC v. Hassan Daieoleslam'," Iranian.com (September 15, 2012), http://iranian.com/main/blog/masoud-kazemzadeh/lawsuit-trita-parsi-and-niac-v-hassan-daieoleslam-0.html.

Kazemzadeh, Masoud. "Post-Khamenei Iran and American National Interests," *The Hill*, (July 11, 2016), http://thehill.com/blogs/pundits-blog/foreign-policy/287175-post-khamenei-iran-and-american-national-interests.

Kazemzadeh, Masoud. "Explaining the Obama Administration Overlooking Iran's Cheating on the Nuke Deal," *Small Wars Journal*, (August 18, 2016), http://smallwarsjournal.com/blog/explaining-the-obama-administration-overlooking-iran%E2%80%99s-cheating-on-the-nuke-deal.

Kazemzadeh, Masoud. "Ayatollah Rafsanjani's Death and Trump Policy on Iran," *Small Wars Journal*, (January 18, 2017), https://smallwarsjournal.com/jrnl/art/ayatollah-rafsanjani%E2%80%99s-death-and-trump-policy-on-iran.

Kazemzadeh, Masoud "Protests in Iran: Characteristics, Causes, and Policy Ramifications," *Small Wars Journal* (January 3, 2018), http://smallwarsjournal.com/jrnl/art/protests-iran-characteristics-causes-and-policy-ramifications.

Kazemzadeh, Masoud "Five Possible Outcomes Following the Mass Protests in Iran," Radio Farda, (February 6, 2018), https://en.radiofarda.com/a/iran-unrest-scenarios-war-revolution-uprising/29023446.html.

Kazemzadeh, Masoud. *Iran's Foreign Policy: Elite Factionalism, Ideology, the Nuclear Weapons Program, and the United States.* London: Routledge, 2020.

Kazemzadeh, Masoud. *The Iran National Front and the Struggle for Democracy, 1949-Present.* Berlin: De Gruyter, 2022.

Kazemzadeh, Masoud. *The Grand Strategy of the Islamic Republic of Iran* (Forthcoming).

Kazemzadeh, Masoud. *U.S.-Iran Confrontation: Alternative Scenarios and Consequences* (Forthcoming).

Kermani, Hussein. *"Zohor Aghazadeh-hay Nogara Va Motarez Beh Pedar Khandeh Nezam"* [The Appearance of the Modernist Children of the Ruling Elite and Their Protests Against the Godfather of the System], Deutsche Welle, (April 10, 2011), http://www.dw-world.de/dw/article/0,,6499727,00.html?maca=per-rss-per-all-1491-rdf.

Keshavarz, Alma. "Iran: al-Qaeda's 'Main Artery for Funds, Personnel and Communications.' The Recently Released Osama bin Laden Letters," *Small Wars Journal*, (March 10, 2016), http://smallwarsjournal.com/jrnl/art/iran-al-qaeda%E2%80%99s-%E2%80%9Cmain-artery-for-funds-personnel-and-communication%E2%80%9D-the-recently-released-o.

Kesten, Lou. "White House monitoring crackdown in Iran," Associated Press, (November 4, 2009), http://hosted.ap.org/dynamic/stories/U/US_US_IRAN?SITE=AP&SECTION=HOME&TEMPLATE=DEFAULT&CTIME=2009-11-04-13-37-52.

Khabar Online, *"Hamsar Shahid Hemmat"* [The Wife of Martyred Hemmat], (May 23, 2010), http://www.khabaronline.ir/news-63698.aspx.

Khabar Online, *"Farmandah Sepah: Mardom Enheraf Az Masir Enqelab Va Rahbari Ra Tahamol Nemikonand"* [IRGC Commander: The People Will Not Tolerate Deviation from the Path of Revolution and Leader], (May 5, 2011) http://khabaronline.ir/news-148846.aspx.

Khalkhali, Ayatollah Sadegh. "All the People Who Are Opposed to Our Revolution Must Die," Interview, *MERIP Reports*, No. 104 (March-April 1982), pp. 30–31.

Khamenei, Ayatollah Ali. *"Bayanat Dar Didar Asatid Daneshgah"* [Remarks in the Meeting with University Professors], (August 30, 2009) http://farsi.khamenei.ir/speech-content?id=7959.

Khamenei, Ayatollah Ali. "Speech," (October 2009) http://www.iranian.com/main/2009/oct/khamenei-islam-humanities.

Khamenei, Ayatollah Ali. *"Bayanat Dar Didar Mardom Qom Dar Salgard Qiyam 19 Dey"* [Remarks in the Meeting with the People of Qom on the Anniversary of January 9 Uprising], Khamenei's official website, (January 9, 2010) http://farsi.khamenei.ir/speech-content?id=8599.

Khamenei, Ayatollah Ali. *"Didar Ba Aazaye Shoray Hamahangi Tablighat Islami"* [Meeting with the Members of the Coordinating Council of Islamic Publicity], Khamenei's official website, (January 19, 2010) http://farsi.khamenei.ir/speech-content?id=8629.

Khamenei, Ayatollah Ali. "Speech," (January 17, 2020), http://english.khamenei.ir/news/7318/Our-Islamic-power-will-overcome-the-superficial-grandeur-of-material.

Khamenei, Ayatollah Ali. *"Bayanat Dar Didar Mehmanan Konferance Vahdat Islami Va Jamee Az Masoulan Nezam"* [Speech at the Islamic Unity Conference and a Group of Regime Officials], (October 24, 2021), https://farsi.khamenei.ir/speech-content?id=48891. Brief excerpts of Khamenei's speech in English is available at his site https://english.khamenei.ir/news/8739/Muslims-unity-necessary-for-realization-of-new-Islamic-Civilization.

Khatami, Hojatolislam Mohammad. *"Hazf Jaryanat Beh Maani An Ast Keh Dar Keshvar Moshgel Vojod Darad"* [The Elimination Of Groups Means That There Are Problems In The Country], Baran Foundation Website, (May 4, 2010) http://baran.org.ir/?sn=news&pt=full&id=2754.

Khatami, Hojatolislam Mohammad. "Speech," You Tube, (2014), https://www.youtube.com/watch?v=KiygQj96DrQ.

Khatami, Hojatolislam Mohammad. (November 14, 2022) https://www.instagram.com/p/Ck7-Ru9sdgd/?utm_source=ig_embed&ig_rid=ba244963-52c6-4f2b-9804-af1daf4170b5.

Khatib, Hojatolislam Esmail. "Interview with the Website of the Supreme Leader," (November 10, 2022), https://english.khamenei.ir/news/9277/Minister-of-Intelligence-analysis-of-recent-hybrid-war-against.

Khavand, Fereydoon. "Interview," Radio Farda, (October 6, 2020), https://www.radiofarda.com/a/30876747.html.

Khavand, Fereydoon. *"Bazaar Arz Iran Taht-e Taasir Entekhabat Amrika"* [Iran's Foreign Exchange Market Under the Impact of the American Elections], Radio Farda, (October 19, 2020), https://www.radiofarda.com/a/30901565.html.

Khazani, Omid. "Just when they're needed most, Iran's doctors are leaving in droves," *The Los Angeles Times*, (May 23, 2021), https://www.latimes.com/world-nation/story/2021-05-23/iran-brain-drain-doctors-exodus-covid-pandemic.

Khomeini, Ayatollah Ruhollah. *"Elamieh Imam Khomeini Beh Monasebat Tahrim Nourooz 1342"* [Statement of Imam Khomeini For the Boycott of 1963 Iranian Persian New Year] (March 1963), https://psri.ir/?id=7fjcxlg1.

Khomeini, Ayatollah Ruhollah. *"Sokhanrani Dar Jame Rouhanioun Qom"* [Speech to the Clerics at Qom], (May 2, 1963), https://emam.com/posts/view/134/%D8%B3%D8%AE%D9%86%D8%B1D8%A7%D9%86%DB%8C-%D8%AF%D8%B1-%D8%AC%D9%85%D8%B9-%D8%B1%D9%88%D8%AD%D8%A7%D9%86%DB%8C%D9%88%D9%86-%D9%82%D9%85-%28%D8%A7%D8%B1%D8%B2%DB%8C%D8%A7%D8%A8%DB%8C-%D9%82%DB%8C%D8%A7%D9%85-%D9%85%D9%84D8%AA%29.

Khomeini, Ayatollah Ruhollah. "Last Will and Testament," (February 15, 1983), released after his death in June 1989, https://www.al-islam.org/imam-khomeini-s-last-will-and-testament.

Khomeini, Ayatollah Ruhollah. "Speech," (1984), the video of the speech available on You Tube, (May 18, 2014), https://www.youtube.com/watch?v=0EmAxl1Ksv0&list=RD0EmAxl1Ksv0&start_radio=1&rv=0EmAxl1Ksv0&t=399.

Khomeini, Ayatollah Ruhollah. "Speech," (no date), posted at You Tube (August 31, 2014), https://www.youtube.com/watch?v=C8nX-IZiWFY.

Khomeini, Ayatollah Ruhollah. "Speech," (1985), You Tube, (May 27, 2015), https://www.youtube.com/watch?v=8uhI1FUeVxA.

Khomeini, Ayatollah Ruhollah. *Aghshar Ejtemaee Az Didgah Imam Khomeini* [Social Strata from the Perspective of Imam Khomeini], (no date), http://www.imam-khomeini.ir/fa/c78_123770/.

Khorsandi, Shappi. "My Family Values," *The Guardian*, (October 23, 2015), interview, https://www.theguardian.com/lifeandstyle/2015/oct/23/shappi-khorsandi-my-family-values.

Klebnikov, Paul. "Millionaire Mullahs," *Forbes*, (July 21, 2003), http://www.forbes.com/global/2003/0721/024.html.

Lake, Eli. "Exclusive: Iran advocacy group said to skirt lobby rules," *The Washington Times*, (November 13, 2009), https://www.washingtontimes.com/news/2009/nov/13/exclusive-did-iranian-advocacy-group-violate-laws/.

Lake, Eli. "Iran's Nobel Laureate Is Done With Reform. She Wants Regime Change," Bloomberg, (April 5, 2018), https://www.bloomberg.com/opinion/articles/2018-04-05/shirin-ebadi-is-done-trying-to-reform-iran-she-wants-regime-change.

Lewis, Paul. "U.N. Inquiry Says Iran Still Abuses Human Rights," *The New York Times*, (November 19, 1989).

Mackey, Robert. "Latest Updates on New Protests in Iran," *The New York Times* blog, (December 7, 2009) http://thelede.blogs.nytimes.com/2009/12/07/latest-updates-on-new-protests-in-iran/?scp=3&sq=Iran&st=cse.

Macleod, Scott, and Azadeh Moaveni, "Confronting the Dark Past," *Time Magazine* Europe, (July 10, 2000) http://www.time.com/time/europe/webonly/mideast/...khoeiniha_intvu.htm.

Maleki, Ammar. "Iranians' Attitudes Towards Political Systems," GAMAAN, (2022), https://gamaan.org/wp-content/uploads/2022/03/GAMAAN-Political-Systems-Survey-2022-English-Final.pdf.

Maleki, Ammar, and Pooyan Tamimi Arab, "Iranians' Attitudes Toward the 2022 Nationwide Protests," GAMAAN, (February 4, 2023), https://gamaan.org/wp-content/uploads/2023/02/GAMAAN-Protests-Survey-English-Report-Final.pdf.

Malherbe, Leon, and Paris Hafezi, "Tens of thousands march in Berlin in support of Iran protests," Reuters, (October 22, 2022), https://www.reuters.com/world/middle-east/irans-guards-warn-cleric-over-agitating-restive-southeast-2022-10-22/.

"*Manshoor Motalebat Tashakolhay Mostaghel Senfi Va Madani Iran*" [Charter of Demands of the Independent Organizations of Civil Society and Syndicates of Iran] (February 20230, https://www.iran-emrooz.net/index.php/news1/more/106294/.

Manzouri, Maryam. "*Mehdi Karrubi Farzand Rahbar Jomuri Islamic Ra Beh Eamal Nofoz Dar Entekhabat Moteham Kard Ayatollah Ali Khamenei Goft Ejazeh Nemidahad Afradi Dar Keshvar Bohran Eajad Konand*" [Mehdi Karrubi Accused the Son of the Supreme Leader of the Islamic Republic of Influencing the Elections, Ayatollah Ali Khamenei Said that He Will Not Allow Individuals to Create Crisis in the Country], Radio Farda, (June 20, 2005), http://www.radiofarda.com/content/article/303458.html.

Mardomak, "*Goftogo Baa Seyyed Hadi Hashemi*" [Interview with Seyyed Hadi Hashemi], (December 25, 2009) http://www.mardomak.biz/news/Interview_with_Montazeri_ExOfficeman/.

Mehregan, Keyvan. "*Goftogoo Ba Mohammad Reza Khatami: Maa Jomhuri Islami Khah Hastim*" [Interview with Mohammad Reza Khatami: We Are Islamic Republicans], *Eatemaad* Newspaper, reposted at Green Wave Blog, August 7, 2009, http://greenwavearchive.blogspot.com/2009/08/blog-post_9237.html.

Mehregan, Keyvan, and Amin Alam-alhody, "'*Pas Az Entekhabat' Dar Goftogoo Ba Alireza Beheshti*" ['After the Election' Interview with Alireza Beheshti], *Eatemaad* newspaper, republished at Iran Emrooz, (August 22, 2009), http://www.iran-emrooz.net/index.php?/news2/print/19156.

Mehr News, "*Roshd Eghtesadi Parsal 2.3 Darsad Bood; Ehtemal Roshd Manfi Ya Sefr Dar Sal 89*" [Economic Growth Rate Was 2.3 Percent Last Year; The Possibility of Growth for the Year 2010 – 2011 Either Negative or Zero], (February 20, 2010) http://www.mehrnews.com/fa/newsdetail.aspx?pr=a&NewsID=1037312.

Mehr News, "Ahmadinejad proposes referendum on subsidy reform plan," (March 20, 2010) http://www.mehrnews.com/en/NewsDetail.aspx?NewsID=1054038.

Mesbah Yazdi, Ayatollah. "*Porsesh Va Pasokh Jam'i Az Daneshjooyan Basiji Ba Alameh Mesbah Yazdi*" [Question and Answer between a Group of Basij Students with Alameh Mesbah Yazdi], Ayatollah Mesbah Yazdi's Official Website, (December 31, 2009), http://mesbahyazdi.org/farsi/?../farsi/speeches/ques-dAns/q-a4.htm.

Mesbah Yazdi, Ostaad Mohammad Taqi. *Hokumat Islami Va Velayat Faqih.* Tehran: Markaz Chap Va Nashr Sazeman Tablighat Islami, 1369 [1991].

Mezzofiore, Gianluca, Katie Polgese, and Adam Pourahmadi. "What really happened to Nika Shahkarami? Witnesses to her final hours cast doubt on Iran's story," CNN, (October 27, 2022), https://www.cnn.com/2022/10/27/middleeast/iran-nika-shahkarami-investigation-intl-cmd/index.html.

Middle East Monitor, "Saudi Arabia blocked Iran from participating in OIC meeting, says ministry," (February 3, 2020), https://www.middleeastmonitor.com/20200203-saudi-arabia-blocked-iran-from-participating-in-oic-meeting-says-ministry/.

Milani, Mohsen. "Iran's Active Neutrality During the Kuwaiti Crisis: Reasons and Ramifications," *New Political Science*, vol. 21–22, (1992), pp. 41–60.

Mohammadi, Hussein. *"Barkhord Ba Jonbesh Daneshjooe Dar Mosahebeh Ba Bahareh Hedayat"* [Confronting the Student Movement in an Interview with Bahareh Hedayat], Rooz Online, (November 25, 2009), http://www.roozonline.com/persian/news/newsitem/article////107/-0742b448ce.html.

Mohammadi, Majid. *"NIAC Darad Jonbesh Mahsai Ra Midozdad"* [NIAC Is Stealing the Movement Inspired By Mahsa], Gooya News, (October 18, 2022), https://news.gooya.com/2022/10/post-69411.php.

Moin, Baquer. "Obituary: Ahmad Khomeini," *The Independent*, (March 18, 1995) http://www.independent.co.uk/news/people/obituaryahmad-khomeini-1611695.html.

Moore, Jr., Barrington. *Social Origins of Dictatorship and Democracy: Lord and Peasant in the Making of the Modern World*. Boston: Beacon Press, 1966.

Motahhari, Ali. "Speech," IRIB, (January 2010), http://www.youtube.com/watch?v=TnuymdsqSC4.

Mottale, Morris M. "The birth of a new class," Al Jazeera, April 22, 2010, http://english.aljazeera.net/focus/2010/04/2010421104845169224.html.

Moussavi, Mir-Hussein. *"Bayanieyh 17, Rah Halhay Panjganeh Baray Khoruj Az Bohran"* [Communique 17, Five Point Plan Solution For Getting Out of the Crisis], Iran Emrooz, (January 1, 2010) http://news.iran-emrooz.net/index.php?/news1/20455/.

Moussavi, Mir-Hussein., *"Goftogoye Kaleme Ba Mir-Hussein Moussavi Piramoon Masayel Mohem Keshvar"* [Discussion of Kaleme with Mir-Hussein Mousavi About the Significant Problems in the Country], Kaleme, (February 2, 2010) http://www.kaleme.org/1388/11/13/klm-10327; the interview has been reposted at http://www.sabztab.blogfa.com/post-161.aspx.

Moussavi, Mir-Hussein. *"Beh Mardom Bazgardid Angah Sobh Omid Fara Khahad Resid"* [Return To The People Then The Morning of Hope Will Arrive], Kaleme, (May 23, 2010), http://www.kaleme.com/1389/03/02/klm-20224.

Moussavi, Mir-Hussein. *"Matn Bayaniyeh Shomareh 18 Va Manshoori Baray Jonbesh Sabz: Ba Qamati Sarafraz Garcheh Majrooh Va Habs Keshideh Eastadehim"* [Content of the Statement Number 18 And Charter for the Green Movement; Standing Tall Although Wounded And Detained], Kaleme, (June 15, 2010) http://www.kaleme.com/1389/03/25/klm-22913.

Moussavi, Mir-Hussein Campaign, *Gozaresh Tafzili Komiteh Sianat Az Araye Mir Hussein Mousavi* [Detailed Report of the Committee for the Defense of the Votes of Mir Hussein Mousavi], (July 4, 2009), available at: http://news.iran-emrooz.net/index.php?/news1/18633/.

Moussavian, Hussein. "Interview," Iran National Front-Organizations Abroad TV, Channel One, (June 20, 2021), https://www.youtube.com/watch?v=XfIRICIejVk.

Moussavian, Hussein. "Interview with Radio Farda," (October 27, 2022), https://www.radiofarda.com/a/32102030.html.

Muir, Jim. "Cleric denounces Iran 'chaos'," BBC News, (July 10, 2002) http://news.bbc.co.uk/2/hi/2119775.stm.

Murphy, Brian. "Iran seeks to quiet critic inside ruling system," Associated Press, (November 25, 2009).

Mussolini, Benito. "The Doctrine of Fascism," (1932), https://sjsu.edu/faculty/wooda/2B-HUM/Readings/The-Doctrine-of-Fascism.pdf.

Naji, Kasra. *Ahmadinejad: The Secret History of Iran's Radical Leader*. Berkeley: University of California Press, 2008.

Nazih, Hassan. "Interview," Harvard University, Iranian Oral History Project, Paris, (April 3, 1984), https://curiosity.lib.harvard.edu/iranian-oral-history-project/catalog/32-nazih__hassan01, audio available at https://www.youtube.com/watch?v=B6uqIUHeMqs; https://www.youtube.com/watch?v=6chtiCr3Hr0; and https://www.youtube.com/watch?v=9rxR17G7qDE.

Nima, Ramy. *The Wrath of Allah: Islamic Revolution and Reaction in Iran.* London: Pluto Press, 1983.

Noorooz News, *"Bar-rasi Tarh Bazdasht Mir Hussein Mousavi Dar Setad kou De Taa"* [Considering Arresting Mir Hussein Mousavi By the Headquarters of the Coup de Etat], republished at Iran Emrooz, (August, 14, 2009), http://www.iran-emrooz.net/index.php?news1/print/19096.

Noorooz News, *"Tanin Allah O Akbar Sabzha Tehran Ra Larzand"* [The Echo of God Is Great By the Greens Shook Tehran], (December 27, 2009) http://norooznews.info/news/15886.php.

Pace, Eric. "Ahmed Khomeini Is Dead; Son of Ayatollah Khomeini," *The New York Times*, (March 18, 1995).

Paidar, Parvin. *Women and the Political Process in Twentieth Century Iran.* Cambridge: Cambridge University Press, 1995.

Pannett, Rachel. "Man with assault rifle arrested near Iranian American writer's Brooklyn home," *The Washington Post*, (August 1, 2022), https://www.washingtonpost.com/nation/2022/08/01/iran-journalist-masih-alinejad-ak47-brooklyn/.

Parleman News, *"Ali Mottahari: Shakhs Ahmadinejad Dar Memaneaat Az Sokhanrani Seyyed Hassan Khomeini Naqsh Dasht"* [Ali Mottahari: Ahmadinejad Personally Had a Role in Preventing the Speech of Seyyed Hassan Khomeini], (June 5, 2010)

Parleman News, "Iran: Grand Ayatollah Dastgheyb Prevented from Traveling to Shiraz,"

Parsine News Site, *"Fatemeh Rajabi Khastar Bazdasht 'Hasehmi, Khatami, Karrubi Va Mousavi' Shod"* [Fatemeh Rajabi Demanded Arrests of 'Hashemi, Khatami, Karrubi, and Mousavi'], (June 14, 2009), http://www.parsine.com/pages/?cid=8335.

Payvand Iran News, "Photos: Iran Students Stage Nationwide Protests," (December 7, 2009) http://www.payvand.com/news/09/dec/1070.html.

Payvand Iran News, (January 3, 2010) http://www.payvand.com/news/10/jan/1023.html, original news in Persian http://www.parlemannews.ir/?n=6862.

Payvand Iran News, "Iran unemployment rate hits 11.3%," (January 11, 2010) http://www.payvand.com/news/10/jan/1106.html.

Payvand Iran News, "Iranian opposition leaders react to deepening crisis," (January 12, 2010), http://payvand.com/news/10/jan/1107.html.

Payvand Iran News, "Khatami: The response to civil protests is not repression, prison, and execution," (February 2, 2010) http://www.payvand.com/news/10/feb/1013.html.

Payvand Iran News, "Ayatollah Rafsanjani said to stand firm on upholding people's rights," (March 1, 2010) http://www.payvand.com/news/10/mar/1002.html.

Payvand Iran News, "Iranian women activists call for end to discrimination," (March 9, 2010), http://www.payvand.com/news/10/mar/1082.html.

Payvand Iran News, "Statement by Iranian Women for International Women's Day," (March 15, 2010), http://www.payvand.com/news/10/mar/1128.html.

Payvand Iran News, "Photos: Assailants attack Iranian opposition leader's home," (March 15, 2010), http://www.payvand.com/news/10/mar/1147.html.

Petrossian, Fred. "Religious Minorities in Iran: Violence, Resistance, and Hope," Religion and IR, International Studies Association, (November 29, 2021), https://religion-ir.org/blog/religious-minorities-in-iran-violence-resistance-and-hope-by-fred-petrossian.

Piltan, Parsa. *"Yek Sal Sarkoob Moaleman Moatarez Dar Iran"* [One Year of Repression of the Protesting Teachers in Iran], BBC Persian, (May 1, 2010) http://www.bbc.co.uk/persian/lg/iran/2010/05/100501_u02-pp-teachers-day.shtml.

Pirvali, Ali. *"Sanat Damparvari Iran Dar Shook Va Soqoot"* [Iran's Animal Husbandry Industry in the Circuit of Shock and Plunge], ILNA, (March 28, 2010) http://www.ilna.ir/newsText.aspx?ID=114469.

Press TV, "Guardian Council: Over 100% voted in 50 cities," (June 21, 2009), available at: http://www.presstv.ir/detail.aspx?id=98711&sectionid=351020101.

Press TV, "Iran's inflation rate falls to 12.2 percent," (February 11, 2010) http://www.presstv.ir/detail.aspx?id=118386&sectionid=351020102.

Posch, Walter. *Prospects for Iran's 2009 Presidential Elections* (Washington, DC: The Middle East Institute Policy Brief 24, June 2009).

Posch, Walter. "Ideology and Strategy in the Middle East: The Case of Iran," *Survival*, Vol. 59, No. 5 (October-November 2017).

Qazi, Fereshteh. *"Hamleh Nirohay Dowlati Beh Manzel Ayatollah Khomeini"* [Government Forces Attack Khomeini's House], Rooz Online, (December 27, 2009) http://www.roozonline.com/persian/news/newsitem/article///107/-e179c444ec.html.

Qazi, Fereshteh. *"Zahra Rahnavard Dar Mosahebeh ba Rooz: Sazesh Nemikonim, Beh Rasmiyat Nemishenasim"* [Zahra Rahnavard in Interview with Rooz: We Will Not Compromise, We Will Recognize], Rooz Online, (January 26, 2010) http://www.roozonline.com/persian/news/newsitem/article/2010/january/26//br-br.html.

Radio Farda, *"Hashemi Rafsanjani: Massael Mojod Ba Tadbir Rahbari Qabel Hal Va Fasl Ast"* [Hashemi Rafsanjani: The Current Problems Can Be Solved by the Wisdom of the Leader], (January 23, 2010), http://www.radiofarda.com/content/o2_rafsanjani_on_iran_crisis/1937710.html.

Radio Farda, *"Rafsanjani: Hokomat Keh Payeh Mardomi Nadashteh Bashad Paydar Nemimanad"* [Rafsanjani: A Governing System Which Lacks Popular Base Will Not Last], (March 11, 2010), http://www.radiofarda.com/content/F8_RASANJANI_DEMOCRACY/1980196.html.

Radio Farda, *"Vakonesh Mokhalefan Va Havadaran Dowlat Beh Qateq Sokhanrani Hassan Khomeini"* [Reactions of Opponents and Supporters of the Government to the Disruption of Hassan Khomeini's Speech], (June 5, 2010), http://www.radiofarda.com/content/f6_Iran_Khomeini_Reactions/2063035.html.

Radio Farda, *"Dabir Setad Markazi Bozorgdasht Ayatollah Khomeini, Joziyat Ekhlal Dar Sokhanrani Hassan Khomeini Ra Montashar Kard"* [The Secretary of the Central Headquarters of the Commemoration of Ayatollah Khomeini Published the Details of the Disruptions of Hassan Khomeini's Speech], (June 8, 2010), http://www.radiofarda.com/archive/news/20100608/143/143.html?id=2065482.

Radio Farda, *"Jafaari: Eqna Pasdaran Hami Fetneh Behtar Az Hazf Anhaast"* [Jafaari: Convincing the IRGC Members Who Support the Sedition Is Better Than Eliminating Them], (July 25, 2010), http://www.radiofarda.com/content/F8_SEPAH_JAFARI_MEMBERS_SUPPORTING_OPPOSITION/2108863.html.

Radio Farda, *"Mokhalefat Rahbar Jomhuri Islami Ba Kenaregiri Heydar Moslehi Az Vezarat Etellaat,"* [Opposition of the Supreme Leader of the Islamic Republic with the Resignation of Heydar Moslehi from the Ministry of Intelligence], (April 17, 2011) http://www.radiofarda.com/content/f7_iran_supreme_leader_acts_against_moslehi_resign/4747130.html.

Radio Farda, "Latest On Continuing Unrest In Iran – Basij Enters The Foray To Crack Down," (December 31, 2017), https://en.radiofarda.com/a/28947733.html.

Radio Farda, "Iranian Currency Roils As Trump Decision Looms," (May 8, 2018), https://en.radiofarda.com/a/iran-currency-drops-ahead-of-trump-nuclear-announcement/29214907.html.

Radio Farda, "Fresh Wave of Protests Starting From Universities Spread to Several Cities in Iran," (January 12, 2020), https://en.radiofarda.com/a/fresh-wave-of-protests-starting-from-universities-spread-to-several-cities-in-iran/30373141.html.

Radio Farda, "Iran's Rial Hits New Historic Low Against US Dollar, Other Currencies," (July 5, 2020), https://en.radiofarda.com/a/iran-rial-hits-new-historic-low-against-us-dollar-other-currencies/30706985.html.

Radio Farda, "Devaluation of Iran's Currency Accelerates With Dollar Hitting 260,000 Rials," (July 19, 2020), https://en.radiofarda.com/a/devaluation-of-iran-s-currency-accelerates-with-dollar-hitting-260-000-rials/30735734.html.

Radio Farda, "Rouhani Says Sanctions Cost Government 900 Trillian Rials in Revenues," (August 26, 2020), https://en.radiofarda.com/a/rouhani-says-sanctions-cost-government-900-trillion-rials-in-revenues/30803859.html.

Radio Farda, "Iran's Khamenei Says U.A.E. 'Betrayed' Islamic World With Israel Normalization Deal," (September 1, 2020), https://en.radiofarda.com/a/iran-s-khamenei-says-u-a-e-betrayed-islamic-world-with-israel-normalization-deal/30814699.html.

Radio Farda, "Dollar Soars to Near Record Level in Iran," (September 9, 2020), https://en.radiofarda.com/a/dollar-soars-to-near-record-level-in-iran-/30829462.html.

Radio Farda, "Iran Condemns Bahrain Deal With Israel," (September 12, 2020), https://en.radiofarda.com/a/iran-condemns-bahrain-deal-with-israel/30834978.html.

Radio Farda, "IRGC Threatens Bahrain with Tough Revenge," (September 14, 2020), https://en.radiofarda.com/a/30838530.html.

Radio Farda, "Iran's Oil Revenue Dropped to Less Than $20 Billion, Rouhani Says," (September 14, 2020), https://en.radiofarda.com/a/30838504.html.

Radio Farda, "*Nerkh Dollar Va Tala Dar Iran Record Dobareh Zad*" [The Price of Dollar and Gold in Iran Hit Another Record], (September 20, 2020), https://www.radiofarda.com/a/30848568.html.

Radio Farda, "*Dollar Beh Kanal 30 Hezar Toman Nazdiktar Shod*" [Dollar Got Closer to 30,000 Toman], (September 26, 2020), https://www.radiofarda.com/a/30859135.html.

Radio Farda, "*Sekkeh Az Marz 15 Million Gozasht; Dollar 30 Hezar Toman Shod*" [Gold Coin Crossed the 15 Million Rial Border; Dollar Became 30,000 Toman], (October 1, 2020), https://www.radiofarda.com/a/30868839.html.

Radio Farda, "Washington Blacklists Iran's Entire Financial Sector," (October 8, 2020), https://en.radiofarda.com/a/washington-blacklists-iran-s-entire-financial-sector/30883130.html.

Radio Farda, "*Gheymat Dollar Az 32 Hezar Toman Gozasht*" [The Price of Dollar Crossed 32 Thousand Toman], (October 15, 2020), https://www.radiofarda.com/a/dollar-Iran/30894913.html.

Radio Farda, "*Kahesh Bish-Az 3 Hezar Tomani Gheymat Dollar Dar Bazaar Arz Tehran*" [Reduction of More Than 3,000 Toman of Dollar's Value at Tehran's Foreign Exchange Market], (October 20, 2020), https://www.radiofarda.com/a/30902739.html.

Radio Farda, "Iran's Net Debt, 44% of its GDP, IMF Says," (October 20, 2020), https://en.radiofarda.com/a/iran-s-net-debt-44-of-its-gdp-imf-says/30903332.html.

Radio Farda, "*Navasan-e Gheymat Dollar Dar Ashofteh Bazaar Iran*" [The Fluctuations of the Price of Dollar in Iran's Chaotic Market], (November 9, 2020), https://www.radiofarda.com/a/30938959.html.

Radio Farda, "*Namayandeh Lahestan Dar Parleman Eropa, Zarif Ra Beh Vazir Omor Kharejeh Alman Nazi Tashbih Kard*" [The Representative to the European Parliament from Poland, Considered Zarif to be Similar to the Foreign Minister of Nazi Germany], (December 18, 2020), https://www.radio farda.com/a/31008036.html.

Radio Farda, *"Rais Kol-e Bank Markazi: Baray Taamin Manabeh Rahi Joz Chaap Eskenas Nadarim"* [Chairman of the Central Bank: We Have No Other Way But to Print Money to Make Payouts], (February 3, 2021), https://www.radiofarda.com/a/31083483.html.

Radio Farda, *"Owjgiri Naghdinegi Va Bedehi Dowlat Iran Beh Bank-ha Dar 9 Mah Aval 99"* [Rise of Liquidity and Iran's Government Debt to the Banks In the First 9 Months of the Year 1399], (February 6, 2021), https://www.radiofarda.com/a/31089592.html.

Radio Farda, *"Enteshar Amar Marg O Mir Dar Aban 98"* [Publication on the Statistics on Deaths During November 2019], (May 27, 2021), https://www.radiofarda.com/a/31276567.html.

Radio Farda, *"Gozaresh Jadid: Jomhuri Islami 'Dast Kam 540 Irani' Ra Dar Kharej Az Keshvar Koshteh Ya Rebodeh Ast"* [New Report: The Islamic Republic Has Murdered or Kidnapped "At Least 540 Iranians" Outside the Country], (July 28, 2021), https://www.radiofarda.com/a/boroumand-foun dation-we-has-identified-more-than-540-iranians-whose-murder-or-kidnapping-is-attributed-to- the-islamic-republic-of-iran/31380796.html.

Radio Farda, *"Nerkh Dollar Az 31 Hezar Tooman Obor Kard; Sooghot 25 Darsadi Arzesh Rial Dar 100 Rooz Dowlat Raisi"* [Price of Dollar Crossed the 31 Thousand Tooman; 25 Percent Fall of the Value of Rial During the 100 Days of Raisi's Government], (December 6, 2021), https://www.ra diofarda.com/a/iran-dollar-rise-raeisi/31596216.html.

Radio France International, *"Vakonesh Reza Pahlavi Beh Ekhtelafha Bar Sar Parviz Sabeti: Az Havadaran Fahash Va Nefaghankan Faseleh Migiram"* [Reaction of Reza Pahlavi to the Events Over Parviz Sabeti: I Distance Myself from Supporters who Insult and Create Divisions], (February 23, 2023), https://www.rfi.fr/fa/%D8%A7%DB%8C%D8%B1%D8%A7%D9%86/20230222-%D9%88%D8%A7% DA%A9%D9%86%D8%B4-%D8%B1%D8%B6%D8%A7-%D9%BE%D9%87%D9%84%D9%88%DB% 8C-%D8%A8%D9%87-%D8%A7%D8%AE%D8%AA%D9%84%D8%A7%D9%81-%D9%87%D8%A7-% D8%A8%D8%B1-%D8%B3%D8%B1-%D8%AD%D8%B6%D9%88%D8%B1-%D9%BE%D8%B1%D9% 88%DB%8C%D8%B2-%D8%AB%D8%A7%D8%A8%D8%AA%DB%8C-%D8%AF%D8%B1-%D8%AA% D8%B8%D8%A7%D9%87%D8%B1%D8%A7%D8%AA-%D8%AC%D9%85%D9%87%D9%88%D8% B1%DB%8C-%D8%A7%D8%B3%D9%84%D8%A7%D9%85%DB%8C-%D8%AA%D9%81%D8%B1% D9%82%D9%87-%D8%A7%D9%81DA%A9%D9%86%DB%8C-%D9%85%DB%8C-%DA%A9%D9% 86%D8%AF.

Radio Zamaaneh, *"Eateraz Tahkim Vahdat Beh 'Apartheid Elmi'"* [The Office for Consolidation of Unity Objects to 'Scientific Apartheid'], (September 21, 2009) http://zamaaneh.com/news/2009/09/ post_10568.html.

Radio Zamaaneh, "Iran universities target of conservative attacks," (October 23, 2009) http://www.za maaneh.com/enzam/2009/10/iran-universities-target.html.

Radio Zamaaneh, "Zahra Rahnavard condemns discriminatory laws against women," (March 6, 2010) http://www.zamaaneh.com/enzam/2010/03/zahra-rahnavard-issued-a.html.

Radio Zamaneh, *"Dollar Az Marz 28 Hezar Tooman Oboor Kard"* [Dollar Crossed the 28,000 Toman Border], (September 23, 2020), https://www.radiozamaneh.com/539959.

Radio Zamaneh, *"Asghar Izadi: Parviz Sabeti Kesi Ast Keh Shekanjeh Rah Beh Nezamyafteh Va Beh Maharat Tabdil Kard"* [Asghar Izadi: Parviz Sabeti is the Person Who Made Torture Institutionalized and an Expertise], (March 1, 2023) https://melliun.org/iran/354076.

Radmanesh, Maziar. *"Seyyed Mojtaba Khamenei Kist?"* [Who is Seyyed Mojtaba Khamenei?], Rooz online, July 4, 2009, http://www.roozonline.com/persian/sotun/sotun-item/article/2009/july/04//-

74f76da028.html republished in Iran Emrooz, (July 4, 2010), http://www.iran-emrooz.net/index. php?/politic2/print/18644.

Rafiee, Bahram. *"Tagheer Gostardeh Masoolin Amniyati Va Nezami Keshvar"* [Massive Changes In The Security and Military Officials], Rooz Online, (August 4, 2009) http://www.roozonline.com/per sian/news/newsitem/article/2009/august/04//-ad05e8de0f.html.

Rahe Sabz, *"Hoshdar Sepah Dar Astaneh Khordad; Cheh Kasi Saran Eslahat Ra Terror Mikonad?"* [Warning Of The IRGC As June Approaches; Who Will Assassinates The Reformist Leaders?], (May 10, 2010) http://www.rahesabz.net/story/15184.

Rahnavard, Zahra. *"Kojayeh Tarikh Sarzamin Maa Bedoon Zan Irani Dar Ooj Ast?"* [Where in the History of Our Land Have There Been Great Heights Without Iranian Woman?], Kaleme, (March 6, 2010) http://www.kaleme.com/1388/12/15/klm-13282.

RAHVA, *"Hameh Farzandan Khanevadeh Hashemi"* [All the Children of the Hashemi Family], (June 15, 2010), http://rahva.ir/104/10267-89.html.

Raisi, Ebrahim. "Biography," https://raisi.ir/page/biography.

Raja News, *"Enteqadat Sarih Ayatollah Yazdi: Mikhahand Baray Rahbari Taain Taklif Konand"* [Explicit Criticisms of Ayatollah Yazdi: They Want {The Power} to Tell the Supreme Leader What To Do], (April 23, 2010), http://www.rajanews.com/Detail.asp?id=48204.

Raja News, *"Kahesh Talafat Chaharshanbeh Souri Emsal/Zedde Enqelab Az Roo Miravad?"* [Reduction of Casualties of This Year's Charharshanbeh Souri/ Will Anti-Revolutionaries Have Shame?], (March 19, 2011) http://www.rajanews.com/detail.asp?id=82236.

Reuters, "Iran detains scores of students, rights group says," (November 25, 2009) http://www.reu ters.com/article/topNews/idUSTRE5AO1ZH20091125.

Reuters, "Arab League labels Hezbollah terrorist organization," (March 11, 2016), https:// www.reuters.com/article/us-mideast-crisis-arabs/arab-league-labels-hezbollah-terrorist-organization-idUSKCN0WD239.

Reuters, "Special Report: Iran's leader ordered crackdown on unrest – 'Do whatever it takes to end it'," (December 23. 2019), https://www.reuters.com/article/us-iran-protests-specialreport/special-report-irans-leader-ordered-crackdown-on-unrest-do-whatever-it-takes-to-end-it-idUSKBN1YR0QR.

Reuters, "Israel's outgoing defence minister says Iran starting to withdraw from Syria," (May 18, 2020), https://www.reuters.com/article/us-israel-iran-syria/israels-outgoing-defence-minister-says-iran-starting-to-withdraw-from-syria-idUSKBN22U2MU.

Reuters, "Rights groups call for prob into Iran's Raisi for crimes against humanity," (June 19, 2021), https://www.reuters.com/world/middle-east/amnesty-calls-investigation-into-irans-raisi-crimes-against-humanity-2021-06-19/.

Reuters, "Iran replaces powerful chief of Guards' intelligence unit-state TV," (June 23, 2022), https:// www.reuters.com/world/middle-east/iran-dismisses-taeb-head-revolutionary-guards-intelligence-unit-state-tv-2022-06-23/.

Rezaee, Mohsen. *"Nameh Dr. Rezaee Beh Rahbar Moazam Enqelab"* [The Letter of Dr. Rezaee to the Esteemed Leader of the Revolution], Rezee's website, (January 1, 2010) http://www.rezaee.ir/fa/pages/?cid=8627.

Robertson, Geoffrey. *The Massacre of Political Prisoners in Iran, 1988, Report of An Inquiry,* Abdorrahman Boroumand Foundation, (April 18, 2011), https://www.iranrights.org/library/docu ment/1380/the-massacre-of-political-prisoners-in-iran-1988-report-of-an-inquiry.

Roostaee, Farzaneh. *"Yek Khanevadeh NIAC Baray Toof Va Laanat Chahar Fasl"* [One NIAC Family for Four Seasons of Condemnation and Spit], (October 19, 2022), https://www.youtube.com/watch? v=A3bDbY1UE1o.

Rooznameh Iran, "Taghdir Khatib Jomeh Tehran Az Talash-hay Diplomatic Dowlat Baray Nejat Ghazeh" [Friday Prayer Speaker Applauding the Government for its Diplomatic Efforts to Rescue Gaza], (January 17, 2009) http://www.iran-newspaper.com/1387/871028/html/internal.htm#s944718.

Rooznameh Jumhuri Islami, "Raah Baaz Ast" [The Path is Open], (January 9, 2010) http://www.jomhour ieslami.com/1388/13881019/index.html.

Rosen, Armin. "America's most prominent group advocating engagement with Iran was hit with a rough court decision," Business Insider, (March 5, 2015), https://www.businessinsider.com/amer icas-most-prominent-group-advocating-engagement-with-iran-was-hit-with-a-rough-court-deci sion-2015-3.

Rouydad News, "Eateraz Mardomi Dar Isfehan: Mardom Mohasereh Manzel Ayatollah Taheri Raa Shekastand" [The Protests by the People in Isfahan: The People Broke Down the Encirclement of the Home of Ayatollah Taheri], (December 24, 2009) http://rouydadnews.com/pages/877.php.

Saeedi, Mehdi. "Bazi Hashiyeh Sazan Bah Manafeh Melli" [Playing with the National Interests by the Band], Sobh Sadeq, http://www.sobhesadegh.ir/Sadegh.htm, republished at Iran Emrooz, April 26, 2011, http://www.iran-emrooz.net/index.php?/news2/28274/.

Salami, Mohammad. "The water crisis and the decline of legitimacy in Iran," Trends Research and Advisory, (October 6, 2022), https://trendsresearch.org/insight/the-water-crisis-and-decline-of-le gitimacy-in-iran/.

Samii, Bill. "Iran: Weak Economy Challenges Populist President," Eurasianet, (July 23, 2006) www.eur asianet.org/departments/business/articles/pp072306.shtml.

Sciliano, Elaine. "Interview," PBS, (April 17, 2002), https://www.pbs.org/wgbh/pages/frontline/shows/ tehran/interviews/sciolino.html.

Shahrooz, Kaveh. "Labigari Jomhuri Islami" [Islamic Republic Lobbying], Iran International, (October 25, 2022), https://www.youtube.com/watch?v=UwZl6O-gsN4.

Shargh Daily, "Niloufar Hamedi, Khabarnegar Shargh Bazdasht Shod" [Niloufar Hamedi, Shargh's Reporter Was Arrested], (September 22, 2022), https://www.sharghdaily.com/fa/tiny/news-856872.

Shariatmadari, Hussein. "Hezb Ya Sotune Panjum?! (Yaddasht Rooz)" [Party or Fifth Column?! (Comment of the Day)], Kayhan, (July 4, 2009), http://www.kayhannews.ir/880413/2.htm#oth er200.

Shojaee, Mitra. "16 Azar Va Ehtemal Dastgiri Mousavi va Karrubi" [December 7 and the Possibility of the Arrests of Mousavi and Karrubi], Deutsche Welle, November 25, 2009, http://www.dw-world. de/dw/article/0,,4929214,00.html?maca=per-rss-per-all-1491-rdf.

Siamdoust, Nahid. "Ahead of Iran Election, President's Rivals Gain Hope," Time magazine online edition, (June 11, 2009) http://www.time.com/time/world/article/0,8599,1903841,00.html.

Siamdoust, Nahid. "Tehran's Rallying Cry: 'We Are the People of Iran'," Time magazine, (June 15, 2009), http://www.time.com/time/world/article/0,8599,1904764,00.html?xid=rss-topstories.

Siami, Ardalan. "Sal 88 Sal Sepahi Shodan Eqtesad" [The Year 2009–2010 The Year IRGC Dominated the Economy], Rooz Online, (March 19, 2010) http://www.roozonline.com/persian/news/news item/article/2010/march/19//88-12.html.

Sikorski, Radoslaw. "Speech," (December 18, 2020), posted on You Tube https://www.youtube.com/ watch?v=YjrnThhS7ZY (December 21, 2020).

Sinaee, Maryam. "Former Iran PM Turned Opposition Has Believers And Critics," Iran International (February 8, 2023), https://www.iranintl.com/en/202302071911.

Sinaee, Maryam. "Leaked Document Reveals Loss Of Loyalty, Insubordination In IRGC," Iran International, (March 20, 2023), https://www.iranintl.com/en/202303192652.

Slackman, Michael. "Iran Protesters Take to Streets Despite Threats," *The New York Times*, (July 10, 2009).

Slackman, Michael. "Purge of Iranian Universities Is Feared," *The New York Times*, (September 1, 2009).

Smith, Lee. "Meet the Iran Lobby," Hudson Institute, (September 1, 2015), https://www.hudson.org/national-security-defense/meet-the-iran-lobby.

Soage, Ana Belen. "Hasan al-Banna or the Politicisation of Islam," *Totalitarian Movements and Political Religions*, Vol. 9, No. 1 (March 2008), pp. 21–42, https://www.researchgate.net/publication/233003241_Hasan_al-Banna_or_the_Politicisation_of_Islam.

Soleymani, Gen. Qassem. "Speech," Fars News, (March 29, 2014). The speech was delivered on February 16, 2014, http://www.farsnews.com/newstext.php?nn=13930108000154.

Stecklow, Steve, and Babak Dehghanpisheh, and Yeganeh Torbati, "Reuters Investigates: Assets of the Ayatollah," Reuters, (November 11, 2013), https://www.reuters.com/investigates/iran/#article/part1.

Stickler, Angus, and Maggie O'Kane, "Former elite officers reveal tensions in Iran regime," *The Guardian*, (June 11, 2010) http://www.guardian.co.uk/world/2010/jun/11/iran-revolutionary-guards-regime.

Stein, Jeff. "Mousavi, Celebrated in Iranian Protests, Was the Butcher of Beirut," *CQ Politics blog*, (June 22, 2009) http://blogs.cqpolitics.com/spytalk/2009/06/mousavi-celebrated-in-iranian.html.

Swash, Rosie. "Arrests and TV confessions as Iran cracks down on women's 'improper' clothing," *The Guardian*, (August 23, 2022), https://www.theguardian.com/global-development/2022/aug/23/arrests-and-tv-confessions-as-iran-cracks-down-on-women-improper-clothing-hijab.

Tabarzadi, Heshmat. "What I See on the Frontline in Iran: Regime Change is Now Our Movement's Rallying Cry," *The Wall Street Journal*, (December 17, 2009).

Tabnak, "*Mohammad Hashemi: Roozhay Sakhti Bar Ayatollah Migozarad*" [Mohamad Hashemi: Harsh Days for the Ayatollah], (August 14, 2009), http://www.tabnak.ir/fa/pages/?cid=59551.

Tait, Robert. "Iran should keep its distance from US, says senior cleric," *The Guardian*, (January 29, 2009) http://www.guardian.co.uk/world/2009/jan/29/iran-us-obama.

Tait, Robert. "Funeral of Iranian cleric Montazeri turns into political protest," *The Guardian*, (December 21, 2009) http://www.guardian.co.uk/world/2009/dec/21/iran-funeral-ayatollah-montazeri-protest.

Tait, Robert. "Iranians' green revolution refuses to wither and die," *The Guardian* online edition, (December 27, 2009) http://www.guardian.co.uk/world/2009/dec/27/iran-tehran-ayotollah-khamenei-protests.

Tajdin, Behrang. "*Eghtesad Iran Beh Ravayat Panj Nemoodar Dar Panjomin Salgard Barjam*" [Iran's Economy According to Five Charts In the Fifth Anniversary of the JCPOA], BBC Persian, (July 13, 2020), https://www.bbc.com/persian/business-53381573.

Tajzadeh, Mostafa. "*Pedar, Madar, Ma Baz Ham Motahamim!*" [Father, Mother, We Are Accused, Again!], Iran Emrooz, (June 15, 2010), http://www.iran-emrooz.net/image1/Tajzadeh20106.pdf.

Talei, Javad. "*Na-aramihay Iran Va Afzaesh Entezarat Mali Police Va Basij*" [Disorders in Iran and the Increased Financial Expectations of the Police and Basij], Deutsche Welle, (January 15, 2010) http://www.dw-world.de/dw/article/0,,5128185,00.html.

Talei, Javad. "*Hazf Yarabeh-ha Va Ehtemal Naa-Aramihay Gostardeh Dar Iran*" [Eliminating Subsidies and the Possibilities for Widespread Instability in Iran], Deutsche Welle, (October 28, 2010) http://www.dw-world.de/dw/article/0,,4835454,00.html.

Tamimi Arab, Pooyan, and Ammar Maleki, "Iran's secular shift: new survey reveals huge change in religious beliefs," The Conversation, (September 10, 2020), https://theconversation.com/irans-sec ular-shift-new-survey-reveals-huge-changes-in-religious-beliefs-145253.

Tayeri, Leyla. *"Goftogoy Rooz Ba Dabir Daftar Tahkim Vahdat: Daneshgah Saket Nemimanad"* [Discussions of Rooz with the Secretary of the Office for Consolidation of Unity: University Will Not Be Silent], *Rooz Online*,(September 21, 2009) www.roozonline.com/persian/news/newsitem/article////107/-62742948d2.html.

Time Magazine, "As Students Return, Iran's Regime Braces for More Protests," (September 17, 2009) http://www.time.com/time/world/article/0,8599,1924412,00.html?xid=rss-topstories.

Times of Israel, "Iran dismisses Netanyahu's nuclear exposé as 'childish' and 'ridiculous'," (April 30, 2018), https://www.timesofisrael.com/iran-dismisses-netanyahus-nuclear-expose-as-childish-and-ri diculous/.

Tisdall, Simon. "Allegations from Tehran straining already rocky relations with the West," *The Irish Times*, (June 23, 2009) http://www.irishtimes.com/newspaper/world/2009/0623/1224249338747. html.

U.N. Letter to the Iranian Government (Geneva, Switzerland: September 3, 2020), https://spcommre ports.ohchr.org/TMResultsBase/DownLoadPublicCommunicationFile?gId=25503.

U.N. Security Council, "Meeting," https://media.un.org/en/asset/k11/k119xlbgct.

United for Iran, "Atena Daemi" (September 2020), https://united4iran.org/wp-content/uploads/Atena-Daemi-Fact-Pattern-and-Legal-Analysis-September-2020.pdf.

U.S. Government, CIA, "Islam in Iran," (August 31, 1979), http://news.files.bbci.co.uk/ws/documents/persian/bbc_persian_islam_in_iran.pdf.

U.S. Government, Department of State, *Outlaw Regime: A Chronicle of Iran's Destructive Activities*, (Washington, DC: 2018), https://www.state.gov/wp-content/uploads/2018/12/Iran-Report.pdf, p. 15;

VOA, *"Hemayat President Trump Az Motarezan Dar Iran"* [President Trump's Support for Protesters in Iran], (December 29, 2017), https://ir.voanews.com/a/us-iran-protest-/4185384.html.

VOA, *"Vakonesh Aazaey Kongreh Beh Eterazha Dar Iran"* [Reaction of Members of Congress to Protests in Iran], (December 30, 2017), https://ir.voanews.com/a/us-iran-congress-/4185301.html.

VOA, *"Vakonesh Hillary Clinton Beh Eaterazha Dar Iran"* [Hillary Clinton's Reaction on the Protests in Iran], (December 31, 2017), https://ir.voanews.com/a/us-iran-protet-pence-clinton-/4186242.html.

VOA, *"Soleimani Ghatel-e Rahbaresh Ham Ghatel-e"* [Soleimani is a Murder, His Leader is a Murderer], You Tube, (January 11, 2020), https://www.youtube.com/watch?v=1bl6ITEoStQ&app=desktop.

VOA, *"Moatarezan Dar Tehran Bilbord Qassem Soleimani Ra Atesh Zadand"* [Protesters in Tehran Set Ablaze Qassem Soleimani's Billboards], (January 12, 2020), https://ir.voanews.com/episode/mtrdan-dr-thran-bylbwrd-qasm-slymany-ra-atsh-zdnd-235040.

VOA, *"Pareh Kardan Bannerhay Tablighati Qassem Soleimani Tavasot Mardom Dar Tehran"* [Tearing Down of Propaganda Banners for Qassem Soleimani by the People, of Tehran], (January 12, 2020), https://ir.voanews.com/episode/iran-235050.

VOA, *"Koshteh Nadadim Keh Sazesh Konim, Rahbar Ghatel Ro Setayesh Konim"* [We Did Not Have Deaths in order to Compromise, And Praise the Murderer Supreme Leader], (January 13, 2020), https://ir.voanews.com/episode/kshth-ndadym-kh-sazsh-knym-rhbr-qatl-rw-staysh-knym-shar-hzar an-mtrd-nfr-dr-thran-235018.

VOA, *"Basiji Sepahi, Daesh Ma Shomae"* [Basij and IRGC You are Our ISIS], (January 13, 2020), https://ir.voanews.com/episode/bsyjy-spahy-dash-ma-shmayy-shar-mrdm-mtrd-dr-mshhd-235013.

VOA, *"Marg Bar Setamgar Cheh Shah Basheh Cheh Rahbar"* [Death to the Oppressor, Whether Shah or Supreme Leader], (January 13, 2020), https://ir.voanews.com/episode/iran-protest-sunday-235014.

VOA, *"Paslarzehay Binatijeh Mandan Mozakerat Vean, Arzesh Rial Iran Beh 'Paentarin Had Dar Tarikh' Resid"* [The Aftershocks of Failure of the Vienna Talks, The Value of the Iranian Rial Reached "Its Lowest Point in History"], (December 5, 2021), https://ir.voanews.com/a/iran-rials-jcpoa-talks/6340254.html.

VOA, *"Goftegoo-e Chaleshi Siamak Dehghanpour Ba Jamal Abdi, Rais NIAC"* [Challenging Interview by Siamak Dehghanpour with Jamal Abdi, President of NIAC], (November 8, 2022), https://www.youtube.com/watch?v=XS-_sS0Ucc&t=3s.

VOA, *"Sezaye Shekanje-garan Va Naghesan Hoghogh Bashar Chist?"* [What are Punishments for Torturers and Violators of Human Rights?] (February 20, 2023), https://www.youtube.com/watch?v=zn4yOHub3R0.

Waldman, Peter. "Clergy Capitalism: Mullahs Keep Control of Iran's Economy with an Iron Hand," *The Wall Street Journal*, (May 8, 1992), pp. 1, 16.

World Bank, "National Accounts Data, GDP Per Capita," (2019), https://data.worldbank.org/indicator/NY.GDP.PCAP.CD.

Worth, Robert F. "Ex-President in Iran Seeks Referendum," *The New York Times*, (July 20, 2009).

Worth, Robert F. "Iran's Chief Cleric Warns Political Leaders Over Election Criticism," *The New York Times*, (July 21, 2009).

Worth, Robert F. and Nazila Fathi, "Opposition in Iran Urges Continuing Challenge," *The New York Times*, (November 2, 2009).

Worth, Robert F., and Nazila Fathi, "Death Toll Rises to 10 as Clashes in Iran Intensify," *The New York Times*, (December 28, 2009).

Wright, Robin. "Latest Iran Protests Show a Resilient Opposition," *Time Magazine* online edition, (December 7, 2009) http://www.time.com/time/world/article/0,8599,1946038,00.html?xid=rss-world&utm_source=feedburner&utm_medium=feed&utm_campaign=Feed%3A+time%2Fworld+%28TIME%3A+Top+World+Stories%29.

Yousef Eshkevari, Hassan. "Interview with Zammaneh Radio's Mohammad Tajdolati," Part I, Zammaneh Radio, (April 28, 2010), http://zamaaneh.com/analysis/2010/04/post_1457.html.

Zeitoon, *"Abaad Jadidi Az Koshtar Aban 98"* [New Dimensions of the Massacre of November 2019], (May 27, 2021), https://www.zeitoons.com/87839.

Zibakalam, Sadegh. "If a referendum is held today, over 70% would say no to an Islamic republic," Deutsche Welle, (January 5, 2018), https://www.youtube.com/watch?v=GuXyEtMgAOI.

Index

https://doi.org/10.1515/9783111280288-010

www.ingramcontent.com/pod-product-compliance
Lightning Source LLC
Chambersburg PA
CBHW020528270326
41927CB00006B/493